THE
FAMILY

THE
FAMILY
A SOCIAL HISTORY OF
THE TWENTIETH CENTURY

Edited by JOHN HARRISS

Oxford • New York
OXFORD UNIVERSITY PRESS
1991

Volume editor Robert Peberdy
Editorial assistant Elaine Welsh
Art editor Ayala Kingsley
Designers Frankie Wood, Tony de Saulles
Picture research manager Alison Renney
Picture research Diana Hamilton (USA), Diana Phillips, Charlotte Ward-Perkins
Cartographic manager Olive Pearson
Cartographic editor Zoë Goodwin
Project editor Peter Furtado

AN EQUINOX BOOK

Planned and produced by
Andromeda Oxford Ltd
11–15 The Vineyard
Abingdon
Oxfordshire
England
OX14 3PX

Copyright © Andromeda Oxford
Ltd 1991

Published in the United States of
America by
Oxford University Press, Inc.
200 Madison Avenue
New York NY 10016

Oxford is a trademark of Oxford
University Press

ISBN 0-19-520844-7

Library of Congress
Cataloging-in-publication Data
The Family: a social history of the
twentieth century/edited by John
Harriss p. cm.
"An Equinox book" -- T.p. verso.
Includes bibliographical references
and index.
1. Family--History--20th Century.
2. Social history--20th century.
I. Harriss, John. HQ518.F325 1991
306.85'09'04--dc20
91-776 CIP

Printing (last digit) 9 8 7 6 5 4 3 2 1

Printed in Singapore by
CS Graphics

ADVISORY EDITOR

Charles Webster   All Souls College, Oxford

MAIN CONTRIBUTORS

Robert Bideleux   University College, Swansea

Nigel Harris   University College, London

Gundi Harriss   Birkbeck College, London

John Harriss   London School of Economics

OTHER CONTRIBUTORS

Tony Barnett   University of East Anglia

Jo Beall   University College, London

Louise Jones   Freelance writer, Oxford

Charles Freeman   Freelance writer, Suffolk

Lucy Newton   University of Leicester

Ruth Pearson   University of East Anglia

CONTENTS

PREFACE

Writers of contemporary history have always had a tendency to see their own times as being at a point of transition from one historical period to another. For someone presenting a social history of the world in the 20th century in the early 1990s the temptation is perhaps especially strong. The idea of "the end of history" has been fashionable because of the apparent collapse of socialist experiments and the supposed victory of market economies with democratic political systems. Certainly the opposition between the ideologies of socialism and of capitalist democracy and between the different attempts made in their names to bring about social change have a major place in the story told in this book. But the fundamental structural changes of the 20th century – the changing social forms of capitalist industrialization, the transition from liberal democracy to mass democracy, and struggles over the role and status of women – are parts of a much longer process of historical change. They are part of the "Great Transformation" of society, brought about by the material forces of industrialization and the development of capitalism, and by the values and ideas associated with the philosophy of the 18th-century Enlightenment. The process of "modernization" to which these forces gave rise has its roots deep in European history. The problems to which it gave birth, however, lying in the impersonality and "dehumanizing" aspects of both market economies and bureaucratic forms of organization, remain with us. This book concludes that they are still unresolved and that they are reflected in some of the striking trends of the late 20th century, such as the resurgence of religious fundamentalism and of nationalisms. There is thus no sign of "the end of history".

The story of social change in the 20th century told here is related as much as possible in terms of the experience of ordinary people, as workers, peasants, women, members of households, and citizens. It aims to represent them as "making their own history", in changing circumstances in which economic, political and cultural elements are all significant, and in which what happens within households and what happens at the level of the state do have some relationships with each other.

The approach is loosely structured around the idea that human actions may be considered as taking place in three main spheres (though these are not necessarily always very clearly distinguished from each other in practice): the sphere of the household; the sphere of work; and the wider society. The world is considered in terms of three broad geographical regions: North America and Western Europe; Russia and Eastern Europe; and Latin America, Africa and Asia. Parts One, Three and Six are presented primarily by theme; Parts Two, Four and Five primarily by region. Robert Bideleux has written most of the material on Russia and Eastern Europe; Nigel Harris has contributed much of the story of the "Third World"; Gundi Harriss has written the history of women, the family and feminism; and I have written the sections on North America and Western Europe (the latter with contributions from Peter Lambert). I am also responsible for the interpretations of the book as a whole and for what is included and what has been left out.

John Harriss   London School of Economics

INTRODUCTION

It was once fashionable to think of social history as history "with the politics and the economics left out". Social history often concentrated on "daily life" and described people's houses, food and clothes. Such an approach is inadequate for a serious consideration of social change in the 20th century, which has been a period of tremendous experiment, with deliberate attempts made to bring about change. Great efforts have been made to *develop* societies by bringing about changes considered "progressive". These efforts have been undertaken in the names of a variety of ideologies, but they have all involved extensive intervention by states, be it to provide social benefits such as old age pensions or to remove "enemy" citizens. The expansion of the state and the history of the state-sponsored social change are fundamental to world social history in the 20th century.

Such a view, however, does not exclude the actions of people. Ordinary people, not just the great ones on whom history-writing used to focus, make their own history. They are active, conscious agents, making decisions which bring about change. Yet people make decisions and act in particular contexts or circumstances which are "social", that is, which are not reducible to the characteristics of individuals nor entirely under their control. The great German philosopher and social scientist of the 19th century, Karl Marx, whose importance should not be denied because of the general discrediting of varieties of "communism" by the end of the 20th century, meant something like this when he argued in a famous passage that "Men make their own history but not in circumstances of their own choosing". He referred to the fact that all of us are in some degree the product of a particular history and set of circumstances, and to the ways in which our possible actions are constrained by society.

Causes of social change
What brings about "social change"? One influential view, associated especially with Marx, is that change in the "economic foundation" of society, that is, change in the ways in which people make their livings, is ultimately what determines change throughout society. This theory is quite persuasive because it clearly is true that people in all societies must produce the material means of their existence and that when they change the way in which they do this it fundamentally affects their knowledge and understanding and the way in which they live. But the problem with this "materialist" explanation for social change is that it rests on the implicit suggestion that the practical activity of human beings can somehow come before thought. Given that what distinguishes human beings from other animals is the capacity for conscious thought this idea that activity comes *before* thought seems inappropriate. If it is accepted that ideas and activity cannot be dissociated then the persuasiveness of materialism begins to weaken.

Historically it is clear that forms of political organization, types of household or ideas about property (for example) exercise as much influence on the way people have made their living as vice versa. Why was it, for example, that the first "industrial revolution" took place in northwest Europe? According to historians all sorts of factors were involved, including religious beliefs which encouraged particular attitudes toward wealth, ideas about the inheritance of property, and family organization. Following from this example, and the general argument against a rigid materialist view of history, then neither economic factors nor politics nor culture should be given causal primacy: all play a part in bringing about change. Different factors assume varying significance at different times.

But there are important connections between control over production and the distribution of products and wider social relations. Thus the idea of social class is important. This is a controversial term in the social sciences, but here is taken to refer to fundamental distinctions between those who own and control production and those who do not, whose employment and livelihoods depend on those who do. On this consideration the principal classes are: the bourgeoisie or capitalist class, the owners of property of different kinds who exercise control over production; the working class or proletariat, those who do the actual work involved in production but who do not own what is produced by their labors; the petty bourgeoisie, the owners of small property such as shopkeepers and some artisans, who themselves work physically with the resources that they own; and peasants, small agricultural producers who also work on their own properties. The distinctions between these groups are not absolutely watertight; it certainly cannot be presumed that people themselves think in these categories. But they are useful shorthand for talking about differences which are important in all societies: who does the work, and who owns what is produced.

There is also another class category which is not of quite the same kind as those just described: that of the middle class. This category is meaningful as the way in which some people identify themselves or others. It usually means having a certain status, given by education or where a person lives; it means not being involved in manual work and probably implies ownership of a small property (especially a house). The middle class or classes include some whom outsiders might define as capitalists; it also includes members of the petty bourgeoisie – shopkeepers, artisans and professional people; and those such as industrial and commercial managers who in the strict terms employed above are really only "workers" because they do not control what is produced through their efforts.

The other important social category is ethnic identity. This refers to the definition of a social group which is important for the way in which people think about themselves and which probably appears to them as "natural". The common bases of ethnic identity are kinship, language, religion, region or ideas of biological "race", any one of which, singly or in combination, may also be linked to a sense of nationality. These are all ideas, potential "imagined communities" in the evocative and perceptive phrase of the leading modern writer on nationalism, Benedict Anderson. People's ideas about their own identity can change, sometimes in dramatic ways. Thus in the late 20th century many people evidently thought of themselves no longer (if ever they did) as "Soviet citizens" but as "Georgians" or "Estonians"; or those who were once perhaps "Yugoslavs" started to define themselves as Croats or Serbs. The connections between these ways in which people think about themselves, the ways in which power is exercised, and the ways in which production is carried on, are extremely important.

The theory of modernization

Though many historians are wary of "grand models" of historical change it can be argued that the 20th century has seen the further working out of the process of "modernization" through industrialization. In the 20th century people in different parts of the world have sought quite consciously, as never before, to modernize by industrializing. This is what "development" has really meant for very many of them. What has latterly come to be described as the guiding conflict of the century, between capitalism and socialism, is substantially about different approaches to modernization. Even the outstanding social trends and problems of the later 20th century, such as the violence and decay of inner cities in the older industrial countries, social conflict in southern Africa, the rise of Islamic fundamentalism and the resurgence of ethnicity and nationalism in many parts of the world can be understood as responses to modernization, or to its failure.

Modernization produces "modernity", a kind of society in which the idea of a distinction between the "individual" and "society" becomes thinkable. In the past, we suppose, and perhaps in some societies still in the present, individual human beings knew themselves essentially as members of social groups, probably based on kinship and neighborhood. In modern society individuals are, as it were, separated out from, and are no longer defined in terms of, particular social relations. Rather they enter into relations with others through things and through economic transactions. It is a change the author John Berger describes in a story about a girl from a small village in the French Alps in the 1950s. Odile Blanc was intelligent and was sent from her village school to one in a nearby town. She says in the story: "ever since I could remember everyone had always known who I was. They called me Odile, or Blanc's daughter, or Achille's last. If somebody did not know who I was a single answer to a single question was enough for them to place me... in Cluses I was a stranger to everyone. My name was Blanc, which began with a B, and so I

▲ Transport for a mass society: a London train terminus about 1910.

9

was near the top of the alphabetical list. I was always among the first ten that had to stand up, or to file out". In town Odile became a name and perhaps a number, and an isolated individual rather than knowing herself, as she did before, as a particular member of a particular family.

The change Berger captures in his story of Odile, the process of individualization, is central to the idea of modernization. Modernization also refers to "secularization", meaning the decline of religious belief; there is a close relationship between secularization and change in the way in which authority is exercised. "Authority" refers to the right to exercise power – to dictate to people what they should do. In many societies in the past, and in some still in the present (such as the Islamic Republic of Iran), authority is based on religious teaching. The idea of modernity connotes, however, a form of authority based on what the great German sociologist Max Weber called rational-legal principles, that is conscious deliberation about desired ends and the best ways by which to arrive at those ends. In "modern" societies authority is bound by laws which are the outcome of thought by people, not by sacred texts which are held to be the word of God. Modern societies, too, are characterized by formal organizations which rest on the same rational-legal principles, and which therefore should not be influenced in the way they work by the whims of individuals. These are the organizations, analyzed by Weber, called "bureaucracies" – a word which has so often come to be used abusively that it is easy to forget that the bureaucratic principle is a fair and efficient way of doing things in complex societies.

philosophy of the 18th-century Enlightenment which established the ascendancy of reason and the value of experience and experiment over religious faith. Industrialization also started in the 18th century, but on a world scale industrial development had not proceeded far by the beginning of the 20th century. Only in Britain was the population more urban than rural; and only a small proportion even of the manufacturing labor force was employed in factories in which it could be subjected to industrial time discipline and reduced to serving machines (rather than controlling tools, which requires skill).

Capitalism, industrialization and modernity

There is another important idea which helps to make sense of social change in the 20th century: the idea of "capitalism". Capitalism was the principal object of study by Marx, and his analysis of *Capital* contains insights of great value. Capitalism refers to an economic system governed by the securing of profits. Unless capitalists secure profits and are able to compete with others their enterprises cease to be viable. It is thus a system with a built-in drive for expansion.

Profits are obtained through exchange, but derive from the ability of those who own the resources, land and equipment used in production (capitalists) to control the product of work carried out by others (workers). Capitalists are able to do this by control of the "labor power" (capacity for work) which they purchase for wages in (more or less competitive) markets. In order to be efficient and compete adequately with others, capitalists have to obtain as much actual work as possible from the labor power they purchase. Perhaps the fundamental dynamic of societies which have capitalist economic systems is the struggle between capitalists and workers for control of the labor power of the latter. At the simplest level capitalists try to ensure that all the labor time they buy is used productively, while workers, because they do not own what they produce, have an equally strong interest in doing as little as possible while they are "at work".

The technological development associated with the Industrial Revolution of the 18th century was driven to a large extent by the need of capitalist manufacturers to establish better control over labor. It was a start to bring weavers, for example, into big workshops where they could be more closely supervised. It was then a much greater advance when, thanks to steam power and invention, it was possible to dictate the pace of work through the use of machinery. Capitalists were thus able to get more work from the labor power they purchased.

Capitalism is not the same as industrialization but it gave rise to it. Capitalism also does not mean quite the same thing as modernization, but the kinds of social relationships, ideas about the self and forms of organization associated with the idea of "modernization" are bound up with capitalism. Capitalism depends upon the existence of what Marx called "free wage labor" – "free" in the double sense of being "freed" from ownership of resources for carrying on production, but also free from feudal or other customary obligations, such as service to the lord of a manor, and so able to sell its labor power to the highest bidder.

These "freedoms" are the basis of the emergence of the isolated individuals of modern societies who no longer know themselves essentially as members of social groups or communities. It is under capitalism that there is a shift from relationships of personal dependence to the predominance of relationships that are impersonal and take place especially through things – things that are bought and sold.

The emergence of societies characterized by individualism, secularism and rational-legal authority is certainly not the same as the process of "industrialization", and historically it clearly anticipates the creation of industrial economies. But there has been such an association between these great trends in history that the industrialized society has been identified as the distinctive type of modern society. It is easy to see why this should be so, for industrialization refers to the raising of the productivity of human labor through the application of science to improve production methods, and modernization to the application of the same kind of reasoning to the conduct of all human affairs.

In the west the development both of rational-legal authority and of modern industry was strongly influenced by the

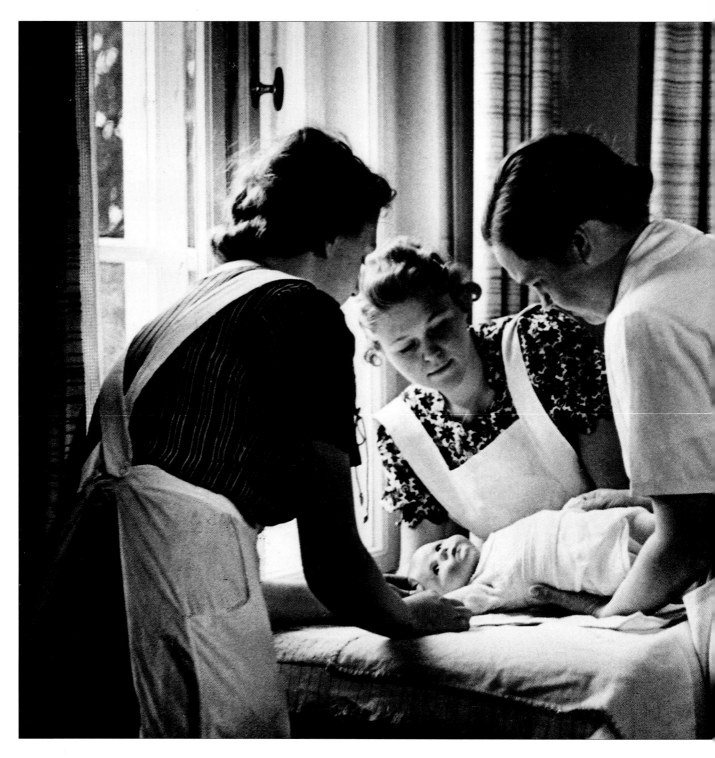

Marx and Weber

The major ideas about modern social change – "modernization", "industrialization" and "capitalism" are *ideas*, abstrac-
tions based on reflection on observations of history. Moreover,
many of them were formed when the proposed social trends
were at an early stage. The two most significant thinkers who
have formed the ways in which social change in the 20th century may be understood are Karl Marx and Max Weber. Marx
developed his theories about the development of industrial
capitalism in the mid-19th century, partly in response to his
observations of industrialization in Britain. Weber, a German
historian and sociologist, produced his major works in the late
19th and early 20th centuries. Whereas Marx in some of his
writings emphasized the economic foundations of historical

change, Weber argued in his most famous work, *The Protestant
Ethic and the Spirit of Capitalism* (1904–05), for the importance of
ideas, specifically that Calvinism (the theological system
developed by John Calvin in the 16th century) inculcated attitudes toward wealth and behavior that gave rise to capitalist
behavior.

There were major differences between the attitudes of Marx
and Weber, but they shared a vision of modernity. For Weber
the modern world came into being as Calvinist religious
beliefs, creating anxiety about individual salvation, led to the
rational, calculating behavior of people who had continually to
review their own conduct. The application of these attitudes to
human organization underlies the rational-legal principles of
modern political authority and bureaucratic organization.

From the "Second Industrial Revolution" to Fordism

By 1900 industrialization involved what has been described as the "Second Industrial Revolution", based on steel, on the steadily increasing use of electricity, and on chemicals and oil. But it also brought a very important change in economic organization, with the development of corporate enterprise. The scale of enterprises started to expand enormously, and in the process ownership and control of production began to separate. Competition was no longer so much between individual capitalists as between large corporations which could monopolize particular areas of industry. Ownership became divided up between shareholders while control of some aspects of industry lay more in the hands of specialist managers. Both in private enterprises and in government the numbers of those employed in bureaucracies, as managers, clerks, typists, accountants, began to increase. "Office work" in bureaucratic organizations, at least as much as "factory work", has been the experience of the 20th century.

The late-19th-century changes in technology and in economic organization prepared the ground for the basic structural change in economic organization in the 20th century, which can be labelled as "Fordism". Marx argued that the development of capitalism would depend upon capitalists' abilities to control the labor power of workers, and he suggested that this involved a shift from *manu*facture, production depending on the skills of individual workers, to *machino*facture, in which workers serve machines which dictate the pace of work. In fact this shift had hardly taken place at all in the 19th century. It was then greatly facilitated by the use of electricity, but also assisted by the ideas of "scientific management". These were worked out especially by an American engineer, F.W. Taylor, around the turn of the century, though they were not put much into practice until after World War I. The implementation of scientific management represented the "deskilling" of labor; it tended to separate the "thinking" aspects of production from the manual, and to allocate the former to management. In practice scientific management meant large increases, relatively and absolutely, in the numbers of semiskilled operatives.

The genius of the American automobile manufacturer Henry Ford was not only to take over these principles and to add to them the technology of the moving assembly line. He also recognized that mass production by these methods required mass consumption. He saw that it was possible for very big enterprises to create and to manage markets, as well as production, through advertising and through influencing the habits and ways of life of workers. This is what we mean by "Fordism" – not only a way of organizing production, involving hierarchical control and sophisticated machinofacture, but a whole culture of consumption and structure of society and politics based around the imperatives of large-scale business corporations.

Fordism is one of the characterizing phenomena of the 20th century (the other is mass democracy). Triumphant in the long boom from 1945 until the early 1960s, Fordism then began to become unstuck in the 1960s.

From Fordism to "flexible accumulation"

"Flexible accumulation" refers to the connected phenomena of a "new international division of labor", in which a number of "newly industrialized countries" (NICS) (previously "developing" countries of the Third World) have taken over major spheres of manufacturing; of apparently new, and, from an

These principles are efficient, but in their very impersonality seem to threaten our humanity. Marx's conception of capitalism involves the same idea of rational calculation and it entails a comparable vision of a world in which humanity is denied as relationships between people are mediated by things and by money. Where the two differed was in that Marx also held a utopian vision of a world in which humanity would be restored through the replacement of capitalism by socialism.

In considering 20th-century change the ideas of Marx and Weber should be used as tools to assist in the understanding of history, not treated as if they *were* history. Like all ideas about historical change they need to be tested. In what follows here, we try to sum up in outline the basic *structural* changes which have shaped contemporary societies.

employer's point of view, more flexible arrangements for the recruitment and management of labor; of new technologies dependent upon electronics and the microchip, which are the basis of modern information technology; of more integrated financial markets; and of a newly resurgent culture of "liberalism" which, oddly perhaps, harks back to 19th-century values. What seems to have happened is that Fordism, as a way of organizing production, and the corporatist political settlement of the postwar period, became subject to increasing rigidity and inefficiency, associated with declining profitability and productivity, and tendencies toward fiscal crisis in states which were by now committed to high levels of welfare expenditure. A crisis was finally provoked by the hike in oil prices in late 1973, and in the turbulence which followed the lineaments of the new "regime" began to appear. Certainly from this time dates the unsticking of the postwar settlement; the decisive rise of new industrial nations and the descent into stagnation and decline of other erstwhile "Third World" economies which became increasingly shackled by foreign debts; and both historically high levels of unemployment and the apparent expansion of "informal" economic activity in the other industrial countries. This is what "flexibility" in labor markets really means from employees' points of view: that jobs are less secure, that there is more part-time working, and more employment in small enterprises which are often linked through subcontracting arrangements with big corporations. These characteristics of people's jobs mesh with the requirements of more flexible production organization, which uses information technology to facilitate "just-in-time" production able to respond very quickly to rapidly changing markets. The new technology has also made possible the organization of production in smaller units. Some of them may be decentralized, and some may require rather high levels of skill.

It all looks like a very different kind of economy from that of the 1950s and 1960s. Politics have undergone parallel changes, shown up in the strength of center-right parties (though some of them still describe themselves as "socialist" or "social democrat") and in popular criticism of state intervention. Western societies seem to be characterized by what the British journalist Peter Jenkins describes as "the new condition in which the relatively prosperous 'haves' constitute a permanent majority over the excluded 'have-nots'", who are increasingly marginalized and are often the victims of a culture of violence. Outside the West the proportions are reversed, but the majority who are "have-nots", subjected to grinding poverty, are equally marginalized victims of violence.

For the history of 20th-century social change what is most important is that long before the 1970s many firms had already pursued a strategy of controlling labor by creating a "core" labor force of privileged workers, trained and quite highly skilled, who were encouraged to believe in their jobs as "careers" and to identify with their firms, while others were relegated to a "periphery" of casual jobs, subject to frequent job changes, and lacking security or "career" prospects. So "flexibility" in labor markets represented an elaboration upon existing practices, and precisely those determining conditions of capitalist production that Marx identified more than a century ago.

The aspects of the sphere of work embraced in the ideas of "Fordism" and "flexible accumulation" help to account for the fact that "class", in the classic sense in which we defined it earlier, has rarely been the most important way in which people defined themselves through the century. In retrospect it appears that the high point of political class consciousness was in the years before and immediately after World War I.

Throughout the century, in "developed" and "less developed" economies, the ways in which production has been organized and labor recruited and controlled have tended to accent ethnic and gender differences; while the ways in which capitalist firms have sometimes encouraged "participation", in different forms, by some employees, and in which societies have permitted *some* social mobility, have blunted the potential for conflict. "Community", too, has remained a more vital part of everyday experience than the theorists thought would be the case. Indeed, in many very different contexts, whether of the slums in which new migrants to the United States settled early in the century, or in the "working class" districts of new cities in the Third World, such as Bombay, or in the old industrial towns of Europe and North America, a sense of community, based on neighborhood, perhaps combined with a sense of shared ethnic identity, has been at least as important in the definition of self as ever it has been.

From liberal democracy to mass democracy

Alongside Fordism the rise of mass democracy is the other defining structural change of the 20th century. Much confusion has resulted from the many meanings of the term "democracy". It means literally "rule by the people", but each of the parts of this statement can be interpreted in different ways. These difficulties have been compounded by the similarly wide usage of the word "liberal". "Liberal democracy" in the 19th century meant a system of government based on a restricted franchise requiring property qualifications – effectively it was an "egalitarian oligarchy" in which "a ruling class of citizens shared in the rights and spoils of political control" (R.M. McIver). The political philosophy of liberalism upheld the notion of a society based on freely contracting individuals, bound by the rule of law, but it did not recognize the contradiction between the equality of individuals in theory and the real inequalities and indignities to which many people were subject in their daily lives. In the later 19th century and early 20th century the contradiction began to work itself out in the transition to "mass democracy", based on a universal franchise, and in the formation of mass political parties.

The accelerated development of industrialization, rapid population growth, and accompanying concentration of people into cities created what came to be recognized as "mass society". And the egalitarian oligarchy that ruled, made up by landowning, aristocratic business people and would-be "gentlemen" bourgeois (for there was an increasing combination and merging of old aristocracy and rising bourgeoisie), felt itself forced to recognize a need to incorporate the masses into political life. A different game of political management was on. Industrialization required a more educated working class and the extension of education both encouraged political participation and the creation of mass-based political parties, and made possible a sense of nationality and of nationhood. The word "nationalism" only acquired currency toward the end of the 19th century, but it has been one of the driving forces of social change in the 20th. Ruling elites created supposedly "traditional" rituals and symbols to encourage nationalism; and the extent to which a sense of national identity outweighed that of class was clearly shown in the way in which workers volunteered to fight each other in 1914.

But labor organization and, outside the United States, mass parties based on the "working class" – heterogeneous though it was in terms of people's experiences of work and living – did become powerful in the early 20th century. For a time, in the

▶ **Laboring life in postwar Germany: workers off home in Bremen, 1950.**

aftermath of World War I, the heralded "proletarian revolution" seemed imminent, encouraged by the success of social revolution in the relatively backward economy of czarist Russia in 1917. But the possibility of radical social upheaval elsewhere vanished with remarkable speed. In part this was because of the interests of the organized labor movement in the success of the capitalist economy, a tendency which has steadily increased through the century. Eventually workers, through investments made by their pension funds and insurance companies, became significant owners of capital. Another aspect of the relative failure of radical labor politics in much of the world has been the often militant hostility of the substantial "middle class", including members of the petty bourgeoisie, self-employed professional people, and sometimes the smallholding peasantry. These groups provided the main support for fascism in the 1930s and sometimes still supported ultraright politics in the later part of the century. Fascism offered an authoritarian system of rule and economic management, often attractive to ruling elites because it has also commanded widespread popular support, stemming from its appeals to a virulent nationalism.

From liberalism to planning and back again?

As one of the founding fathers of contemporary history writing, Geoffrey Barraclough, wrote: "communism, fascism and the modern western multiparty system are all different responses to the breakdown of 19th-century liberal democracy under the pressure of mass society". For all their substantial differences they have involved a common challenge to liberal values, because all have espoused a philosophy of state intervention. States began to intervene in economy and society much more extensively around the turn of the century, in order to try to make capitalism work better, for example by controlling monopolies, and in order to incorporate the masses through provision of welfare. These tendencies crystallized in the Depression of the 1930s and in World War II, following which the necessity of planning and of state regulation of economy and society were almost universally accepted. The competing systems of "capitalist democracy" and "communism" shared this philosophy to a remarkable extent. This seemed to confirm at last the implication in the writings of the French philosopher Saint-Simon on industrial society, at the beginning of the 19th century, that industrialism entails socialism, at least in the sense that it rests on the rational, scientific, efficient organization of society for production.

The triumph of Fordism after 1945 was associated with an alliance, often uneasy though it was, between business, the state and organized labor – a "corporatism" which tended to move decision-making from parliamentary assemblies to negotiation and bargaining between the state and these major organized interest groups. The settlement, which led some to talk of "the end of ideology" and of class conflict, brought an undreamt-of level of welfare provision for the mass of the people, just as the success of capitalist industrialization finally created mass consumerism. A British prime minister, Harold Macmillan, could claim with justice in 1959 that "You've never had it so good".

Yet not long after this time the consensual model of triumphant progress was torn up by conflict, as those excluded from the corporatist settlement, notably blacks and other ethnic minorities in western societies, young people and women rose up in rebellion. It was subjected to radical criticism from within by those who questioned the values of bourgeois society or – for example with "the Limits to Growth" debate of the early 1970s – the extent to which economic growth was morally justified or physically sustainable in the long run. It

◀ Dark side of an Asian "little tiger": a slum block in Hong Kong.

was not so much these critics, however, as the economic events of the 1970s and 1980s, which brought a resurgence of 19th-century values. Fordism had erected rather rigid, inflexible production systems. State intervention under the corporatist settlement had created enormous fiscal burdens, partly in paying for high levels of welfare, and so, it was argued, had stifled both individual feedom and enterprise. Part of the reorganization or "restructuring" which took place under the regime of flexible accumulation was the drive to "roll back the state" associated especially with President Ronald Reagan in the United States and Prime Minister Margaret Thatcher in Britain. By the end of the 1980s the desirability of planning was no longer unquestioned; public sector organizations had often been privatized; and market principles were being introduced into the delivery of education, welfare and all public services. The former "socialist" economies in Eastern Europe awaited the deliverance of the market economy.

The structural changes which have affected societies outside the western, industrialized nations and Japan, have to an important extent been determined by their relationships with the leading capitalist economies. The first communist regime to come into being, in Russia, quickly took an authoritarian turn, partly perhaps because of old Russian concepts of rule, but also because of the demands of defense against what was often perceived to be a greater threat from outside than really existed. But the underlying reasons for the moral and economic bankruptcy of that system, and the extraordinary speed with which, at the end of the 1980s, the erstwhile Soviet satellites rejected this form of communism, had to do rather with the foundations of Soviet society in a rigid, authoritarian system of government and the lack of humanity in the construction of societies around principles of bureaucratic rationality.

Such was the discrediting of socialism in the late 1980s that it is quite difficult to remember that not long before this time socialism was seen as the "natural" form of government and social organization, not least in societies which were seeking to "develop" following the defeat of imperialism by nationalist struggles for freedom from colonial rule. Colonial rule had implanted some capitalist production, but in the colonies both the local bourgeoisies and the working class were usually very small. Most people remained peasant producers for whom the notion of "the nation" was rather remote. The political movements which led the struggle for freedom were dominated by professional people and minor functionaries of the colonial state, for whom alone the idea of "nation" had meaning. Not unnaturally, when these elites took power they were inclined to the view that the state had to play a leading role in development. They took over the government institutions created by the former colonial powers and they were encouraged in their beliefs by the economic theories and political philosophy of the time.

In practice the regimes which succeeded in colonial states were rarely at all "socialist", because they mostly came quite quickly to depart from democracy and because they sought to control the economy rather than to run it through effective popular participation. "Socialism" was a guise for expanding state control, often in a way which meant that political imperatives in the management of political support undermined economic interests. Because of the kind of economic policy pursued, which created inefficient industries behind protective tariff barriers, and neglected agriculture or ran it down in seeking to take resources from it, the story of "development" in much of the Third World has not been one of great success. It is possible to be too pessimistic, however, and to forget the progress that there has been in terms of such fundamental criteria of human well-being as life expectancy or literacy.

The great successes of the former "Third World", the newly industrialized countries such as South Korea and Taiwan, and (increasingly) Malaysia, owe their achievements to a whole range of factors. Amongst them is *not* the fact that they have had noninterventionist states. Their states have been highly interventionist. Where they differ from other, still "less developed" countries is in the nature of state power and the effectiveness of intervention. Elsewhere the failures of "modernization" are significantly to do with the attempt to extend bureaucratic control but in circumstances in which rational-legal authority is undermined by the political system.

The failures of modernization through economic development based on industrialization are at least partly responsible for some of the outstanding social phenomena of the end of the 20th century – nationalism, violent conflict between groups of people who define themselves in terms of linguistic, tribal, caste or religious affiliation, and the resurgence of religious fundamentalism. It would be much too simple to suggest that these can all be explained as just the responses to economic failure, though this failure does have a part to play in explanation. More broadly, trends such as the rise of Hindu nationalism in India have to do with the inability of political classes to live up to the modernizing ideals they had set for themselves.

Women, households and family life.

This brief account of the determining structural changes of the 20th century has so far failed, just like the great social scientists of the 19th century, to take account of half of humanity – of women or of the households of many different forms in which most people live. Marx's theory of capitalism, for example, largely ignored the fact that this economic system depends on upaid labor, mainly of women in the household, for the reproduction of the labor force. The other great structural tendency of this century, as yet far from complete, concerns the increased resistance of women to their subjection under patriarchy. The struggle did not start in this century, but it derived major impetus from the fight for the extension of the fanchise which took off around the beginning of the century. Almost throughout there has been an ever developing contradiction between the idea of women as citizens, as members of society with the same rights as men, on the one hand, and deeply held beliefs on the other, that women's primary role must be as mothers, and because of this essentially "in the home". A constant theme of social policy in most countries has been the need to ensure the stability of family life, and whenever social and political elites have felt at all threatened a part of their response has been to argue for revival of "stable" family values.

There has often been a simple contradiction, therefore, between political rhetoric about women's rights and the social policies that governments have pursued. In spite of this, and in spite of the persistence and sometimes the deepening of the real inequality of treatment of women as opposed to men everywhere, women have become increasingly organized in both "developing" and "developed" countries. The women's movement(s) form the most important of the new political movements which have grown up toward the end of the century which include also peace movements and "green" or environmental movements. Some of these organizations, especially the women's movement, are "new" in the sense that they reject incorporation into the existing political system, as for example by constituting a party, or being affiliated to a party, and because they aim to resist the pervasive control

exercised by the state over all spheres of life, rather than to take it over. In their methods of organization too, some of them aim resist the tendencies of bureaucratic organization toward a dehumanizing, hierarchical rationality. They stand out, too, against another of the tendencies of this century: the isolation of families and individuals in an increasingly *sub*urban, rather than urban or rural existence.

Continuity and change

The "grand model" of modern, industrial society of the 19th-century philosophers has proven an imperfect guide to the changes of the 20th century. "Industrial society", in the way they envisaged it, never really happened; "community" did not die away, though what people imagined as communities

changed a great deal so that "tribes", "caste", religious sects and "nations" have acquired a salience that our forebears did not anticipate; and the whirligig of time seems latterly to have made both religion more significant and the idea of society as rationally administered by the state more remote, as well as unpopular. Meanwhile "property owning democracy, middle class in structure" and the sovereign national state remain anchors of our social lives. The values of 19th-century liberalism, celebrating the notions of individual equality and liberty before the law and of order as emerging from the interactions of freely contracting individuals, have reemerged with vigor. A popular conception has it that socialism, which some 19th-century philosophers thought the likely partner of industrialization, is if not dead then at least on its last legs.

Yet the 19th-century philosophers, notably Marx and Weber, did provide us with powerful ideas for exploring the social changes of our own time. Their concern about the dark inner lining of modernity, the way in which it threatens to dehumanize people through the impersonality of markets and of bureaucracies, remains with us. The problems socialism has sought, inadequately though it has thus far turned out, to address in the 20th century, problems of inequality and poverty which make a mockery of the theory of equality before the law, and of the effective exclusion of large numbers of people from exercising significant control over their own lives, also remain. Social history shows no signs of having come to an end.

▲ **Muslims in an age of resurgent Islam: pilgrims in Mecca, 1980.**

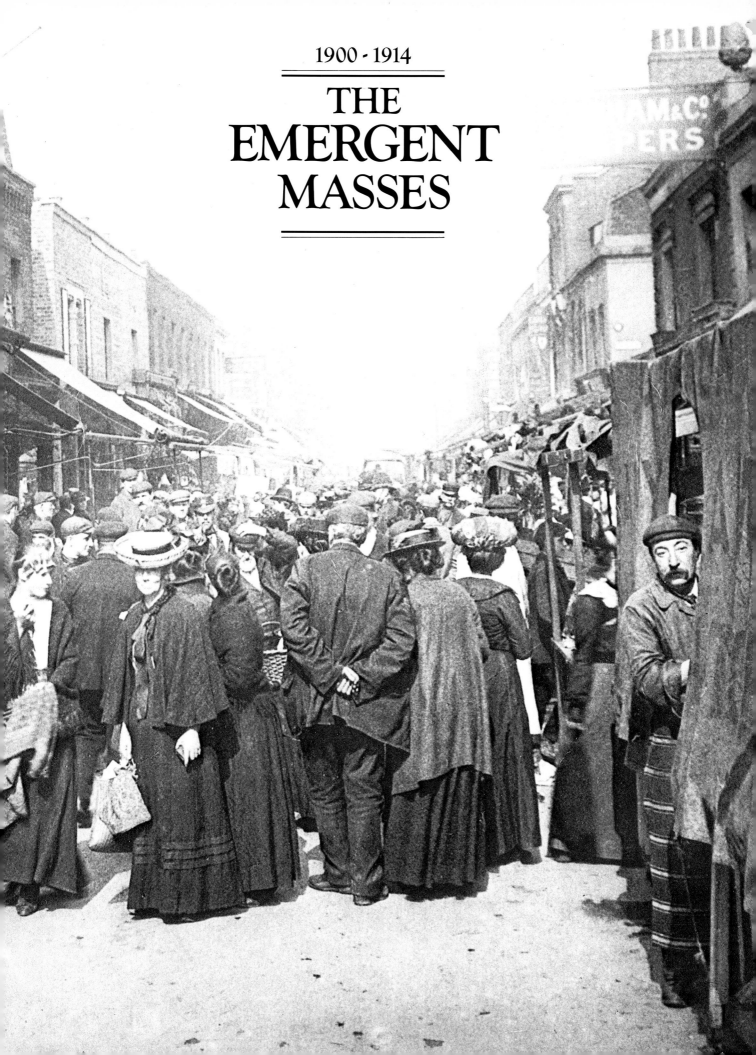

1900 - 1914

THE EMERGENT MASSES

Time Chart

	1900	1901	1902	1903	1904	1905	1906	1907
Rural life	• Irrigated cropland totals 100 million acres worldwide, up from 20 million in 1880	• By May, 1.25 million have died in famine in India. British report blames over-population	• National Reclamation Act encourages family farms (USA) • Dec: Protectionist tariff enforced in Germany, restoring higher duty on imported agricultural products	• Russian harvest fails, creating a famine which claims the lives of millions	• First caterpillar tractor produced in California (USA)	• 1 Feb: US President Roosevelt creates a Bureau of Forestry within the US Department of Agriculture • Foundation of the International Agricultural Institute in Rome	• Prime minister Pyotr Stolypin reforms the *mir* system by distributing communal land among the peasantry (Russ) • China pledges to suppress cultivation and consumption of opium over ten years	• Four million people starving in China due to famine caused by heavy rains and crop failure • 20 million starving Russia's worst ever famine
Industry and labor	• Feb: Formation of Labour Representative Committee (UK) • Sep: Fifth Congress of the Socialist International in Paris • Dec: National Civic Federation formed in the USA, for the arbitration of labor disputes • American Federation of Labor (AF of L) is formed from 216 trade unions • Only 3.5% of the US workforce is unionized	• Jul: Beginning of a steelworkers' strike in USA • Dec: Unemployed workers demonstrate and riot in Budapest (Aust-Hung) • Foundation in Amsterdam of the International Trade Union • Taff Vale Ruling: House of Lords rules that unions can be sued (UK)	• Jan–Feb: Strikes of Mediterranean Railway employees demanding recognition of their union • 7 Apr: Foundation of the Texas Oil Company (Texaco) (USA) • 12 May–13 Oct: United Mine Workers strike demanding a nine-hour day and wage increase (USA) • Oct: Two-thirds of French miners are out on strike	• Apr: Week-long general strike in the Netherlands, put down by the military • Nov: Spanish miners strike, demanding their wages be paid weekly • Legislation for the regulation of children's labor in the USA and Germany • 50,000 Chinese coolies are imported into the Transvaal, but prove to be disorderly so are repatriated in 1907 (SA)	• 27 Apr: Australia elects a minority Labor government • Aug: End of disruption in the petrol industry at Boryslaw (Aust-Hung) with the demand met for a reduction of working hours	• Sep: Trades Union Congress demands provisions for free trade and an eight-hour day (UK) • Foundation of the Bethlehem Steel Company (USA) • China boycotts US goods as a protest against the latter's restrictive immigration policies • Strike of miners in the Ruhr and Belgium, demanding a reduction of working hours (Ger/Bel)	• Mar: Series of severe strikes begins in Germany • Dec: Trade Disputes Act reverses the 1901 ruling in the Taff Vale case (UK) • Labour Representative Committee becomes the Parliamentary Labour Party (UK) • Upton Sinclair's *The Jungle* exposes the terrible conditions in the meat packing industry (USA)	• May: Sailors in Marseille proclaim a general strike for improved working conditions (Fr) • Formation of the Confédération Générale des Vignerons, an organization of vineyard workers, after a decline in wine prices in 1906 caused an epidemic of strike and unrest (until 191 (Fr)
Government and people	• Mar: French legislation limits working day for women and children to eleven hours • May: First trial of proportional representation, in Belgium • Jul: Canada forbids the immigration of paupers and criminals	• Sep: Congress of the International Association for the Legal Protection of Workers agrees on a package of workers' legislation for all countries • 21 Dec: Women vote for the first time in Norwegian local elections	• 1 Feb: Working day for women and children reduced from 11 to 10.5 hours (Fr) • 5 Feb: Miners' working day is fixed at nine hours (Fr) • Dec: Education Act places elementary and secondary education under the control of county councils	• 14 Feb: US Congress votes to create a Department of Commerce and Labor • 22 Mar: Coal Commission suggests shorter hours and higher pay (USA) • Aug: International Miners' Conference calls for minimum wage and eight-hour day	• National Child Labor Committee created by reformers to promote protective legislation (USA) • Interdepartmental Committee on Physical Deterioration reports on bad living conditions and ill-health in British slums	• May: Meeting of the International Conference for the Protection of Laborers discusses night work for women • Eight-hour day introduced for all miners under 18 years (UK)	• May: US government prohibits any further expansion of the Rockefeller Oil Trust by passing the Sherman Act • School Meals Act provides free meals for children (UK) • US Pure Food and Drug Act prohibits misbranding of and tampering with foods	• Feb: US Congress legislates to limit entry of Japanese laborers after immigration peaks at 1.29 million • 15 Mar: First woman elected to parliament in Finland • May: First meeting of the Women's Labou League chaired by M Ramsay MacDonald (UK)
Religion	• Aug–Apr 1901: Anti-Jewish riots in Odessa (Russ) • Shintoism is reinstated in Japan to counter Buddhist influences	• Feb: Spain is swept by anti-Jesuit riots • Apr: Pope Leo XIII condemns the European trend toward state regulation of the Catholic Church	• Harvard professor William James writes *Varieties of Religious Experience*, an attempt to reconcile science and religion (USA)	• 18 Mar: French government refuses all applications to teach from religious orders • Aug: Accession of Pope Pius X on the death of Leo XIII • Unification of the black churches in South Africa to form the Ethiopian Church		• 8 Nov: Pogroms are initiated by the "Black Hundreds" terrorists in Odessa. By 1909, 50,000 Jews have been killed (Russ) • 9 Dec: French law decrees the separation of Church and State, a move condemned by Pius X	• American Jewish Commission founded to protect the rights of Jews and fight prejudice • Publication of Albert Schweitzer's *The Quest for the Historical Jesus* (Ger)	• 8 Sep: Pius X issues papal encyclical *Pascendi gregis*, condemning liberal modernists who recently were calling for a revision of Church policy and dogma to square them with modern scientific scholarship (It)
Events and trends	• Dec: British deaths in the Boer War reach 11,000 • Freud publishes *The Interpretation of Dreams*, a work which revolutionizes understanding of the human unconscious (Aust-Hung) • Kodak introduces the Box Brownie camera, thus popularizing photography (USA)	• 11 Dec: Marconi transmits the first transatlantic wireless signal • European population exceeds 400 million • First Nobel Prizes awarded in Sweden • Oldsmobile, the first mass-produced gasoline-driven car, is introduced (USA)	• 15 Feb: Berlin underground railroad (U-bahn) opens • 4 Mar: Foundation of the American Automobile Association • Dec: Completion of the first Aswan Dam (Egy) • Publication of J.A. Hobson's *Imperialism*, a work whose ideas later becomes part of Leninist ideology (UK)	• Aug: Sixth Zionist conference in Basel (Swi) rejects a British proposal for a Jewish homeland in Uganda • 10 Oct: Foundation of the Women's Social and Political Union by Emmeline Pankhurst (UK) • "Typhoid Mary" is discovered to be the carrier of the disease during an epidemic in New York (USA)	• Mar: Publication of color photographs in London's *Daily Illustrated Mirror* (UK) • 27 Oct: Opening of the New York Subway • Thomas Sullivan pioneers the teabag (USA)	• 4 Apr: Earthquake in Lahore, India, claims over 10,000 lives • English suffragettes step up their campaign with hunger strikes and acts of violence • Publication of Max Weber's *The Protestant Ethic and the Spirit of Capitalism*, arguing that Luther and Calvin are among the wellsprings of modern capitalism (Ger)	• 19 Apr: Severe earthquake in San Francisco kills 1,000 people and destroys much of the city (USA) • Roman Catholic clergyman John Ryan condemns insufficient wage systems in *A Living Wage* (USA)	• Bubonic plague kills 1.3 million in India • Lord Baden Powell founds the Boy Scout Movement (UK) • Mohandas Gandhi begins a campaign of passive resistance (*satyagraha*) to the Asiatic registration bill of 22 Mar (Ind) • Mothers' Day first celebrated, in the US
Politics	• Jun–Aug: Boxer Uprising against the foreign presence in China is put down by an international task force	• 22 Jan: Death of Queen Victoria and accession of Edward VII (UK) • 6 Sep: Theodore Roosevelt becomes president after the assassination of McKinley (USA)	• 31 May: Boer rebels surrender to the British in South Africa • 28 Jun: USA pays $40 million for the Panama Canal	• 18 Nov: Signing of the Panama Canal Treaty • Bolsheviks led by Lenin split from the Mensheviks at the London Congress of the Russian Social Democratic Party	• 8 Feb: Beginning of the Russo-Japanese War	• 9 Jan: First revolution in Russia begins on Bloody Sunday • 5 Sep: Treaty of Portsmouth ends Russo-Japanese War after the Russian defeat	• Rehabilitation of Alfred Dreyfus after it is proved that the charges of treason brought against him in 1894 were false (Fr)	• 10 Jun: Franco-Japanese Treaty ensures open door economic access to China

1908	1909	1910	1911	1912	1913	1914
• 90% of horsepower on English and Welsh farms still provided by horses • Rural population of USA falls to 50% of total	• First kibbutz started at Degania Aleph (Pal) • US lumber production reaches its peak	• Mexican social revolution is led by Madero against President Diaz who had allowed Indian and mestizo land to be taken by whites • R. Biffen breeds Little Jos, a wheat suitable for British climate and resistant to the yellow rust fungus	• Famine reduces 30 million Russians to starvation, even though 13.7 million tonnes of Russian grain is exported	• New Homestead Act reduces residence requirement from five to three years (USA) • Department of Justice orders the dissolution of the International Harvester Trust (USA)		• Revelation that British farmers produce less than 25% of the nation's grain needs • George Washington Carver reveals experiment results showing how peanuts and sweet potatoes can replenish soil fertility (USA)
• 18 Feb: Plan for the restriction of Japanese labor emigration to the USA mooted by Japan, to settle disputes between the two countries • Sep: International Conference for the Protection of Labor demands prohibition of night-work for children • Supreme Court imprisons three AF of L leaders for violating an injunction against a boycott (USA)	• Apr–May: Paris postal workers on strike over demands to unionize and to affiliate with the Confédération Générale du Travail (Fr) • Aug: One-month general strike in Sweden over economic conditions • Three-month strike by 20,000 garment workers (USA)	• Jan: British miners strike for an eight-hour day • Aug–Sep: Dockers strike for higher wages (Ger/UK) • Oct: Strike of French railroadmen nearly leads to a general strike	• Jan: Miners' strike in the Belgian coal district • 15 May: Supreme Court breaks up Rockefeller's Standard Oil Company (USA) • Aug: British railroadmen go on strike • Olivetti Company founded (It)	• Jan: General strike in Lisbon over dissatisfaction with the new regime • Mar: Miners' strike in the Ruhr ends in failure • Apr: Army suppresses goldminers' strike in Siberia (Russ) • May–Jun: Transport strike in London causes a sympathetic strike by 100,000 dockers (UK) • Textile workers' strike in Lawrence, Massachusetts, demonstrates the power of the International Workers of the World (IWW) (USA)	• 14–24 Apr: 100,000 miners strike in Belgium demanding a revision of the franchise laws (achieved May 1919) • Department of Labor is created by the Wilson administration in response to AF of L pressure (USA) • United Federation of Labor and of the Social Democratic Party founded in New Zealand, providing for the interests of industrial workers	• Jan: General strike initiated by South African gold and diamond miners and railroadmen • Jan: Ford Motor Co introduces profit-sharing and higher wages to avoid threatened labor trouble (USA) • May: Trade unions of miners, transport workers and railroadmen found a common committee for collective bargaining (UK) • 15 Oct: Clayton Anti-Trust Act strengthens government stand against combinations (USA)
• Invalid and Old Age Pensions Act passed in Australia	• Apr: Lloyd George introduces the "People's Budget" with new taxes to fund welfare provision (UK) • May: Old Age Pensions Act provides for noncontributory pension of five shillings per week for those over 70 years (UK) • Federal old age pensions awarded to those over 65 and resident in Australia for over 25 years	• Apr: First majority Labor government in Australia continues the program of heavy taxation and allowing "desirable" white immigrants into the Northern Territory • Old age pensions introduced in France • China abolishes slavery	• 30 Apr: Constitutional court establishes female suffrage in Portugal • Dec: Lloyd George's National Insurance Act provides unemployment insurance for 2.25 million workers (UK)	• 29 Mar: Minimum wage enforced after a strike of 1,500,000 miners (UK) • Massachusetts institutes a minimum wage law for women and children (USA) • Russia adopts workmen's insurance • French *Code du Travail* issued	• 25 Feb: US introduces federal income tax via the Sixteenth Amendment • Apr: Suffragette leader Emmeline Pankhurst is sentenced to three years imprisonment (UK) • 29 Jun: Norwegian parliament grants women equal electoral rights with men	• Jan: General Hertzog founds the Nationalist Party in South Africa, which becomes a platform for Boer separatism • 26 May: UK House of Commons passes the Irish Home Rule Bill for the third time, bypassing the Lords by way of the 1911 Parliament Act (enforced 1920)
• Completion of the Hejaz Railroad to the holy places of Mecca and Medina after eight years (Ott Emp)			• 19 Apr: Provisional government in Portugal separates Church and State		• 13 Jan: Pope bans films from churches and forbids films of a religious nature • Rudolf Steiner founds the first Goetheanum, for the teaching of anthroposophy, at Dornach (Swi) • B'nai B'rith founds the Anti-Defamation League to fight antisemitism (USA)	• May: Reports of extreme cruelties by Serbians against Albanian muslims • Aug: Death of Pope Pius X, succeeded by Benedict XV
• Creation of the Federal Bureau of Investigation (FBI) (USA) • Aug: Ford introduces the Model T automobile • *The Times* newspaper of London is acquired by Viscount Northcliffe who also publishes the *London Daily Mail* and the *Daily Mirror* (UK)	• Jun: National Negro Committee founded in New York, becoming the National Association for the Advancement of Colored People (NAACP) in 1910 (USA) • Selfridge, the first large department store in Britain, founded by US businessman H.G. Selfridge, opens in London (UK) • Girl Guides established in the UK	• Boy Scouts and Campfire Girls of America are founded • Pathé Gazette pioneers the film newsreel (USA/UK) • Fathers' Day first celebrated, in Spokane, Washington DC (USA)	• 17 Apr: New York's Ellis Island records a record influx of 11,745 immigrants in a single day (USA) • 16 Dec: Roald Amundsen raises the Norwegian flag over the South Pole, two months ahead of Robert F. Scott • Founding of *Union or Death* (The Black Hand), an anti-Austrian propagandist society, in Serbia	• 15 Apr: Sinking of the *S.S. Titanic* on her maiden voyage across the Atlantic Ocean; 1,513 lives are lost • Journal *Pravda* begins to voice the ideas of Russia's underground Communist Party • Benito Mussolini becomes chief editor of the Italian Socialist Party newspaper *Avanti* • Mar: Girl Scouts of America founded	• Marcus Garvey founds the Universal Negro Improvement Association (Jam) • Dr Henry Plotz discovers a typhoid vaccine (USA)	• Oct: George Eastman announces the invention of the color photo process (USA) • US feminist Margaret Sanger introduces the term "birth control" in *The Woman Rebel* and exiles herself to England to avoid prosecution
		• 31 May: Union of South Africa becomes a Commonwealth dominion under Louis Botha • 22 Aug: Japan annexes Korea and renames it Chosen	• 10 Aug: Parliament Act restricts House of Lords veto power (UK) • 10 Oct: Revolution begins in China leading to the end of the Manchu dynasty	• 12 Feb: Abdication of boy-emperor Pu Yi, and a provisional government takes control in China (15 Feb) • 18 Oct: Outbreak of First Balkan War	• 4 Mar: Woodrow Wilson becomes 28th US president (until 1921)	• 28 Jun: Assassination in Sarajevo (Bosnia) of Archduke Franz Ferdinand of Austria creates war crisis • 1–3 Aug: Germany declares war on Russia and France, and invades Belgium

23

Datafile

The systematic study of society began in the 19th century partly in response to anxiety among ruling groups about the social impact of industrialization and urbanization. The breakdown of "social order" was widely feared. By the beginning of the 20th century the "second industrial revolution", based on electricity and chemicals, was under way. Big corporations were becoming established, and industrial work was beginning to be subject to new methods of control under "scientific management". Yet most people, even in the advanced industrial nations, were still peasant farmers, agricultural workers or employees in small enterprises. "Industrial society" was not yet fully formed.

Industrial countries 1900

Pig iron output

- USA
- UK
- Germany
- Russia
- France
- Others

◄ **By 1900 industrial leadership, reflected here in the relative output of a basic industrial product, had passed to the United States. The world economy, however, still depended on British financial and shipping services, and was based on sterling.**

◄ **Only in the United Kingdom was there an "industrial society" in which more were employed in manufacturing than in agriculture. But the United States produced more with fewer manufacturing workers.**

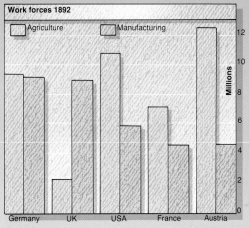

Work forces 1892

- Agriculture
- Manufacturing

Millions

Germany UK USA France Austria

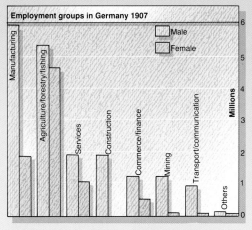

Employment groups in Germany 1907

- Male
- Female

Millions

Manufacturing, Agriculture/forestry/fishing, Services, Construction, Commerce/finance, Mining, Transport/communication, Others

◄ **By 1907 among German men manufacturing had overtaken agriculture as the chief source of employment. But the proportion of the whole work force employed in manufacturing was only to increase from 29 to 33 percent by 1939. Meanwhile the services sectors (including finance, commerce and transport) increased from 22 to 32 percent. Where agriculture has declined worldwide in the 20th century, "services" has usually become the predominant employment sector – not manufacturing.**

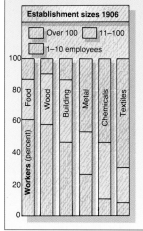

Establishment sizes 1906

- Over 100
- 11–100
- 1–10 employees

Workers (percent)

Food, Wood, Building, Metal, Chemicals, Textiles

◄ **In 1906 59 percent of all industrial workers in France were still employed in establishments with less than ten employees. But the proportion in big factories was much higher in the modern industries based on machine production.**

► **Europe's rural areas encompassed a wide range of economies, as is suggested by this information for prewar France. Local agricultural practice could influence social structures, producing distinctive local areas or *pays*.**

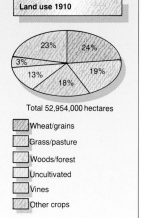

Land use 1910

Total 52,954,000 hectares

- Wheat/grains
- Grass/pasture
- Woods/forest
- Uncultivated
- Vines
- Other crops

At the beginning of the 20th century parts of northwest Europe and North America were caught up in profound social change as a consequence of industrialization – the process in which the productivity of human labor is raised through the harnessing of power and the application of science to improve production methods. Industrialization was organized by capitalists: private owners of wealth who invested it to earn profits and who employed the labor of others. For these employees, industrialization meant that they lived in big cities (rather than villages or small towns), worked in factories or offices (rather than in agriculture), and that the pace of work was determined by machinery (rather than individual capacity).

Industrialization and employment

How far had capitalist industrialization proceeded by the beginning of the 20th century? The first and for a time the only industrial society was that of Britain, where industrialization had first gathered pace toward the end of the 18th century. But by 1900 Britain's industrial supremacy had given way in the face of competition from the United States and from Germany. By 1913 the United States accounted for about one-third of the world's manufacturing output, equal to the shares of Germany, Britain and France combined. But even in these, the advanced industrial nations of the world, the extent to which societies had become dependent on industry was limited. A contemporary British statistician, Michael Mulhall, wrote as follows, referring to what he called "the nations of Christendom": "One half of the world is engaged in agricultural pursuits, one fourth in manufactures, one-tenth in trade and transport and the remainder [15 percent] in professions, public service and other useful occupations". It is true that by 1914 less than half of the labor force was employed in agriculture in Britain, France, Germany, the Low Countries and the United States, but in France the proportion so engaged remained 43 percent and in Germany 35 percent. Only in Britain was it as low as 8 percent.

In spite of the rapid growth in the number and size of cities which had taken place in the 19th century, there was no country apart from Britain where the total urban population exceeded that of the rural areas. Not until 1920, indeed, did the urban population of the United States outstrip that of the rural areas.

Outside the west the most important industrializing state was Imperial Russia. There industrialization was being telescoped into a few decades by drawing on foreign technology, skills and investment. Between 1909 and 1913 alone industrial output rose by 54 percent and the factory work force increased by 30 percent.

NEW WORLDS OF WORK

The world of manufacturing itself, however, remained in some ways remarkably unchanged from the conditions previously found in craft workshops, even in the advanced industrial nations. It has been said of American industry at the beginning of the century that "the factory remained a congeries of craftsmen's shops rather than an integrated plant". In London the 8,500 factories using power employed an average of only 41 workers each. Large-scale industrial enterprises were in fact more prominent as a proportion of new industry in Russia, though this suggests a misleading impression of advance given that it reflects the labor intensity and lower productivity of Russian industry.

Before the Industrial Revolution industrial work had largely consisted of "manufacturing", literally understood as "the process of making by hand" and thereby subject to dependence upon skills of individuals. In factory production work consisted of a system of "machinofacture", in which the pace of work was dictated by machines and was thereby more under the control of employers or owners. Yet by 1900 the transition from manufacture to machinofacture had not in fact proceeded very far.

Social order and change in the countryside

In the late 19th century, partly in response to fears about the breakdown of "social order", the study of human social institutions – sociology – had become established as an academic discipline. Its first practitioners, notably the Frenchman Emile Durkheim (1858–1917), considered that many of the social problems of their time had been caused by the spread of industry and the expansion of cities. The pioneering academic sociologists sought to interpret these changes. Durkheim suggested that there had been a change in the basis of the social order: from "mechanical solidarity"

▼ A production line at one of Henry Ford's automobile plants c. 1913, where "the pace was inexorable, the pressure for ever-better production insistent".

to "organic solidarity". In traditional rural societies people did the same kind of work and generally had the same kinds of experiences and identities but in societies where there was a great range of specialized jobs, people were related to each other by each performing a necessary inter-related task. By implication, even if the range of occupations increased and people became more individual, a stable social order could be maintained because of people's economic inter-dependence.

Durkheim's theory seems to have presupposed that the process of industrialization was more complete than it actually was around 1900. In fact most of the world's people, even in the advanced industrial nations, remained agricultural workers, many of them still peasants – owners or tenant cultivators of small landholdings and some other assets which they worked with their own labor and with that of their household members. Moreover, some agriculture was proving to be

more flexible and adaptable than anyone had expected.

In the mid 19th century the radical German social thinker Karl Marx had suggested that the growth of large units of production in industry would be associated with a similar development in agriculture and that small-scale producers would be forced out. But again, another idea about likely social and economic changes proved incorrect. Several developments gave peasant agriculture a new lease of life: the establishment of peasant cooperatives; the gradual extension of political rights to peasants; protection of agricultural markets; increased education; and cheap transport. They expanded the potential for such activities as intensive small-scale livestock rearing, dairying and horticulture. Indeed, the long slump in international grain prices, from 1874 to 1896, hit the largest farms hardest and benefited the smallholders. Large farms had depended on wage laborers, who only did what they were told

▲ Smallholding peasants, seen here at a market in France, still made up much of the work force over most of Europe. The establishment of the wholesaler and distiller seen in the background, however, reflects the penetration of commerce into agriculture. The expansion of the railroad network had begun to break down isolated rural communities.

(and no more) and who would slacken their effort when no one was watching. The price depression dented the profitability of such farms and caused a reduction in the proportion of agricultural workers employed on them. By contrast, as a contemporary Russian economist, A.V. Chayanov, argued influentially, labor on the small peasant family farm was more motivated and flexible, and also responsive to changing conditions. In the late 19th and early 20th century peasant agriculture was sometimes becoming increasingly successful commercially.

The creation of big business

Even though capitalist industry had not taken over societies in the way in which many thinkers thought it must do, capitalism itself had by 1900 entered a new phase. Sometimes called "monopoly capitalism", it was a phase characterized by competition between a small number of rival large-scale firms rather than between individual small capitalists, and by imperialist rivalry between capitalist countries. The economic depression after 1870 had given rise to protectionism and to a quest for new markets. There were also needs for new products, such as oil and rubber, and an expanding mass demand for tropical foodstuffs like bananas among the increasing numbers of people who lived by purchases in the market and were no longer dependent on self-provisioning.

The search for markets and for commodities, or sometimes political compulsion alone, drove the expansion of colonial empires. All these trends had considerable impact on the kind of employment available in many countries and on the organization of industry and business.

In the early 20th century new industries of the so-called "second industrial revolution" were emerging in the major industrial countries that were to dominate the century – oil and petrochemicals, electrical equipment, radio and communications, vehicles and many other forms of metal manufacture, synthetic materials, etc. Many of these industries could only be developed with major initial capital investment or, after the initial

New farm implements were being bought and they were costly. In the end it would perhaps be an economy but how could one be certain...? The most ignorant, that is to say the majority, evidently relied on the experience of the more prosperous and better educated. They copied them full of wonder at their knowledge and began to think that...it would be a good thing to be able to think things over, pen in hand.

R. THAUBAULT

Life in European Villages

In 1900 the majority of Europe's population lived in rural societies, usually in villages which had an average population of about 500. Strongly contrasting ideas about village life still persist. On the one hand there is an attractive picture of villages as "communities" regulated by values which supply physical and emotional security. On the other rural life is seen as backward and even rather brutish. Marx, for example, spoke of its "idiocy", and an observer of Russia in 1917 wrote that villagers "wallowed like pigs in the pestilential atmosphere, blended of the excretory putrescences exhaled from men and animals".

It is generally thought that traditional rural society, with all the virtues of the community, was in decline by the beginning of the century, due to the impact of schools, railroads and military conscription. Military service accustomed young peasants to urban values and tastes. Peasant families learned the uses of literacy and the transport revolution accelerated rural-urban migration. In 1861 11 percent of Frenchmen lived outside their native department; by 1918 25 percent. Bicycles extended the mobility of young men and allowed them to spend their evenings in cafes and bars in town. Modern sports replaced older village pastimes; folk-dancing began to be ousted by dancing by couples of waltzes and polkas; and folk songs were collected by folklorists to save them from extinction. But the historian of the French peasantry, Eugen Weber, believes that on balance the changes taking place were progressive as education encouraged greater independence from the old rural elite and standards of diet and health began to improve.

It is, however, possible to exaggerate the decline of the "traditional" society. In some ways the changes around 1900 made the countryside *more* rural, for urban competition hit precisely those groups in rural society who had previously provided the contacts between the peasantry and the world of the towns. Even by mid-century social mobility in the countryside was still often restricted. A study of one French village shows that three-quarters of the residents in 1946 had

been born in the village or less than 20km (12.5 mi) away, and that of the 4,000 children born there since 1821 only 50 had finished secondary school. The standard of living remained modest. Three-quarters of the villagers' income was spent on food and their staples were bread and soup.

The image of the self-regulating village community has been extremely powerful in ideas about social development and change, and it is sometimes sought to be renewed through progams of "community development". In practice, however, village societies are often deeply divided by differences of interests.

▲ A village council in Russia, where communal land ownership and organization of farming still survived. It is said that "The commune was a sort of democracy, but a democracy of minority – male heads of household (like those seen here) under whose interests were subsumed the interests of the majority".

development, by attaining great economies of scale. Production rapidly became very concentrated and in some cases companies developed into monopolies. Thus, the tendency to seek control of national markets was considerably enhanced in comparison with the 19th century. In the United States the process of concentration was associated with particular individuals, the "robber barons", and with their business empires which often dominated particular industries: Andrew Carnegie, Henry Ford, Cornelius Vanderbilt, J.P. Morgan etc. John D. Rockefeller made prodigious monopoly profits from the fledgling oil industry.

Great size of firm implied that the enormous mass of shareholders could no longer play any serious role in directing a company. Ownership and management separated. The majority of shareholders became passive "rentiers" or "coupon clippers", with no role in the company except privileged access to a share of profits (and even that was determined by those who managed the company). Giant companies were controlled by those with the largest block of shares, often

financial institutions, banks and insurance companies, with professional managers (who only became "owners" by virtue of being given the company's shares as part of a salary payment). Firms thus often assumed a life and stability independent of the personal fortunes of particular businessmen. They also presented a quite different image from what had gone before. The old competitive markets with a mass of firms scrambling for advantage gave way to large-scale managerial and bureaucratic hierarchies, from the Individual to the Corporation, from the ethics of the jungle to those of status.

The growth in the size of firms was paralleled by the increasing importance of the State. As businesses grew larger and became more sophisticated the demand for educated labor increased enormously. "White collar" workers were becoming increasingly important and a mass phenomenon (unlike the few clerical staff a half century earlier). A mass educational system and universal literacy were becoming necessary, and with it other underpinnings of rising labor productivity – health and welfare schemes.

▲▼ Clerical black coats (like these at Cadbury's in England) were a badge of respectability. Working conditions were improved by inventions such as the electric fan (below), though office jobs became routinized like industrial production.

New organization of work

The depression of the 1870s and 1880s revealed to many industrialists the inadequacy of their control over labor in the workplace. In America this was observed by the pioneer of "scientific management", F.W. Taylor. He wrote that "in most of the shops in this country, the shop [is] really run by the workmen and not by the bosses". Though prices fell during the depression, workers were able to maintain the level of money wages, so that labor costs rose and profits were squeezed. In response employers developed what was known as the "drive system" of production, involving mechanization and decreased reliance on skilled labor, and closer supervision by foremen.

The application of electrical power contributed to the development of the drive system. The machine tools industry was transformed by the introduction of automatic lathes and riveting machines, reducing the level of skills necessary in the manufacture of ships and machines, and encouraging a more rapid pace of work.

The key symbol of the new technology – combining both new methods of organization and new technologies – was the continually moving assembly line. It was introduced by the American automobile manufacturer Henry Ford in 1913. He employed nearly 14,000 people at his plants in Detroit, and from this time the majority were semi-skilled workers using electric-powered equipment to repeat simple operations within a complex manufacturing process. In the words of the sociologist Hugh Beynon, "The machines were the masters and the men had to keep pace with them" – a pattern of work depicted movingly in Charlie Chaplin's film *Modern Times* (1936).

The efforts of employers in the United States to increase their control over labor were met with resistance, reflected in increasing labor unrest toward the end of the 19th century. Then, however, the rise of big corporations saw the introduction of policies to undercut worker opposition. These included the establishment of centralized personnel departments, cooperation with and sometimes cooptation of craft unions and manipulation of ethnic differences among workers.

The last was assisted by fresh waves of immigration. For the most part the immigrants (mainly from the backward regions of eastern and southern Europe) were prepared to take on the most disagreeable jobs and to endure long hours and ruthless exploitation. Mechanization and the simultaneous expansion of the supply of cheap labor undermined craft skills and served to reduce more and more jobs to the level of the semi-skilled. After 1900 the proportion of the industrial labor force made up by such operatives increased and the ratio of their wages to those of skilled workers declined, while the numbers of supervisory workers increased in proportion to those engaged in production.

The growth of industrial bureaucracy, as of public bureaucracy, was assisted by such recent innovations as the typewriter and the adding machine. In offices too work became more routinized, faster paced and noisier.

Bureaucracy

Karl Marx argued that industrial capitalism is the fundamental determinant of modern social change. The German sociologist Max Weber (1864–1920), however, thought that the development of capitalism is itself an effect of a deeper process, which he referred to as that of "rationalization". This means the reorganization of social and economic life according to principles of efficiency, on the basis of technical knowledge. The application of these principles to administration creates bureaucracy which, Weber said, "means fundamentally the exercise of control on the basis of knowledge". Bureaucracies have a clear hierarchy of authority to coordinate decision making; they have written rules of procedure; and they are staffed by salaried officials. They should act according to the rules of the organization so that its functioning is made independent of their individual characteristics. Weber's belief that bureaucracy is the best way of organizing large numbers of people has been borne out by the growth in importance of the white-collar workers who staff bureaucracies.

▲ Early bureaucrat with symbols of authority.

Of course you know I thought I was somebody when I got a job because jobs under an employer were just a thing almost unheard of...They were just engaged and their own craft and suchlike, but get work outside of the home and under an employer and just at a specified job – you thought yourself somebody then.

PETER HENRY
GOODS CHECKER

▼ A dormitory of a Russian factory, c. 1900. Conditions in Russia's large-scale industries were typical of those to be found in most industrializing countries. Factories were overcrowded and stifling; workers were closely supervised; accidents were frequent. The working week was six days, the working day over 11 hours. Forty percent of workers lived in factory dormitories, the remainder packed into rented rooms or apartments. Relief from a monotonous and hard existence was provided by religious holidays, by playing cards and by bouts of heavy drinking.

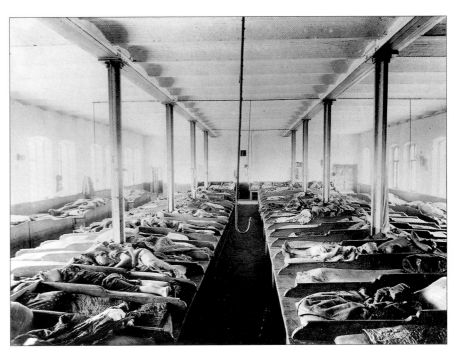

Datafile

The prewar period saw the consolidation in Europe (though not in America) of mass political parties based on the working class as well as of a range of organized interest groups, including trade unions. The development of these institutions was matched by increasing state intervention in education, health care and social welfare. The middle class, meanwhile, distinguished by access to secondary education, developed a new leisure ethic.

Ownership of capital c.1905

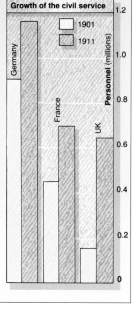

Poorest
Lower middle
Upper middle
Richest

Prussia · France · UK · USA (Wisconsin)

Total wealth (percent)

Income distribution 1910

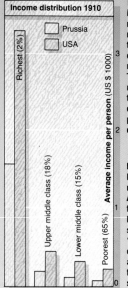

Prussia
USA

Richest (2%) · Upper middle class (18%) · Lower middle class (15%) · Poorest (65%)

Average income per person (US $ 1000)

▶ There was sharp inequality in wealth, measured here by the money value of property. In the UK the richest 2 percent owned nearly three times as much as the rest of society. These disparities were reflected in the life style of the plutocratic "leisure class", which also permeated the middle classes.

◀ Average incomes were higher in the USA than in Prussia, but not notably more equally distributed. America offered opportunity for European immigrants but not necessarily upward social mobility. The "rags-to-riches" thesis of economic and social advancement has been found wanting in historical studies of American cities.

US Labor Union membership 1913

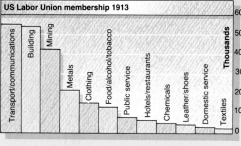

Transport/communications · Building · Mining · Metals · Clothing · Food/alcohol/tobacco · Public service · Hotels/restaurants · Chemicals · Leather/shoes · Domestic service · Textiles

Thousands

◀ Trade unionism faced more determined resistance in the USA than in Europe but by 1913 the American Federation of Labor (a loose federation of national unions made up especially of skilled workers) had more than 2 million members. Unionism was especially strong in transport, mining and construction.

Social structure 1897

3%
24%
73%

Russian Poland

5%
11%
84%

European Russia

Peasants
Burghers
Others
(nobles/high officials/clergy/
merchants/foreigners)

◀ The western parts of the Russian Empire, including Poland, were more commercialized and industrialized than the Russian heartland. This lent force to Russian nationalist movements. The more diversified social structure of Poland is reflected here in the higher proportion of townsmen or "burghers".

▶ Governments now took on many more functions, becoming more involved in economic management, providing infrastructure, education and welfare services. They thus needed more information and to monitor and police the population more closely. Consequently public bureaucracies expanded rapidly.

Growth of the civil service

1901
1911

Germany · France · UK

Personnel (millions)

I f capitalist industrialization – based on the 18th-century Industrial Revolution – is one of the great forces which has shaped 20th-century society another is the struggle for democracy, which was powerfully influenced by that other revolution of the late 18th century, the French Revolution. Both the French Revolution and the Industrial Revolution were animated by the same currents of individualism and rationalism in 18th-century European thought. Although there is no inherent or necessary connection between industrialization and the development of a political system in which "the people" rule (the basic meaning of democracy), it was generally believed among thinkers and most statesmen in the early 20th century that industrialization had to be accompanied by the involvement of the mass of the people in political life.

There were still great variations in patterns of social and economic life, which the French geographers of the time sought to explain in terms of the concept of *pays* – referring to distinctive regional cultures at quite a small scale. But there was also a strong trend of standardization, encouraged by the growth of factory organization and of cities, by the beginnings of mass consumption (marked, for example, by the success of F.W. Woolworth's "five and ten cent stores" of which there were over 1,000 in the United States by 1911), and by the spread of primary education. Industrialization and its administration required the expansion of literacy and basic education, and the numbers of schools, pupils and teachers multiplied even in the more backward parts of Europe. The general level of education was higher in the United States, though even there in 1910 more than 90 percent of children still only received an elementary education lasting on average for just six years.

These standardizing forces seemed to some, in the words of the 19th-century French statesman Alexis de Tocqueville, "to be rendering people into a uniform mass, alike in their thoughts and attitudes". The relationships between, first, this "mass" and the elites, marked in the early part of the century by a widening economic gap, and, second, between the masses and the state were a matter of major concern. Some feared the threat the masses seemed to pose to the established order, others the extent to which standardization represented a threat to individual liberty. Yet the trend of democratization – of widening franchises with the relaxation of property and educational qualifications for voting rights, and even of the extension of the franchise to women (pioneered on the margins of the western world in Wyoming (USA), New Zealand and South Australia in the 1890s) – was generally accepted outside Spain and eastern Europe. Even so, by 1914 electorates were

MASSES AND ELITES

Standardization in
ordinary life

The growth of the
working class and the
labor movement

The response of the
state: the beginnings of
welfare programs

Ruling classes of Europe
and America

Social structures in
Russia and Eastern
Europe

Peasant-based mass
movements

still usually restricted to between 30 and 40 percent of the adult population. The persistence of autocracy in Russia was regarded elsewhere as a matter of shame, and in other countries, in spite of their fears, rulers did not seriously contemplate a return to authoritarian rule.

Imperial Russia remained a vast multinational peasant society dominated and held together by an absolute monarchy, an all-pervasive state bureaucracy, a relatively small commercial-industrial sector, a large standing army of mainly peasant conscripts, the Russian Orthodox Church and a privileged landed nobility. The established church and the nobility were for the most part servants and guardians of the state. They derived their power and position from a long history of obsequious service to the czarist autocracy. As with its Soviet successor, but unlike most western states, the authority and legitimacy of the Imperial Russian state were based upon a strong and monolithic official ideology, known as that of "Orthodoxy, Autocracy and Nationality", which was deliberately critical of democratic liberalism.

▼ The solidarity of their communities helped to make miners the vanguard of the labor movement. In mining villages the "pub" was a center of community and it was here that Welsh coal miners discussed the progress of a national strike in 1912.

Workers, the labor movement and mass culture
The British historian Eric Hobsbawm argues that "Democracy created rather than followed political consciousness amongst workers and peasants"; the expansion of democracy in the late 19th and early 20th centuries brought about the political mobilization of the masses by and for electoral competition. By 1900 the growth of the mass party-cum-movement, based on the working class and involving a complex of local branches and associations, marked the development of civil society in place of the fragmented, localized and personalized loyalties of the past.

Who were the masses who were organized by the new parties? The "working class" – those dependent upon work for wages – was far from homogeneous, though there were some massive groups including notably the miners (who numbered 800,000 in Germany and more than a million in Britain in 1907). Important differences in the organization of production persisted between large-scale factories and small workshops, and workers were divided by differences

of skill and in the nature of the work they did, as well as by ethnic differences of nationality, language and religion; for example, the powerful Western Federation of Miners in the United States was divided by antagonisms between skilled Methodists from Cornwall and less skilled Catholics of Irish origin. There was also an increasingly significant intermediate stratum of the old small property-owning class of artisans, craftsmen and small shopkeepers, and the new middle class of nonmanual and white-collar workers-for-wages. The growth of this lower middle class perhaps helped to define "working class" identity.

In spite of the differences among them, manual wage workers were receptive to socialist ideas. Their recognition of themselves as a collectivity was assisted by the widening gap in wealth and incomes between workers and owners of capital. The latter now came to be identified, as employers had not been before, with "the privileged", the old target of radical political attack. Awareness of class identity was reinforced by the residential segregation of workers and others in the expanding cities. There were towns like Bochum in Germany, or Middlesbrough in northeast England, built around heavy industry, in which most of the population was of manual workers who might rarely meet people from other backgrounds. In the great cities working-class areas like Wedding in Berlin or West Ham in London grew up, their dwellings clearly distinguished from those of the new middle-class quarters or suburbs.

A further element in the formation of the working class was increasing state intervention. For workers' struggles for the regulation of the length of the working day, and of conditions in the workplace, to be effective required the intervention of the state. But this then in turn called forth

▶▶ The Carnegie company built this steel town at Homestead, Pennsylvania, USA. For the European immigrants in the work force, industrial work meant the acceptance of factory discipline; but this was usually preferable to their previous servile dependence. Real wages rose slightly to 1914, and the working week was reduced from 66 to 55 hours.

▶ The front page of a special German paper for May Day 1900 celebrated the advance of the labor movement.

▼ The powers of American unions, meanwhile, were eroded by the courts. Strikes were bitterly fought, leading here (in Philadelphia, Pennsylvania, in 1910) to street violence.

an increasingly organized response by workers. As Hobsbawm puts it, "the state unified the class", and no other class had such consistent need for state action.

The modern labor movement had begun to take shape in Europe and North America in the 1880s, assisted by the relaxation of laws limiting strikes and the formation of unions, notably in Britain (where unions acquired a legal status not seriously challenged until the 1980s), and to a lesser extent in France and Germany. The Federal Government of the United States, by contrast, remained more willing to intervene on the bosses' side, and employers there were able to use court injunctions to break strikes up until the 1930s. In the industrial states of Europe direct action was not illegal as it had been before (though there were continuing struggles, as over the right to picket); this, together with increasing literacy and, until the 1900s, increasing workers' incomes, encouraged the growth of the labor movement.

In the 1890s a new kind of industrial unionism arose, showing much less hesitation about strike action than was the case with the older craft unions. The industry-based unions grew up among miners and transport workers, especially dockworkers. Coal-miners became the group of workers most likely to conduct repeated, massive strikes, encouraged by their sheer numbers, the conditions of their work and the cohesiveness of the communities in which they lived.

By the first decade of the 20th century union membership was massive. In Britain unions had more than 3 million members, those in Germany 1.5 million and in France about 1 million. Industry-wide strikes took place in mining and in transport; national general strikes occurred in some countries (in Belgium, Holland and Sweden), and in Britain at least nationwide collective agreements were quite common.

In the United States trade unionism made more faltering progress because of government support for employers, ethnic divisions among workers, and the tenacity of the American Dream – that no one needed to remain a hired worker. Workers themselves thus supported capitalist values. Yet the American Federation of Labor (the AF of L) was formed in 1881, mainly by skilled workers. It was dominated by the moderate Samuel Gompers from 1886 until his death in 1924, and his pragmatism, rejection of socialist influences and of the idea of a separate labor party did much to secure the acceptability of the AF of L in a political environment which was very hostile to labor organization.

The development of the drive system of management meant that unionism lost ground in the 1900s, but by 1914 the AF of L had more than 2 million members. This was in spite of the challenge posed by the revolutionary movement of the International Workers of the World (known as "the Wobblies"), which had been founded in Chicago in 1905 and intended to unite all wage-earners in class war against capitalism. Never a large organization, the IWW still provoked fears and singular hostility amongst employers, to which it quite soon succumbed leaving a rich legacy only in American folklore.

Diet and Social Differences

In all societies food is a sensitive indicator of differences of wealth and status. In England at the beginning of the 20th century a well-known high-society hostess wrote: "No dinner should consist of more than eight dishes: soup, fish, *entrée*, joint, game, sweet, *hors d'oeuvre* and perhaps an ice, but each dish should be perfect of its kind". In the British city of York, according to the 1901 survey of poverty in the city made by the industrialist and social researcher Seebohm Rowntree, average consumption among the poor represented on average 2,069 calories per day. This was less than some experts believe to be necessary for good health among working adults, and comparable with intakes of dietary energy observed in large parts of the "Third World" today. Similarly in rural Russia early in the century, "In the diet of poor households the basic position is occupied by bread, potatoes and other cheap foodstuffs while in the diet of rich households wheaten bread is more important and so are meat and fat, milk, confectionery and so on". But the diets of the poor were improving in the industrial countries. Surveys showed that, in England at least, even rural laborers were able to spend more on meat than on bread.

Later, in the years after World War I in the West, consumption of fruit, vegetables and eggs in particular increased while that of bread declined. But still the main meal in poorer working families in Britain was supper, "consisting of strong tea, bread and margarine, tinned salmon or sardines – if this could be afforded – or otherwise fish and meat pastes". Yet by 1927 slimming had become fashionable among the better-off, and concerns about "healthy eating" took off. The medical journal *The Lancet*, for example, introduced the idea of the importance of "roughage" in a healthy diet. There immediately appeared "roughage" breakfast foods such as bran to supply this need. Toward the end of the century in the rich countries diet and health became a major preoccupation, reflected in the increased consumption of foods such as pasta and poultry, but alongside the popularity too of "fast" or "junk" food.

The growth of the civil state

In industrial Europe meanwhile, the increasing strength of the labor movement – reflected in an unprecedented wave of labor agitation and strikes between 1905 and 1914 and in the electoral advances of labor and socialist parties – drew forth a different response from governments. Following the German chancellor Bismarck's example, when in the 1880s he introduced social insurance to undercut support for socialism, European governments deployed what has been called "the strategy of the soft embrace"; they initiated programs of social welfare and reform. Austria, Denmark and Italy introduced programs modeled on the German example before 1900. In Britain old age pensions, public labor exchanges, health and unemployment insurance were all introduced between 1906 and 1914. Old age pensions were introduced in France in 1911. In the USA no such legislation existed by 1914 and even child labor remained uncontrolled by Federal law, in spite of the reforming intentions of the Progressive politicians. It is too early yet to speak of the "welfare state" in Europe, for the coverage of legislation like the National Insurance Act of 1911 in Britain was still restricted, and the amount of income redistributed very little. But the social reforms of the early 20th century mark a major departure from the liberal values of the previous century and a shift toward collectivism, prompting concerns amongst some politicians and philosophers about the erosion of individual liberty. They involved too, growth in the size of public bureaucracies. In Britain, for example, government employees increased threefold between 1891 and 1911.

The very success of the labor movement and of disciplined class parties in western Europe in wresting concessions from governments and rulers in fact helped to undermine revolutionary aspirations. The future was increasingly seen in terms of successful working-class collectivism within the structures of industrial capitalism rather than in those of revolutionary change. Ruling classes discovered that democracy was compatible with the stability of industrial capitalism. The success of their efforts at incorporating the masses by means of political and social reforms and by appeals to patriotism, the thrills of empire, and a "tradition" that was deliberately created – as in the institution of new festivals like the Fourteenth of July in France – was finally demonstrated in the way workers volunteered to fight each other after August 1914.

The democratization of political life in industrializing societies gave rise not only to the consolidation of working-class identity but also to nationalism. The word itself only acquired currency toward the end of the 19th century, when it seems that the imaginary community of "the nation" could fill the gap left by the weakening of ties of kinship, community and religion, and the depersonalization of social relations. Democracy, especially elections, gave opportunity for groups to mobilize as Czechs, or Germans, or Italians, and attempts were made by left- and right-wing politicians alike to combine their appeals with those of nationalism. States sought to use

▲ Public baths where children might be bathed, like these in London, helped to improve urban living standards. But research by Seebohm Rowntree in the English cathedral city of York in 1901 showed that 30 percent lived in poverty. In the United States at this time about 40 percent of wage-earning families lived below the official poverty line.

◀ Payment of old-age pensions started in Britain in 1909, 20 years after their introduction in Germany. The British scheme was paid for from taxation and thus represented a departure from principles of self-help, but it still involved a means test. In France the unions protested that pensions which began at age 65 would come too late.

This was the heyday of vaudeville and music hall, and of popular music and humor which by gently mocking class divisions accommodated rather than threatened them.

The existence of these activities was an expression of the new ethics of the workplace, which created a clear distinction between "work" and "leisure". Workers increasingly sought fulfilment outside work itself. Organized religion largely failed to provide a framework for their lives, and the strength of organized religion lay elsewhere. Even in America, in spite of investment in church building, and increasing church membership, active church-going became increasingly middle class.

Elites and middle classes

Who were the rulers of the industrializing societies of the West? Though monarchies survived in most of Europe, the 19th century is sometimes described as "the bourgeois century" because of the new ascendancy of capitalist owners of industry, business and finance. But historians now differ in their views as to the eclipse or the persistence of the power of the old landed aristocracies.

It is clear that the formerly dominant values ascribing high status as a right of birth and social position had given way before those associated with the market, and that social power was closely correlated with wealth. Equally there is no doubt that members of the "big bourgeoisie" sought to take on aristocratic standards. Self-made American millionaires, for example, married into European noble families. It is probably best to think of the ruling classes of the European industrial nations as being formed by landed noblemen who had often developed commercial and industrial interests, and by the industrial and financial bourgeoisie whose politics and attitudes were susceptible to aristocratic influences.

They were relieved of anxiety. They were suddenly rich. Independent for life! At first when they went down to the Post Office to draw it [their first pension], tears of gratitude would run down the cheeks of some, and they would say as they picked up their money, "God bless that Lord George!"

FLORA THOMPSON

▼ Expanded access to elementary education, standardized under state control, assisted in the foundations of nationalism. Here a German teacher leads cheers for the Kaiser in the first week of World War I. German primary schools encouraged hard work, obedience and piety, not critical thought, in order to create the perfect *Untertan* (subject).

the idea of "the nation" as ideological cement – a process both made necessary and facilitated by the spread of elementary education. This in turn helped to make language into a primary condition of nationality as the official language of the state and the medium of instruction marked out social groups as they had not been before. It was the period in which, according to one seminal history, "peasants turned into Frenchmen". National identities competed with and complemented the sense of class consciousness and both, similarly, might combine with consciousness of religious community as among Poles and Irish Catholics.

Consciousness of class was thus only one kind of identity fostered by industrialization and the spread of democracy. But workers' sense of belonging to a separate social world is shown too in the formation of a distinct culture, characterized by distinctive clothing – the ubiquitous peaked cap became a badge of working class membership; by involvement in particular sports and recreations – football and gardening (listed, with "country walks", as their favorite leisure pursuit by German workers in a survey before World War I); and by choice of entertainments.

At the upper end of society there were the phenomenally wealthy, pilloried by contemporaries as "the plutocracy" and described by the American economist Thorstein Veblen (in a book published in 1899) as "the Leisure Class". They were distinguished by their conspicuous consumption and conspicuous leisure. There was then a range of people clearly distinguished at the ends of, on the one side, smaller industrialists and businessmen, or high-ranking civil servants and professionals, and at the other the "old" "petty bourgeoisie" of tradesmen and artisans, but who were not very clearly differentiated from each other between these extremes. Much of their behavior came to be concerned with establishing social boundaries, marking out differences. Literacy and increasing individual self-consciousness tended to diffuse bourgeois values, and the criteria for membership of the bourgeoisie (availability of time for leisure, filled with distinctive activities, notably sports like racing or yachting, or the somewhat more popular golf and tennis, and formal education beyond the elementary level, which clearly showed the ability for adolescents to postpone earning a living) permeated the middling ranks of society. The big bourgeoisie had to keep itself open, also, to new recruits and needed to conciliate the middle classes. Further down the social hierarchy the members of the new lower middle class of white-collar workers and the "middle" middle class of managers sought to distinguish themselves from the working class, sometimes by the adoption of reactionary politics. It was often among them, as among "the little men" of the old small property-owning petty bourgeoisie, that nationalism took a particularly strong hold, and with it antisemitism and virulent dogmas of racial supremacy.

Social structures in Russia and Eastern Europe

In the West social structure and class configurations determined the nature of the state; in Russia, the autocratic state determined the nature of the social hierarchy and social relations and prescribed the functions, obligations and prerogatives of each legally defined "social estate" (*soslovie*). Everyone was registered as belonging to a particular social estate at birth – to the nobility, the clergy, the peasantry, etc – and normally remained there till death, although there was some upward mobility through state-service or through entrepreneurial success recognized by the state. This formal hierarchy was, however, slowly giving way to a more variegated and autonomous class structure.

Advancing commercialization and occupational specialization in the economy were accompanied by a gradual increase in class consciousness, culminating in a socially divisive flowering of class-based organizations in the 1890s and 1900s. These interlocked explosively with the simultaneous emergence of significant autonomist and separatist movements among ethnic minorities: Poles, Finns, Jews, Latvians, Estonians, Lithuanians, Georgians, Armenians, Azeris and Volga Tatars. Parts of the Russian Empire's western borderlands, especially the

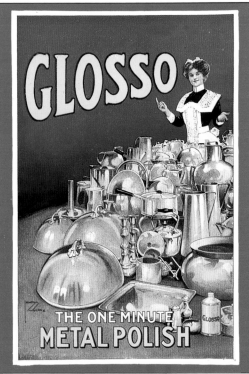

◄ **Cleaning the silver was a job for servants even in lower middle-class families. In a provincial British city 29 percent of families belonged to the "servant keeping class". Domestic service was the major occupation open to women. But numbers of female servants trailed urban growth and in France even began to decline in the 1890s.**

They [servants] accept social inequalities as one of the consequences of human existence and they firmly believe that it is above all by faithful duty that they can improve the general lot.
SERVANTS' TRADE UNION NEWSPAPER, 1907

▲ By 1900 the expanding European middle classes had begun to relax. A leisure ethic replaced the earlier emphasis on hard work. Idling in a fashionable restaurant (here at Vichy in France) was among their pursuits. But these also included cycling, new styles of dancing and organized sports. Devotion to religion declined – in response one pastor even suggested drive-in sevices for cyclists! Attitudes toward sex were loosened and the whole notion of what a woman should look like – slender and a little athletic – evolved as part of the leisured life style.

Baltic provinces and Poland, were more commercialized and/or industrialized than the Russian heartland. Capitalism accelerated the emergence of increasingly assertive "national bourgeoisies", as well as peasantries and proletariats among the ethnic minorities and intensified the social disruption and distress that normally accompany rural commercialization and the early stages of industrialization. It also ended the nationalities' parochialism, raised national and class consciousness, and fostered mass support for nationalist and class-based movements. These class and ethnic divisions, further inflamed by religious tensions, were the major ingredients in the seething caldron which boiled over in the 1905 revolution, aptly described by Lenin as the "dress rehearsal" for 1917.

The peasantry as a class

From the 1860s to 1914, from Ireland to the Urals, peasants were emerging as a conscious class with specific interests and aspirations. At first these were often articulated on the peasants' behalf by bourgeois politicians or members of the intelligentsia who sometimes wanted to use peasants for their own ends, but other social changes awakened peasants to the need to articulate

their interests and organize themselves: the long-delayed dissolution of serfdom in Russia and Eastern Europe (1840s to 1880s); the slowly increasing availability of rural schooling; growing contact with the expanding ranks of village teachers, doctors and local government officials, and with the rural industrial proletariat (railroadmen and miners); the eye-opening experiences provided by more universal military service and occasional employment in towns; the opening of the peasants' world and widening of their horizons by national market integration and railroad networks. By 1905–07 there were major peasant-based mass movements in Ireland, France, Denmark, Sweden, Finland, Latvia, Estonia, Lithuania, Georgia, Poland, the Ukraine, Russia and Romania. The great Romanian peasant revolt of 1907 was partly inspired by peasant revolts in the Russian Empire in 1905–06. Moreoever, during 1906–14 there was a spectacular growth of peasant cooperatives, consciously modelled on the trail-blazing Danish cooperatives of the 1880s–90s. Peasantist movements were also reaping the harvest of the 19th-century romantic, folkloristic, philological, "Völkisch" and Slavophil "rediscoveries" or "reinventions" of vernacular peasant cultures.

CHILDHOOD

Today childhood is seen ideally as a protective time, during which children should have the chance to flourish and learn within the security of a united and loving family. This does not hold true for all children, and has not always been the case. Before World War I in Europe, childhood for many ended abruptly at 12 when children could legally begin work. Many earned their keep even younger. It was only the children of the rich who could enjoy workfree lives devoted to a combination of education and play. While working-class children entered premature adulthood through labor, childhood was often curtailed, even for the better-off, by authoritarian parents who instilled strict codes of conduct in their "little adults" and taught them to control their emotions.

Following the war, women became more intimately involved with their children. They were offered a glut of "expert" advice on "mothercraft", ranging from the strict regime of four-hourly feeds for babies, promoted in the 1930s by the British pediatrician Frederick Truby King, to the atmosphere of indulgent affection encouraged by the 1950s American child-expert Benjamin Spock. Today many Western parents elect "natural childbirth", though supported by the technological professionalism of hospital births which has done much to reduce the dangers to mother and child alike. There is also greater informality between children and adults, with fathers playing a greater role. Increased rates of divorce and single-parent families mean family forms are more varied, but all tend to be child-centered.

For many, grinding poverty means that the birth of a child represents if not a new contributor to the family work force then yet another mouth to feed. The consequences can be dire. City centers throughout the world abound with street children who live by their wits, begging, ragpicking, washing cars or engaging in petty crime. Most vulnerable among them are the child prostitutes and "rent boys", victims of pimps and pedophiles alike.

Despite poverty and deprivation, many Third World children work alongside family members in the home, fields or workplace. In some instances this may give rise to strong bonds of affection and a sense of identity and security, learning skills and values that equip them for life. This can be contrasted with children in the West, who often face increased competition and parental expectations of achievement which can lead to psychological stress and sometimes a sense that love is conditional on their performance.

▲▶ Better-off children in pre-1914 Europe were raised to be "seen-and-not-heard". Boys were sent to boarding schools at the age of seven or eight. Girls were taught beauty and deportment and encouraged in genteel accomplishments such as music and needlework.

▶ In wealthier homes at the turn of the century, parents were distant figures. Children were brought up by nannies who took them from the nursery, bathed and dressed in their best clothes, to their parents for an hour or so a day. Children formed close bonds with their nannies.

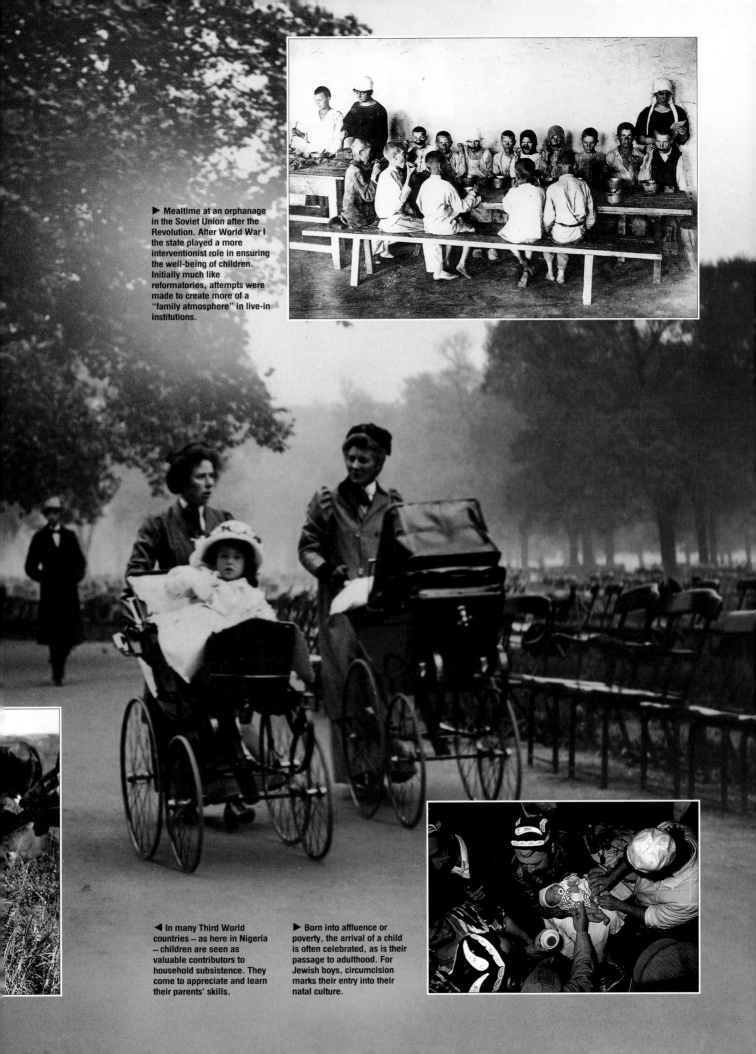

► Mealtime at an orphanage in the Soviet Union after the Revolution. After World War I the state played a more interventionist role in ensuring the well-being of children. Initially much like reformatories, attempts were made to create more of a "family atmosphere" in live-in institutions.

◄ In many Third World countries — as here in Nigeria — children are seen as valuable contributors to household subsistence. They come to appreciate and learn their parents' skills.

► Born into affluence or poverty, the arrival of a child is often celebrated, as is their passage to adulthood. For Jewish boys, circumcision marks their entry into their natal culture.

Datafile

There was widespread anxiety around 1900 about the collapse of "social order". Industrialization and urbanization were thought to be destroying the family and the communities which had supposedly characterized rural society. In practice working people developed new communities in the cities, based on novel organizations rather than on recreation of the old. Contrary to popular belief, small "nuclear" families had been the norm before the Industrial Revolution; both patriarchy – male dominance in the family – and parental control over children were still strong. The dissociation of work and family life was beginning to change the expectations men and women had of each other.

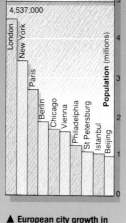

Ten largest cities 1900

4,537,000

London, New York, Paris, Berlin, Chicago, Vienna, Philadelphia, St Petersburg, Istanbul, Beijing

Population (millions)

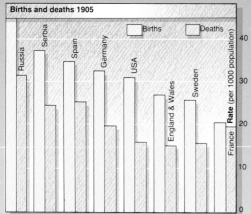

Births and deaths 1905

Births ☐ Deaths ☐

Russia, Serbia, Spain, Germany, USA, England & Wales, Sweden, France

Rate (per 1000 population)

▲ European city growth in the last part of the 19th century resulted particularly from the natural growth of their populations consequent upon the fall of the death rate; American cities grew because immigrants settled in them. The great cities were found also in the old civilizations of Ottoman Turkey and China, while the expansion of colonial capitalism created disproportionately large urban centers. Melbourne, Buenos Aires and Calcutta were all bigger than Amsterdam, Milan, and Munich.

▲ Death rates had been quite sharply reduced in the industrialized countries. Birth rates for a time remained high and so populations grew rapidly. France led the way in reducing birth rates (perhaps because peasants wished to prevent the division of landholding between numerous heirs), and had experienced the so-called "demographic transition" to low birth and death rates and a stable population. Generally in western Europe population growth had slowed; not so in the east and south.

▼ ▶ Population growth in western Europe had been rapid by historical standards. But its distinctive pattern of later marriage and a high proportion of bachelors and spinsters, seen here (below) in data for Belgium and Sweden, meant that growth was more modest than it has been in the contemporary Third World. The effects of a tendency for earlier marriage in the early 20th century were offset by increasing practice of birth control, partly reflected in the reduction in household size in the USA (right).

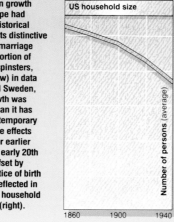

US household size

Number of persons (average)

1860   1900   1940

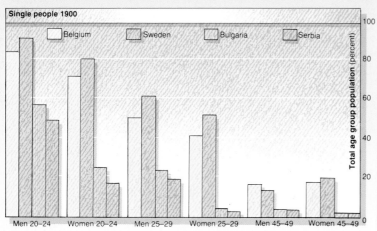

Single people 1900

Belgium ☐ Sweden Bulgaria Serbia

Total age group population (percent)

Men 20–24   Women 20–24   Men 25–29   Women 25–29   Men 45–49   Women 45–49

At the beginning of the 20th century there was already a firmly established belief that the family was in decline and decay as a result of the growth of industrial society. Members of the middle classes and conservative commentators of that time expressed particular concern about the family life of the urban working classes. They blamed the perceived deterioration of the qualities of life and sentiments experienced within the family for declining standards in society at large. The spread of women's labor in the cities, the growth of organized youth and women's movements and the political mobilization of women and children by the new political forces on the Left – all of which removed women and young people from the orbit of the family – were seen by the ruling classes as a byproduct of the destruction of family life by industrialization.

Despite a shared concern at both ends of the political spectrum for its integrity and stability, the family became the focus of conflict between rival ideologies. The ruling classes saw the stable family as a major bulwark against the radicalization of industrial workers and believed that socialists, feminists and other radicals were destroying marriage and family life by undermining the patriarchal assumptions of the dominant culture of bourgeois society. The promotion of emancipatory aspirations, which threatened established norms of male authority within the family, was thus a constant source of anxiety to those who sought to uphold social stability by maintaining the "traditional" blessings of hearth and home. Such concern is illustrated by the fact that by the end of the 19th century a theory about "ideal family types", (developed especially by the French sociologist F. Le Play, 1806–82) firmly upheld the so-called "stable" large patriarchal peasant family of preindustrial times as a model of authority for the whole of society, while declaring the "new" smaller urban family to be the "unstable" product of industrialization.

Family life in the cities

The *modern* nuclear family was in fact not so much the product of structural changes within the domestic group in industrializing societies as the notion of the large preindustrial family would suggest. It is now generally accepted that throughout most of western Europe and the United States, and even among the Russian peasantry, the *conjugal* (rather than "extended") family, consisting of husband, wife and four or five children, with servants, lodgers or apprentices where appropriate, has been the common family form since at least the 16th century. It has even been suggested that the existence of the so-called *modern* nuclear family prior to the Industrial Revolution made the social transition to a new

THE FAMILY UNDER THREAT?

Industrial society and
the family

Immigrant communities
in the United States

Parents and children in
towns and cities

The new role divisions
between men and
women

Feminism in the early
20th century

way of life far easier for people as they gathered their children and packed up their belongings to seek a new livelihood in the cities. What they had to leave behind – old and diverse community values of neighborhood and friendship, or family relationships – they tended to reconstruct in their new environment or they adapted old values to new needs. Nowhere else was the tenacious struggle to preserve traditions greater than in the family. Thus the cities offered a varied picture of rural people come to town, all with their own strongly local customs, family traditions and rituals.

During the times of large-scale migration it was common for whole communities to plan together their exodus to a nearby city or to seek a new life by emigrating to North or South America. The majority were peasants and all of them had their own particular national or regional identity. In the cities, or in the new country, a new and often more urgent dependency on relatives or neighbors, especially in hard times, made people seek out the support of those they had known before

▼ A British family. In Europe not only authoritarian familial ideals, but also preindustrial notions of honor, social standards and moral codes set the tone for society's attitudes toward the family – an ideology that proved extremely hostile to women's emancipation in particular.

the misery of unemployment, poverty or illness began to threaten their sheer existence, rather than rely on poverty relief or charity.

With the tremendous housing shortage in the new industrial cities, relatives helped each other to find lodgings and work, and working-class women who were forced to contribute toward a family income reestablished support networks of childminding, or caring for the sick and the old. The street began to replace the market center or the village common for gossip and meetings among women on their way to do their shopping or while they idled for a while watching their children play. Men, on the other hand, increasingly drifted into a separate male world of leisure; the sports ground and the tavern, or the music hall – places where respectable women were rarely seen, and if so then usually only to claim the pay-packet before it had turned into beer or spirits.

Among the immigrants in America, close-knit Italian communities, for example, recreated a "little Italy" in their new surroundings. Old history

Life in American Ethnic Neighborhoods

By 1910 one-third of the population of the 12 largest American cities was foreign born. Different groups of immigrants tended to be concentrated in particular industries, for example the Italians in construction and textiles. Whatever the industry, they undertook the more disagreeable jobs and worked long hours in poor, often hazardous conditions. To find work non-English speakers tended to rely on compatriots who had preceded them. These established men who acted as intermediaries became "work-bosses" – *padrones* among the Italians; they were paid commissions by the men to whom they gave jobs. Not all *padrones* cheated, but enough did to give the system a bad name.

By the beginning of the century peasants from southern and eastern Europe formed the overwhelming majority of immigrants. Their adjustment to urban, industrial life was eased by the tendency of different groups to occupy particular neighborhoods within the congested slums in which they mostly lived. Here, despite appearances, they did not so much recreate the communities from which they had come as establish them afresh. An Italian immigrant and community leader, Constantine Panunzio, said of the colony in Boston in which he lived that though it was "in no way a typical American community neither did it resemble Italy". The sociologist Robert E. Park wrote in 1920 that "In America the peasant discards his habits and acquires ideas. In America, above all, the immigrant organizes". Characteristic of Italian communities were mutual-benefit societies, Italian-language newspapers, Italian theater, opera and marionette shows, the celebration of religious festivals involving elaborate processions and an allegiance to Catholicism that was combined, however, with strong resistance to Irish domination of the Church in America. Mutual-benefit societies, of which there were for example 150 in Manhattan alone in 1900, required small but regular financial contributions from their members and provided notably for medical and funeral expenses. But the importance of the societies went beyond the merely instrumental, for the fraternities they

▲ **An immigrant Jew. By 1910 New York had more Jews than the whole of western Europe. Unlike other immigrants they usually came in families and brought a high level of skill.**

Ethnic Areas in Chicago

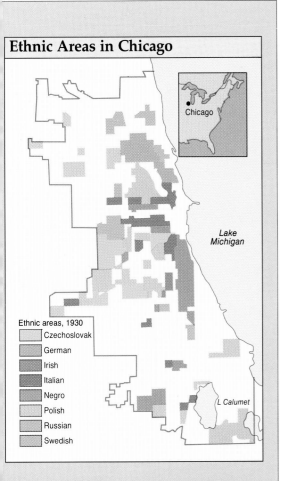

Ethnic areas, 1930
- Czechoslovak
- German
- Irish
- Italian
- Negro
- Polish
- Russian
- Swedish

◀ **An Italian family in New York's teeming Lower East Side.** Immigrants craved Old World dishes partly because they could now afford them. The production or import from Italy of olive oil, spaghetti and salami became important for the immigrants' well-being.

▲ **City neighborhoods in Chicago.** The immigrants' desire to retain their identities and their search for emotional security led different groups to occupy distinct residential areas, creating a mosaic of ethnic neighborhoods, like this one in Chicago, 1930.

established filled a social and psychological void for those uprooted from familiar surroundings and ways of life. One society described itself as an organization that "unites us and gives us strength, and will make us more acceptable in the eyes of the American people". The ethnic press also served as a bridge between life in the European village and that in the American city, providing leadership and voicing group demands and complaints. The Italian newspapers were not like those of Europe but were "addressed to the common man" (Park) and much more popular in language. The Italian theater, too, acquired a distinctive "Italian-American" style and idiom.

Exploited though they may have been, the immigrants enjoyed more abundant and varied food than they had known before. Part of what has become known internationally as "Italian food" – notably pizza – is rather an Italian-American creation. Saints parades were to Italian immigrants, in the words of an American social worker, "what a returned heroes parade is to us – a bond, a reminder, and the thrill of the uncommonplace". Over time these community organizations gave way to American counterparts, but they were vital in the early stages of immigrant adjustment.

and old values were maintained with pride and new ones were only gradually adopted when circumstances dictated. Paternal power remained unimpaired, and family loyalty carefully controlled any expansion into a so-called American culture. Confessional differences similarly marked out subcultural boundaries both in the "New World" and in Europe. In Germany, for example, the Catholic Church built for its members a kind of "ghetto-existence" within which authoritarian values and family rituals were carefully kept alive and the new values of industrial living decried.

In theory the authoritarian structure of the patriarchal household changed as soon as a family no longer possessed its own means of production (such as land or a family workshop), especially among the new working classes where property obligations or expectations to inherit a small shop or a farm no longer regulated the relations between father and son or daughter. While among the property-owning classes the old obligations to the family continued to regulate marriage arrangements, and channeled sons into suitable professions to enable them to take over the family business, the authority of the wage-earning head of household in theory remained intact only for as long as his dependents were reliant on his income. But family ties among workers often remained strong, born out of their insecure and unstable dependence on the market and their employers. Lack of housing meant that many of the working youth remained at home as lodgers while beginning to pursue their own life and leisure, separate from that of their fathers. Yet fathers still tended to initiate their sons into the world of men and factories, seeking positions for them, not infrequently transferring on to employers that aspect of parental control which once the master had had over the apprentice. The system of apprenticeship itself continued alongside the new relationship between worker and employer. The increasing stress on a more formal education, and longer years of schooling – designed to prepare sons (and only a small number of daughters) for an independent life in the world outside – also created new financial dependence on the head of household, delaying or postponing the time when youngsters would leave the parental home often far beyond the ages at which children once became apprentices or farmhands.

For others in the rural areas or the small market towns, those remaining on their farms or those who continued well into the 20th century to run their small craft enterprises, their shops or a small business, change was slow and uneven. For them marriage remained an economic institution and both husband and wife continued to work for their mutual support. Seemingly untouched by the debates over women's rights and by feminist issues (so much part of the urban Protestant middle-class scene of the late 19th and early 20th century), women continued in the traditional division of labor, serving behind the counter or even doing the book-keeping, milking the cows, growing vegetables and taking care of children, their menfolk's clothes and their stomachs.

However, there too patterns and the period of

Hold fast, this is most necessary in America. Forget your past, your customs, and your ideals. Select a goal and pursue it with all your might. No matter what happens to you, hold on. A final virtue is needed in America – called cheek...Do not say, "I cannot; I do not know."

HANDBOOK FOR IMMIGRANTS

▲ **"Urgent warning to girls emigrating! Don't accept any position abroad without first making close inquiries! If in need or danger apply to the captain of this ship"** – a poster of The German National Committee for the International Campaign against the White Slave Trade. Between 1899 and 1910 males aged between 14 and 44 accounted for nearly 75 percent of the emigrants to the new world. The consequent small numbers of women traveling alone gave rise to fears for their moral safety.

parental control did change as more and more of the young – both sons and daughters – left the farms, daughters often to take up domestic service, the principal occupation open to women of the lower classes until World War I, and sons to work in the factories. While many girls from poor agricultural areas went to cities such as Paris, London or Berlin to follow the increasing demand for domestic labor among the middle classes, others tended to move into towns not far away and parents kept a watchful eye over possible exploitation of their labor or person by their employers, illustrating a fairly mutual distrust between the two classes.

With compulsory education, girls too began to form their own circles of friends outside the home, dream of a different life and seek companionship among peers to a far greater extent than they had been able to in the 19th century. They read the new novels and magazines and gradually new expectations of love and marriage formed as they prepared themselves for their future roles as wives and mothers. Once married, however, the 19th-century pattern of family life repeated itself with the familiar stress on the essential quality on which women's moral worth depended, on "self-denial" or the "renunciation of self", embodied in its most perfect form in maternal love.

Middle-class social norms which idealized women's *natural* profession as mothers, ideally to the exclusion of paid employment outside the home, stood in stark contrast to the material needs of the vast majority of working-class women; their household budgets dictated that most of them needed to contribute income at

▲ A French miner being washed by his wife, c. 1900. In France, where there was no tradition of women working underground in coal mines and little other employment in mining areas, women concentrated on their menfolk and homes. A degree of living style, ornaments and photographs on the wall give some sense of settled existence, but it could easily be shattered by a mine disaster, such as that at Courrières in 1906 when 1,100 men were killed.

some stage of their lives. By 1900 family commitments, but more fundamentally the idealization of the family as the female domain, had clearly influenced patterns of women's employment. On the whole women were confined to more marginal activities in or associated with the household. Only a small number of women had qualified as professionals by the turn of the century, most of them as teachers (compare, however, the 4,500 women physicians in America in the 1890s with 93 in France in 1903), more so as semiprofessionals in health and child care. The majority of lower-class women worked as domestic servants or in laundries, hotels, restaurants or shops, in the textile or clothing industry, or in food processing. Although it became fairly usual for single girls in the lower classes to earn part of their upkeep, women's wages rarely reached a level that might have kept a woman alone. Up to 70 percent or more of single women were fully occupied by the early 1900s, but most left work on marriage, especially in the cities. In Berlin, for example, only 11 percent of married women were fully employed in 1907, compared with 26 percent for the whole of Germany or 45 percent of all widows.

It was among the middle classes that the official idealization of family life appeared perhaps even more contradictory. Late or loveless marriages or marriage contracts dependent on property had created a massive demand for the sexual services of prostitutes. This service was generally drawn from the family circles of the poor and was often better paid than the more legitimate forms of employment open to women. Already in the 1870s such "double morality" had sparked off crusades among feminists against the legalization of prostitution. Yet official concern over the moral threat of urban prostitution (seen to constitute one of the main social problems of city life alongside illegitimacy and alcohol abuse), which brought disease and humiliation on thousands of women, was leveled at the need to regulate this vice through legislation rather than at addressing its more fundamental causes. While middle-class wives had been elevated onto a pedestal of irreproachable purity by the 19th-century bourgeois male, their sexuality repressed or stifled in the family context, it was notably middle-class men who argued that prostitution was an efficient safety valve and therefore should not be abolished. The outcry against the so-called sexual liberation after World War I follows closely in the footsteps of such a model of official morality, and of course of the 19th-century role model of women as wives and mothers.

Women's closely defined sphere of activity within the home as it emerged in the 19th century was the result of a gradual transformation of the roles of both men and women. By 1900 the transition toward a *new* role division was complete. The new sexual division of labor was not determined by the needs of the family as a unit of production but rather by "natural" character traits ascribed to men and women. Attributing to women distinctive moral qualities led to a reevaluation of women's domestic roles and raised their status within the family. But it also

offered a new rationale for subordination within the context of industrialization by suggesting that these qualities of "innocence of spirit and purity of heart" could only blossom in the right setting – the home. As women's nature was viewed as being governed more by feeling than reason, making women more receptive and yielding, loving and caring and selfless than men, they were also ideally equipped for the care of the home and husband, the sick and old, the rearing of children and their socialization, acting as moral guardians of the home and of society at large.

Woman's destiny for a domestic role was further underscored by the lesser points of her irrational and passive nature which made her naturally dependent on the male who was seen as more of a thinking creature, bold and certain of purpose. Lack of analytical powers and ambition were also seen as naturally excluding women from the public world of business and politics. Portrayed as evil and corrupt, this was a world in which women needed the protection of the male,

◀ Pediatrics and new child-care methods were well established by the 1890s. Prenatal care and the instruction of pregnant women to reduce birth defects and problem deliveries were introduced around 1900. New knowledge in obstetrics and gynecology greatly reduced the number of women dying in childbirth. Here a nurse is instructing young mothers in London in 1908.

▼ Until mechanical labor-saving household appliances were developed, the physical load of the housewife was considerable. Even the use of this new mangle required strength.

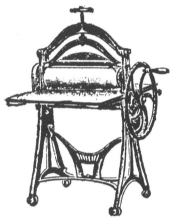

▼ Some industrial workers, especially coalminers, lived somewhat outside urban experience. Here miners' wives in an English mining village talk in the lane at the backs of their small houses. Industrial housing was often badly built.

FLORÉINE
Crème de Beauté

▲ France pioneered the manufacture of cosmetics and French women used makeup long before it was accepted in polite society elsewhere. In other countries the open use of cosmetics by women "to impose or seduce into matrimony… by scents or paints" was generally looked upon with disfavor. Not until after World War I did such opinions disappear.

▼ A lady in the Ottoman sultan's harem, 1906. Harems were common in Muslim countries in the early decades of the 20th century. In some large households each wife had her own set of rooms and servants, in others three or four wives lived together and children were brought up as one family. In Turkey polygamy became illegal in 1926, in India (by the Hindu Marriage Act) not until 1955.

of the state and society. The understanding of women's need for protection in a morally corrupt world, despite their unique power as regenerators of society, was to have far-reaching and ambivalent consequences for their position in the public sphere throughout the 20th century. Thus protective policies for women and their roles as wives and mothers, rather than truly emancipatory ones, were to regulate their participation in the labor market, while the idea of their natural role continued to define educational opportunities, their work or professional prospects.

Increasing concern over the declining birthrate after 1900 added a new dimension to the interest in maintaining not only an ideology of separate spheres or the notion of female dependence, it also raised motherhood to a new level of social recognition. It received an aura of "professionalism" with new stress on child care and children's needs through the impact of science and psychology. As increasingly pronatal political concerns were now added to the moral imperatives of motherhood, the case for women's equality naturally had to be shelved. Even the developments in the women's movements bear out a fairly general trend toward accepting marriage and motherhood as women's primary role, a strengthening of domestic life and a sharpening of the two separate spheres of activity for men and women.

This polarization of sexual stereotypes was not simply the product of a revolution in the sphere of formal ideas, or of a new interest in the individual and his and her "natural" rights. It was an important byproduct of the dissociation of work and family life and thus a direct result of the changing economic structure of the industrializing world. The commitment to life-long marriage, the maintenance of family stability, a secure and affectionate context of home life and careful upbringing of children with reciprocal feelings of love and care became those maxims which were to govern family life once its function as an economic institution began to disappear, and the very basis of marriage and the nature of dependency of family members on each other began to change.

The Origins and Rise of Feminism

Women have always protested against their oppression. In the 18th century, when philosophers rejected old sources of truth (God) and offered a new secular model of family relationships, the nature and role of women received new attention. Feminism in a literary form was born. All the themes writers then introduced were to recur in feminist propaganda a century later. The word feminism itself appeared first in French in the early 19th century.

Organized feminism began by addressing itself to women's economic dependency and resulting exploitation. The two major objectives of moderate feminism around 1850–60 were the right for married women to own property and the admission of unmarried women to the professions. There followed demands for better educational opportunities (access to secondary schools and universities) which were necessary for the pursuit of a profession or the maintenance of middle-class status.

In Russia feminism emerged in the 1860s among the intelligentsia of the provincial nobility or the merchant class. The concentration of Russian feminists on educational rather than economic objectives reflects this background.

The most important social development underlying the rise of feminism in the West was the growth of the middle classes, and the

increasingly more prominent role they played in social and political life. Feminists virtually everywhere shared their liberal, Protestant-based values of independence, self-sufficiency, careers open to talents and equality before the law. This alliance with liberalism remained central to the politics of feminism. By the 1930s the general decline of liberal beliefs and values also sealed the fate of liberal feminism. When feminism reemerged in the 1960s–70s it had a new voice. A combination of socialism and sexual liberation clearly distinguished the ideology of the Women's Liberation movement from that of its predecessor.

The rise of socialism and of communist movements in the late 19th century was to have profound and often unexpected consequences for liberal feminism. By the end of the century the socialist women's movements formed the major and almost the only alternative forms of women's movements to that developed by middle-class feminists in the 19th century. The largest socialist women's movement was in Germany. Under the leadership of Clara Zetkin (1854–1933) it pioneered many advanced policies on female equality. Above all it represented the plight of working-class women who had often been overlooked in the feminists' struggle to emancipate the female sex.

▲ This running race for American young women on a company outing in 1908 reflects their greater personal freedom, strengthened by education and employment opportunities – including the professions. Feminists' demands from the 1850s focused on the disparity between men's and women's education which effectively barred women from professional jobs.

◀ Representatives of a German women's academic league, 1914. The power of authoritarian political systems to stunt the growth of reform movements such as feminism is clearly illustrated in Germany. The admission of women to universities after 1900 was not due to pressure exerted by the women's movements, but rather to reluctant concessions following the examples of other industrial nations.

EDUCATION

During the 19th century, education was given a vital role in creating a prosperous and united nation-state. By 1900 many European states had taken responsibility for providing a national educational system that was compulsory for all, at least in the elementary stages.

Schools of the early 20th century were usually very formal. Children sat in their desks in ranks under strict discipline, often enforced by physical violence. There was the feeling that knowledge and skills, national pride and moral values, had to be forced into reluctant minds. This view of education persisted into the 1920s and 1930s and beyond. It acquired a new form and intensity under the communist and fascist dictatorships of the interwar years when children were indoctrinated into becoming model citizens in the service of an overpowering state.

There was already a reaction against such views in the early 1900s. In the United States the educationalist John Dewey (1859–1952) saw the child as an individual with his or her own worth. In his view, the purpose of education was to draw out what was already there rather than force it into a new mold. In Italy Maria Montessori saw the ideal school as an environment where each child was encouraged to develop his or her own freedom. She echoed Dewey's idea that the teacher should be a fellow-worker with the child rather than an authority figure. Although the number of truly progressive schools remained few their influence was strong. By the 1950s many schools in the Western world had become less formal and more child-centered.

As society became increasingly complex and technologically advanced the demands made on the education system grew in other ways. While traditionally education had served to support the ruling elites of society, now there had to be a massive expansion of higher education to provide the intellectual and scientific elite needed to keep society running. Because society was changing so rapidly, continual updating through adult education for people of all sorts was needed and flexibility in acquiring new skills became as highly prized as knowledge itself. Opportunities for women in education also grew rapidly as traditional barriers between the sexes were broken down.

A high level of education brought power, access to elite jobs and thus status. Though this was the case universally, nowhere was this more obvious than in the newly independent countries of Asia and Africa. The small minority who progressed beyond secondary education found their efforts richly rewarded. However, elementary education was often formal and academic, with little emphasis on the skills needed for survival and development at village level. It is not surprising that a major development in the poorer world has been to provide education programs in basic skills such as literacy, nutrition and hygiene which can be taken to children and adults alike.

◀ The urge for formal classroom education in newly independent nations drew many young people away from their farms. Here, in the Sudan in the early 1960s, the balance is redressed with practical education on the recognition of healthy crops.

▼ A traditional school in Germany at the outbreak of World War I. German schools had stern discipline but high achievement.

► "Like butterflies, mounted on pins, each one fastened to his place," was how Maria Montessori (1870–1952) described children in traditional academic schools. Montessori, here visiting one of her schools in old age, aimed to draw out the natural creativity of children by designing materials from which they could learn by self-discovery. Informality was the keynote of the Montessori classroom.

► Caught in one of the most competitive education systems in the world, this harrassed-looking boy, like the majority of his age-group in 1980s Japan, is off to attend nightschool (*juku*).

◄ Everyday hygiene education in China is encouraged through a poster campaign. After the Revolution of 1949 there were massive attempts to educate China's peasant population into new skills and correct behavior. Public education campaigns, especially in health matters, have been undertaken in most countries.

Datafile

The increasing integration of the world economy at the beginning of the 20th century is reflected in the growing volume of trade and the near doubling in size of the world merchant fleet between 1890 and 1914. The expansion of commerce and of colonialism, driven by the rivalry of the Great Powers, and the first steps in industrialization outside Europe and America helped to bring about social change in the "Third World" of Africa, Asia and Latin America. The formation of a working class began. The pattern of change depended also on the social structures and value systems of the colonial territories and on the way in which these were understood or misunderstood by the colonists.

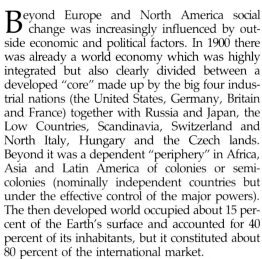

South African gold miners

▲▼ Part of the drive behind colonial expansion was demand for commodities such as oil and rubber and, with the growth of the electrical industry, copper. Mexico's status as an informal colony of the United States is shown in the response in 1907–08 of its copper production – developed by foreign capital – to a down turn in the US economy (below). The demand for precious metals created the largest black labor force of all in South Africa (above), drawing in men from surrounding territories.

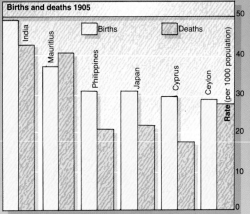

Births and deaths 1905

▲ Birth rates in "Third World" countries were in some cases no higher than in the West. Death rates were much higher so that population growth rates were often modest. The diversity in the demographic patterns of the colonial territories is striking, and there is evidence that they have varied also over time.

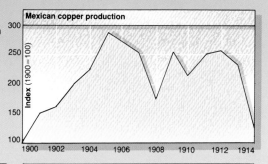

Mexican copper production

Caste occupations 1891

- Agriculture/fishing etc
- Muslims
- Leather workers/menials
- Artisans
- Professionals
- Traders
- Others

Brahman population of Indian provinces 1911

◀ British colonial attempts to classify and measure the Indian population in terms of castes (named groups of people defined by intermarriage and in part by distinct hereditary occupations, ordered in a district hierarchy) are reflected in the 1891 census. Such exercises made Indians themselves more conscious of caste.

▲ Variations in the social structure in different parts of India are shown in the wide differences that existed in the share in the whole population of the Brahmans, the priests who are at the top of the caste hierarchy. British administrative and legal arrangements ignored these differences, sometimes causing social change.

Beyond Europe and North America social change was increasingly influenced by outside economic and political factors. In 1900 there was already a world economy which was highly integrated but also clearly divided between a developed "core" made up by the big four industrial nations (the United States, Germany, Britain and France) together with Russia and Japan, the Low Countries, Scandinavia, Switzerland and North Italy, Hungary and the Czech lands. Beyond it was a dependent "periphery" in Africa, Asia and Latin America of colonies or semi-colonies (nominally independent countries but under the effective control of the major powers). The then developed world occupied about 15 percent of the Earth's surface and accounted for 40 percent of its inhabitants, but it constituted about 80 percent of the international market.

The competition between the Great Powers increased colonial governments' attention to economic questions as the costs of empire rose. Increased concern with the economy took the form of improvements in agriculture, veterinary services and irrigation. In India, almost 65,000km (40,000mi) of canals were built to irrigate 8 million ha (20 million acres) of the Indus Basin in the late 19th century.

IMPERIALISM AND SOCIAL CHANGE

- The influence of European and US economic power
- Taxes, land seizures and mining in Africa
- Industrial expansion in Latin America and India
- Colonial governments and change in local societies
- The origins of native middle classes

The expansion of colonial work forces

To expand exports of agricultural and mining goods from colonies required infrastructure – roads, railroads, ports. This called for a substantial waged labor force, and colonial administrations devoted much ingenuity throughout the world to secure an adequate supply of workers – from the imposition of cash taxes (forcing peasants to undertake wage labor to secure cash with which to pay them), the use of terror or, as in the 19th century, instituting large-scale labor migrations – Indians to Africa, the Caribbean and Malaya; Chinese to Malaya, Australia, the Caribbean; Europeans to North and South America, southern Africa and Australia.

In Africa the period was one of active colonization and settlement, punctuated with wars of popular resistance, such as the Herero war in German South West Africa in 1905–06 and the Maji Maji rebellion of 1906 in Southern Tanganyika. They were put down with great force. Administrations sought steadily to increase revenues from direct taxation; for example, poll taxes were imposed on unmarried Kikuyu men in British East Africa (Kenya) to force them to work (desertion from work was simultaneously made a criminal offence). Expatriate administrations and

◀ ▶ "France brings the blessings of civilization to Morocco" (right) according to a popular view of 1911. In practice the "civilizing mission" included the construction of railroads, here (below) in Madagascar, by laborers recruited and controlled by harsh and repressive means. The conditions of native employment in the colonies attracted criticism – sometimes censored – even in the colonial metropolises.

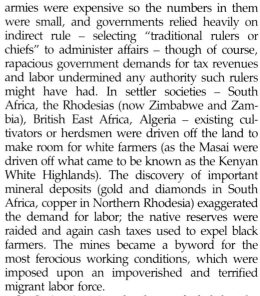

LA FRANCE VA POUVOIR PORTER LIBREMENT AU MAROC LA CIVILISATION LA RICHESSE ET LA PAIX

armies were expensive so the numbers in them were small, and governments relied heavily on indirect rule – selecting "traditional rulers or chiefs" to administer affairs – though of course, rapacious government demands for tax revenues and labor undermined any authority such rulers might have had. In settler societies – South Africa, the Rhodesias (now Zimbabwe and Zambia), British East Africa, Algeria – existing cultivators or herdsmen were driven off the land to make room for white farmers (as the Masai were driven off what came to be known as the Kenyan White Highlands). The discovery of important mineral deposits (gold and diamonds in South Africa, copper in Northern Rhodesia) exaggerated the demand for labor; the native reserves were raided and again cash taxes used to expel black farmers. The mines became a byword for the most ferocious working conditions, which were imposed upon an impoverished and terrified migrant labor force.

In Latin America the boom fueled by the overseas demand for raw materials was considerable, and supplied the means to absorb an enormous wave of immigration which created fashionable European cities across the continent. In Mexico, however, the pattern of growth produced a devastating social explosion. Under the long dictatorship of President Porfirio Díaz, foreign capital poured into the country to develop the northern silver and copper mines, the oil

▲ "A good specimen of a taxed hut", reads the contemporary caption. The picture was taken in Sierra Leone during a rising against the abolition of slave-dealing under British rule and the imposition of hut taxes. These were a widely favored system of colonial taxation.

▼ In the Congo, according to an account of 1911, "in the place of work the tax was assessed as so many kilograms of rubber. If the stated quantity was not delivered there were several methods of enforcing compliance, including the use of the *chicotte* – a rawhide whip".

industry (the 10,000 barrels of crude of 1901 rose to 13 million in 1911 by when Mexico was one of the leading oil exporters), agricultural exports (sugar and henequen from Yucatán), and major extensions to the transport system and to ports. US and British capital were said to own a fifth of the Republic's land by the turn of the century. The vast expansion in output seemed to be associated with increased landlessness and poverty; although three-quarters of the population lived off the land, 95 percent of them were landless and virtually enserfed to the 8–9,000 very large Mexican and foreign plantation owners. The scale of oppression – and the speed with which the land had been expropriated – explains the ferocity of the Mexican revolution; in the decade after 1911, possibly a quarter of a million people died.

In Latin America and in densely populated Asia (where the possibility of plantation agriculture was limited), industrialization was also becoming significant. By the turn of the century, some 18 percent of Argentina's national output was derived from industry, 14 percent of Mexico's. Employment in the Brazilian textile industry rose from 2,000 in 1895 to 26,000 in 1905 and 53,000 in 1907. The Indian textile industry was already of world significance by the turn of the century. Bombay alone then employed just over 80,000 workers (including 19,000 women and 2,000 children), and this rose to 105,000 by the outbreak of war. In 1911 the Indian Tata business group initiated the building of India's first iron and steel mill at Jamshedpur in the northeast, the same year in which Japan's first steel mill, Yawata, was begun. China, starting from a much lower base point, also began a modest industrialization, based upon a "putting-out" system to villages in the regions around the ports (for cloth, carpets, silk, tea, grass mats and flour). But in due course, a separate industrial sector emerged.

World Population c.1900

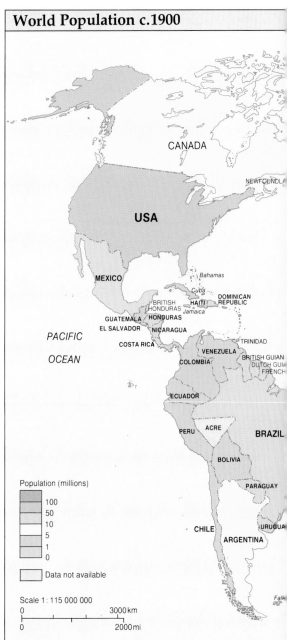

Population (millions)
100
50
10
5
1
0

Data not available

Scale 1 : 115 000 000
0   3000 km
0   2000 mi

In general the new workforces were most often recruited through agents. Employers hired agents to scour towns and villages to find members for work gangs. Sometimes they turned these over to the employer, but more often the agent became a ganger, supervisor of his group and often a subcontractor to the employer to deliver a certain volume of output in return for a fixed price; the ganger then paid his gang on whatever basis he chose.

Such a system tended to create loyalties to the gang rather than loyalties to either the collectivity of workers or to the firm, particularly where the gang was distinguished by a common language, caste, village of origin, religion, etc. This made it very much more difficult to organize trade unions. Furthermore, the system gave great power to the ganger who often took bribes to favor the recruitment of one worker rather than another, and also received a cut of what the workers saw as their earnings.

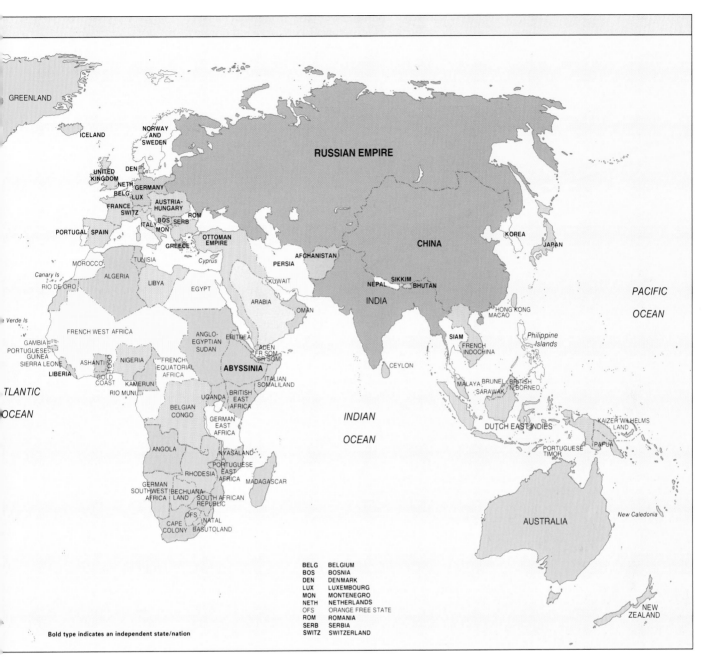

GREENLAND

NORWAY
AND
SWEDEN

ICELAND

RUSSIAN EMPIRE

UNITED
KINGDOM

DEN

NETH
GERMANY
BELG LUX
FRANCE AUSTRIA-
SWITZ HUNGARY
ITALY BOS SERB ROM
MON
PORTUGAL SPAIN GREECE OTTOMAN
EMPIRE

KOREA

JAPAN

MOROCCO
TUNISIA
Cyprus

Canary Is
RIO DE ORO
ALGERIA
LIBYA
EGYPT

AFGHANISTAN

PERSIA

KUWAIT

CHINA

ARABIA

OMAN

SIKKIM
NEPAL BHUTAN
INDIA

HONG KONG
MACAO

PACIFIC

OCEAN

Verde Is
FRENCH WEST AFRICA

GAMBIA
PORTUGUESE
GUINEA
SIERRA LEONE
LIBERIA

ASHANTI
GOLD
COAST

TOGO

NIGERIA
KAMERUN
RIO MUNI

FRENCH
EQUATORIAL
AFRICA

ANGLO-
EGYPTIAN
SUDAN

ERITREA

ADEN
FR SOM
BR SOM

ABYSSINIA

ITALIAN
SOMALILAND

CEYLON

SIAM
FRENCH
INDOCHINA

Philippine
Islands

MALAYA BRUNEI BRITISH
SARAWAK N BORNEO

TLANTIC

OCEAN

UGANDA

BELGIAN
CONGO

BRITISH
EAST
AFRICA

GERMAN
EAST
AFRICA

INDIAN

OCEAN

DUTCH EAST INDIES

KAIZER WILHELMS
LAND

PORTUGUESE
TIMOR

PAPUA

ANGOLA

NYASALAND

RHODESIA
PORTUGUESE
EAST
AFRICA

MADAGASCAR

GERMAN
SOUTHWEST
AFRICA
BECHUANA
LAND
SOUTH AFRICAN
REPUBLIC
OFS
CAPE NATAL
COLONY BASUTOLAND

AUSTRALIA

New Caledonia

NEW
ZEALAND

BELG BELGIUM
BOS BOSNIA
DEN DENMARK
LUX LUXEMBOURG
MON MONTENEGRO
NETH NETHERLANDS
OFS ORANGE FREE STATE
ROM ROMANIA
SERB SERBIA
SWITZ SWITZERLAND

Bold type indicates an independent state/nation

Despite what seemed to be dramatic changes in the output of agriculture, mines and manufacturing in the "Third World", the overwhelming majority of people remained peasant cultivators or herdsmen. But colonial intervention did not leave them as "subsistence" producers outside the market economy. The need for cash to pay taxes and increasing needs for money to buy simple consumer goods brought in by European traders, drew these producers into the market and commonly into indebtedness and dependence upon traders and moneylenders.

The timing of government tax demands, sometimes at a time of the year when peasants had nothing left to sell, contributed to this process. A major share of colonial cash crops was produced by such apparently "independent" peasant producers, in circumstances which tended to break down arrangements which had previously provided them with some insurance against the effects of drought and other hazards.

Colonialism and the making of "tradition"

In his writings on India in the middle of the 19th century Karl Marx suggested that British colonial rule was bringing about the first major social transformation that the subcontinent had experienced. Modern historians have doubted this judgment on the impact of colonial rule in India and elsewhere and have found evidence of continuity, or of the adaptation, of supposedly traditional social institutions to modern purposes. A classic instance of this was thought to be the use of caste or tribal connections for political mobilization after electoral politics were introduced. But more recently historians have argued that much of what has been thought to be the "traditional" social structure in Asia and Africa is itself really the outcome of local responses to colonial rule, and sometimes the result of the way in which colonial administrators imposed their understandings of "native" societies upon the people they ruled.

▲ World population c. 1900
Thanks to lower death rates in the 19th century there were now relatively more Europeans than ever before (excluding the Russian Empire, about 16 percent of a total world population of about 1,640 million people), though Asians still made up more than half of the global population. As a result of the extraordinary population mobility of the 19th century there were now more Americans than Africans. Europeans and North Americans moved quickly to low birth and death rates and thus low demographic growth rates, whereas those in the "Third World" increased and have remained high for a longer time.

In India the British attempted to count the population by caste titles in the decennial census and thereby probably made caste more important for Indians themselves than it had been before. Certainly the legal system established by the British imposed ideas about the regulation of social relations from north India on the south, helping to change southern society in the process. And the economic circumstances of colonial rule also made caste affiliations more important. As labor scarcity gave way to labor surplus and indigenous owners of capital profited as never before by exploiting workers to the bone, those who were thus oppressed found some security for themselves by calling on the assistance of those to whom they could claim to be related by caste ties. Thus for them caste title became more important. Wealthier people sometimes found it expedient even to change rules about caste membership through marriage, as they sought to build up networks of alliances across much larger areas than before. Social collectivities or "communities" were constructed by the circumstances of colonial rule in much the same way, in fact, as they were by those of emigration to North America or movement to towns in Europe. In Africa too, it has been said that "tribes came into being on the way to town", referring to the way in which networks of kinship and neighborhood were built up by migrant workers and the new townsmen.

In much the same way that in Europe the sense of national identity or of membership in a group of people identified by common religious affiliation became important in the new circumstances of industrialization and democracy, so in the colonial territories religious loyalties could acquire new significance. Relations between Hindus and Muslims in India were not usually marked by conflict until late in the 19th century when competition over opportunities for salaried employment gave birth to rivalry amongst middle-class Hindus and Muslims, and workers in the Calcutta jute mills began to be drawn into bloody conflicts on communal lines.

New middle classes and rising nationalism

In the older imperial possessions the growth in the size of administrations (particularly in land administration and irrigation, highways and railroads and in tax collection) as well as the emergence of modern professional classes (for example, in India, lawyers, journalists, business management, etc), created a small but influential Westernized middle class by the end of the 19th century. In the Ottoman Empire and elsewhere the officer corps of the armed forces often provided the source of a comparable modernizing elite. The Westernized middle classes were the children of traditional rulers and gentry, the staff of traditional courts or the priesthood, bound together by the common experience of Western education, of becoming in most respects European.

At the same time, the lower echelons of the civil and military bureaucracies (the local officers, the operating engineers on the railroads and in shipping and commerce), small businessmen supplying local markets, and some of the children of richer peasants who benefited from the extension of vernacular education also merged as a significant force: a non-Westernized middle class. Their rebellion was against not only imperial rule, but against those with Western education who excluded those with vernacular education. There was rising interest in the creation or recreation of traditional values, cultures and religions. Whereas the Westernized had an ambiguous relationship to imperial power, hostile but dependent, demanding access to power by being accorded equality with the Europeans, the non-Westernized were entirely excluded from participation and thus much more aggressively nativistic, religious (as a form of secular politics) and anti-imperialist. Furthermore, the Westernized tended to regard traditional culture – and the mass of the population – with contempt in their attempt to prove themselves as good as the Europeans.

India provides the clearest example of the parallel development of two social classes, in part embodied in the factions of the nationalist movement, the Indian National Congress (founded in

◄ A South Indian Christian family. Christian missionaries had urged their converts to give up Hindu habits and culture. At this time members of the Indian elites, Christian or not, usually wore Western dress and through their education were quite anglicized in manners and outlook. But by 1900 there was a strong Hindu revivalist movement, responding to the challenge of Western influence. Christianity did not advance much beyond the lower castes.

My first contact with British authority was not of a happy character. I discovered that as a man and an Indian I had no rights. More correctly, I discovered that I had no rights as a man because I was an Indian.

M. K. GANDHI

▼ A classroom in Dar es Salaam, German East Africa, in 1905 with a German teacher. Financial provision was sufficient to provide for the education of only a small African elite, of clerks, teachers and a few who became independent professionals. They eventually became the leaders of the African nationalist movements.

1885). At first Congress had been led by an aloof and sophisticated group of lawyers who, in general, scorned traditional India and Hinduism (except in its sanitized reform versions); however, the most effective movement to link with mass agitations were the Hindu nationalist supporters of Bal Gangadhar Tilak. In the Dutch East Indies (Indonesia), meanwhile, the Sarekat Islam movement focused a nativistic opposition.

In China education in the treaty ports and elsewhere spread quickly as the new century dawned. Western missionaries were particularly important here, and as a result many of the significant figures in interwar nationalist politics were Christians. Gentry and merchant families began sending their children abroad for higher education; by 1906 there were 12,000 Chinese students studying in Japan. When, in 1911, after a long period of decomposition, punctuated by rebellions, the Manchu imperial dynasty fell, a small middle-class nationalist movement under Sun Yixian (Sun Yat-sen) – himself long exiled in

Japan – was one of the political alternatives on offer. The gentry, the former instrument of imperial power, was unable to supply an alternative order, and its families tended to ally with the fragments of the imperial and provincial military forces; the country disintegrated after World War I into what became known as the period of warlords. But the main social issue – the hideous oppression of the mass of the peasantry – still scarcely concerned any of the aspirant political alternatives.

In Latin America the emergence of new professional classes in the more advanced republics profoundly influenced politics, producing the beginnings of movements favoring representative democracy as opposed to rule by dictators, landowning oligarchs and foreign capitalists. But to achieve representative government a much wider stratum of the population had to be mobilized: this was the beginnings of mass populist politics in the big cities (frequently dominated by new immigrants from Europe).

▲ The watchful anxiety of these Mexican women reflects the confusion in their country following the downfall of the modernizing dictatorship of Porfirio Díaz (1911). The Mexican Revolution, involving agrarian unrest in the south led by Emiliano Zapata and dissidence in the dynamic but anarchic north, where Pancho Villa emerged as a revolutionary general, stemmed from the economic developments initiated by Díaz.

THE
UTOPIAN
VISION

Time Chart

	1915	1916	1917	1918	1919	1920	1921	1922
Rural life	• German War Grain Association confiscates all wheat, corn and flour stocks at fixed prices and suspends private grain transactions as the blockade of Britain begins • US wheat crop tops one billion bushels	• 20 Aug: US Congress creates the National Park Service • France sets a new wheat price and controls on butter, cheese and oil • Potato blight causes starvation which kills 700,000 people	• Drought begins in the Western Plains of USA • US Food Administration Grain Corporation buys, stores, sells and transports wheat at a fixed price	• Government report proposes a Forestry Commission to ensure that Britain will have sufficient timber in the future	• Fiat begins manufacturing tractors (It) • Poor harvest and lack of manpower lead to famine in eastern Europe. Increased demand for US wheat pushes prices to $3.50 per bushel	• American Farm Bureau is established to mobilize US farmers' political efforts • Massive drought begins in Russia • A mere 20% of virgin forests in USA remain uncut	• Aug: Russia suffers devastating famine with up to 18 million starving • E.M. East and G.M. Shull perfect a hybrid corn (maize) strain that will greatly improve crop yields	• 14 Oct: Agrarian law in Finland distributes land among the peasantry • Lenin allows for the existence of small private farms to boost production (USSR)
Industry and labor	• 15 Sep: TUC resolves to oppose conscription (UK) • 10 Dec: One millionth Ford motor automobile leaves the assembly line (USA) • International Workers of the World (IWW) organizer Joe Hill is executed by firing squad (USA)	• 13 Jan: UK miners vote overwhelmingly against conscription • During the first seven months of the year there are more than 2,000 strikes by US workers • 7 Sep: Workmen's Compensation Act brings protection for 500,000 federal employees (USA)	• Apr: 200,000 Berlin factory workers strike for a week to protest against reduced bread rations • Mining magnate Ernest Oppenheimer founds the Anglo-American Corporation of South Africa • Phillips Petroleum Company is founded • Union Carbide and Carbon Corporation is created (USA	• Jan: Strikes in the German armaments industry • 26 Feb: Labour Party Constitution declares common ownership and state control as objectives (UK) • IWW leaders found guilty of conspiring and of prosecuting the war (USA)	• Jan: Miners' strike in favor of nationalization and a six-hour day (UK) • May: Establishment of the International Labor Organization (Swi) • 2 Mar: Foundation of the communist Third International • Steelworkers strike in the USA until 1920	• 1 Mar: US returns railroads to private ownership • 1 Apr: German Workers Party becomes the National Socialist German Workers Party • 16 Oct: Coal miners strike begins (UK) • Unemployment insurance introduced in Austria and Britain	• 13 Jan: General Confederation of Labor (CGT), the heart of the syndicalist movement in France, dissolved by court order • Feb: UK unemployment surpasses one million • 31 Mar–1 Jul: Coal strike due to the rejection of nationalization proposals (UK)	• Feb: Strike of German railroadmen • 6 Mar: General strike breaks out in Johannesburg (SA) • 1 Apr–4 Sep: UMW leads a massive coal miners' strike (USA) • Montecatini chemical company is founded and grows to become Italy's second largest industry
Government and people	• 18 Mar: Government appeals to women to take positions in trade, industry and agriculture (UK) • Sale of absinthe is outlawed in France, after the liquor has produced blindness and death among heavy users • Income tax rises to an unprecedented 15% (UK)	• 2 Sep: US Senate passes a bill introducing the eight-hour working day • House of Commons votes in favor of conscription (UK)	• 6 Apr: Kerensky government in Russia introduces the eight-hour day for all workers • 15 May: Congress passes Selective Service Act (USA) • New US immigration laws ban all Asians except Japanese and requires all immigrants over 60 years to know 30–80 English words	• Jan: Representation of the People Act gives the vote to all women over 30 and all men at the age of 21 (UK) • Mar: House of Commons raises the school leaving age to 13 (UK) • 21 Apr: Denmark adopts universal suffrage	• Dec: UK Sex Disqualification Removal Act opens professions to women • Eight-hour day introduced in France, Netherlands and Spain • Women enfranchised in Czechoslovakia, Belgium, Germany, Netherlands and Sweden	• 28 Aug: Ratification of 19th Amendment enfranchises women in federal elections (USA) • 10 Sep: Indian National Congress votes in favor of Gandhi's program of noncooperation with the Indian government • Abortion is legalized in Soviet Russia but outlawed in France	• 8 May: Sweden abolishes capital punishment • 19 May: New immigration legislation strictly limits entry in proportion to the nationalities already present (USA)	• 13 Feb: Campaign of civil disobedience suspended by Indian National Congress due to violence • 22 Sep: Women granted the same citizenship and naturalization rights as men (USA) • Empire Settlement Act Britain pledges to promote emigration to Australia
Religion	• 7 Jan: Reports of Poles and Cossacks slaughtering Jews • 31 Oct: 1.5 million Jews reported starving in Russia	• New York's "Father Divine" organizes the Peace Mission movement. It stresses renunciation of personal property, racial equality and a strict moral code	• 7 May: Reports from Palestine suggest Jews being terrorized by Muslims throughout the region • Jun: Promulgation of the codification of canon law by Pope Benedict XV • 9 Nov: Britain declares its support for a Jewish homeland in Palestine	• 25 Aug: Hungary expels Jews and seizes their assets • 2 Dec: Reports disclose the murder of 3,200 Jews in Lvov (Pol) • Fundamentalist International Church of the Four-Square Gospel is founded in Los Angeles (USA)	• 28 May: Romanian Jews are emancipated and given rights of full citizenship • 18 Jul: Reichstag votes against the separation of Church and State (Ger) • Benedict XV revokes a decree forbidding Catholics from participating in politics	• 12 Jan: Reports suggest the massacre of up to 12,000 Jews in the Ukraine • 11 Aug: First ecumenical conference brings together Eastern, European and US churches in Geneva	• 1–6 May: Anti-Jewish riots by Arabs in Palestine, in protest at the increased influx of Jewish immigrants	• Jan: Death of Pope Benedict XV, succeeded by Pius XI • 27 May: Vatican objects to Britain's proposed mandate in Palestine, because of the privileged position it gives to Jewish concerns • 1 Nov: Mustapha Kemal abolishes the sultanate in Turkey
Events and trends	• 25 Nov: William Joseph Simmons starts a new Ku Klux Klan in Georgia (USA) • 14 Dec: Reports from Central Asia suggest that a million Armenians have been killed by Turks • Theosophist leader Annie Besant founds the Benare Hindu University and organizes the Home Rule League in India, agitating for home rule	• 20 Mar: Rationing begins in Germany as food shortages becomes acute • 29 Sep: John D. Rockefeller becomes the world's first billionaire • France imposes taxes on milk, coffee, sugar and other foodstuffs	• 8 Jul: Government assumes control of exports, food, fuel and war supplies (USA) • Oct: US government confiscates all German properties in the USA • Typhus epidemic begins to sweep Russia and kills three million people within four years • US population passes 100 million	• 4 Jul: Pan-Russian Congress adopts a socialist constitution • Devastating influenza pandemic sweeps Europe, America and the Orient killing 21,640,000 people (1% of the world's population) • By the end of World War I, ten million people are estimated to have been killed	• 6 Mar: UK Board of Trade Report reveals that women in paid employment has risen 1.2 million since 1914 • 28 Oct: National Prohibition Act passed in the USA, severely restricting sale and manufacture of alcohol (taking effect 16 Jan 1920) • 28 Nov: Nancy Astor is the first woman MP in the UK parliament	• Feb: Hitler and the National Socialist German Workers Party publish their program for a Third Reich • 13 Jun: International Feminist Conference opens in Geneva (Swi) • Social reformers found the American Civil Liberties Union	• 13–22 Jan: Italian Socialist Party splits into moderates and radicals at a congress in Livorno • 17 Mar: London's first birth control clinic opens to bitter opposition (UK) • Height of Gandhi's civil disobedience movement in India; though the movement is nonviolent, terrorist violence occurs frequently	• 10 Mar: Gandhi is arrested and sentenced to six years imprisonment (Ind) • 31 Dec: US figures reveal a total of 57 lynchings for the year • Country Club Plaza, the world's first shopping center, opens in Kansas City (USA) • Radio is used as an advertising medium for the first time (USA)
Politics	• 7 May: Sinking of the S.S. Lusitania by a German U-boat • 19 Dec: Britain abandons the Gallipoli campaign against Turkey, and begins to withdraw	• 1 Mar: J.J. Pershing's US forces defeat Pancho Villa's rebels in Mexico • 24 Apr: Beginning of the Easter Rebellion in Ireland	• 6 Apr: USA enters the war on the Allied side • 7 Nov: Bolsheviks seize power in Petrograd (Russ)	• 8 Jan: US president Wilson outlines his Fourteen Points for peace • 11 Nov: Armistice declared, ending World War I	• 23 Mar: Mussolini forms the Fascio di Combattimento (It) • 28 Jun: Treaty of Versailles creates several new European states	• 10 Jan: League of Nations is founded in Geneva (Swi) • Mar: UK parliament passes the Home Rule Bill dividing Ireland into North and South	• 17 Mar: Lenin announces his New Economic Policy (NEP), introducing partial capitalism • 10 Apr: Sun Yixian elected president of China	• 28 Oct: Fascists march on Rome, and Mussolini becomes prime minister of Italy on 25 Nov • 6 Dec: Establishment of the Irish Free State

1923	1924	1925	1926	1927	1928	1929
• 26 Mar: 15,000 Norfolk farmhands go on strike for higher wages (UK) • Dec: 73,500 animals have been slaughtered during a foot and mouth epidemic (UK) • Continued export of corn after the recent famine in the USSR	• Oct: Up to seven million people reportedly starving after failure of the harvest (USSR) • Introduction of the first effective chemical pesticides	• 16 Sep: Liberian land is opened to rubber cultivation by Harvey Firestone • 28 Dec: Land law in Poland passed to provide for the distribution of 500,000 acres of land to the peasantry annually for ten years	• Trofim Lysenko first gains notice in the USSR by putting ideology ahead of science in farm policy	• Perfection of the mechanical cotton picker in Texas reduces the need for field workers, thereby spurring black migration to the urban north (USA)	• Jan: International Famine Relief Commission reports that Chinese peasants are selling children to obtain food • Oct: Stalin launches land collectivization with the first Five-Year Plan. Millions of kulaks (farm landlords) are murdered or exiled to Siberia (USSR)	• 15 Jun: Congress passes the Agricultural Marketing Act encouraging farmers' cooperatives • Africa's Serengeti National Park formed after complaints about hunters using Model T Fords in the bush
• Jul–Aug: Seven-week dock strike in London (UK) • United States Steel Corp reduces the working day from twelve to eight hours • Wilhelm Messerschmidt establishes his aircraft manufacturing firm (Ger)	• 29 Jan: End of an eight-day rail strike (UK) • 16 Feb: Dock strike closes every port in the UK • Nov: Railroadmen strike in Austria • International Business Machines (IBM) Corp is organized in New York (USA)	• Jul: British government grants miners special wages and establishes an arbitration committee to avoid a strike • Aug: Tram and bus employees strike in Paris (Fr) • 12 Aug: Reports of numerous deaths during riots by striking cotton workers in Tientsin (China) • Miners' strike for 170 days in the USA	• 12 Mar: Italian senate passes an industrial relations law abolishing strikes • 3-12 May: General strike cripples Britain, after sympathy strikes by those supporting the refusal of coal miners to accept wage cuts • 2 Nov: Formation of Imperial Chemical Industries (ICI) is announced (UK)	• 18 Feb: 65,000 Shanghai workers strike to protest against the presence of foreign soldiers (China) • 23 Jun: UK Trade Disputes Act outlaws sympathetic strikes and compulsory political levies • 10 Nov: Dividend of $62 million is announced by General Motors, the largest in US history • Pan-American Airways is founded (USA)	• 1 Aug: Morris Motors begins a new model, the Morris Minor (UK) • Merger creates the Colgate-Palmolive-Peet Co (USA) • General Motors (USA) takes over Opel Werke (Ger) • Wave of strikes by textile workers, railway workers and others in Bombay, indicating the influence of the communists (Ind)	• 1 Dec: Ferrari founded at Modena (It) • Lufthansa is organized as the German national airline • British unemployment tops 12%; in Germany, 3.2 million are unemployed • Grumman Aircraft Engineering Corp organized (USA) • World Congress of Women's Labor opens in Berlin
• Apr: National Birthrate Commission recommends the teaching of sex education in schools and homes (UK) • 3 Jun: Bill approved by Mussolini gives women municipal voting rights (It) • First forced labor camp established by Lenin in the Solovetsky Islands; slave labor will be used extensively in construction projects (USSR)	• 12 Apr: Congress approves the Johnson-Reed Immigration Act restricting Japanese immigration (USA) • 13 Nov: Mussolini introduces a bill granting women the vote in national elections (It) • Mongolian women enfranchised on equal terms	• Apr: Britain and Australia begin funding the migration of British families to Australia • 8 May: Bill passed making Afrikaans the official language of the Union of South Africa • Jun: MPs pass a bill excluding blacks, coloreds and Indians from skilled or semiskilled positions (SA)	• 5 Jan: First widows pensions paid out at British post offices • 2 May: India allows women to stand for election to public office • 25 Nov: Mussolini restores the death penalty (It)	• 17 Oct: Norway elects its first Labor government • Italian Fascists introduce the labor card • German government warned by the agent for reparations to increase public expenditure	• 29 Mar: House of Commons passes the Equal Franchise Bill giving the vote to all women over 21 years (UK) • 12 May: Italy reduces its electorate to three million by abolishing female suffrage and limiting male suffrage to those paying over 100 lira in rates • Soviet Union introduces compulsory military service	• 11 Jun: Soviet working day reduced to seven hours • 10 Mar: Egyptian government grants women limited rights of divorce • 6 Dec: Turkish women enfranchised • Romanian women granted equal voting rights
• 27 Jun: Pope Pius XI condemns Franco-Belgian military occupation of the Ruhr • Jul: Treaty of Lausanne begins a huge transfer of population including the removal of 388,000 Muslims from Greece to Turkey	• 3 Mar: Abolition of the Caliphate (Islam's spiritual leadership) by Mustapha Kemal (Turk) • 28 Sep: Gandhi starts a 21-day fast in response to Hindu-Muslim rioting (Ind)	• 30 Jan: Turkish government expels Constantine II (Greek Orthodox Patriarch of Constantinople) from Istanbul • 1 Apr: Hebrew University in Jerusalem opened by Lord Balfour (Pal) • 6 Oct: Archbishop of Canterbury blames low church attendance on poor teaching and outdated clergy (UK)	• 11 Feb: Calles government nationalizes all Church property (Mex) • 31 Jul: Mexican priests begin a strike after enforcement of anticlerical clauses in the 1917 constitution (until 1912) • 2 Apr: Martial law is declared in Calcutta after the outbreak of Hindu-Muslim rioting. Similar disturbances occur in Rawaplindi in June (Ind)	• 3 May: Sikhs and Muslims clash during riots in Lahore (Ind) • 19 Aug: Orthodox Church recognizes the Soviet government (USSR) • 15 Dec: House of Commons rejects the new Book of Common Prayer (UK)	• 9 Apr: Turkey abolishes Islam as state religion • Papal Secretary requests that Catholics not associate with Fascists (It)	• 11 Feb: Lateran Treaty establishes The Vatican as a sovereign city state • 4 Aug: 250 killed in Arab-Jewish clashes over Jewish demands to exclusive use of the Wailing Wall • 11 Aug: Chaim Weizmann forms the Jewish Agency in Zurich (Swi)
• Jun: Ku Klux Klan claims to have one million members (USA) • Nov: Germany crippled by inflation, with a loaf of bread costing 200 billion marks (US$1 = 4 trillion marks) • Mothers' Day first celebrated in Europe • Gregorian calendar introduced in the USSR, replacing the Julian calendar	• Aug: Severe floods in China kill 50,000, leaving two million homeless • 4 Nov: Texas elects Miriam Ferguson, the first woman state governor (USA) • Foundation of Imperial Airways (UK)	• Mar: State of Tennessee bans teaching of the theory of evolution. A violation of this law brings the highly-publicised "Scopes Monkey Trial" (USA) • Apr: Founding of the SS (Schütz Staffel) in Germany • 8 Aug: First National Congress of the Ku Klux Klan (USA) • American Medical Association endorses birth control	• 21 Jan: Makwar Dam opens on the Nile in Egypt, due to fears that irrigation in Sudan might deprive Egypt of enough water for its crops • 28 May: 1,200 reported killed by a cyclone and tidal wave in Burma • 31 Aug: 15,000 people reported heading for the new diamond field in the Transvaal (SA)	• 12 Aug: 80,000 Bolivian Indians revolt against the government • First World Population Conference is organized by Margaret Sanger • UK petrol prices drop to 1902 levels • Borden Co introduces homogenized milk (USA)	• 15 Feb: Oxford English Dictionary, the world's biggest etymological dictionary, published in twelve volumes • 5 Aug: International Socialist Congress opens in Brussels • 3 Nov: Latin alphabet introduced in Turkey – all Turks under 40 years are obliged to learn it • More than 1,500 Americans die from drinking bad liquor	• Jan: King Amanullah restores the veil for women and abandons European clothing (Afg) • May: 3,000 die in Persian earthquake • 22 Sep: Confrontations between armed groups of communists and Nazis in Berlin (Ger)
• 11 Jan-26 Sep: French troops occupy the Ruhr, and a policy of passive resistance is instigated by the German government	• 22 Jan: Ramsay MacDonald forms the first (minority) Labour government (UK) • 6 Apr: Fascists win sweeping victory in Italian general election	• 12 Mar: Death of Sun Yixian (China)	• May: Marshal Jozef Pilsudski becomes dictator of Poland • 25 Dec: Death of Japanese emperor Yoshihito, succeeded by Hirohito (until 1989)	• 31 Jan: Control over Germany turned over from the Allies to the League of Nations	• 8 Jun: Beijing surrenders to Jiang Jieshi, and the capital is moved to Nanking (China) • 27 Aug: Kellogg-Briand Pact renouncing war is signed by 63 nations (Fr)	• 22 Oct: $30 billion in capital disappears as Wall Street collapses on Black Friday. Beginning of the Great Depression

Datafile

Before World War I it looked as though Western capitalist industrialization was destined to conquer the world. But the Russian Revolution ushered in a new social and economic order planned and imposed by a doctrinaire one-party state. Despite the first communist regime's initial failures and the human cost of forced social change, the Soviet "model" would eventually reshape the destinies of one-third of mankind.

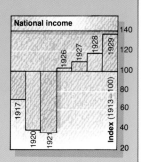

National income

Index (1913=100)

Wartime money supply

◀ World War I forced up public expenditure and reduced tax revenues. In Russia, as elsewhere, the gap was bridged by printing ever more paper money. The ensuing rise in wages, however, was more than offset by accelerating inflation, shortages and curtailment of civilian production, exacerbating hardships and frustrations.

▲ The Russian Revolution was a cause, not a consequence, of a massive drop in national income and output. Until 1917 levels of output, employment and income held up well. But by 1920 gross industrial output and employment were only 14 percent and 47 percent of prewar levels, while agricultural output had halved.

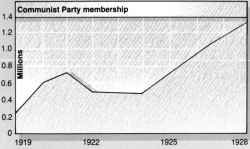

Communist Party membership

◀ Communist party membership soared after 1917, particularly in 1918–20 when half was in Trotsky's Red Army, and after Lenin's death in 1924. Many who had joined the party for opportunistic reasons were "purged" in 1921–23, while others left in disappointment or disgust at its failure to live up to its promises.

▼ Although the Revolution was enacted in the name of the proletariat, wage-earners and their dependents made up under one-fifth of Russia's population. Many workers, moreover, had recently arrived from a village world with which they kept close economic or family ties. They were aptly called "peasants in factories".

▼ In 1917 Russia's peasant farmers finally routed landlordism, threw off official and ecclesiastical tutelage and (through local land committees) radically redistributed the main agricultural means of production. From 1917 to 1928 the peasants were masters of their domain, before their "reenserfment" under Stalin.

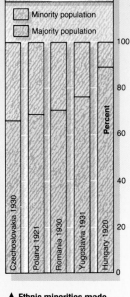

E European minorities

- Minority population
- Majority population

Percent

Czechoslovakia 1930 | Poland 1921 | Romania 1930 | Yugoslavia 1931 | Hungary 1920

▲ Ethnic minorities made up around one-third of the population in interwar Poland, Czechoslovakia, Romania and Yugoslavia and over one-tenth in interwar Hungary and Bulgaria. The ethnic patchwork meant that no amount of redrawing of frontiers could completely resolve all competing territorial claims.

Russian workers 1917

40% | 60%

Total 2,093,862

- Males
- Females
- 12–17 year olds

Russian peasant households

9% | 22% | 69%

1917

6% | 2% | 92%

1920

- Poor/middling
- Well-to-do
- Kulaks

In 1929 the Hungarian historian Oscar Jászi wrote: "War is sometimes a kind of revolution"; World War I "destroyed four petrified political structures, those of the Habsburgs [Austro-Hungarian Empire], the Romanoffs [Russian Empire], the Hohenzollerns [German Empire] and the Sultans [Ottoman Empire]. In consequence a great number of state embryos in Central Europe, in the Balkans and in the Baltic grew into independent life and for many millions of people the road was opened toward national and social emancipation." In Russia the collapse of imperial authority led to the triumph of a socialist party, which presented an opportunity to impose the kind of radical social change envisaged by 19th-century socialist thinkers.

Wartime social change in Russia

In Russia, as elsewhere, labor problems were the catalysts of many social changes ensuing from World War I. To surmount labor bottlenecks and secure maximum effort, cooperation and adaptability from industrial workers (especially in defense-related industries), governments and industrialists courted, recognized and bargained with workers' representatives and leaders whom they had previously disdained or despised. Even in czarist Russia, workers' representatives were elected in May 1916 to serve on 20 regional and 98 district war industries committees.

The massive expansion of war industries and of bureaucracies and office work caused overcrowding, acute accommodation shortages and large rent rises in munitions towns, above all in Petrograd (formerly St Petersburg). Tenements and town houses were converted into workers' "rabbit warrens". Petrograd's industrial work force expanded from 250,000 in 1913 to 417,000 in 1917; Moscow's from 148,000 to 206,000. Russia's total industrial work force increased by 13 percent between 1913 and 1916. By 1917 65–75 percent of factory workers were in defense-related industries. As 20–30 percent of the 1914 industrial work force were drafted into the armed forces by 1917, the war involved a big influx of less experienced and less skilled recruits into the industrial work force. Coming on top of the 30 percent expansion in the factory work force in 1909–13, by 1917 recent recruits comprised over half the industrial work force and 40 percent of all factory workers were women. By then, moreover, three-quarters of the inhabitants of both Petrograd and Moscow were formally members of the peasant social estate. So when revolution occurred in 1917 it is conceivable that, even in Petrograd and Moscow, those involved were more peasant than proletarian and not surprising that when workers had the opportunity to take over industry they had little readiness to do so.

THE BOLSHEVIK EXPERIMENT

From war to revolution

In 1915–16 social unrest and morale were not palpably worse in Russia than in other belligerent states. Indeed, the Russian war effort, production and employment held up well. There were military successes against Austria-Hungary. There was little loss of ethnically Russian territory. Italy and Austria-Hungary seemed to be in greater trouble than Russia. Yet in March 1917 (old style, February) revolution broke out in Russia. It involved bread riots in Petrograd, strikes, the mutiny of city garrisons, the abdication of the czar, the reemergence of workers' soviets (councils) and the emergence of a self-appointed Provisional Government. Why did this occur?

It has been argued that revolutions do not just "happen", that they must have instigators and that any talk of "spontaneity" masks a failure or unwillingness to identify the culprits. But, despite allegations of wartime "subversion" from various quarters, and much political agitation and propaganda, the March revolution was a spontaneous outburst and caught politicians off guard.

The March revolution was mainly a product of wartime dislocation of transport and urban provisioning; a six-fold increase in prices since 1913; the discreditable conduct of government (including the antics of the court mystic Rasputin); and local difficulties caused by Germany's naval blockade of Petrograd. However, the spontaneous activities of self-appointed war industries committees, Red Cross committees, the union of local government bodies, cooperatives and village communes in support of Russia's war effort meant that "Without realizing it, the Russians were beginning to govern themselves. The revolution had not yet been thought out, but it existed in fact" (M. Ferro).

The unstable outcome of the March revolution was that the workers, soldiers and peasants who had toppled czarism became the main powers in the land, yet they expected the relatively impotent

▼ Putting on brave faces, Moscow workers celebrate May Day 1918. The Bolshevik "workers' state" had already started down the road of brutal repression of other socialist and revolutionary groups and dissident workers.

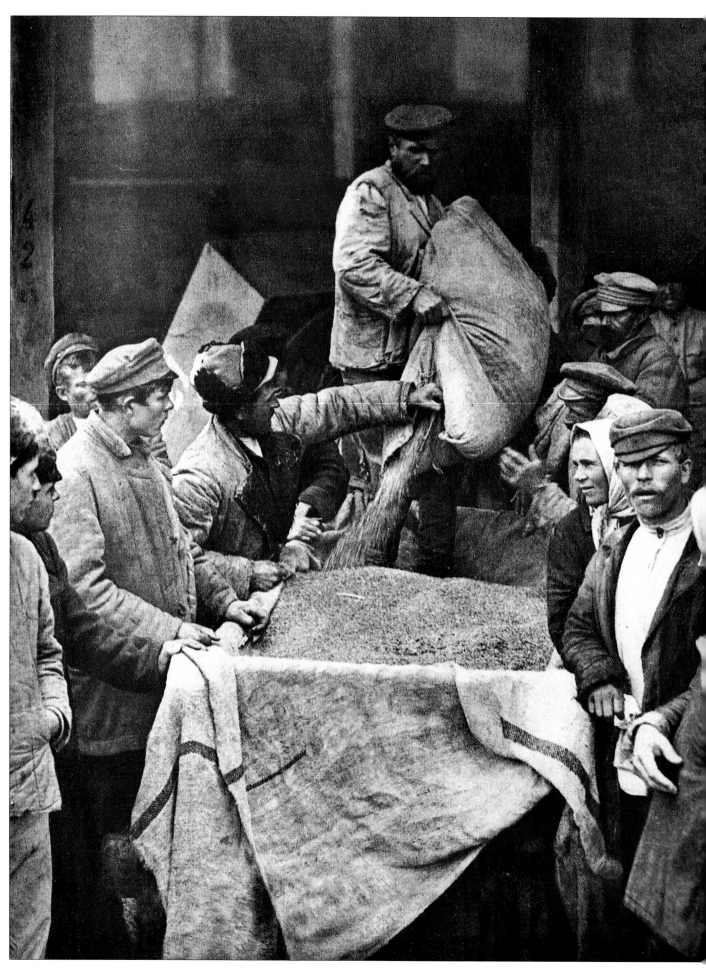

properted classes to keep the responsibility of governing. The instability of "dual power" ended with the Bolshevik socialists' seizure of power from the Provisional Government in November 1917 (old style, October). Lenin – the Bolsheviks' leader – claimed to be taking power for the soviets and on behalf of the proletariat – the mass of laboring men and women.

Social consequences of the Bolshevik coup

Lenin launched the Bolshevik bid for power with schemes for social reconstruction in mind. The basis was to be the nationalization of land, industry and the controlling financial apparatus. As Lenin wrote in 1918, "Capitalist culture has created large-scale production, factories, railways, the postal service, telephones etc., and *on this basis* the great majority of the functions of the old state power have become... reduced to such exceedingly simple operations of registration, filing and checking that they can be performed by every literate person." Thus "We, the workers, shall organize large-scale production on the basis of what capitalism has already created, relying on our experience as workers."

The Bolshevik seizure of power through and for the soviets and factory committees momentarily reflected the interests and wishes of many industrial workers. In November 1917–January 1918 (new calendar) there was a honeymoon period, during which workers and factory committees enthusiastically used up remaining stocks of materials, fuel and capital. But workers' support for the Bolsheviks, soviets and factory committees rapidly dwindled, as it proved impossible to deliver on the promises made and expectations raised. Employment, food supplies and real wages not only did not increase, but from January 1918 began to fall catastrophically. The truce between the new Bolshevik government and the Central Powers (signed on 3 December 1917), the ensuing peace negotiations and cessation of Russia's war effort caused a 70–80 percent reduction in employment in defense-related industries. Unplanned spontaneous demobilization of the 7-million strong armed forces further swelled unemployment and threw transport and distribution into deeper chaos in the winter of 1917–18. Since mounting hardships could no longer be blamed on capitalism, millions of starving, unemployed and disillusioned workers blamed incompetent Bolsheviks, soviets and factory committees for their desperate plight and for having cheated them with promises and panaceas. Peace, workers' control and the Bolshevik policy of "All power to the soviets" had solved nothing and had rendered the crisis even more insoluble.

During 1918 the Bolsheviks increasingly resorted to repression of workers' protest, forcible dissolution of hundreds of workers' soviets and imprisonment, exile or execution of opposition socialist leaders. This struggle played a critical role in the emergence of a one-party police state. The party and the security police decided who was a "counterrevolutionary", a power that was freely abused. Already by May 1918 Lenin was publicly demanding "unquestioning obedience... to the one-man decisions of Soviet directors, of

◀▲ Sickening contrasts between official Soviet propaganda pictures of well-stocked shops and granaries (left and opposite) and the grim realities of widespread malnutrition, destitution and disease (above) added insult to injury. They reinforced a growing popular revulsion against the consequences of revolution and civil war: regimentation, requisitioning and repression. In 1920-21 grain output was only half the prewar level, and in 1921-22 Russia was ravaged by famines and epidemics centered on the Volga basin. They caused around 5 million deaths. Women and children suffered terribly. Gangs of abandoned children roamed towns and villages, begging, scavenging and stealing.

the dictators elected or appointed by Soviet institutions, vested with dictatorial powers". As Lenin told the 1919 congress of the Communist party (as the Bolsheviks had renamed themselves in 1918) "the Soviets, which by virtue of their program are organs of government by the working people, are in fact organs of government for the working people by the advanced section of the proletariat", meaning the Communist party. Dictatorship of the proletariat became dictatorship over the proletariat and, if proletarians resisted, against the proletariat.

The Bolshevik police state

The Bolshevik coup led by Lenin resulted in the execution of some 200,000 opponents in his six years in power (compared with 14,000 executions under the last czar) and to the creation of a one-party police state. (The political police expanded from 15,000 under the last czar to 250,000 in 1921.) Worst of all, Lenin plunged Russia into a wholly avoidable civil war in 1918–21, by forcibly suppressing in January 1918 a new constitutent assembly (his party had won only 25 percent of the 42 million votes in the November 1917 elections).

It is painful for me...to see how the peasants are ordered around in the localities.... You have to explain and prove things to peasants, not simply use rigorous and iron discipline against them, not beat them into submission; you have to have the patience to talk to the peasants. It's no good just terrorizing the peasants. Is that not right, comrades?

RED ARMY COMMANDER
JULY 1919

Lenin also unleashed an uncontrollable "Red Terror" against rival socialists and against massive peasant and proletarian opposition in 1918 (ostensibly against the relatively insignificant and peripheral "counterrevolutionaries" and "foreign intervention"). This civil war and the ensuing famine and economic collapse were to cost over 12 million lives in 1918–21, about four times the 3.2 million lives lost by Russia in 1914–17 and over twice the 5.5 million lives lost in 1926–39 (in Stalin's Purges, rural collectivization, epidemics, and the 1932–34 famine), according to the sober calculations of F. Lorimer, B. Kerblay and S. Wheatcroft. As the radical historian Yuri Afanafiev told the Supreme Soviet in February 1990, the Soviet state was founded on violence and terror, which its founder elevated into principles of government.

One of the principal reasons for the enormous human and economic costs of the early years of Soviet rule was that the Bolsheviks seized power with no agreed or worked-out blueprint for the "socialist" society they hoped to build. Marxist orthodoxy had never envisaged that the first and only "proletarian dictatorship" could arise in a peasant society. The Bolshevik leadership seized the opportunity to take power in November 1917 because it might never have arisen again. However the vast number of Marxist writings offered no thought-out or unambiguous guidance on policies that should be pursued by a "dictatorship of the proletariat" in an industrialized society, let alone in a predominantly peasant society. Marxists had embraced the idea of "planning" as a panacea for the "anarchy" and "waste" of commodity production. But until 1924 they remained blissfully ignorant of *how* to plan, of the various possible *forms* of planning, and of the various possible relationships and contradictions between central and local planning and workers' control and the market, or even of where to start. Until the 1930s planning was just one of many socialist slogans, devoid of real substance; planners were just groping in the dark.

Soviet society and the New Economic Policy

By 1921 Russia's civil war (which had raged since 1918), the Russo-Polish War of 1920 and the reabsorption of the Ukraine, Transcaucasia and Central Asia had reduced Russia to a state of economic collapse, epidemics and famine. The industrial work force had been more than halved in size. The Revolution had devoured its children.

To provide a breathing space to enable Russia to recover, Lenin launched his New Economic Policy (NEP) in March 1921. Its essence was the restoration of a market-based, mixed economy, in which only the "commanding heights" of finance, transport, large-scale industry and foreign trade remained in state control. Simultaneously, however, Lenin set out to consolidate one-party rule. Party appointees replaced elected officials, and there were prohibitions on "factions" within the ruling party and on independent trade unions, professional associations, schools and publications and on opposition parties. But, having monopolized political power in the hands of the party leadership and especially in those of the general secretary (a post which Joseph Stalin's astute exercise of patronage quickly elevated to the status in effect of party boss soon after he obtained it in 1922), the party felt a growing need to try to convince the public that this was still their revolution rather than exclusive "party property".

To promote broader identification with and support for this Soviet regime, the party promoted (within officially prescribed parameters) an unprecedented eruption of experimentation, iconoclasm, creativity, festivity, revolutionary cinema and mass organizations. It made particular efforts to increase peasant, female, ethnic minority and intelligentsia support for and commitment to the party and the Soviet regime.

The Indian summer of the commune system

Under NEP the Russian peasantry enjoyed a large measure of autonomy. Some 90 percent of all peasants used the opportunity to hold their lands and to administer their villages on a communal

◀ **Bolshevik caricature of Orthodox priest.** The Bolshevik state was fiercely atheist and anticlerical from the outset. In 1918 Lenin's government outlawed religious instruction in schools, nationalized all church and monastic properties and ended legal recognition of religious marriage and divorce procedures. It also denied clergy any right to vote, to public office, to state employment, to full ration cards, to post-primary education for their children and to subsidized rents. Moreover it subjected clergy to discriminatory taxation. By 1920 673 orthodox monasteries had been dissolved; by 1923 over 1,000 orthodox clergy had been killed; by 1929 over 15,000 orthodox churches had been closed. In 1929 proselytizing and instruction of children by priests were outlawed completely.

▼ **According to the 1926 Soviet population census,** only 71.5 percent of males and 42.7 percent of females (aged 9–49) could read. In the mid 1920s, therefore, 20 percent of local education expenditure was earmarked for adult literacy classes. The classes were staffed mainly by volunteer women recruited from the radical intelligentsia. Their endeavors helped to raise literacy to 93.5 percent for males and 81.6 percent for females (aged 9–49) in the 1939 census. For the Soviet regime literacy campaigns provided one "safe" way of mobilizing women into active service to the state while they were increasingly excluded from politics after 1922.

Soviets and Social Organization

The Bolshevik party seized power in November 1917 behind Lenin's slogan "All power to the soviets." But what were the soviets? The word *soviet* simply means "council." Soviets or councils of workers' deputies first arose in the 1905 Revolution, when factories in St Petersburg and Moscow elected delegates to coordinate strike movements. The soviets became embryonic organs of popular power, establishing workers' militias and printing presses.

Suppressed after 1905, soviets reappeared in 1917 after the March Revolution, but this time peasants and soldiers imitated the workers and formed soviets. As various soviets coordinated opposition to the Provisional Government an improvised national network and hierarchy of soviets emerged with an All-Russian Congress of Soviets at the top which elected a 300-member All-Russian central Executive Committee.

"All power to the soviets" was never understood to mean "All power to the Bolshevik party." Soviets were originally seen as organs of dispersed, decentralized power and direct democracy, in which Bolsheviks could coexist with other parties. But the Bolsheviks quickly monopolized and centralized power in the Soviet system. Local budgets and appointments came under central control, rival parties were terrorized and suppressed, lower soviets became passive executors of the policies of higher tiers; key policy-making decisions and debate shifted to the ruling Party. The soviets became the official structure for the Bolshevik state, yet it has never been imitated by other communist states.

▲ A village soviet in the Volga region, c.1930. A nationwide network of village soviets (*selosoveti*) was established in 1918-20, in a political endeavor to wean the Russian peasantry from their peasant-administered village commune system. The village communes or "land societies" (as they became under Soviet law) were seen by the Bolsheviks as irritating obstacles to party penetration and control. However, village soviets failed to attract much peasant support.

basis in accordance with peasant custom. They farmed their fields on an independent family basis and carried out widespread "land reorganization" involving division and resettlement of communes and villages scattered over excessively large areas, and the consolidation of scattered and excessively narrow strips (reorganizing 27 percent of cropland by 1927). From 1913 to 1929 the sown area rose by 13 percent and production of cash crops and potatoes rose two and a half times. The average size of peasant farm allotment in the Russian federation rose from 14ha (35 acres) in 1913 to 18ha (44 acres) in 1927, and in 1925–29 average Soviet grain yields per hectare were 12 percent higher than the 1909–13 level.

It might have been expected that this agricultural policy would have led to the reemergence of the so-called *kulaks* or rural "bigmen". But the cumulative concentration of agrarian capital, land and production in the hands of a rural wealthy class was inhibited by the prohibition of the private purchase and sale of land, legal restrictions on private employment of hired labor, and by the strength of communal landholding. Even official Soviet accounts generally concede that the so-called kulaks comprised only 2–5 percent of the

The Bolshevik Revolution and Women's Emancipation

The Bolshevik Revolution was a milestone in the struggle for women's emancipation. It was the first occasion on which complete economic, political and social equality of males and females became an officially proclaimed goal of a state.

World War I had greatly expanded the roles, public recognition and self-confidence of women in Russia, as elsewhere. Thousands of Russian women had distinguished themselves as army nurses, auxiliaries and doctors. In industry, women took over jobs vacated by male conscripts. Malnourished women nevertheless staged serious food riots in April and June 1915, and food riots and strikes by working-class women were the catalysts of the Revolution of March 1917. During 1917 leading feminist organizations redoubled their support for Russia's war effort. In return, the Provisional Government enfranchised all adults over the age of 20 in July 1917. Russia was thus the first *large* country to confer equal political rights. In mid 1917 Russia's women also won rights to serve as lawyers and jurors and to equality of opportunity, pay, benefits and titles in public employment *before* the Bolshevik takeover.

The successes of liberal feminism in 1917 galvanized Russia's ailing socialist women's movement. In 1917 leading Bolshevik women established a Bureau of Women Workers, resurrected the Bolshevik women's newspaper and founded new publications. The same women organized the First All-Russian Congress of Working Women in November 1918. There Lenin declared that "A primary task of the Soviet Republic is to abolish all restrictions on women's rights", as "the success of a revolution depends on the degree to which women take part in it". Out of this congress arose the energetic *Zhenotdel* (women's department) of the Communist Party (1919–30).

In late 1917 and early 1918 Bolshevik family reforms established a basic juridical framework around which equality of the sexes could gradually be built or attained, primarily within marriage. The reforms conferred legal recognition only on marriages recorded in civil registry offices; completed the equalization of male and female rights to hold and inherit property, be household heads, take employment, conduct business and reside where each chose, begun in 1912–14; equalized the rights of legitimate and illegitimate children; established liberal, equal, quick civil divorce (at the request of either spouse and subject to alimony for unemployed exspouses); and proclaimed equal male and female rights and obligations to work. The revised Family Code of 1926 further liberalized divorce procedures, permitting "postcard divorce" (postal notification of divorce in uncontested cases).

However, heated public debate during the revision of the Family Code in 1925–26 revealed significant peasant hostility to the liberal divorce laws, not so much on religious as on practical grounds. Divorce might be relatively straightforward in towns and cities where divorcees could often move to new accommodation and jobs. But for multigenerational peasant households which were also production units, divorce could be economically disastrous for the divorcees and their dependent relatives, splitting up peasant family farms. The same debate revealed a widespread tendency to blame Soviet family

reform for alarming crises in family life in 1918–26: soaring divorce rates and juvenile delinquency; resurgent prostitution; endemic sexual promiscuity and venereal disease; and millions of homeless waifs and orphans and abandoned, destitute wives. Such phenomena were mainly consequences of World War I, the Civil War, economic collapse, famine and epidemics, but many people blamed the Communists' attacks on the family and religion, and their "free-living" and "free-loving" moralities.

Marxism and Leninism were committed to encouraging high birth rates and to the idea of motherhood as a social duty. Abortion was legalized in 1920, not to increase women's freedom to choose whether or not to have

children (although women had the final say in practice), but as a "lesser evil", to reduce the health and mortality risks attendant upon illegal "backstreet" abortions. (Unqualified abortionists were made liable to criminal prosecution.)

In Russia, unlike the West, the struggle for women's emancipation was joined to a quest for total reconstruction of society. The ascendant intelligentsia increasingly saw women's emancipation not as a discrete goal in its own right but as one element in a wider transformation of society. This gave women's emancipation greater initial prominence in post-revolutionary Russia than in the West, but it also contributed to the subsequent subordination of women's emancipation to economic, political and military goals.

ОВЛАДЕВАЯ ТЕХНИКОЙ, БУДЬ В ПЕРВЫХ РЯДАХ СТРОИТЕЛЕЙ СОЦИАЛИЗМА

agrarian population in 1928–29, as against 15 percent in 1914, and that they produced 20 percent of peasant grain in 1926–27, compared with about half before 1914; Western estimates are much lower. Either way, it is difficult to take seriously the Bolshevik alleged notion of a kulak threat to the Soviet regime.

On the reverse side of the same coin, there was almost no rural proletariat or "semi-proletariat" and the soviets could hope to attract much class-based rural support. Many peasants were put off or perplexed by the party's obsessive class-rhetoric, and also by its "militant atheism", its closure and desecration of thousands of churches and mosques, its persecution of Christian and Muslim clergy and its formal (albeit skin-deep) commitment to women's emancipation.

NEP as "New Exploitation of the Proletariat"

Relative to other groups, the main loser under NEP was the much-diminished working class. Many workers felt betrayed, denied the deference they deserved in the dictatorship of the proletariat, and exploited and manipulated by a self-serving bureaucracy. Some saw the restoration of a market system as an unpalatable restoration of capitalism, a sell-out and a defeat, rather than as a welcome escape from the rigors and privations of a siege economy. Many resented the growing powers and privileges of the bureaucracy, the continuing decline of "workers' control" in industry and of democratic accountability in public administration, the rampant corruption and nepotism, and the regime's concessions to the peasantry, to "Nepmen" (traders and industrialists), to the intelligentsia and to ethnic minorities, allegedly at the workers' expense. Real wages remained well below the paltry 1913 levels until as late as 1926.

In 1928 the statutory working year was lengthened from the 267 days of 1913 to 300 days. Workers felt threatened by serious urban unemployment. The number of unemployed hovered around 1.2 million in 1924–28, jumping to 1.7 million in April 1929. In mid 1929 45 percent of the unemployed were women, 17 percent were youths and many were peasants who had recently left their land in search of new opportunities. Even in 1928 the number of wage and salary earners was only just above prewar levels at 11.6 million (versus 11.2 million in 1913). The number of industrial wage earners was 2.8 million (versus 2.5 million in 1913) and women comprised 28.5 percent of factory workers (versus 31 percent in 1913 and 40 percent in 1917).

As elsewhere, it seems that 1920s unemployment bore most heavily on female workers, seriously undoing their wartime occupational advancement. Only in teaching, nursing, medicine, office work and as students in secondary and higher education did the 1920s see Russian women making further major advances. Peasant and working-class women were still confined to drudgery and looking after Soviet males.

Workers also felt exploited by Leninist enthusiasm for piecework and F.W. Taylor's "scientific management". A Central Labor Institute was formed in 1920, especially to promote "scientific

▲ **An Uzbek woman removes the veil. In the predominantly Muslim and Turkic Republics of Soviet Central Asia the near-complete absence of industrial workers encouraged the Bolsheviks to seek alternative sources of support. Most notably, they mobilized Muslim-Turkic women. Sweeping social reforms, however, met fierce resistance or caused widespread social problems.**

organization of labor" based on time and motion studies, the definition of output quotas or work norms for each job, and remuneration of workers in accordance with the degree to which they "fulfilled" or "overfulfilled" their norms. Work norms based on time-and-motion studies were introduced from 1924 and by 1928 62 percent of all industrial workers were on piecerates. These favored the fittest workers at the expense of the unfit, the old, the inexperienced, etc. Most unpopular were the differential or "progressive" piecerates, rewarding above-quota work at progressively higher rates, which became widespread under Stalin. Workers were not enamored of NEP, but there was far worse to come.

The springtime of nations

After the Bolshevik Revolution the Russian Empire in effect broke up. Separate states emerged from once imperial territories in Eastern Europe (Poland), along the Baltic (Lithuania, Latvia, Estonia and Finland) and in the Ukraine, Transcaucasia, Central and East Asia. Between 1920 and 1921 the Communists reestablished control over all these states except those in Europe and the Baltic and in July 1923 adopted an all-union constitution. The initial plans for a federation and the subsequent Communist nationalities policy were directed by Joseph Stalin.

The forcibly reincorporated Ukrainian, Transcaucasian and Central Asian nations were first of all thoroughly subjugated and then permitted significant areas of cultural autonomy. Each of the major ethnic minorities (except Jews) was in due course granted its own separate Soviet Socialist Republic. Especially under NEP, these Republics vigorously promoted vernacular education, literature, art, architecture and music. The 1920s saw a remarkable flowering of national cultures which, while a surrogate for true independence, occurred on a scale that would have been unthinkable under czarism. With hindsight, one can see that this period sowed the seeds of the long-term survival and growth of nationalism and separatism in the Soviet Union by fostering the "emblems" of nationhood.

In 1924, as people's commissar for nationalities, Stalin set forth guiding precepts for the "eastern" Soviet Socialist Republics. These included the aims to "develop national culture [but also] training Soviet, party, technical and business cadres from the local population". These were to

▶ **In 1926 the Soviet Union was a multinational federation comprising 147 million people, 47 percent of whom were non-Russians. The 31 million Ukrainians were the largest European nation to have been denied full sovereignity and independence since the 1920s. The Soviet Union contained 17 million Turkic peoples and about 19 million Muslims (13 percent of the total population). Except for the 4 million Turkic, Muslim and largely nomadic-pastoral Kazakhs and 2.7 million widely dispersed Jews, each major nation within the Union had its own "Union Republic" or "Soviet Socialist Republic" (SSR) with its own "Republican" government and formal rights of self-determination and secession. But the bundle was tightly bound together by the Communist party's monopoly of power and decision-making.**

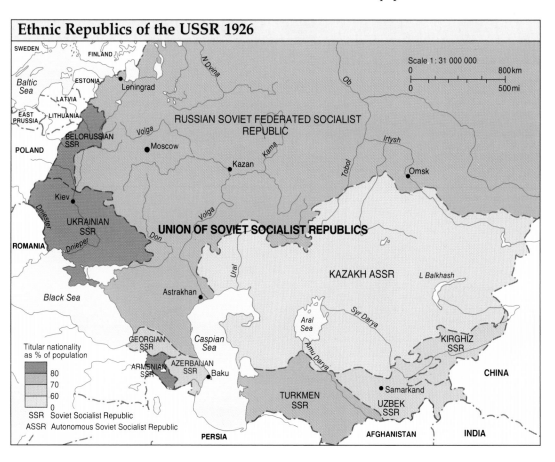

Ethnic Republics of the USSR 1926

SWEDEN
FINLAND
Baltic Sea
ESTONIA
Leningrad
LATVIA
EAST PRUSSIA
LITHUANIA
N Dvina
Ob
Scale 1 : 31 000 000
0   800km
0   500mi

RUSSIAN SOVIET FEDERATED SOCIALIST REPUBLIC

BELORUSSIAN SSR
Volga
Moscow
Kazan
Kama
Irtysh
POLAND
Omsk
Tobol
Kiev
UKRAINIAN SSR
Dniester
Dnieper
Don
Volga
UNION OF SOVIET SOCIALIST REPUBLICS
ROMANIA
Ural
Black Sea
Astrakhan
KAZAKH ASSR
L Balkhash
Aral Sea
Syr Darya
GEORGIAN SSR
Caspian Sea
KIRGHIZ SSR
Amu Darya
ARMENIAN SSR
AZERBAIJAN SSR
Baku
CHINA
Samarkand
TURKMEN SSR
UZBEK SSR
PERSIA
AFGHANISTAN
INDIA

Titular nationality as % of population
80
70
60
0
SSR Soviet Socialist Republic
ASSR Autonomous Soviet Socialist Republic

become, in effect, foot troops of the Soviet regime. "Proletarian in content, national in form – that is the universal culture towards which socialism proceeds... Proletarian culture does not abolish national culture, it adds content" – the national cultures of the new Soviet national republics were to be inbred with the Soviet as well as national foundation myths, emblems and values. Moreover, Stalin maintained that socialist revolution, "by stirring up the lowest sections of humanity and pushing them into the political arena", was responsible for a national awakening of hitherto submerged nationalities. Finally, Stalin warned against mechanical attempts "to transplant models of economic construction comprehensible and applicable in the center of the Soviet Union, but totally unsuited to conditions in the so-called border regions". those "guilty of this deviation fail to understand... that, if work is not adapted to local conditions, nothing of value can be built" and "they degenerate into Left phrasemongers", divorced from the masses. The opposite "deviation" lay in "exaggerating local features...hushing up socialist tasks, adapting to the tasks of narrow nationalism" (*Pravda*, 22 May 1924). Stalin thus left himself plenty of scope for accusing local Soviet elites of either excessive or insufficient nationalism and served notice that either "deviation" could land them in political hot water. Stalin was laying a minefield which would claim many victims during his long reign.

The "Green Rising" in peasant Europe

The working classes were not the only people "on the move" in post-1917 Europe. There was also a groundswell of peasant-based movements right across Europe, from Ireland and Scandinavia through Germany and the Slav world. This "Green Rising" was accelerated by the emergence of self-consciously peasant nation states in Ireland, the Baltic littoral, Eastern Europe and the Ukraine, by the largely peasant revolution in Russia in 1917, by the growing politicization of peasantries during and after World War I, by electoral competition between rival mass movements, and by the international ideological appeal of "blood and soil" nationalism and Russian agrarian socialism (the latter mainly among Slavs and Romanians). Moreover, the widespread adoption of universal suffrage and elementary schooling in Europe after 1917 benefited peasants more than any other class, as did the continuing spread of cooperative networks.

In Eastern Europe peasants achieved new social prominence thanks to radical land redistribution. In all countries except Poland and Hungary large estates were eliminated. Both native and foreign estate-owners were expropriated. Their lands were transferred to peasants in the form of small freeholdings. As the British writer G.K. Chesterton wrote in 1923 "what has happened in Europe since the war has been a vast victory for the peasants".

▲ Young and old reading a local newspaper in Yakutsk, Siberia, 1929. While failing to precipitate "international proletarian revolution" in the West (which Lenin had hoped would come to the aid of Soviet Russia), the Soviet regime more successfully championed "national liberation" in the East, starting with the creation of SSRs and ASSRs (Autonomous Soviet Socialist Republics) in Soviet Asia and the People's Republic of Mongolia in the 1920s. By instigating "national liberation" in the East, Lenin set out to tip the balance of world power against Western imperialism.

DEVIANTS

Deviants are societies' scapegoats. Every community has its "nuts, sluts and perverts" although life-styles and motives which are ridiculed or discriminated against in one epoch might become conventional or at least acceptable in the next. Having a child outside marriage once caused a woman to be utterly rejected; it is now common in many societies.

Some deviance has always been tolerated; for example the "court fool" or the "village idiot" of the rural past and, more recently, teenage rebellion. Defining deviance is a power struggle between contending groups over where the line should be drawn between acceptable and unacceptable behavior. If deviants lose, at best they face ostracism, at worst legal sanction – both intended to punish the offender and to act as a deterrent to others. Over time this has meant death, arrest, prosecution, imprisonment or compulsory treatment. If deviants win, the boundaries of tolerance shift.

Deviance takes many forms. Moral deviance often becomes political opposition. Suffragettes chaining themselves to fences in the early 20th century were seen as scandalous. Today in most countries the vote for women is beyond contention. In the 1980s the stand taken by British women against the siting of cruise missiles at the US air base at Greenham Common in England was initially ridiculed, but the missiles were eventually removed. The concern for environmental issues is no longer just the hobbyhorse of an eccentric few but a matter of international concern.

All societies have their economic deviants. Over half a century of centralized planning did not purge entrepreneurs and black marketeers from socialist countries. In capitalist societies some have eschewed competition by adopting alternative life-styles while others have survived by operating in the underground economy, avoiding regulation and as pedlars of contraband or sexual services.

Social deviants offend because they subvert prevailing and reassuring certainties about normality. Alcoholics, psychiatric patients, drug abusers, homosexuals or prostituted women are regarded by the moral majority as not just outrageous but prone to trouble and crime. They are thought to prey on innocent and unwary victims and some forms of deviance do have serious social consequences, dragging families into poverty, transmitting venereal disease, thieving to sustain drug habits and the spread of the AIDS virus through needle sharing by heroin addicts. But deviants not only offend, they also suffer, from discrimination in jobs, social services and the courts. The stronger amongst them have challenged their victimization. Prostituted women in the developing world have formed organizations to fight toward decriminalization and for protection, homosexuals in the West have challenged pejorative labeling and stereotyping. The weak, however, are still ultimately dependant upon the slow shift of social perception.

▶▶ **Inside a mental hospital.** Many such institutions are located far from city centers, removing from society the sense of embarrassment felt at the plight of the mentally ill. Isolated locations provide tranquility for patients but also add to feelings of alienation.

▶ **A member of the Salvation Army visits old people.** Dedicated members of voluntary organizations have shown some of the greatest concern for marginal members of society.

▼ **The "old man of the road"** – attractive at a distance, an outcast if he approaches.

▼ *Three Prostitutes on the Street* by Otto Dix, 1925. In the 1920s antiestablishment culture in Germany celebrated outcasts such as prostitutes and homosexuals. It was repressed by the Nazis.

▲ At the state level, pressures to conform have been strongest in the 20th century in totalitarian societies. For example, Soviet governments have removed and imprisoned millions of supposed enemies of communism, such as these prisoners engaged in forced labor near Tiflis in Georgia.

▼ Members of a gang of "Hell's Angels" who use appearance, behavior and contrary values to shock the rest of society. Their self-confidence, however, is based on the creation of conformity within their own groups.

Datafile

Throughout Western Europe the war of 1914–18 brought devastation but also hastened the passing of social welfare legislation, of which there was a wave in the early 1920s. The period saw greater personal freedom as social conventions were relaxed, and also saw real advances in the conditions of labor in both Europe and America. There was more time and scope for home life, modest prosperity, and the concept of "leisure" began to have meaning even for workers. Yet at the same time it was a period of reaction in which, after initial reverses, ruling classes reasserted themselves and, in America especially, sought to impose a moral conformity quite at odds with the carefree image of "the roaring twenties".

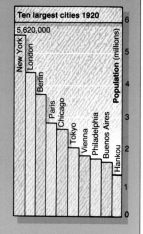

Ten largest cities 1920

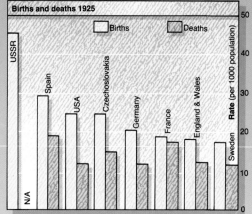

Births and deaths 1925

◀▲ By 1920 American prosperity was reflected in the fact that New York had become the largest city in the world (above). Some cities outside the West were also growing fast. In Europe the 7 cities of more than 1 million inhabitants of 1910 were to be 16 by 1940. Birth and death rates continued to fall (left) but the pattern of much higher rates in the east and south than in the north and west of Europe became even more pronounced. The proportion of children in the Western European population was disproportionately low.

▶ The period immediately after World War I witnessed unprecedented labor unrest with British workers leading the way. The British government used troops against strikers. In Italy industrial unrest culminated in some large-scale factory occupations. However, militancy there and in other countries was generally short-lived.

▶ Disillusionment with Europeans after the war heightened American fears of being swamped by poor immigrants from Europe. The National Origins Act of 1924, designed to stabilize the ethnic composition of the population, reduced immigration but represented the repudiation of America's tradition as a haven refuge.

▶ Lloyd George's scheme of building "homes fit for heroes" after the war was a turning point for the public provision of housing in Britain, even though it was soon dwarfed by the boom in private house-building. Houses were relatively cheap, costing on average about twice the annual salary of a lower professional man.

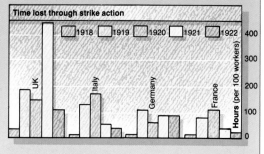

Time lost through strike action

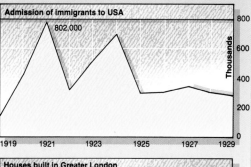

Admission of immigrants to USA

802,000

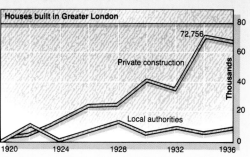

Houses built in Greater London

72,756

Private construction

Local authorities

For those in the West who lived through the war years of 1914–18, the war they called the "Great War" was a catastrophe. Yet now it seems that contemporary perceptions exaggerated the extent of change caused by the war. There certainly were major changes, perhaps especially the end of European ascendancy in the world economy. In the 1920s the United States emerged as the dominant economic power, offering unparalleled prosperity to its people and a style and way of life to the world. But the lines of social change are more difficult to discern.

In Europe it is most helpful to think of the war as having etched out and emphasized particular changes that were already underway. In general it enhanced the power and improved the position of organized labor. It threw further into doubt the future of the middling classes. It encouraged unprecedented intervention by governments and thereby hastened change in state–society relationships, while at the same time helping to ensure the continuity of social power in Western Europe.

In the United States the war encouraged a mood of disillusionment and reaction and introduced an era of political conservatism and social conformity. This was all in spite of the popular image of a new, freer way of life.

Population movements and family policies

Precisely how many lives were lost during the war is debated – a common estimate is that 9 million combatants were killed. The losses of war fell particularly heavily on France, the population of which had been growing more slowly than that of other powers. By the late 1930s it no longer really counted as a major power because of its loss of manpower. The postwar period saw a major influx of immigrants, accounting for three-quarters of the increase in the population in France between 1920 and 1930 – mainly Poles, Spaniards, Belgians and Italians. French governments pursued policies to encourage population growth.

Yet the war and the later economic depression accelerated the long-run trend toward smaller families in Western Europe and North America – also extending it to the working classes. They also encouraged the practice of contraception. Contraceptives had already been quite widely used amongst the middle classes but during World War I working-class soldiers were issued with them as a protection against venereal diseases. As a result there was a sudden diffusion of knowledge of contraception. Marie Stopes' *Married Love* was published in the UK in March 1918 and her *Wise Parenthood* in November of the same year – marking a greater openness about sexuality. The long-run differences between the richer north and west of Europe, with their smaller families and slowing rate of population growth,

LIBERTY AND REACTION

and the poorer south and east became much more marked.

The growth of large cities went on in Europe and North America. Suburbia expanded. The population of the French department of Seine-et-Oise, outside Paris, for example, increased by 50 percent between 1921 and 1931 as transport became easier. In Britain there was a significant drift of population to the southeast around London, and away from the areas of the older heavy industries. Meanwhile the great movement of Europeans to North America came to an end. There was now widespread feeling that the "Anglo-Saxon" stock of America was being swamped by the "new immigrants" from poorer parts of the Old World. The National Origins Act of 1924 reduced immigration to 165,000 a year and extended national quotas in a way which discriminated against the "new" immigrants.

World War I and social change

The changing position of labor movements

Life in English suburbia

The spread of Fordism in the United States

Organized crime in the United States

Marriage as a career

The "roaring twenties"

▼ The entombing of the unknown soldier beneath the Arc de Triomphe symbolized for France the loss of one-tenth of its menfolk in the war.

The onward march of labor?

The urgency of wartime production demands strengthened the hand of organized workers generally. In Britain, at least, the living standards of the working class also rose, especially among those at the bottom end of the scale. As a result there was considerably less poverty after than before the war. Elsewhere in Europe, especially in Germany and Austria-Hungary, the war usually brought greater material suffering than in Britain but everywhere workers became more organized and more militant. Even in a country outside the conflict like Spain the war years were part of "a revolution of rising expectations" which also led to a rush among employers to form associations.

The war period itself and especially the period immediately afterward saw an enormous surge in union membership and quite unprecedented industrial conflict. Regimes feared the prospect of

imminent revolution following the Bolshevik example in Russia. Yet as early as 1922 the threat of the contagion of revolution had receded as the varying mix of repression and conciliating reform applied by governments took effect. A notable effective reform was the granting of the eight-hour working day, which became nearly universal. It seems likely that popular support for revolutionary social change was anyway much weaker than contemporaries believed. A study of workers in the Ruhr, for example, has shown that their demands at this time were essentially economic and that "theirs was much more a social protest movement than a wish to achieve major political and other structural changes". Critically, too, the left in Germany split between reformist/revisionist wings aiming to work within the existing system, and the revolutionaries. The German Communist party (KPD) broke away from the Independent Social Democrats (USPD) in December 1918 and continuously challenged the SPD-dominated government during a period of near-revolution. It was met with sometimes brutal force as the SPD, in its effort to secure stability and the independence of Germany, was driven to reliance on the army and conservative forces profoundly mistrustful of socialism. There was direct repression of worker militancy in Britain and France too. Police forces were used to break up demonstrations and strikes, and in Britain wartime legislation allowed the government to declare a state of emergency to deal with the rail strike in 1919 and again in 1920–21. The left split in Britain and France in 1920 and in Italy and Spain in 1921.

One reason for the divisions in working-class movements was that social reforms started in some countries before the war, and extended during and after it, increased the interest of organized labor in the existing economic system. Concessions made by ruling groups to a large extent worked. The early 1920s saw a wave of social legislation throughout most of Europe, extending social insurance for the elderly, widowed and orphaned, making provision for unemployment and for subsidizing housing. Reform went farthest in the country where organized labor was strongest – Britain. A ministry of health was established in 1919 and national health insurance became universal for the working class in 1920. The Housing Act of 1919 obliged local authorities to meet housing needs and so established the "council house" in the social landscape. The Unemployment Insurance Act of 1920 extended that of 1911. The years to 1939 saw more and more legislation which brought real benefits: by 1935 the working class received 91 million pounds more from the state than it paid in taxation.

Labor militancy in the 1920s

After the storms of 1919–20 workers were increasingly pushed onto the defensive politically, and were variously absorbed in economic reconstruction and modestly increasing living standards, or in confronting unemployment. The nine-day General Strike of 1926 in Britain, which has sometimes been seen as the high watermark of labor militancy, was essentially a defensive action. It developed as a response to attempts by mine owners to extend working hours and cut pay. Its defeat was followed by antiunion legislation and a great drop in militancy (fewer working days were lost because of strikes in the whole period between 1927 and 1939 than in 1919 alone).

In Germany many of the workers' gains had been lost by 1924. Unemployment increased and union membership declined. Business amalgamations created huge firms and units of production in iron and steel and chemicals. The increased strength of employers was shown in November 1928 when a quarter of a million iron and steel workers were locked out during a dispute. French unions were weaker anyway, and cheap immigrant labor kept down wage increases. But France also had the fastest growing European economy in these years and average incomes rose by nearly 40 percent (1913 to 1929). The establishment of Fascist power in Italy, meanwhile, saw the removal of the rights of opposition trade unions by 1925, and thereafter the incorporation of workers' organizations into the Fascist movement. In Spain the socialist leadership cooperated with the dictator Primo de Rivera (1923–30).

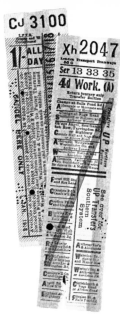

▲▼ Tickets for London trams (above); and the fight of suburban travelers to get home by tram during the national rail strike of 1919. In this one year 35 million days were lost to strikes in Britain and revolution seemed near.

European elites and middle classes

A leading historian of the 1920s, C.S. Maier, argues that "European social hierarchies have proved remarkably tenacious". It is widely accepted that after the upheavals of the war and its immediate aftermath the social order of western Europe emerged more or less intact. The war enhanced the position of workers, brought benefits to some members of the upper classes and assisted the upward mobility of others – notably those businessmen whose activities related to the war effort and who were drawn more directly into government. But the war also precipitated the decline of those aristocrats and gentry who had remained dependent upon title and landed wealth alone, and it had a particularly damaging impact upon the middle classes.

Together with the aristocracy, the middle classes lost relatively more men during the war than the working classes. Increased taxation in wartime affected them too and those who depended on rents or fixed incomes were especially hard hit. Wartime and postwar inflation eroded the savings of all the middle classes and the reduced spending power of others also hit the incomes of shopkeepers and craftsmen. Though middle-class incomes, relative to those of workers,

▲ Mounted police in action against strikers in London during the nine days of the General Strike in May 1926. Class divisions never stood out more strongly in Britain. Working-class communities showed immense solidarity in support of miners who were threatened by proposals for the reorganization of the coal industry. On the other hand middle-class volunteers helped the (well-prepared) government to maintain essential services. Yet both sides sought to avoid violence and it became clear that the labor leadership did not seek revolutionary change.

◀ The establishment of the 8-hour day, for which these workers from the Paris Metro demonstrated, was achieved at last in France in 1919. The limitation of the working day marked both new industrial time discipline and the clearer separation of work and leisure.

Life in English Suburbia

Suburban development around London began before the end of the 19th century, when a contributor to *The Architect* described the modern suburb as "a place which is neither one thing nor another; it has neither the advantage of the town nor the open freedom of the country, but manages to combine in nice equality of proportion the disadvantages of both". In spite of such disdain many common people preferred a semidetached house with a bit of garden to tenement flats in the city. The housing boom after World War I, and the extension of the Underground and Metropolitan railroad systems – beginning with the continuation of the Hampstead line out to Hendon beyond North London in 1923 – saw the development of huge new housing estates around the city, served by new multiple stores, banks and branches of the building societies. The local Woolworths "was increasingly the focus of popular life", and by bringing down retail prices Woolworths, together with the building societies and the "Never-Never" (the instalment system of payment for consumer goods such as sewing machines, vacuum cleaners and wireless sets) "made it financially possible for people of small means to take over new houses" (R. Graves and A. Hodge). Houses built mostly of red brick, costing around £1,000, belonged to people with incomes of £5-10s per week, and were given individuality or "personality" by their architects with pebble-dash, half-timbering and unexpected minor features. The poorer classes were given less fanciness in council estates and new tenements built in slum-clearance schemes. Though there was jerry-building, housing regulations brought better standards which resulted in improvements in health and "the elevation of slum-dwellers to lower middle-class rank by virtue of such amenities as gas, electricity, bathroom and water-closet". Yet still the new suburbs attracted scornful upper-class comment. The remark of the writer Osbert Lancaster is characteristic: "It is sad to reflect that so much ingenuity should have been wasted on streets and estates that will inevitably become the slums of the future". In practice social classes were increasingly separated by the layouts of the new estates, and the effects of the Town Planning Act of 1932 were to perpetuate this cleavage. Status divisions were almost literally built in to British society at this time.

The life of English suburbia has been supposed dull and restricting, and to have encouraged "a privacy of loneliness and tedium". Thus the British writer George Orwell wrote: "Do you know the road I live on? Even if you don't you know fifty others like it. You know how these streets fester all over the inner-outer suburbs. Always the same. Long, long rows of little semi-detacheds... The stucco front, the creosoted gate, the privet hedge and green front door". And yet, just as the country house on the green outskirts of the city met the aspirations of the wealthy, so a semidetached in the suburbs seemed the way to independence and social consideration for the lower middle-class and many workers. A larger proportion of the population emerged from World War I with these aspirations of home ownership, a quiet family life, leisure activity and domestic comforts. "The home" became for them the supreme object of attention, to be embellished with labor-saving devices like the Hoover vacuum cleaner. These

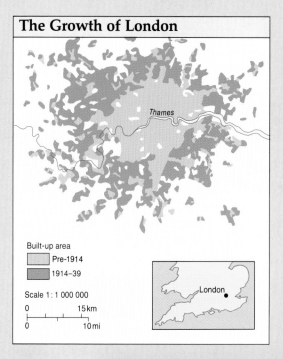

The Growth of London

Thames

Built-up area

Pre-1914

1914–39

Scale 1 : 1 000 000

0   15km

0   10mi

London

◄ About one-third of the increase in the English population between the wars was found in Greater London. Suburbs grew rapidly on all sides of the city in response to the demand for new housing which attracted much adverse comment, though it was evidently what people wanted.

▼► The new suburban houses were smallish, semi-detached, usually tiled and lighter and airier than Edwardian houses had been (below). They had larger gardens and space for sheds and garages. There were over one million privately owned cars by 1930, of which the favorite model was the "Baby" Austin (right).

aspirations were fostered by developments in retailing. The provision and advertising of branded goods simplified shopping, and fast-cooked foods (like "Quick Quaker Oats") arrived in the shops. Packaging changed too, and in the 1920s cellophane wrapping came into general use, banishing the flies from grocers' shops. There was, contemporaries wrote, "a new found pride" among young women "who wished everything to conform in cleanliness and respectability to their new domestic standards". The same young women now dressed in clothes made from the new fabric – artificial silk – called "rayon", which made both for a quicker turnover of fashions and for their adoption even by relatively poor people. "It was now at last possible to mistake working-class girls for titled ladies, if one judged by dress".

The suburban growth was fostered by the growth of productivity in the 1920s and 1930s, especially in new industries based on electricity and the automobile. But these developments took place mainly in the Midlands and Southeast, which accumulated wealth and population and power. A social gulf opened up between these areas and the older industrial regions which persisted through the century. The divide was remarked upon by the British novelist J.B. Priestley when, in 1933, he described three different Englands: the "old country of history"; the England of 19th-century industrialization; and then 20th-century England, "springing up unplanned and shapeless – an England of...thousands of semi-detached houses, with advertising hoardings everywhere". Here there is another hint of disdain. Yet, as the historian K.O. Morgan says, "The majority of the population found that life was acceptable and in many ways agreeable. If one explanation for the lack of social change amidst unemployment and depression lies in the lack of political power vested in the old industrial areas, another lies in the increased commitment to a pleasing form of suburban life by larger and larger sections of the population".

had generally recovered by the mid-1920s, the undermining of their positions during the war led many members of the middle classes to support the "new European right" – "comprising distressed farmers, retired officers, intellectuals and university youth, clerical employees and hard-pressed small businessmen and traders [who had, even before the war] embraced a strident chauvinism, anti-semitism and anti-parliamentarism" (Maier). It was such people, or sometimes members of Catholic groups, who formed the ranks of the various volunteer corps which fought against socialists in Germany, France and Spain. They thus contributed to the defense of bourgeois Europe while posing a sinister threat to liberal institutions.

The way in which regimes achieved or maintained stability after the war represented an important change in the way in which power was exercised, marking a shift from the ideals of 19th-century liberalism. The urgency of wartime production had required harmonious industrial relations. The war thus both established the legitimacy of unions and their leaders and increased the significance of employers' associations. It had also caused states to intervene and acquire new powers to control prices, allocate materials and regulate labor. The autonomy of markets thus tended to be eroded, and decision making to shift from parliamentary assemblies to negotiation and bargaining between the state and major organized ("corporate") interest groups. In sum the war produced a trend toward "corporatism" in which key decisions are made by corporate groups, or these groups and the state jointly, and individuals have influence only through their membership of corporate bodies (such as trade unions, professional associations or business corporations). Corporatism is reflected in the Stinnes-Legien agreement between union leaders and employers' representatives in Germany, which was made on 15 November 1918 – only four days after the Armistice. In return for recognition of many trade union bargaining rights and the eight-hour day, manufacturers were assured of their leadership of industry. Similar sorts of agreements were at least considered in Britain at this time; and somewhat later in the 1920s corporatism became established as a principle of rule in fascist Italy. But the extent of the trend toward corporatism in the 1920s should not be exaggerated. In Germany, for example, the Ruhr lockout of 1928 showed how far power had swung back to employers and the old privileged groups which had in fact run things throughout.

Industry and workers in America

Across the Atlantic, in the United States, the war had encouraged an inward-looking, intolerant nationalism, known as "100 percent Americanism". In the name of the war effort, there was an assault on civil liberties and repression of dissent. The pro-business Harding administration after 1920 sided with employers. Union membership fell from 5 million in 1920 to 3.5 million in 1929.

At the same time, as industrial production almost doubled in the 1920s, industrial workers

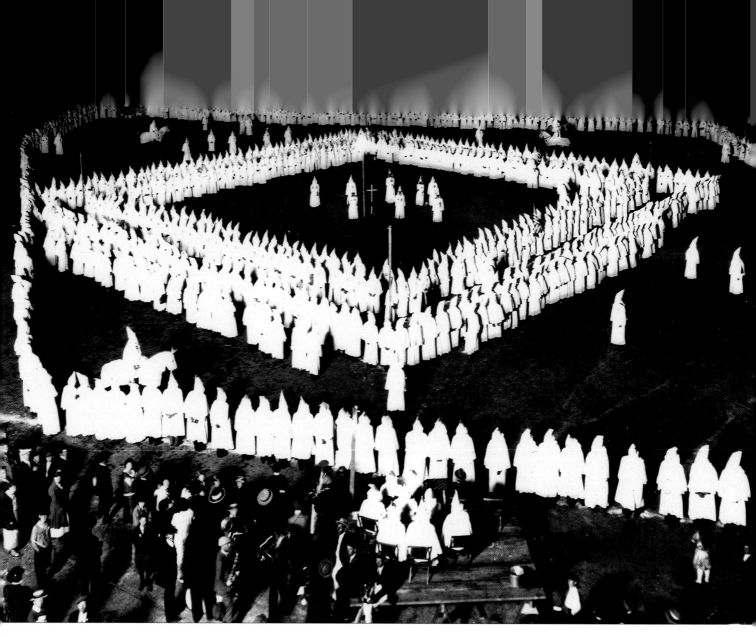

achieved new prosperity. Working conditions were improved as employers, in order to head off labor unrest, developed "welfare capitalism" – including profit-sharing, life insurance and pension plans, and company recreational facilities. The mix of repression and conciliation applied in America as it did in Europe. But as in Europe, some areas of old heavy industry lay outside the general prosperity. Agriculture was generally depressed and the countryside in America (as in Europe) lagged behind in the rise in living standards.

America's prosperity was based on the chemicals industry and the manufacture of new synthetic textiles (rayon) and plastics. The electrical industry was also important: in 1912 only 16 percent of the population lived in dwellings with electricity, but 63 percent in 1927. Electrical household appliances – cookers, irons, refrigerators, toasters – were mass-produced for the first time. Meanwhile the production of automobiles trebled in the 1920s.

Industrial growth in this period was based upon increased productivity resulting from technological innovation and the application of "scientific management". Its key idea – to take

control of production away from workers by making it independent of their knowledge and skill – had been elaborated by F. W. Taylor before the war, but actually implemented in only a very small number of plants. The approach required detailed study of industrial processes to break them down into simple operations. It began to come into its own in the 1920s – in both the United States and Europe – together with the principles of mass production pioneered by Henry Ford: flow (assembly line) production of highly standardized products, often involving special-purpose machinery.

Such mass production presupposes mass consumption, in which advertising plays a crucial role, and market management – of which a bold example was the purchase by General Motors, Standard Oil and Firestone Tires of urban electric trolley systems. They then dismantled the systems to ensure the dominance of motor transport. Mass production also involves intensely hierarchical, top-down management and authoritarian work relations. These features of "Fordism" – mass production and consumption, centralized organization with rigid job specifications, reliance on semiskilled workers and collective

▲ A gathering of the Ku Klux Klan in West Virginia, 1924. Open only to "native born, white American citizens" the Klan by then had more than 2 million members, mainly among disadvantaged blue-collar workers, clerks and small business people in fast-growing cities of the mid-West, Southwest and the Pacific Coast. Its hostility was at first directed not so much against blacks as against Catholics, Jews and "foreigners" who "with drink, dancing and short skirts" were accused of undermining American values.

▼ A last drink before
Prohibition made drinking
illegal in America in
1920. Rural Protestant
fundamentalists were strong
supporters of what President
Hoover described as "a great
social and economic
experiment", sought by the
high-minded idealists of
American Progressivism
since the Civil War had
boosted alcohol consumption.
But it proved impossible to
enforce because so many
people, including the very rich
and the immigrant working
class, were strongly opposed
to it.

bargaining, and commitment to standardized products (cultural products like films as much as chocolate bars) – together constituted the dominant economic culture of the middle part of the 20th century. It powerfully influenced experiments in the construction of socialism (usually obsessed with scale) – as well as market societies until later in the century when it was challenged by more flexible production methods.

Conformity and reaction

The defensiveness of American society was shown in the "Red Scare" of summer 1919 and was also reflected in the terrible outbreak of racial violence which followed the influx of blacks into northern factories during the war. In the postwar recession white workers felt that blacks threatened their jobs and homes.

From this time onward race became a crucial factor in urban labor markets, dividing workers against themselves. The colorful founder of the Universal Negro Improvement Association, Marcus M. Garvey, won a following for a time among the black urban masses when he sought to stimulate pride in black achievements. But his movement was undermined and had collapsed by 1923, leaving only "garveyism" as an inspiration for later black nationalists.

Defensiveness also manifested itself in an intolerant moralism rather at odds with the image of the age of jazz and the automobile and of greater social freedom and leisure. The attempt to enforce moral and intellectual conformity by law is epitomized by Prohibition and by anti-evolutionism, first established in law in Tennessee in March 1925. The legislation reflected the strength of religious fundamentalism and anxiety in the south about the basis of white racial supremacy. Ethnic and racial tensions also underlay the rise of the Ku Klux Klan, founded in Georgia in 1915, as a vehicle of militant patriotism.

Organized Crime

▲ The studied calm of Al Capone.

Alphonse Capone, born in New York in 1899, became the most famous gang boss of all in the 1920s, the violent but formative years of organized crime in America. Capone was reputed to have owned banks, real estate firms, hotels and other investments, bringing in more than 60 million dollars annually. His imprisonment in 1931 for tax evasion may, however, have been engineered by more progressive syndicate groups because he attracted too much publicity and attention from the law, which obstructed the development of organized crime.

Ethnic criminal groups like the Mafia, with their origins in the armed bands of Sicilian landowners, laid the foundations of 20th-century criminal syndicates. Prohibition then marked a turning point, for the supply of illicit liquor to a national market with deliveries to thousands of "speakeasies", meant that criminals had to become businessmen owning distilleries and breweries and distribution networks, albeit with protection rackets enforced by their private armies. Their operations taught the gangs the need for national cooperation. Johnny Torrio, a Neapolitan, was elected president of the Unione Siciliane, and brought together a convention of major crime groups in 1929 to formulate a national policy. Capone perhaps stood in the way of this rationalization of crime. Organized crime was in some ways an outgrowth of the corrupt economic practices of late-19th-century America, and there has been close liaison between the syndicates and the political and business establishments. But organized crime has also been encouraged, paradoxically, by America's Protestant tradition, for attempts to legislate morality, as with Prohibition, have always created criminal opportunities in their evasion. The crime syndicates, described by a presidential commission as "a society that seeks to operate outside the control of the American people...working within structures as complex as those of any large corporation" have extended their operations from the traditional lines of gambling, loan-sharking, labor and business racketeering, and narcotics, into new ones such as credit-card and real-estate fraud, as well as into legitimate business operations.

Women and the family

After the war the great social and cultural trends of prewar industrial society continued. Although differences were to persist between urban and rural settings, between rich and poor, with increasing urbanization notions of personal happiness and the desire for security began to change the goals and nature of marriage more widely.

For women, marriage was to become increasingly their "career". It denoted status and security, both of which were absent in most fields of employment open to them. The media began to promote motherhood and better housekeeping in advertising and women's magazines. Fashion journals and designers followed suit: "How to attract a man" and "How to please one's husband" were the kind of maxims which channeled women's interests, their expectations and aspirations. This renewed focus on women's reproductive roles after the war was accompanied by a retreat of feminism from the doctrine of individual equality toward an acceptance of sex-role divisions in society. The programs of the women's movements thereafter sought to protect the interests of mothers and housewives, abandoning earlier demands such as the right to abort or the right of married women with children to work outside the home.

Complex reasons underlie this shift. The increasing obsession with the birthrate after the war, for example, put feminists on the defensive. It was suggested that it was women's moral or even national duty to "cooperate in the preservation of the nation". In all the industrialized countries the low birthrate was widely attributed to the growing independence of women. In Germany feminists were accused of undermining the nation; in others they were stigmatized for wanting to destroy the family.

In nearly all countries feminists responded by mounting pro-family campaigns in an effort to halt the downward trend of birth rates. Other agencies helped along and the celebration of "Mother's Day" (in the United States from 1914, in Germany from 1922) became a great commercial success. In France mothers of numerous children were awarded the *medaille de la famille*. Already by 1920 employment figures for women had "normalized" and now varied little from those before the war. Except for some advances in the professions such as medicine and law, women's positions seemed not to have been changed by the war at all. In many countries women were granted the vote, but on the whole it brought them only symbolic equality.

Yet there were some important if limited changes resulting from the war. They mainly affected younger women who, during the war, had been "out in public" on their own as never before. This undoubtedly fostered new expectations of personal freedom and independence, especially as the whole notion of women in public (as distinct from the home) had become more respectable during the war. Supporting the national effort and working in new surroundings also raised women's consciousness and made them more confident. These less concrete yet threatening changes to the traditional image and

role of women were difficult to offset, especially as a whole new industry of recreation and fashion now began to "market" the modern trends. Thus motherhood, or rather the perceived lack of it, received new attention.

Married women were increasingly barred from the professions or dismissed upon marriage. In the postal services in Germany, for example, the total number of married women was reduced between 1922 and 1923 from 2,718 to 21. Among the workers, married women in the labor force were stigmatized and accused of taking men's jobs away. Would-be working women were channeled into so-called "caring" occupations in social welfare, child or health care – or at universities into the "female" professions. In secondary education, the curriculum for girls continued to incorporate an emphasis on housekeeping and childcare. "New opportunities" for women began to mean better conditions in the home, improved child and maternity welfare, and a better education for their children. While new welfare legislation and extended family benefits on the whole improved the quality of material life within the family, they also served to reinforce women's traditional roles.

In this decade of so-called moral decadence, and of a general erosion of acquiescence, the family was blamed, as it had been and was to be again and again, for all the social and moral ills of society. The family was held to be at risk: "it was weakening". Parents were seen to be losing control over their offspring as adolescence was emerging as a distinct phase in the life of individuals. It was the result of a delay of his or her entry into the sphere of productive work through longer education. Social concern that children should be brought up according to cultural and social ideals and the increasing attention paid to them created what the historians Mitterauer and Sieder called a "kind of hiatus", a period of initiation into society by external institutions (schools, job-training, clubs or youth organizations).

▲ Modern technology was soon to become indispensable for the wife and mother. This advertisement shows the leisurely pace of washday with an *Easy* machine.

▶ In spite of war, defeat and social democracy, German society in the 1920s still bore the stamp of its aristocratic traditions. Guests at the wedding of the grandson of Count Otto von Bismarck (German chancellor until 1890) to Anne Marie Tengbom are waving the newly married couple off to their honeymoon.

▼ Holidays abroad remained the privilege of the rich during the 1920s, but lower-middle-class and even some working-class families were beginning to have holidays in their own country, as did this German family seen at a seaside resort.

It's sheer enjoyment dancing to -

Columbia
New Process RECORDS

"NEW PROCESS" means NO SCRATCH

▲ Mass production of records transformed the leisure time even of the poor, as the introduction of gramophones to pubs and cafés brought to them the newest fashions in music and dance.

▼ In some American municipalities "indecent bathing" was banned in the 1920s; in others "petting" was made a crime. Anything authorities deemed obscene or immoral was liable to suppression or seizure, as for example these unfortunate women bathers.

By the end of World War I the young had begun to form an important social group through which nations hoped to transmit their "cultural heritage" of work ethics or moral values. The extent to which they could be influenced in order to ensure socio-cultural continuity became more pressing, once young people were beginning to be organized by political parties, or formed their own organizations. This seems to have happened on a wider scale in Germany than elsewhere, where a youth movement began to emerge before the war. In other countries the young grouped together after the war often out of protest against conformity and authoritarianism. In prosperous America such youthful rebellion has been described as a reaction against the prevailing social norms, sexual taboos and double standards of "Victorianism".

A significant feature of the 1920s was the spread of Freudian ideas throughout Europe and America. This also increased the number of apostles of sexual freedom. Although profoundly anti-feminist, Freudian ideas eventually proved to have a generally liberating effect also on young women, pointing the way beyond feminism. The "advocates of women's rights" of that time gave short shrift to "radical" women such as Victoria Woodhull, Marie Stopes or Helene Stoecker who promoted sexual freedom. Instead they joined the ranks of those who expressed indignation over the new "immorality" of the twenties. They also supported the new moves to make the diffusion of knowledge of contraception illegal (in Sweden such a law had been passed already, in 1911). Yet the use of contraceptives increased despite statutory obstacles – to what extent among the unmarried is difficult to assess. The existing trend of rising nonmarital intercourse certainly continued, but the number of illegitimate births also continued to fall until World War II (as it had done, with variations from country to country, from the mid-19th century or so, though not in Sweden until the 1930s).

"Nothing and no one was in its place anymore, everything was possible", reflected the German philosopher Helmut Kuhn, in response to the changes in Europe after the war. Change was too fast. Although individual morality had already become a matter of public concern long before the war, bringing along new types of social reform through state intervention, the postwar period saw the convergence of more active forms of state control, as expediency, class or political interest began to replace the notion of "the rights of the individual". With regard to women, this can be clearly sized up by the way in which, even among the feminists, vocabulary such as "rights" or "justice" had begun to recede as a justification for female suffrage, and moral imperatives moved into the forefront of the struggle.

Feminist ideas of the 1920s

The granting of female suffrage in most Western countries soon after the war was celebrated by women as a main victory on the road to their liberation. At the same time, however, it was seen by politicians and suffragists alike as a means of controlling society in the interests of the "stable" part of the population, the middle classes. In the end women were given the vote either to stave off a proletarian revolution, or as Sir John Hall, the main advocate of votes for women in New Zealand, put it, because female suffrage would "increase the influence of the settler and family man, as against the loafing single man".

The feminists' promotion of motherhood as women's primary role after the war was illustrative of a more long-term reorientation of feminist ideology. Feminists had started off as liberal individualists, asserting that there were no innate differences in reason or ability between men and women, and had fought for "equal" opportunities on "equal" terms for women, only to retreat to a position where these innate differences became the basis for feminist demands. This was to be a crucial development in all industrializing nations, as it endorsed the concept of separate spheres of action for men and women. The feminists' new rationale built on that 18th- and 19th-century proposition that women's moral superiority was inborn and a consequence of their function as mothers. Thus suffrage had been widely demanded on the grounds, that once in government, women could help curb immorality and disorder.

This move toward the right with the feminists' retreat from liberalism was part of a general change in the nature of liberalism itself. At this time liberals came to endorse state interventionist and collectivist solutions to social problems in order to preserve social peace – often in order to preempt solutions suggested by the left. Liberalism became a "Janus-faced political ideology", as Richard Evans termed it, and feminism shared its characteristics: "The way in which problems of social control featured in the actual granting of female suffrage illustrates the extent to which the feminists owed what many of them saw as the crowning victory to these more conservative implications of the liberal creed".

▲ **A much publicized aspect of women's revolt against the restrictions placed on their behavior and appearance was that they demanded and sometimes asserted the right to drink or smoke in public, as in this English restaurant.**

▼ **The images on these powder compacts convey a sense of the new freedom young women claimed in the 1920s. The use of cosmetics no longer implied a wearer's easy virtue. Advertising now reminded women of their duty to keep young and beautiful and face powder promised an "irresistible complexion".**

The freedoms of the "roaring twenties"

A new trend of leisure and youth culture took its cue from the cinema as the new "movies" from Hollywood began to offer notions of "another life". America's jazz, played by New Orleans black musicians, grew increasingly more popular. It inspired new dance forms – the Charleston and "Black bottom" – all visually suggestive, which was proof for the period's moralists to believe that the collapse of all morality was imminent. Most parents felt lost in the face of such rapid change among the young; and most young people did think of themselves as wild and daring. There were probably fewer changes in sexual behavior than contemporaries believed, but there was experimentation, and new romanticization of love as the notion of sexual fulfillment in marriage was being discussed more openly.

The "modern" young woman, who no longer behaved as she used to do, filled a special niche in society's concern for stability, as she threw off the restrictions which traditions had placed on appearance and behavior. The "new" woman smoked in public, took part in entertainments outside the home, at cinemas, the dance halls; she wore boyish hairstyles, makeup and shorter dresses. She seemed to prefer carefree pleasure-seeking rather than preparing herself for her serious duties as future wife and mother. New employment opportunities in the expanding service sector, where young women worked as typists, telephonists, secretaries, or as clerks, had made this short period of carefree life between school and marriage possible. It was a period of idealized freedom and temporary independence and of equally idealized dreams of marriage – a form of escapism, reinforced by Hollywood cinema and the new novel.

PLAY AND GAMES

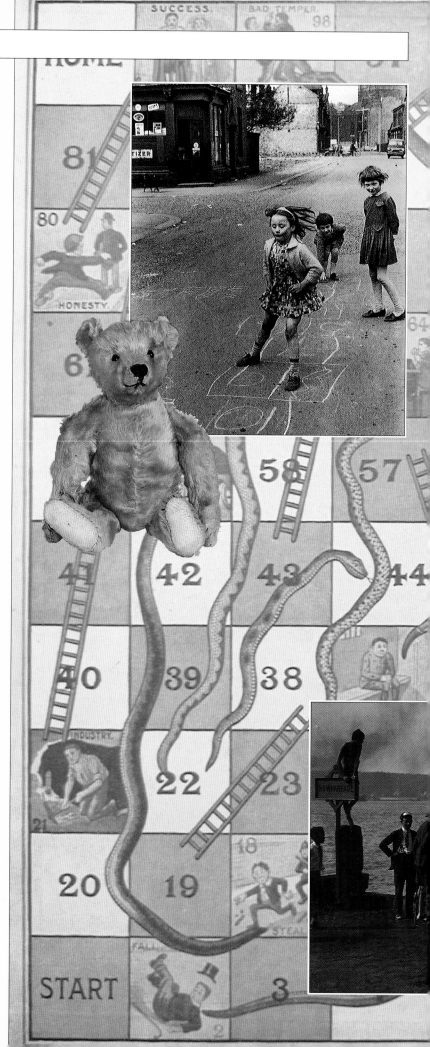

The idea that the world of the child is entirely separate from that of the adult is a relatively recent one. A hundred years ago, blind man's buff was a game for the whole family, and even today, in many parts of the world, adults and children play games together – charades, cards, ball and board games. It is usually through games that adults find it easiest to spend recreation time with their children, because "playing by the rules" imposes a structure and competition that resemble aspects of daily life. In this way, games teach children valuable life skills, not least of which is that when they lose, the world does not come to an end.

But play is also about freedom from all but self-imposed rules. Playing statues, trying not to blink in staring contests, or avoiding cracks in the pavement are all children's attempts at mastery; they are common for many cultures and periods. Moreover, children need fantasy play to allow them to integrate their inner and outer worlds harmoniously and independently of adults. For children in societies where myth and magical beliefs are a normal part of daily reality, the capacity for creative fantasy is fostered; where adult impatience or the constraints of modern life reduce the long hours of leisure necessary for valuable day-dreaming, this ability may be curtailed.

Middle-class children have always been subject to greater adult control over their play. This was extended to working-class children during the century; for example by the introduction of boy scouts and girl guides and the construction of municipal playgrounds in many countries from the 1920s. Shop-bought toys too, were once the preserve of better-off children. In the interwar years mass-market toy manufacture flourished with the introduction of the cheap clockwork motor, although the wholesale commercialization of children's play was only a feature of the affluent postwar years.

Toys mirror societies' values and technological progress. Television has undermined the importance of books, or so it is often claimed. Walkie-talkies and moon buggies have replaced the lead or tin soldiers of the 1900s and the train sets of the interwar years, while the delicate porcelain dolls of Edwardian times have given way to gregarious plastic teenage "Barbie" and "Cindy" dolls, dressed for the discothèque and the beach. Today there is growing concern about the pressures of fashion and crazes on children's toys and play, largely a result of television advertising which exploits children's need to be accepted by their friends.

▲ ▶ Rather than gardens or playgrounds, urban children often favor streets or building sites as the center of their play, like these girls engaged in a game of hopscotch in the 1950s. Outdoor play such as skipping, ball games, tag and hide-and-go-seek have a universal appeal; many such games endure unchanged for generations of children.

▶ ▲ Teddy bears are an invention of the early 20th century. Soft toys provide children with safe objects of affection which they can alternately cuddle and control. They can act as parent substitutes in the long hours of the night. While real bears might be threatening to children, teddies protect them from harm.

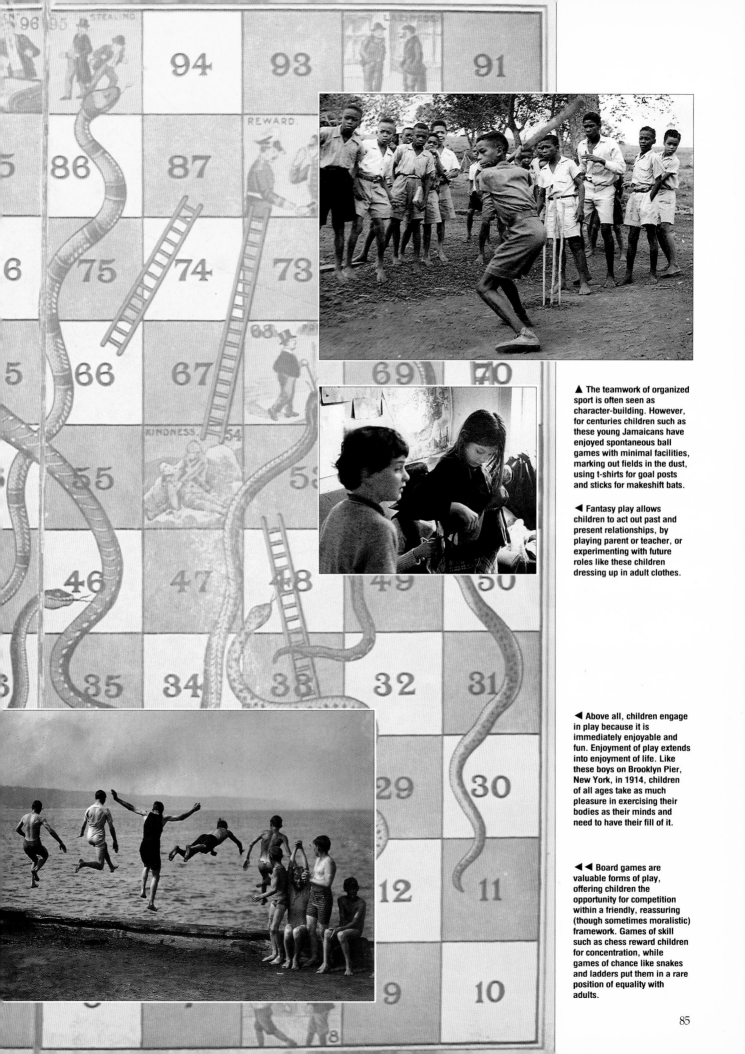

▲ The teamwork of organized sport is often seen as character-building. However, for centuries children such as these young Jamaicans have enjoyed spontaneous ball games with minimal facilities, marking out fields in the dust, using t-shirts for goal posts and sticks for makeshift bats.

◄ Fantasy play allows children to act out past and present relationships, by playing parent or teacher, or experimenting with future roles like these children dressing up in adult clothes.

◄ Above all, children engage in play because it is immediately enjoyable and fun. Enjoyment of play extends into enjoyment of life. Like these boys on Brooklyn Pier, New York, in 1914, children of all ages take as much pleasure in exercising their bodies as their minds and need to have their fill of it.

◄◄ Board games are valuable forms of play, offering children the opportunity for competition within a friendly, reassuring (though sometimes moralistic) framework. Games of skill such as chess reward children for concentration, while games of chance like snakes and ladders put them in a rare position of equality with adults.

Datafile

World War I unleashed rapid social and economic change in parts of the "Third World", which threatened the ultimate breakup of the European empires. The spread of manufacturing and modern communications accelerated the growth of towns. The concentration of workers provided the basis for mass trade unionism, major strikes and the development of mass nationalism, often begun by students in higher education. Where governments had political autonomy – as with Turkey, Mexico and Brazil – the state undertook radical social change. Turkey's reforms foreshadowed the programs of state-initiated development in much of the Third World after 1945.

▼ Most Indians depended on agriculture, often within an oppressive system of land tenure with great landlords and princes at the top. The structures of land tenancy and subtenancy were complicated. There was usually little return for the actual cultivator. Despite 60 years of industry – particularly the development of an enormous textile industry – only 10 percent of India's 96,623,000 workers were employed in industry in 1921.

Births and deaths 1925

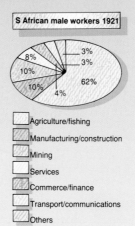

▲ Birth rates were beginning to rise in "Third World" countries and rates of population growth to increase, but with great variations between countries. Egypt's rate, for example, was two-thirds larger than that of Cyprus. This in part reflected considerable differences in relative prosperity and diet, influencing how many children survived birth. Death rates also varied widely. Modern medicine had had as yet little effect, and public health measures in the great and growing cities were still limited.

► The South African economy was boosted by World War I. The Rand became a key supplier of raw materials to Europe, sustained by a continuing inflow of white immigrants. The 2,593,000 workers of 1921 depended on the core activity of exporting minerals. Black and white workers constituted two societies – a high-income white minority and a miserably poor black majority. South African employers purchased white worker loyalty with special privileges, later to be rationalized in apartheid.

Indian male workers 1921

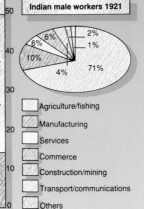

- Agriculture/fishing
- Manufacturing
- Services
- Commerce
- Construction/mining
- Transport/communications
- Others

S African male workers 1921

- Agriculture/fishing
- Manufacturing/construction
- Mining
- Services
- Commerce/finance
- Transport/communications
- Others

Employment in Turkey

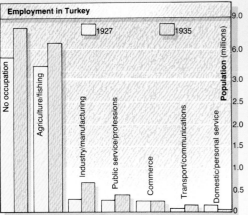

◄ In 1929 Turkey set out to protect its economy against imports and the effects of the Great Depression in Europe and North America, using the state to foster widespread industrialization and the development of infrastructure (particularly railroads). This approach was embodied in the 1934 Five Year Plan and the declared aim of the state to pursue state capitalism. Perhaps as a consequence, as the labor force grew in a very difficult period for the world economy, Turkish manufacturing employment also expanded.

World War I was prodigiously demanding in its need for manpower, raw materials and finance. One consequence of this was an economic boom. For the countries of Africa, Asia and Latin America it entailed the creation of an apparently insatiable European appetite for raw materials and, to a lesser extent, men. Furthermore the supply of European manufactured goods to the rest of the world dried up, so overseas countries were obliged to manufacture substitutes. The war thus contributed to a profound breakdown in the 19th-century world division of labor. With this growth came the creation, with remarkable speed, of new working classes, concentrated in a handful of rapidly growing cities. The concentration itself enhanced the potential social power of these work forces, and the 1920s in the area that came to be called the Third World are characterized for the first time by battles between capital and labor.

Urban labor forces around the world

In China, India and much of Latin America the growth in the urban labor force continued, with greater fluctuations, throughout the 1920s. Take, for example, Bombay's textile industry: it had 105,000 workers in 1914 and a peak of 151,000 in 1922. By the early 1920s it was estimated that 11 percent of the city's population was dependent upon the industry. India's textile industry as a whole had become the third largest in the world in the size of its labor force and the second in the volume of production. Only about a quarter of the labor force were born in Bombay, and the rural kinsmen of many immigrant workers called them back to the villages at harvest time or marriage season, or when slump cut employment. The rural base and divisions based upon different origins weakened the capacity to organize trade unions. But the close links between cities and the countryside also provided a channel of refuge against urban disasters, and, as happened in China, a means whereby urban conflicts were swiftly spread to the countryside.

Nonetheless, despite all the divisions, Indian workers did organize. The railroad workers were particularly important here; they were above average in education, and saw the country as a whole. They provided an example for others, particularly as aspirations rose. The Bombay textile workers agitated for a 12-hour day in 1905, and a 9-hour day in 1919. The 1920s saw two general strikes (one in 1928 lasting six months) and an increasingly effective union organization. In the first instance, the work of trade union organizing was not clearly distinguished from general political and social reform or charitable work – "uplift" as it was called by middle-class volunteers in India. Thus some of the leading political figures

THE BEGINNINGS OF MODERNIZATION

were also leading trade union leaders, especially if they were lawyers and could combine trade union work with advocacy of labor's cause in the courts. For example, some of the earliest nationalist work by Gandhi in India was championing the grievances of textile workers in Ahmadabad. Critics, especially the colonial government, argued that the workers could not properly be represented by those who had no direct experience of being workers. But while the outside leadership posed serious problems for workers, in many cases it was the only form of representation they could get against powerful and ruthless employers. Once real mass movements developed, worker leaderships emerged with great speed, as was shown in the 1920s in the Bombay textile industry.

In the turbulence of China, where a republic had replaced the Qing (Ch'ing) empire in 1912, industrial workers made an even more spectacular debut. Their role was the more effective politically because they were so heavily concentrated in a handful of cities (42 percent of modern factories were in Shanghai). Conditions were appalling; impoverished peasants still sold their children into semislavery in the textile mills.

The first major mass movement in China, the May 4th Movement of 1919, was student-led and directed against some of the provisions of the Versailles Treaty, but six years later the May 30th Movement was a workers' campaign. It was initially directed against Japanese factory practices but then spread into protests against all foreign capital. It produced ultimately a long general strike in the south and an effective boycott of British goods which closed Hong Kong. Many workers spread out in the countryside, and one by-product of these events was an extraordinary growth in peasant associations and, later, attempts to seize the land and overthrow landlordism. Membership of the Communist party soared, and trade unions for the first time became effective forces.

When the new armed forces of the Nationalists, the Guomindang (Kuomintang), set out from their southern base in Guangzhou (Canton) on a Northern Expedition to conquer China proper, in 1926, it was the new mass organizations of trade unions and peasant associations that fanned out before the troops, seizing towns, cities and installations along the way. The great trade union federation of Shanghai seized that city in order to present it to the army chief, Jiang Jieshi (Chiang Kai-shek). Those that glimpsed the reality of the violence being unleashed were further horrified when Jiang turned on the unions and the Communist Party to destroy them. In the late 1920s possibly 120,000 union and peasant activists were liquidated or imprisoned.

In Africa somewhat similar processes were at work. In South Africa the white working class doubled in size during World War I and emerged radicalized. However, the ferocious competition between poor white and black workers, enhanced by shrewd employers, provided the basis for a racial division of the labor force. Even then, the need for a mass of low-paid migrant labor on the farms and in the mines was beginning to collide with the need of manufacturing for a higher level of productivity in a settled labor force. The slow development of apartheid smothered these tensions. The Urban Areas Act of 1929 sought to segregate the black labor force and control black movement into areas nominated for white occupation. The 1924 Industrial Conciliation Act recognized what were then overwhelmingly white trade unions and set up industrial councils (with representatives of trade unions and employers) with the power to exclude Africans, Indians and Coloreds from apprenticeships and skilled jobs; closed shop provisions further strengthened the power of white unions to exclude black workers.

▼ Evening meal for Indian soldiers, France 1916. Over 3 million served worldwide with the European armies. Possibly 150,000 died in Europe. "Many natives", Albert Schweitzer noted in the Congo, "are puzzled…how… the whites who brought them the Gospel of Love are now murdering each other".

Elsewhere in Africa the wartime growth of the industrial labor force was less significant. The retention of land rights and the control exercised over peasant production by merchants and their capital meant that the rise of the wage labor force did not generally divorce workers from the land. But incorporation in the cash economy and pressure from the colonial state – taxes were still an important instrument for forcing Africans into employment – threw up an immense migrant population, pressing men (and more slowly, women) into towns to lead a marginal life searching for patrons and work. Resistance involved shirking or desertion rather than strikes, though skilled workers on the Gold Coast or in Senegal began to unionize after the war.

Nationalism and mass movements

World War I and the 1920s offered the first real glimpse of the likely course of future events in what became the Third World: the national assertion of countless peoples who had hitherto been submerged in the misleading uniformity of empire. It still concerned in the main the larger and more advanced countries, but it presaged the emergence of a host of new sovereign powers. The range of nationalist reactions was wide – from the struggle of independent regimes in Latin America to assert the rights of sovereignty, to limit the role of foreigners, and to use social reform to incorporate a much larger proportion of the population; to the pressure in the Dutch East Indies, in French Indochina or more sporadically in Africa to open government structures to natives; to a war of national unification in China against not only the domestic warlords, but also against foreigners who financed them.

Latin America's independent republics had much greater power to pursue the sorts of reforms already current in Europe. For example, José Batlle y Ordónez as president of Uruguay set about creating what would later be called a welfare state. He instituted an eight-hour working day, pensions for the aged, and expropriated many public services and basic industries; he enshrined in the law the right of women to divorce and abolished capital punishment.

The Mexican government, under a new constitution of 1917, took into state ownership land and water. It assumed powers to control all private

▲ Women workers collect iron ore for the steel works at Jamshedpur in northeast India. The Tata family conceived the project of India's first steel plant in the 1880s; production started in 1911. By the 1920s 53,000 workers were employed in steel production and raw material supply, with 150 Europeans and Americans. Most of the workers were local tribespeople.

▶ World War I blocked imports from Europe so there was a surge in industrial output in the rest of the world. The easiest industry to start was textiles, but steel production opened the way to make machines. The new workers worked long hours for miserable pay. Employers in China purchased the daughters of impoverished peasants and locked them in the mills as virtual slaves. Workers were drawn off the countryside and packed into appalling shanty towns.

property, nationalized all mineral assets, introduced an advanced labor code and excluded the church from education. Much legislation was mere declaration and not implemented, but nonetheless some land was expropriated and redistributed to the cultivators, and rural education was extended. Under President Plutarco Elías Calles – a Bolshevik monster to the shareholders of North America – foreign holdings in the oilfields were converted into 55-year leases (a measure superseded by nationalization in the 1930s). More land was expropriated and redistributed. In Argentina, in 1916, the first radical president proposed to limit working hours and institute a minimum wage level. Throughout Latin America reform was part of the process of incorporating a much larger proportion of the inhabitants into the nation – and in doing so, embracing where relevant a mythical pre-Columbian history rather than Spanish roots.

In India World War I saw the issue of home rule become almost universally accepted as an aim. B.G. Tilak with his band of energetic nationalists took control of the Indian National Congress and reached, for the first time, an alliance with the Muslim League in the Lucknow Pact that seemed likely to frustrate British attempts to divide followers of the two religions. With the arrival in India of a famous Indian agitator and lawyer from South Africa who was to become known as Mahatma Gandhi, a quite new style of politics was promised which would go well beyond the urban middle class to reach out to the mass of the peasantry. Gandhi abandoned the mark of the lawyers who had hitherto run Congress, formal European dress, for an Indian

dhoti and shirt. The great upsurge of feeling towards the end of the war, the belief that India had earned its right to self-government, all added to the sense that a new age was dawning.

Gandhi's role in welding together the contradictory social forces of Indian nationalism – tenant cultivator and landlord, borrower and moneylender, worker and employer – now became vital as the movement of agitation expanded. But it was brief. The economy floundered, stamina was exhausted. The British through the 1920s were slowly able to reestablish their position. They were helped by Congress disunity, by the growing pessimism about the prospects for home rule, by communalism (adherence to antagonistic religious groups) and

▲ **The other India.** Machine-made textiles threatened village spinners like this one. Mahatma Gandhi, the independence leader, opposed modern industry because, he said, it enslaved the workers and made impossible *swaraj* or "self-rule" on an individual as much as a social level. His followers met their own need for clothes by spinning yarn.

The Spread of Industrialization 1929

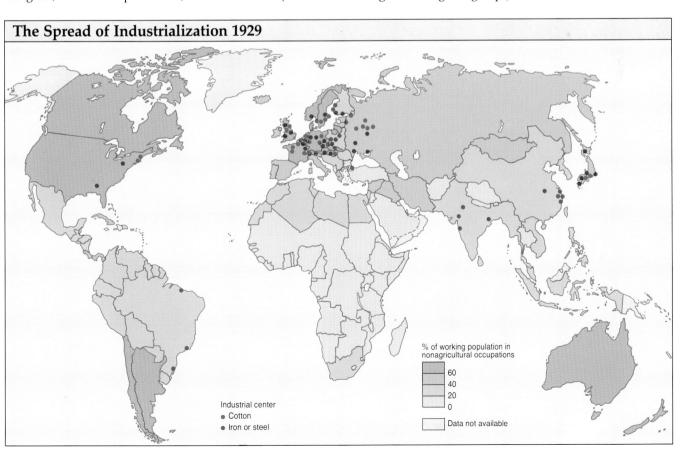

% of working population in nonagricultural occupations

60
40
20
0

Industrial center
● Cotton
● Iron or steel

Data not available

its periodic terrible blood-letting. The British employed reform judiciously to strengthen their support – mildly protectionist tariffs to limit imports for businessmen, more public works and education and the promise of extensions of the franchise. By the late 1920s the upsurge in feeling in the immediate postwar years had been dissipated.

Unlike India, where a national industrial and commercial bourgeoisie began to flourish in the 1920s, in Africa – outside South Africa – such a bourgeoisie was barely discernible. Petty commerce was extremely important, and those who were higher up in the labor hierarchy – railroadmen and clerks – often sought to use their jobs as a means of entry to trading. But except in some parts of West Africa – notably the Gold Coast – there was little development of an African bourgeoisie and little interest in entering into capitalist production. The educated elite, created by the need of colonial states for a substantial class of petty bureaucrats, was at best only an incipient bourgeoisie, though it began to become an important group of power-brokers. This class started to form associations reflecting its members' sense of belonging to a distinct interest group. The National Congress of British West Africa was briefly influential in the 1920s, agitating for improved education, especially at higher levels, and for promotion of Africans in the civil service. But it failed to link up with the working masses who sometimes organized to resist colonial rule. The East African Association, an intertribal group formed in Nairobi by a telephonist, Harry Thuku, was briefly more threatening to colonial rule in 1920-21. But the educated elite, as the historian Bill Freund has put it, "remained too deeply rooted in the colonial structure to question the colonial order very profoundly".

Social change in Turkey

A new style of politics, social change and economic policy was being shaped in the 1920s which was to achieve full expression in the newly independent regimes of Asia and Africa in the 1950s and 1960s. It became known as "economic nationalism". The policy presupposed a mass popular basis to government, a nation, and a governmental responsibility for popular welfare. Government embodied, it seemed, the single clearcut interest of the nation, and on that basis could intervene in all fields, particularly the source of popular livelihood, the economy. Because there was only one national interest, only one political party was required and possibly only a single leader.

The carving out of a new Turkish Republic from the domains of the Ottoman Empire provided new opportunities to experiment with social and economic development. The new and overwhelmingly powerful president Kemal Atatürk (elected in 1923), with his successors, undertook a wide-ranging series of measures to create a modern European state and society in Turkey. A new single political party, the People's Party of the Republic, was established in 1919. In 1934 women were given the vote and permitted to hold public office; by 1935 there were 17 women members in the National Assembly.

▲ Boys at school, Turkey 1934. Atatürk's regime made education a priority – to the point, in principle, of punishing adults who remained illiterate. The alphabet was romanized and religious education abolished. Atatürk's theses – on History (that the Turks of Central Asia were the source of the world's great civilizations) and on the "Sun Language" (that modern languages were descended from Turkish) – made education the basis for a new Turkish nationalism.

In a country where over 80 percent of the population was dependent upon agriculture, agrarian reform and improvement were vital. Atatürk established an agricultural bank to provide credit for agricultural exports, and later encouraged credit cooperatives for farmers. He set up a purely Turkish bank, the Ish Bank, in 1924, designed to finance public works, manufacturing, construction and commerce. (It was followed by the foundation of the Sümer bank in 1933 and the Eti bank in 1935.) During the 1920s and 1930s Turkey developed cotton and woolen mills, sulfur and coal mines, iron- and steel-making, and many other industries.

The government eliminated the old religious primary school system and through a newly created ministry of education endeavored to spread a secular educational system. The Arabic script was changed to roman (rendering much of the old order illiterate), and a system of adult night schools was introduced to reduce the level of illiteracy (92 percent of the population). Sports education was begun for the first time and Turkey began to participate in international sporting events. Women's ordinary and professional education was encouraged.

Many of these measures collided directly with an Islamic inheritance and had the potential to promote much discontent. Religious reform was therefore a necessary part of the program from forbidding women public employees to wear anything but Western dress (without the veil), banning for all men anything but Western dress (and allowing ecclesiastical dress only in places of worship), to the abolition of the Caliphate and of Islamic Shariat law. A modern legal system was introduced and all references to Islam removed from the constitution; Sunday, not Friday, became the weekly day of rest.

In sum, the reforms constituted, the governing party decided in 1935, a "Turkish form of State socialism". The appearance of Turkey was transformed and the Turkish model of economic policy persisted up to the great liberalizing and privatizing swing of the 1970s and 1980s.

◀ Turkish women greeting the government's grant of rights to women to vote and hold office in municipalities, 1930. The same happened later for national elections and office (by 1935, 17 women sat in the National Assembly). The women wear Western dress, which was strongly encouraged in Atatürk's Turkey as a means to modernization; it was compulsory for women in government jobs. Women were also encouraged to gain education and enter the professions; there were women judges, lawyers, bank directors, etc. Polygamy was abolished and the right to divorce established. The strongest progress was made among urban educated women. Many in the villages experienced little change.

1929 - 1945

THE
FADING
DREAM

	1930	1931	1932	1933	1934	1935	1936	1937
Rural life	• Feb–Mar: Reports of 40 kulaks per day murdered by agents of Stalin. Thousands of peasants flee to Poland • Southern and midwestern USA hit by unprecedented drought	• 10 Jan: Molotov, head of the Council of Commissars, predicts half of Soviet agriculture will be collectivized by 1932 • UK, USA, France, Belgium and Canada join to stop Soviet grain dumping	• Feb: France begins an assistance program for agriculture • New farmland opens up in the Netherlands with the drainage of the Zuider Zee • Famine in the Caucasus and the Ukraine (USSR)	• 12 May: Agricultural Adjustment Act becomes law (USA) • World price of wheat hits an historic low point	• May: Dust storms blow 300 million tonnes of topsoil from Kansas, Oklahoma, Texas and Colorado into the Atlantic (USA) • "Okies" and "Arkies" (farmers from the Dustbowl) begin the trek to California	• Apr: Increasingly severe dust storms in Kansas, Colorado, Wyoming, Texas and New Mexico (USA) • Resettlement Administration is created by executive order to move people to better land (USA)	• Nazi Germany undertakes a four-year program to replace raw materials such as fats and livestock fodder with synthetics (ersatz) • Drought reduces the American harvest	• Drought finally ends in the USA but stem rust attacks the wheat crop
Industry and labor	• 12 Mar: All-India Trade Union Congress authorizes Gandhi to commence civil disobedience demonstrations • Majority of USSR production is industrial (53%) • Unemployment passes two million in the UK, and four million in the USA	• 15 Sep: 12,000 Royal Navy sailors at Invergordon strike against pay cuts (UK) • 30 Nov: Merger between His Master's Voice and Columbia creates Electrical and Musical Industries (EMI) (UK) • Unemployment reaches 4.75 million in Germany, 7 million in the USA, and 2.66 million in the UK	• Jan: Reconstruction Finance Corporation established to finance the creation of work and to encourage business activity (USA) • 14 Apr: New Zealand sees its worst riots in history after cuts in civil service pay • 20,000 US businesses go bankrupt and 1,616 banks fail	• 18 May: Tennessee Valley Authority is created in Roosevelt's New Deal to develop the area's resources (USA) • 5 Aug: Roosevelt establishes a National Labor Board under the National Recovery Act to ensure the right of collective bargaining • 30 Aug: Air France is created	• Sep: Industrial League prevents the introduction of the 40-hour week (UK) • 1 Sep: 400,000 US textile workers begin a three-week strike • Italy establishes a corporatist economy. Confederations of employers and employees act as supreme economic associations	• 5 Jul: Labor Relations Act takes effect and guarantees the freedom of trade unions (USA) • Nov: France nationalizes the mining industry • Germany introduces the eight-hour day	• 26 Feb: Hitler opens the first Volkswagen factory • 5 Oct: Jarrow Protest March begins with 200 unemployed men and a petition bearing 11,572 signatures (UK) • United Rubber Workers of America pioneer the sit-down strike in action against the Goodyear Tyre and Rubber Company	• 2 Mar: United States Steel allows its workers to join unions • 29 Mar: US Supreme Court upholds the minimum wage principle for women • 30 Apr–26 May: 30,000 London bus workers strike • German Jews are excluded from positions in industry
Government and people	• 31 Mar: Congress enacts the Public Road Building Act, providing funds for state highway building jobs (USA) • 1 Apr: Government abolishes the Poor Law Guardians (UK) • 30 Apr: Women's insurance law enacted in France • 19 May: White South African women given the vote; coloreds remain without vote	• 16 Jan: Electoral reform eliminates plural voting in the UK • 31 Jul: May Committee recommends £96 million in spending cuts (UK) • 16 Oct: Spanish government legalizes divorce • Universal suffrage introduced in Ceylon	• 17 Apr: Emperor Haile Selassie abolishes slavery in Abyssinia • 24 Sep: Poona Pact is signed, after Gandhi's fast in prison, giving voting rights to untouchables • Brazil, Thailand and Uruguay extend voting rights to women on equal terms with men	• 14 Mar: Nazis ban kosher meat and leftwing newspapers • 8 May: First gas chamber execution carried out in the USA • 6 Jun: Congress approves the National Industry Recovery Act. Congress gains tremendous control over industry, administered by the National Recovery Administration (USA)	• 19 Jan: Roosevelt orders $21 million for US war veterans • 29 Sep: Conscription is introduced in Poland for both men and women • 30 Oct: Mussolini orders all 6–8 year olds to join a special premilitary training corps (It) • 20 Nov: Depressed Areas Bill introduced in the UK	• 6 May: Beginning of the Works Progress Administration, to provide employment for millions in a series of public works programs • 27 May: US Supreme Court declares the majority of US president Roosevelt's "New Deal" legislation illegal • 27 Nov: NZ Labour government enacts a major program of social reforms	• 21 Feb: New Spanish government grants amnesty to 30,000 political prisoners • 7 Apr: Blacks are barred from office in South Africa by the Native Representation Act. Instead, they are represented by three elected white representatives • USSR revokes a 1920 decree which legalized abortion	• 9 Jan: Italian government bans interracial marriages in its African colonies • Jan–Feb: First general elections held in India • Fatwa issued by Islam's Grand Mufti permits Muslims to use contraceptive measures to which both men and women agree
Religion	• 31 Dec: Birth control proclaimed a grave and unnatural sin by Pope Pius XI • Haile Selassie, new Ethiopian emperor, is hailed as the living God by Rastafarians, thus fulfilling the prophecy of Marcus Garvey	• 25 Mar: Muslim and Hindu riots at Cawnpore kill hundreds (Ind) • 31 May: Pius XI condemns fascism after priests are attacked (It) • Joseph Franklin Rutherford renames his group Jehovah's Witnesses (USA)	• 30 Sep: Pius XI condemns Mexican anticlericalism	• 7 Feb: Mustapha Kemal bans Arabic prayers and "Allah", the Arabic word for God (Turk) • 27 Oct: Protests against Jewish immigration in coastal towns of Palestine	• Jan: Pastors denounce the Nazi regime but homes of such clergy are attacked by the police (Ger) • 5 Aug: 100 Jews and Arabs are killed during rioting in Algeria • Nazis rewrite the Psalms to minimize reference to the Jews	• 19 Mar: British troops fire on a crowd of Muslims rioting against Hindus, killing 27 people (Ind) • 15 Sep: German Nuremberg laws legitimize antisemitism • 17 Sep: Jews are denied German citizenship	• 19 Apr–25 May: Riots in Tel Aviv between Palestinians and Jews leads to eleven deaths and 50 injuries. The Arab rebellion continues until 1939 (Pal) • Oct: Hindus and Muslims riot in Bombay (Ind)	• May: Government decree forbidding the veiling of women leads to riots by Albanian Muslims • 7 Jul: British government Peel Report suggests a partition of Palestine into Arab and Jewish states
Events and trends	• 12 Mar–6 Apr: Gandhi's march to the sea in protest against British laws controlling salt production (Ind) • May: Stewardesses first employed, by United Airlines (USA) • Abortion becomes a crime in Fascist Italy • First supermarket opens, on Long Island, New York (USA)	• 22 Jan: Doctors in London claim the discovery of a vaccine against polio (UK) • Feb: Japan is first to televise a baseball game • 1 Jun: Mussolini bans all Catholic youth organizations (It) • 11 May: Austrian Kreditanstalt goes bankrupt	• 30 Jan: Prohibition of alcohol is lifted in Finland • Jul: With 230 seats gained in an election, the Nazis become the biggest party in the Reichstag (Ger) • Oct: Iraq enters the League of Nations, thereby gaining full independence from Britain	• 22 Mar: Roosevelt signs bill legalizing wine and beer, thus ending the Prohibition (USA) • 25 Jul: Hitler announces plan for a compulsory sterilization program to racially purify Germany	• 15 Jan: Serious earthquake in the Bihar Province of India and in Nepal kills 10,000 people and leaves 500,000 homeless • 3 Sep: Evangeline Booth becomes the first woman general in the Salvation Army (UK) • Durex condoms for men first produced	• May: Yellow River floods drowning 50,000 and covering hundreds of square miles • Alcoholics Anonymous founded in New York • Amended Irish criminal code makes the sale, importation or advertisement of any birth control device a felony	• Tampax Inc is founded to commercially produce tampons (USA) • Great purge begins in the USSR as Stalin eliminates his political enemies • Publication of J.M. Keynes' The General Theory of Employment, Interest and Money (UK)	• Publication of George Orwell's The Road to Wigan Pier (UK) • Jamaicans riot against British rule • Nationalist riots in Trinidad and Tobago
Politics	• 21 Jan–22 Apr: Five Power Naval Conference agrees to limit size and quantity of naval ships and submarines	• 14 Apr: King Alfonso leaves Spain, and the country is declared a republic • 11 Dec: Statute of Westminster creates a Commonwealth of equal and autonomous Dominions	• 18 Feb: Japan establishes a puppet state (Manchukuo) in Manchuria	• 30 Jan: Hitler becomes Chancellor of Germany and proclaims the Third Reich (Mar) • Falange, the Spanish fascist party, is founded by Antonio Primo de Rivera	• 30 Jun: Hitler wipes out rival leadership of the Nazis during the Night of the Long Knives • 2 Aug: Hitler assumes the title of "Führer" on the death of Hindenburg (Ger)	• 19 May: Sudeten Party, many of whose members are Nazis, becomes the second strongest party in Czechoslovakia • 3 Oct: Mussolini's troops march into Abyssinia	• Mar: Germany remilitarizes the Rhineland • 18 Jul: Beginning of the Spanish Civil War with the Nationalist insurrection	• 7 Jul: Japan attacks and later occupies northeast and east China • Irish Free State renamed Eire, with a new constitution and dominion status with the Commonwealth

1938	1939	1940	1941	1942	1943	1944	1945
• By pooling milk from various herds, US dairies eliminate the occasionally fatal "milk sick" disease • Crop planting restrictions eased in a new Agricultural Adjustment Act (USA)	• 3 May: UK farmers offered £2 per acre to plow up and reseed unused pastures • Swiss chemist Paul Müller introduces DDT as an effective, inexpensive pesticide		• Stem rust reduces the Mexican wheat harvest by 50% • Rockefeller Foundation sponsors a program to improve Mexican agriculture	• Fungus disease ruins the rice crop near Bombay; subsequent famine kills 1.6 million Bengalese (Ind) • Cultivation of back gardens and communal plots begins with "Dig for Victory" (UK) and "Victory Gardens" (USA)	• Japan's worst rice crop in 50 years means difficulty for those on subsistence level • UN Conference on Food and Agriculture makes provision for a Food and Agriculture Organization (FAO)	• A "Green Revolution" advances in Mexico • New uses for soybeans pushes US production up to twelve million acres • Bengal's rice crop fails again and millions starve	• Jun: German troops demobilized and sent to work the land to aid food production • First selective plant killer 2,4D is patented as a general weed killer by the American Chemical Plant Co
• 18 Mar: Mexico nationalizes its petroleum industry and expropriates US and UK oil companies • Apr: US president Roosevelt establishes a 4.5 billion work program • 27 Jun: Employers in Vienna give all Jews two weeks notice (Aut)	• 19 May: Trades Union Congress decides not to oppose conscription (UK) • Aug: More than 30 industrial plants are transferred to Manzhouguo (Jap) • 22 Dec: Female arms workers in UK demand the same pay as males	• Mar: British and French war industry and production are unified • 5 Jun: Ban on all strikes in Britain • Pétain dissolves all trade unions and employer organizations in Vichy France • Eight-hour day and six-day week reestablished in Soviet industry	• Jan: New wage system for collective farms takes effect in the USSR • 25 Jun: Roosevelt creates a Fair Employment Practice Committee after 50,000 black members of the Sleeping Car Porters Brotherhood threaten to march in Washington • Dec: UK announces intention to call up women aged 20–30	• 17 Apr: Burma's main oilfields are destroyed to prevent them falling into Japanese hands • 3 Oct: Roosevelt orders a freeze on wages, rents and farm prices • 1 Nov: Vichy forced recruitment of labor for Germany leads to protest strikes in Haut-Savoie (Fr)	• Apr–May: Roosevelt uses threats to narrowly avert a coal strike (USA) • 29 Oct: Troops take over for striking London dockers (UK) • Payment for women's employment has increased 80% since 1938	• Feb: Forced labor in Germany now applies to all Frenchmen aged 16-60 • Mar: 87,000 Welsh miners go on strike; UK government agrees on a four-year pact • Jul: Germany implements a total war economy with a 60-hour week in industry	• France nationalizes Renault, Air France, the Bank of France and other private banks • Sep: UK Labour government puts forward a five-year plan for increasing production in the coal and iron industry • Rockwell Manufacturing Co is created (USA)
• 3 Jun: UK government announces its intention to distribute gas masks to all schoolchildren • 30 May: All Czechs and Slovaks aged 6–60 must undergo defense training • 1 Sep: Mussolini orders the expulsion of all Jews who entered Italy after 1918 • Social Security Act provides state medical service in New Zealand	• 1 Jan: All women under 25 years ordered to do one year's civilian service for the Reich (Ger) • 5 Apr: Government announces plans for the evacuation of 2.5 million to the country in the event of war (UK) • 30 Aug: Beginning of the evacuation of children from cities in France and Britain	• 1 Jan: UK calls up two million 19-year olds • 22 May: Emergency Powers Act gives government almost unlimited authority over people and property during mobilization (UK) • 16 Sep: US makes military service registration obligatory for all men aged 21 to 35	• Mar: Minister of Labor Ernest Bevin urges 100,000 women to volunteer for jobs in auxiliary services and industry (UK) • 7 Apr: UK war budget raises income tax to an unprecedented 50%	• 3 Mar: 110,000 Japanese Americans living on the West Coast are interned in concentration camps (USA) • 14 May: Congressional Act creates the Women's Auxiliary Army Corps (USA) • 1 Dec: Publication of the Beveridge Report which forms the basis of the future UK welfare state	• Jan: Hitler orders the mobilization of society aged 16–65 (Ger) • 2 Feb: House of Commons urges war compensation be equal for both males and females (UK) • 3 May: Government makes part-time work compulsory for women aged 18–45 (UK) • 17 Dec: Chinese Act repeals Chinese Exclusion Acts of 1882 and 1902 (USA)	• Jan: Hitler mobilizes all children over the age of ten • Apr: Britain institutes a Pay-As-You-Earn (PAYE) income tax program • 3 Apr: In Smith vs Allwright the Supreme Court rules that voting rights cannot be denied because of color • Enfranchisement of French, Jamaican and Albanian women	• Foundation of United Nations Educational, Scientific and Cultural Organization (UNESCO) in Paris • World Bank and International Monetary Fund are established • Enfranchisement of women in Mali, Monaco Indonesia and Portugal • Cooperative for American Remittances to Europe (CARE) founded as a private relief organization
• 14 Jul: Italy officially adopts antisemitism • 9 Nov: *Kristallnacht*: 7,000 Jewish shops looted and hundreds of synagogues burned during a night of Nazi violence (Ger)	• 20 Jan: King Farouk declared the Caliph (spiritual leader of Islam) (Egy) • 27 Feb: British White Paper issued outlining plan for independent Arab-Jewish state in Palestine • 28 Oct: Jews are required to wear the Star of David	• 22 Feb: Coronation of the five-year-old Dalai Lama in Tibet • 27 Mar: Himmler orders the building of a concentration camp at Auschwitz • Vichy regime strips Jews of citizenship and bans them from public service (Fr)	• May–Jun: Thousands of Jews arrested by Vichy French police and turned over to the Nazis • Hitler orders the "Final Solution" to the Jewish question at the Wannsee conference in Berlin, and the program of genocide begins	• Jun: All French Jews over six ordered to wear the Star of David • 16 Jul: 30,000 Parisian Jews arrested by police and sent out to concentration camps • Sep: Nazi SS empty the Warsaw ghetto, killing 50,000 Jews while doing so	• 19 Jun: Goebbels proclaims Berlin "free of Jews" (Ger) • 19 Oct: Archbishop of Canterbury warns against moral laxity as the incidence of venereal disease continues to rise during wartime	• Apr: Nazis begin deporting Jews from Hungary • 6 Nov: Zionist terrorists murder Lord Moyne, the British Minister-Resident in the Middle East	• Nazi genocide program has murdered 14 million people including nearly six million Jews (Ger) • Sep: British government refers the issue of Jewish immigration to Palestine to the newly-formed United Nations
• 22 Oct: First xerographic image is produced, by Chester Carlson (USA) • 21 Dec: UK announces plans to spend £200,000 on air raid shelters • Nestlé Company of Switzerland introduces Nescafé coffee	• 20 Feb: Nylon stockings go on sale for the first time (USA) • 23 Jun: Irish government outlaws the Irish Republican Army (IRA) • British government begins delivery of free air raid shelters to thousands of homes	• Jan: Britain faces food rationing for the first time since 1918 • 21 Aug: Leon Trotsky is assassinated in Mexico City by a Stalinist agent • Extended period of military dictatorship begins in Paraguay	• 11 Mar: Roosevelt signs a lend-lease pact with Britain • 8 Sep: Vietnamese nationalist leader Ho Chi Minh forms the Viet Minh (French Indochina) • 16 Sep: Reza Shah abdicates, succeeded by his son Muhammad Reza Pahlavi who promises constitutional reform (Iran)	• 15 Jan: Gandhi names Pandit Nehru as his successor (Ind) • 31 Jul: Formation of the Oxford Committee for Famine Relief (Oxfam) (UK) • Rationing of fuel, sweets, coffee, petrol and numerous other items (UK)	• 10 Feb–1 Mar: Gandhi fasts at Poona (Ind) to protest against his imprisonment • Apr: Publication of J.M. Keynes' plan for post-war economic reconstruction and an international bank • Shoe rationing stands at three pairs per year (USA) and one pair per year (UK)	• Jul: Bretton Woods Agreement to establish an International Monetary Fund (IMF) and International Bank for Reconstruction and Development (World Bank) • Dec: 20 million Germans reported homeless in the wake of Allied bombing	• 30 Jan: Food riots break out in Berlin • 22 Mar: League of Arab States is formed (Egy, Syr, Iraq, Leb, Saud, Transj, Yemen, Arab Pal) • 15 Aug: End of the rationing of fuel oil and petrol in the USA • World War II has claimed the lives of 55 million people
• 30 Sep: Munich agreement between Britain, Germany, France and Italy allows for the German annexation of Sudetenland (Czech)	• 1 Sep: German troops invade Poland, causing Britain and France to declare war on Germany on 3 Sep	• Jun: Hitler successfully invades France and signs an armistice with the Vichy Pétain government • Aug–Sep: Battle of Britain	• 22 Jun: Beginning of the German invasion of the USSR • 7 Dec: Japan bombs the US fleet at Pearl Harbor, Hawaii, thus drawing the USA into the war	• Oct–4 Nov: Second battle of El Alamein ends with the triumph of Montgomery over Rommel's panzers • 22 Aug: Beginning of the battle of Stalingrad (USSR)	• 25 Jul: Mussolini deposed, and the Fascist party banned three days later (It) • Germans defeated at the battle of Stalingrad, and the war in the east turns in favor of the Russians	• 6 Jun: D-Day invasion of France by the Allies opens a second front • 25 Aug: Liberation of Paris by the Allies	• 7–8 May: V-E Day: Germany surrenders unconditionally • 15 Aug: Japan surrenders after US atomic bombs are dropped on Hiroshima (6 Aug) and Nagasaki (9 Aug)

Datafile

The 1930s saw challenges to capitalism as an economic system and to political liberalism. Right-wingers as well as Marxists saw in the world crisis of the Great Depression the imminent demise of capitalism; and the authoritarian politics for which the crisis provided fertile ground fundamentally questioned political liberalism. The upshot was that the planning of economic development and social change, with the state intervening in most spheres of life, became widely accepted. For ordinary people the effects of these years were contradictory and sometimes divisive, as some experienced long-term unemployment while others benefited from falling prices and the increase of domestic comfort.

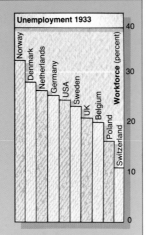

Unemployment 1933

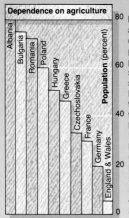

Dependence on agriculture

◀ Eastern and southern Europe remained primarily agricultural. Almost everywhere the traditional peasant economy had been proven an adaptable system. Big estates survived in Poland and Hungary. Change was taking place, however, and the "sociographer" Gyula Illyes wrote in 1936: "The 'wind of progress' blew keenly over the *pusztas* (the Great Plain of Hungary), breaking in through the farm servants' windows and scattering [them] like chaff" – referring to the modernization of agriculture.

▲ The 1930s were "the time of troubles". Among the major powers Germany was hardest hit, largely because of its heavy dependence on international credit. By 1933, the year in which Hitler came to power, almost one-third of the working population was unemployed. It was *not* amongst the groups most affected by unemployment, however, that Hitler's support lay, but rather among the large self-employed labor force in agriculture and in handicrafts.

▶ Following the passing of the National Labor Relations Act in the United States in 1935, which gave government backing to rights to join trades unions, there was massive growth in union membership. The history of labor in Europe in this period, in contrast, is generally one of defensiveness, at least until the war years.

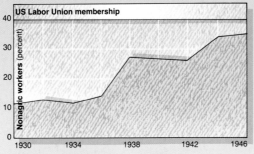

US Labor Union membership

New Nazi members 1930–33

7%
5%
22%
34%
32%

Total 670,000

- Manual workers
- Self-employed
- White collar workers
- Public servants
- Domestic employees

◀ What was most striking about the membership of the Nazi "workers" party was the underrepresentation of the working class (then 45 percent of the German population). Around half of the new manual worker members were unemployed. Peasants provided the Nazis with their overwhelming support after 1929.

▶ The industrialization of the Soviet Union under "Five Year Plans", launched in 1928, led to an enormous and rapid expansion of the nonagricultural work force. This permitted a great deal of social mobility. The 1939 Party Congress plausibly claimed that "The Soviet intelligentsia is yesterday's workers and peasants".

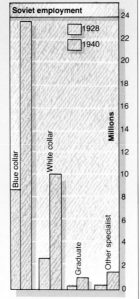

Soviet employment

1928
1940

In the 1930s different approaches to social change crystallized and came into conflict. The assumptions of democratic liberalism in industrial societies were threatened. Fascism and Nazism, born from the social tensions generated by industrialization and liberal democracy in Italy and Germany, came to offer an alternative, authoritarian model of social change. In Eastern Europe and the Soviet Union, meanwhile, there were radically opposing experiments in changing economically backward societies – one building on existing peasant communities; the other on centralization of authority to bring about rapid industrialization.

The responses of the capitalist democracies established the notion of the possibility of planning economic development and social change – even in the United States. The central issue left by this period was that posed to himself in his diary in May 1940 by British prime minister Winston Churchill's private secretary: "Will state control, once instituted, ever be abandoned?" By 1945 the world confronted two models of development and change, that of Soviet communism and that of capitalism. But by then both involved state intervention in a way which challenged liberal values.

Social consequences of the world crisis

"On the morning of October 24, 1929", wrote the American author Fredrick Lewis Allen, "the towering structure of American prosperity cracked wide open". The fall of New York's Wall Street stockmarket dragged the economy of the whole world into the Great Depression. It led to a sharp reduction in industrial production, slashed the already deficient demand for primary commodities, and threw millions of industrial workers into unemployment. It also destroyed the livelihoods of millions more peasant producers, even in parts of the world remote from Wall Street – bringing far-reaching changes in their societies and hastening the overthrow of colonialism.

The American economy spiraled downward from the day of the crash through to mid-1932. As industrial production dropped there were as many as 5 million vagrants, with (in the words of the historian M.A. Jones) "jobless men roaming the countryside looking for work or congregated on the outskirts of big cities in colonies of cardboard shacks known as Hoovervilles" – a play on the name of the then president (Herbert Hoover), who spurned state intervention. Meanwhile in industrial Europe Germany was hardest hit. In Britain unemployment remained at over 1.5 million throughout the 1930s, stretching the system of unemployment relief to the limit and leading to the introduction of a bitterly resented means test for benefits. France, with its more autonomous

UPHEAVAL AND UNCERTAINTY

economy, was affected later but then saw unemployment remain high from 1932 right up to World War II.

European and American agriculture was already depressed in the 1920s. Farmers everywhere struggled because of falling prices. In France, where farmers still made up a third of the work force, small peasants were those hardest hit as prices for farm produce fell much more sharply than those of industrial products. Between 1931 and 1935 peasant incomes fell by a third. A Peasant Front was formed in 1934, seeking a political system more in sympathy with agriculture. There were demonstrations and a milk strike which saw peasant landowners (as opposed to farm laborers) banding together in collective action for the first time. The Depression brought great hardship to German peasants too, and their similar grievances over falling prices were allied with resentments against both big business and

The social impact of the Wall Street Crash

Fascism and its supporters

Antisemitism

France and Britain under threat

Socialism in one country

Collectivization in Stalin's Soviet Union

The peasant societies of Eastern Europe

▼ Unemployed workers in the United States waiting for relief payments. For the millions of unemployed in North America and Europe the 1930s were the "hungry thirties".

socialists, making many of them strong supporters of Nazism. In the United States decline in foreign demand and the withdrawal of government price support saw prices falling from 1920. Part of the New Deal legislation in the 1930s was the Agricultural Adjustment Act (1933) which attempted to increase prices by curtailing production. Benefits went mainly to larger farmers.

Amongst the deeper and longer-run causes of the slump was the fact that by 1929 productive capacity had far exceeded the level of consumer demand. This in turn reflected the inequality of income distribution in America as in Europe. An important aspect of the responses of governments to the slump was intervention to stimulate demand in the economy. In America Franklin D. Roosevelt's New Deal entailed the massive expansion of Federal expenditure. Part was for the employment of several million people in work relief projects. Blacks, who had been especially

hard hit, benefited from these and began to vote massively for the Democrats for the first time. State recognition of the needs of the under-privileged was expressed also in welfare legislation in which the United States had hitherto lagged behind Europe. In 1935 the Social Security Act and the National Labor Relations Act were passed, the latter encouraging unionization to raise wages and purchasing power, and expanding the role for government in labor relations.

In America the minority of trade union leaders who formed the Committee on Industrial Organization (CIO) in 1935 had some success, against the craft traditions of the American Federation of Labor (AF of L), in organizing all workers in particular industries into single unions. By the end of 1937 it claimed to have more members than the AF of L and pioneered a new technique of industrial action, the "sit-in". The growth of industrial unions accelerated the decay of the old "drive system" of labor management. Corporations encouraged the integration of unions into a new collective bargaining structure. They also began to experiment with the development of "internal labor markets", that is the incorporation of a section of the work force in a secure and privileged career structure. The increasing importance of blacks and of women in the work force – notably during and after World War II – made for a growing heterogeneity, giving employers an opportunity to manipulate sex and race differences to enhance their bargaining power.

Experiences of fascism

The rise of fascist movements predates but was later intensified by the economic crisis. Contemporary Marxists saw in fascism the "death agony" of capitalism. Many representatives of landed and business interests took a similar view, regarding the economic crisis as opening up opportunities

to bolshevism; but they also considered it to be insoluble within the confines of parliamentary democratic rule. They therefore looked to authoritarian means to quash organized labor. At the same time, however, the elites required mass support in order to establish authoritarian rule, or at least to legitimize it. A potent base for such support existed in the eclectic mixture of nationalism and racialism that characterized Benito Mussolini's first steps to build a fascist movement in Italy.

Who supported fascism in Italy, and what kind of a regime was established? The fascist movement in its early phases was predominantly young and radical. "Old men of power", and notably the corrupt oligarchic politicians of the rural south, were targets of the anger of the petty-bourgeois fascist base described by the historian J. Steinberg: "young ex-officers, now students without degrees, lawyers without clients, doctors without patients, accountants without accounts". In the Tuscan city of Livorno in April 1921, for example, over 48 percent of fascist activists were lower middle-class (largely white-collar employees), compared with a working-class presence of just 8.5 percent (and that in an industrial city). Peasant smallholders, especially share-croppers in what became the fascist stronghold in Central Italy, supported the fascists; landless laborers did not. Italy had no major conservative party in which a scared, angry middle class might take refuge. Liberalism itself remained fatally fearful of mass-participatory politics, while the propertied classes were also mistrustful of the main Catholic party, the Partito Populare, because it was a socially radical peasants' party. Thus, even as early as 1921, the middle and upper ranks of the middle classes were prominent among the fascists (19 percent of members in Livorno). The working class had been seen as a threat to state and church alike, and to the material interests of the defenders of each. Fascism, and the restoration of law and order which it promised, provided the ruling elites, even at the eleventh hour, with an opportunity to recover much of the ground they had lost.

Mussolini seized power in Italy in 1922 and in 1926 established a one-party fascist dictatorship, when all opposition parties were formally abolished. Only working-class organizations, however, felt the full force of "totalitarianism". Borrowing from Fordism, the regime encouraged new techniques of production, but in contrast with the USA, Italy's industrial innovators after 1926 no longer had an independent labor movement to contend with. In theory the regime favored "Corporatism", in which key decisions are supposedly made through negotiation between organized interest groups. In fact in fascist Italy corporatism was an illusion: workers could not choose their own leaders and management was given a free hand. While the Italian economy clawed its way out of depression after 1929 this situation allowed wages to be depressed and consumption to be sacrificed to the needs of heavy industry. But it took the strains imposed by war finally to cause the fragmentation of the coalition of interests represented by fascism.

◄ A Nazi election poster, promising "Work, Freedom and Bread". Similar imagery and slogans were used in the Soviet Union, but here the literal message was less important than the impression of purposefulness and strength. The breakdown of law and order was an issue on which the Nazis successfully appealed to a frightened middle class which had lost confidence in the institutions of the German republic. Paradoxically the one serious prospect for the restoration of order lay in the suppression of Nazi violence.

The authoritarian regimes imposed in Portugal from 1932, in Austria in 1934-38 and by the Francoite forces in Spain in 1938-39, were instances of long-established Catholic, military and landlord conservatives adopting a fascist coloring.

Fascism offered order, efficiency and strong government. It rejected pluralism in favor of "corporate" or "organic" national unity and solidarity. It promised a new social order based not on birth or economic status, but on service to the nation and to the fascist movement – a kind of meritocracy. Like socialism it rejected the insecurity of the unregulated market economy and it favored state and corporate regulation. But in contrast to socialism it did not contemplate wholesale expropriation of private property, and it repudiated class as an organizing principle. Instead, it aimed supposedly to transcend class divisions and to enforce national solidarity and consensus. It capitalized on the widespread disenchantment with "old-style" party politics, and repudiated economic and political liberalism. Fascism thus constituted a fundamental challenge to smug Western assumptions that as other countries "developed" they would become more and more like pluralistic Western democracies pursuing liberal policies.

German society in the thirties

Nazism was both a more virulent and more consistently totalitarian variant of fascism. The democratic history of the "Weimar Republic" in Germany was effectively ended with the onset of the world economic crisis in 1929, when, in the

▲ A young mother and her child, migrants from Oklahoma to California, 1937. Drought, dust storms and erosion together with the unintended effects of state intervention drove small farmers from the Dust Bowl of the Great Plains in Oklahoma and Arkansas to become migrant laborers in California. Their plight, which became legend in John Steinbeck's novel *The Grapes of Wrath*, was shared by many others in different parts of the world. Jobless men roamed America. Poor farmers everywhere suffered notably during the Great Depression.

▲ Children in Rome give a priest the fascist salute. The Italian fascist regime gave Roman Catholic religious instruction a central role in elementary education. The church enjoyed a position of autonomy in relation to fascism; its organizations – such as Catholic Action – were not subsumed by the party. In return the church worked within the framework set by the fascist regime. Mussolini's concordat with the Vatican in 1929 ensured the blessings of the church for most fascist policies.

absence of a stable coalition in the German parliament, the Reichstag, traditional political and military elites sought to fill the power vacuum that was left. It was the failure of those elites to manage the political crisis of the early 1930s that caused them to look to the Nazi leader Adolf Hitler to bolster the narrow base of their rule.

In the early 1920s the Nazi party had been only one among a number of small racialist groupings on the fringes of German politics. In 1923 it had attempted to overthrow the Bavarian government but after 1925 it demoted violence to a tactic and shifted its emphasis to the ballot box. The Nazis appealed to nationalism and racism and presented demands which included reduction in taxation and increases in food prices appealing above all to the middling classes and peasantry. They came to form its mass base. Big business threw its weight behind the Nazis relatively late in the day. The Depression had served to reinforce industrialists' determination to dismantle

the Weimar welfare state and to put an end to independent trade unions. It was not actual trade union power they baulked at but merely its potential as an impediment to the dismemberment of social welfare provision. Neither those business interests who rallied to Hitler at the last, nor the many conservatives who voted Nazi in the elections of 1932 and 1933, fully understood the nature of the power they had helped set in motion. But the destruction of the political and economic wings of the labor movement was welcomed.

As had happened in Italy a decade earlier, the revolutionary rhetoric of much of the left had given both the working class and its enemies an exaggerated impression of its strength – in fact now reduced because of the split between communists and social democrats, and by the sheer weight of unemployment (one-third of the work force in 1932). Labor's real weakness was exposed by the passivity of its responses to Nazi power.

The Nazis were aware of proletarian hostility to the new regime from its inception. They responded first with brutal coercion and then by attempting to integrate the working class within the fabric of the "Third Reich". Unemployment was rapidly reduced and real wages increased by 19 percent between 1932 and 1938. The all-out offensive on workers' living standards which some industrialists had hoped for was a luxury the regime felt it could not afford. Indeed, wages were augmented by new social provision on the part of the state (though capital gained far more than labor from economic recovery). Most workers reacted to the Third Reich with indifference or passive consent, or with a mute but stubborn resistance to its ideological claims.

The dictatorships at war

Until the very last months of World War II, the Nazi regime maintained order and morale remarkably well. Although levels of absenteeism rose and the authorities worried about falling productivity, there is little evidence of a working-class attempt to undermine the war effort. (Britain, too, experienced these phenomena – and more militant forms of industrial action). What impresses in the end is the Nazi regime's ability to mobilize labor for the war. Only the attempt to drive women back into the labor market (which flew in the face of the Nazis' own family policy) failed. The shortage of labor was made up instead by the massive recruitment of foreign labor from occupied territories, foreshadowing postwar dependence on immigrant labor. In wartime most served under conditions of virtual slavery.

It is a chilling testimony to the coercive power of the Third Reich that resistance activities remained marginal and largely individual to the very end. In Italy and Austria ordinary people did play some part in their own liberation; in Germany a flowering of anti-fascist committees postdated the war.

▲ A button from the tunic of a young woman, who was obliged to perform a "Year of Duty" for the Nazi state, before starting regular work. The year was usually spent in either agriculture or domestic service. It was not enforced thoroughly and was strongly opposed by industrialists who feared it would lead to cuts in labor supply.

Jews and Antisemitism

The fate of the Jews in 20th-century European societies can be traced back to prohibitions and privileges imposed on Jews in medieval Europe. They were determined not by Jews themselves but by Christian elites, which accorded Jews unique religious toleration – on condition that they engaged in usury (moneylending at interest) with which Christians would not demean themselves. Medieval church rulers built on scriptural authority to portray Jews as the killers of Christ and to encourage pogroms (unprovoked violent attacks). The Lateran decrees of 1215 obliged Jews to distinguish themselves from Christians by their clothing so that their separateness might be regulated. Racial elements began to contribute to the antisemitic arsenal. The association of Jewishness with long, hooked noses dates from this time.

While persecution of the Jews therefore long predated the modern world, the social position of Jews and the dynamics of prejudice against them altered dramatically during the 19th century. In 1800 most of the large Jewish population in Central Europe was economically peripheral and rural, but as the 19th century proceeded liberal sentiment increasingly approved their emancipation (removal of civil disabilities) and social assimilation. But emancipation was slow and uneven.

Three specific factors contributed to the emergence of a genuinely popular antisemitic movement from around 1880. First, Jews proved remarkably adept at using the educational avenues for advancement now open to them. Second, where they had previously been dispersed, Jewish communities now concentrated in the growing industrial cities. Third, the mass immigration of Jews into Central Europe to escape persecution in the Jewish "pale" (settlement area) of western Russia caused widespread resentment. Where Jews had once been despised for their poverty and ignorance, now they were envied for their wealth and education. In the new conditions of mass participation in politics, the pressures of small-town and peasant prejudices forced the adoption of antisemitic rhetoric by threatened conservative and even liberal political elites,

which reached its culmination in the antisemitism of the German Nazi party.

The role that antisemitism played in the growth of the Nazi party has, however, frequently been exaggerated. Much of the German electorate voted Nazi in spite of rather than because of racial rhetoric. The execution of the Nazi holocaust in World War II, when about 6 million Jews were systematically murdered, owed far more to planners and technocrats than to the brutish violence of the perpetrators of pogroms.

After World War II antisemitism was suppressed, but it revived in the late 1980s when across Europe attacks on synagogues and the desecration of Jewish cemeteries became commonplace. The antisemitism of the early 1990s shared one characteristic with that of the late 19th century: both were concomitants of nationalism, which needs to draw attention to aliens at home in order to forge the bonds of new cultural and ethnic communities.

▲ Nazis organize the boycott of Jewish shops in prewar Germany (top). *Cahier Jaune* (above) was a wartime French antisemitic journal produced by collaborators in occupied France.

France, Britain and the fascist threat

Though French society was shot through by political turbulence and bitterness, in the 1930s, and in spite of the war-time Vichy regime's fascist sympathies – as in its antisemitism – French political culture as a whole remained resistant to fascism. In Britain contemporaries widely anticipated that political "extremism" would flourish as a consequence of the Slump, but in the event parliamentary government in general and the Conservative Party in particular adapted easily to the challenge. The economic hardships of the 1930s did give rise to a more humane and also more technocratic approach to social issues. But if the intellectual high ground moved to the left in the course of the decade, it took the war to translate it into political effect.

It is possible to exaggerate the leveling effects of the war, even within the working class. Although women entered the workforce to an unprecedented degree, there was no recognition of the principle of equal pay for equal work, let alone of equality of opportunity. Yet there was an undoubted general leveling of incomes and a significant improvement in wage levels. The permanence of these changes and of the welfare reforms instituted under the auspices of the wartime coalition government in Britain help to explain the popularity of the Labour Party in 1945 and its victory in the general election of July 1945.

Stalin's revolution from above

From 1929 to 1953 social change in the Soviet Union was directed by Joseph Stalin, whose 50th birthday in 1929 was used to launch the "cult of personality", ie of the party leader. Thereafter, even those Communist party faithful who believed in more humane forms of socialism were unable to halt the Stalinist juggernaut. This was

partly from fear of the dreaded security police. More fundamentally, however, the party faithful shared the belief that, in the ousted Bolshevik leader Leon Trotsky's words, "The Party in the last analysis is always right, as the Party is the sole historical instrument given to the proletariat for the solution of its fundamental problems".

Stalinism grew out of the doctrine of "socialism in one country", which Stalin elaborated following the economic collapse and political retreats of the early 1920s. He warned that "the land of proletarian dictatorship cannot remain independent if it does not produce the instruments and means of production in its own country". Hence "industrialization is to be understood above all as development of heavy industry, especially machine-building". With this came a reductionist interpretation of socialism as state-regimented industrialization, collectivization of agriculture and military modernization, to which all other goals should be subordinated.

Soviet agricultural development, however, failed to keep pace and this, together with a state

▲ This English advertisement reflects the centrality of "the home" and the commitment to a form of suburban life which was found pleasing by more and more people in Britain. This was the "age of disguise". Surburban architecture simulated past grandeur, while the restricted space of suburban homes meant that furniture now had the trick of folding away into nothing or revealing unexpected secondary uses.

► Watching the coronation procession, London, 1937. The enthusiasm of the British people for their monarchy was undiminished by the abdication of Edward VIII (1936). The coronation of King George VI was an occasion of national unity. The idea of the nation as a family was one which the new king aimed to depict.

◄ Loading bicycles at the Gare St Lazare, Paris, for the holidays in 1936, the year in which holidays with pay were introduced in France. The same rights were extended to 11 million people in Britain in 1938. Now the common people, too, could go for seaside holidays which had long been fashionable for others. The 1930s also saw a great vogue for hiking and the development of an interest in the conservation of the countryside – nowhere more so than in Hitler's Germany.

policy of holding down bread and grain procurement prices for the benefit of townspeople, caused a growing shortfall in peasant grain deliveries to the towns. "What is the way out for agriculture?" Stalin asked the December 1927 party congress. "Perhaps to slow down our industrial development...? Never!... The way out is to convert small scattered peasant farms into large amalgamated farms based on...collective cultivation of the land on the basis of new higher techniques". It was time to "systematically eliminate" capitalists from agriculture and craft industries.

According to an official *History of the USSR* (1977), "As of 1928, there were more than 1 million kulak farms [farms held and run by relatively rich farmers]... In two years around 600,000 kulak farms were expropriated and more than 240,000 kulak families were deported... At the end of 1932 there remained approximately 60,000 kulak farms". Since kulaks were prohibited from joining collective farms, and since kulak households were relatively large, so-called "dekulakization" presumably left at least 5 million people (including Russia's best farmers) either destitute or languishing in labor camps. Indeed, any peasant opposing rural collectivization was liable to be denounced as a "kulak". Thus "dekulakization" also served to intimidate the

Collective Farms and Rural Development

◄ **Members of a collective farm prepare a tractor.** "All the objections raised by science against the possibility...of organizing large grain factories of 40,000 to 50,000 hectares each have collapsed", Stalin proclaimed in 1929, "We can now accomplish...what was considered fantasy several years ago." He later declared that collective farmers could "utilize neglected land, obtain machines and tractors and thereby double or even treble labor productivity".

▲ **"Peasant woman, go to the collective farm"**, urges this Soviet poster. For peasant women, however, the problem was not so much going to the collective farms as ever getting out again. In the 1930s the Soviet Union introduced internal passports and residence permits which severely restricted peasant mobility. By the 1940s most collective farmers were women, with little hope of escape from their allotted stations in life.

peasantry at large into joining either collective farms (*kolkhozi*), in theory autonomous agricultural cooperatives, or state farms (*sovkhozi*), which were funded and controlled by the state. The autonomy of collective farms was more formal than real. In practice they were controlled by local party cells and were assigned mandatory plan targets and delivery quotas.

By 1935 most peasants had reluctantly joined *kolkhozi*, which they rightly regarded as a form of serfdom, on account of the attendant regimentation, supervision and restricted household autonomy. Even the system of workdays or workpoints used to tot up each person's labor con-

In the 19th and early 20th centuries communists cherished the idea of creating social equality and increased efficiency in rural societies by forming large, communally run "collective" farms not in private ownership. The Soviet Union was the first state to implement this idea, between 1929 and 1935. After World War II other communist states pursued similar policies. However, among the millions of words of early communist theory about agriculture and peasantries there was little guidance on how collective farms were to be structured and managed. In practice the collectivization of Soviet agriculture was carried out by hundreds of thousands of urban workers, party officials and Red Army soldiers with little knowledge or experience of farming. They threw together landholdings into large farms, which were subject to party and state control. Collectivization included the "liquidation" of several million of the most successful farmers, the so-called *kulaks*. So it is not surprising that Soviet agricultural output, productivity and incomes fell sharply instead of rising as communist "economists" had naively anticipated.

Nevertheless it is difficult to sustain dogmatic verdicts "for" or "against" rural collectivization. As with private agriculture the forms, contexts, objectives and results have been extremely varied. It is more meaningful to refer to specific forms and circumstances in which rural collectivization has been successful or unsuccessful in promoting rural development. There has been a widely held but mistaken belief that rural collectivization embodies a particular rural development strategy or option. It really embraces a wide range of strategies and options which have widely differing results. Rural collectivization has assumed a wide variety of institutional forms: (1) "collective farms", formally self-managed and self-financing agricultural producers' cooperatives; (2) "state farms", financed by the state, employing workers who are state employees with statutory benefits; (3) China's vast "people's communes" (1958-80), federations of collective and state farms with increasingly centralized services, local government functions and burgeoning rural industries; (4) Bulgaria's giant unwieldy "agrarian-industrial complexes", 170 of which were established in the 1970s; and (5) various "transitional forms", such as "mutual aid teams" and purchasing or marketing cooperatives. In some cases collectivization has built upon existing village or communal institutions and practices, as in North Vietnam; but in others it has set out to destroy and supersede them, as in the Soviet Union under Stalin.

◀ A prison camp for the wives and children of Western Ukrainian "rebels". In squandering so many millions of lives in forced labor camps and prisons and through brutal collectivization of agriculture, the Soviet regime profoundly alienated and demoralized the peasantry, especially in the Ukraine. After the famine in rural areas in 1932–34 many Ukrainians came to believe that the Soviet regime was pursuing deliberate policies of genocide or "war by starvation" against the Ukrainian peasant nation. The ordeals of the 1930s were so terrible that when the Germans invaded the Soviet Union in June 1941 many Ukrainian and Byelorussian villagers greeted them as "liberators".

tributions and entitlements was adapted from Russian serfdom and subsequently transmitted to other communist states! In the process of collectivization, however, the Soviet Union experienced major famines in several regions and lost half its livestock. According to the careful estimates of F. Lorimer and S. Wheatcroft, "excess mortality" totalled 5.5 million in the 1930s.

Stalin's "Workers' State"

In the 1930s the Soviet regime enjoyed great prestige from its lasting elimination of mass unemployment – in dramatic contrast to the mass unemployment in the capitalist world. The industrial work force in fact grew much more than expected because Plan targets were repeatedly and arbitrarily raised. Labor productivity did not rise as rapidly as expected. (Enterprises found it easier to meet increased targets by taking on additional workers than by raising the productivity of a largely inexperienced and untrained work force.) The consequent labor shortage encouraged enterprises to hoard scarce labor, and planned industrialization spawned a mushrooming bureaucracy. These became enduring features of the Soviet planned economy.

This expansion of the "modern sector" work force permitted massive upward mobility. Between 1926 and 1939 some 23 million peasants moved into town work and 10–15 percent of Soviet workers were recruited into administrative, managerial and technical posts. Under Stalin, there was always room at the top for those prepared to live dangerously, never knowing when it would be their turn to be arrested and imprisoned. According to S. Fitzpatrick, " the essence of the special relationship between the Party and the working class...was that the regime got cadres [administrators and managers] from the working class" and "the regime's commitment to the working class had much less to do with workers *in situ* than with working-class upward mobility".

Operations shall begin at daybreak. Upon entering the home of the person to be deported, the senior member of the operative group shall assemble the entire family of the deportee into one room...In view of the fact that a large number of deportees must be arrested and distributed in special camps and that their families must proceed to special settlements in distant regions, it is essential that the operations of removal of both the members of the deportee's family and its head shall be carried out simultaneously, without notifying them of the separation confronting them.

SOVIET SECRET POLICE
ORDER FOR DEPORTATION

◄ **Peasants outside a church in Yugoslavia.** In 1942 representatives of Eastern Europe's peasant movements met to produce a joint statement of their philosophy and goals. "Believing, in the words of the Bible, that we are all members of one body", it began, "we maintain that the raising of the peasant's standard of life is the necessary precondition for the progress of the whole nation... The main basis on which a sound and progressive agricultural community can be built up is that of individual peasant-owned farms. We do not, however, believe that the peasant can live in isolation, and we recognize the desirability of voluntary cooperation in land cultivation." However, "peasants themselves should control marketing, credit and the supply of agricultural equipment by their own institutions, democratically organized."

We work fourteen hours a day in the fields, and we have no money.... A kilogramme of oil for my lamp now costs me sixty eggs. It is too much, for to sell eggs I must walk to Czernowitz, or take the horse out of the fields for a whole day. It is not worth it, just to get some oil, so we sleep when it is dark.

PEASANT FARMER'S WIFE
ROMANIA, 1932

Peasantist movements in Eastern Europe

In Eastern Europe in this period major peasant movements emerged in almost every state. They were engaged in a common quest to end "feudal" landlordism and to build in its place democratic societies based on peasant proprietors united in cooperative movements. The natural constituency for peasantism was still considerably larger than that for Marxist socialism or fascism or liberalism. Only in Slovakia, Slovenia (in Yugoslavia), Hungary and Poland did agrarian parties remain strongly under ecclesiastical (Catholic) influence, and only under the reactionary Sanacja and Horthy regimes in, respectively, Poland and Hungary did landed oligarchies survive almost intact. But even here peasant parties eventually united in support of radical programs prior to their electoral victories in 1945. The peasantist Agrarian party was the dominant party in successive governments in interwar Czechoslovakia, the Romanian National Peasant party dominated Romania in 1928–31, and interwar Croatia (in Yugoslavia) was dominated by the radical Croatian Peasant party.

In Europe since the late 19th century large-scale industrialization and the spread of Marxist socialism had increasingly distanced urban-industrial workers' movements from peasants and fostered often bitter ideological divisions between them. However much Marxist parties attacked the exploitation and alienation inherent in capitalist industrialization, they fully intended to move or "progress" in the same direction as capitalist industrializers, only their industrial society would be under the control of socialists or communists. It would be capitalist industrialism without the capitalists.

By contrast, the peasantist movements aspired to move in an altogether different direction. They envisaged a "cooperative society", distinct from both capitalism and Marxist collectivism. In their view, full democracy would only be achieved if peasants were to break the political monopoly of the urban and rentier classes, so that society could be governed "from below, not from above". Voluntary, democratic village cooperation was expected to address every need of village life, though collective agriculture on the Soviet model was rejected because of its suppression of peasant autonomy.

The very survival of peasant movements and democracy were closely intertwined in Eastern Europe. Both were under recurrent threat from the fascist or royalist authoritarian right and from the Marxist left. But unfortunately, except in liberal Czechoslovakia, the peasantist movements failed to retain and expand their footholds in government. They were mainly the victims of the singularly vicious conjuncture of world Depression and fascism. In Eastern Europe, as elsewhere, the Depression and plummeting tax and export revenues scuppered schemes of democratic social reconstruction by causing public expenditure cuts, widespread bankruptcies and foreclosures, and increased ethnic tension. As in Western Europe such conditions were a fertile breeding ground for both urban and rural fascism. Furthermore, the continuing popularity of the peasantist movements and their proven ability to make effective use of the democratic rights written into most East European constitutions, frightened the ruling groups as the socialists never had done and made them prime targets of the political malpractice and persecution perpetrated by monarchs, dictators, fascists and corrupt urban "machine politicians".

These political and economic setbacks forced the peasantist movements into a period of intense introspection and self-renewal from which they reemerged strengthened in 1945, though not before they had undergone the ordeal of fascist domination and war, during which millions of peasants demonstrated extraordinary capacities for active and passsive resistance.

► **Threshing in progess in Poland.** Vladko Maček, leader of the Croatian Peasant party in the 1930s, declared that East European peasants who had only recently freed themselves from "feudal serfdom" would not readily accept forms of collectivism which "turn the peasant into a serf of the state". However, "it is possible to turn the village into an economic unit." Peasants produce "partly for the needs of the family and partly for the market". The former "should remain the business of the peasant family", but the latter was already evolving "toward cooperative production as a common concern of the village as a whole."

An ethnic group is one held together by common traditions based on race, religion, language, culture, or a combination of these. These traditions act as a force for unity within the group, providing it with an identity which it seeks to maintain against outsiders. Often the group is a minority one, under pressure from a mainstream culture which seeks to devalue or destroy its heritage; in such cases the need for a common identity becomes all the stronger.

Such ethnic minorities originate in many ways. Some, the Australian Aborigines or North American Indians for example, were the original inhabitants of their continents but were almost overwhelmed by an irresistible influx of European settlers. The Jews were scattered from their homeland in the Middle East and existed as minorities throughout Europe and elsewhere for many centuries. Their communities were particularly successful in maintaining their religious and cultural traditions in face of long periods of persecution. The ancestors of today's American blacks were forcibly transported from Africa as slaves. In the 19th and 20th centuries many millions of voluntary migrants have sought new lives in the richer parts of the world. Their own ethnic traditions have traveled with them.

There is a common feeling among minority ethnic groups that their traditions are undervalued by the majority culture. All kinds of subtle discriminations can exist in order to exclude a minority culture from a full life in the host community. In extreme cases, as in the Nazi treatment of the Jews in Europe in the 1930s and 1940s, a long-established and economically successful group may even face extermination.

In the United States for many years there was an active policy of breaking down ethnic roots in an attempt to create an all-American culture from the melting pot. Many second-generation immigrants were torn betweeen the cultures of their parents and the mainstream American life which seemed to offer the only path to economic success. Often it was the third generation who reacted and successfully rediscovered their ethnic roots.

Although discrimination and persecution are common experiences for ethnic minorities, some succeed in both maintaining their traditions and achieving economic or political success. Chinese communities overseas have achieved a dominance as traders in many Asian countries. In South Africa, the Afrikaners, forming only ten per cent of the population, achieved absolute political control of the country from the 1940s.

▲ ▶ The gypsies are one of Europe's oldest and most persistent ethnic minorities. With no national home and living nomadically, gypsies have faced discrimination and persecution over centuries. This picture shows traveling gypsies in central Europe in the 1930s.

▶ Jews throughout Europe had been forced in medieval times to live in segregated "ghettos". Even when they became free to move, many chose to remain in the ghetto areas, such as this Jewish community in Poland in the 1930s. Such ghettos were common in central Europe.

◀ In the 1970s and 1980s the Aborigine peoples of Australia have become increasingly aware of their cultural heritage and the way that their land rights and traditions have been devalued by the white majority. These children have joined a demonstration for their rights.

▼◀ The white Afrikaner minority in South Africa fought to defend their traditions and livelihood against other whites and the black majority. They achieved political supremacy in the 1940s, instituting the policy of apartheid. This farmer's wife illustrates Afrikaner defiance.

▼ Many cultures have fought to maintain their identity and Muslims have felt particularly affronted by Western cultural dominance. The picture shows a single sex girls' school in Britain run on traditional lines for Muslim girls.

Datafile

The arrival in the 1930s of new consumer goods like instant coffee and potato crisps prefigured the postwar development of consumer society. For many people in the West, outside agriculture and the old industrial areas, in which unemployment bit deep, this was a period of increased comfort, more leisure and a pleasing domesticity. This was the context of declining fertility, smaller families and a new awareness of the relationships between men and women as individuals. Yet states were concerned about the sheer numbers of their peoples, and a renewed emphasis on the roles of women as mothers conflicted with the trend toward greater freedom for women as individuals.

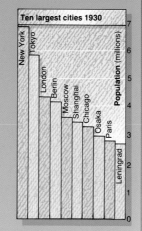

Ten largest cities 1930

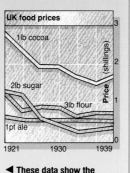

Births and deaths 1935

◀▲ The changes which had taken place in the world economy are marked by the growth of New York and Tokyo well beyond the great European cities. The relative slowing down of the expansion of the latter's populations reflected the fact that western Europe began to complete the "demographic transition" to low birth rates and low mortality. Children were no longer considered an economic advantage. The French population started to decline, in spite of the encouragement of populationist policies.

▼ The British National Insurance Acts of 1920 and 1921 established unemployment insurance (known as "the dole"), but it was severely stretched by high and persistent unemployment. Yet, though the dole was often near the margin of adequacy, it was usually just sufficient to keep people from desperation.

▶ After 1920 retail prices fell almost continuously until 1934, and only gradually thereafter. Thus real wages generally increased. In Britain those employed in new industries (mainly in the Midlands and Southeast) became better off and a social divide opened between this area and those of old heavy industry.

UK food prices

◀ These data show the high level of aspiration for higher education among young Americans (and, considering it was wartime, a surprising lack of interest in military service). The belief that higher education was the right of all Americans was encouraged by the "G.I. Bill of Rights", which provided for tuition fees and maintenance grants for ex-servicemen. By 1956, when it ended, it had permitted several million to go through college. The war years in America especially ushered in expansion of higher education, which would later make the idea of "the meritocracy" – a new elite, recruited by merit rather than by birth – seem realistic.

UK family dole budget 1934

Total £1 9s 0.5d

- Food
- Rent
- Fuel
- Insurance
- Balance

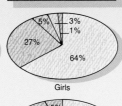

US students' plans 1943

Girls

Boys

- Further education
- Work
- Armed services
- Marriage
- Don't know

In spite of the impact of the Great Depression upon the millions who experienced unemployment in Europe in the 1930s, average living standards improved modestly. Prices fell faster than wages so that average real wages increased and there was more money available to spend on modest luxuries. With the expansion of chain and department stores the range of foods on sale increased. Canned and processed foods became more widespread. Instant coffee, breakfast cereals and potato crisps attracted consumers and diets improved as the consumption of meat, milk, vegetables and fruit increased. But scientific investigations still suggested that (in Britain) a high degree of poor nutrition and ill-health was intrinsic to the lives of the poor, especially children, whether or not their parents were unemployed, while in the United States the heavy toll of the Depression is reflected in the finding in 1940 that almost half of the first batch of 2 million conscripted men was medically unfit, largely because of malnutrition. Yet death rates in the United States continued to decline, reflecting higher standards of medical care.

The domestic use of electricity increased further, and with it that of electrical gadgets. The radio became the center of home entertainment. In Germany by 1932 one house in four possessed a radio; in France before the outbreak of World War II there were about 5 million sets. The political use of broadcasting became very significant. In the USA President Franklin D. Roosevelt's "fireside chats", initiated in 1933, played a part in his construction of a new consensus in American politics; the propaganda uses of the radio in the war are notorious. Cinema-going expanded hugely – in Britain in 1939 new cinemas were opening at the rate of three a week. For the mass of the people holidays became a feature of life for the first time. When holidays with pay were introduced in France in 1936 many families made their first visit to the seaside. The idea that suntanned bodies were attractive began to take hold.

Demographic decline and the family

By the 1930s the industrialized world had seen the last stages of what has been called the "demographic transition": a move from high birth rates and high death rates to a pattern of low birth rates and low mortality. Fertility was being limited; fewer children were created; and people lived longer. This development, which began roughly during the later 1870s changed family life and the position of women in particular.

From about 1900 onward the main effect of fertility limitation had been to compress childbearing into the early years of marriage. Thanks to the lower birth rate and the general fall in adult mortality, women could now expect to live far longer

STATES AND FAMILY LIFE

The "demographic transition"

Family policies in the Soviet Union

Youth movements

The Nazi revival of motherhood

World War II and social change

after the birth of their last child (30–35 years compared with 20 in the 1850s). For the first time in history both parents could look forward to a period together without the cares of bringing up children. Falling adult mortality also meant that the duration of marriage, unbroken by divorce, had risen from about 20 to 35 years by 1900 (45 in 1990), with all the obvious implications of the need for readjustment between marriage partners. Sexuality gradually became dissociated from biological reproduction. At the same time improving standards of living encouraged the desire to limit fertility.

The way in which marriage, the family and women's roles were defined and regulated in the 1930s through population policies, illustrates how unprepared most nations were to accept the interrelationship between industrialization and low birth rates. These policies affected women in particular. Their struggle to control their own fertility

and sexuality was directly opposed by political and ideological policies and pressures to bear more children.

After the huge losses of men killed in World War I the 1920s began to show a conclusive fall in the rate of population growth and the world economic crisis of the early 1930s accentuated the established trend toward smaller families. Overall population structures were changing throughout the industrialized world, but changes were more apparent in those countries that had suffered especially large losses of life in World War I. In France, Germany and Romania people noticed a disproportionate number of old people and a "surplus" of women (1 million in Germany), for whom there were no husbands, giving rise to concern about so-called "population deficiencies". Rational demographic thinking changed into populationist obsession notably in Germany, where the maintenance of racial purity added a

▼ The arrival of the family car greatly changed people's leisure options. Here a family had traveled from their small town to a "community sing" at Pie Town, New Mexico, USA.

sinister element to the generally reactionary measures employed to encourage larger families. Populationist thinkers in many countries featured propaganda supporting the cult of the family and advocated fiscal encouragement for large families. In France, where abortion had been relatively widespread, laws were enacted to forestall further "race suicide": both abortion and the sale and supply of contraceptives were forbidden. Generous family allowances and medals for large families were introduced to encourage motherhood. In 1931 the papal encyclical *Casta Conubii* declared all except "natural" family limitation to be sinful. In Catholic countries population policies thus simply swam with the tide – or were pursued for militaristic or political reasons, as in Italy, despite its relative overpopulation.

In America as in Britain the response to family limitation and planned parenthood was in general no more favorable. While contraception continued to become more widely available in a few American states, and the number of advice centers set up also increased (from 29 in 1929 to 746 by 1941), about half of the states maintained the Federal Comstock Law of 1873 which forbade the import and distribution of contraceptives, many until as late as 1968. In Britain family planning became more respectable through Marie Stopes' advocacy of contraception as a means to improve the race. In 1930 the British government accepted that birth-control information should be provided "on specific medical grounds" for controlling the fertility of women "unfit" to have children. It was not until 1949 that this was extended to all married women. Thus in Britain the emphasis remained on family policy, on insurance benefits and on unemployment assistance to support and strengthen the family during the long years of high unemployment and financial hardship, rather than to help control the number of mouths that had to be fed. In Scandinavia policies were more enlightened. Sweden began to provide public finance for contraceptive clinics in 1936, together with new family benefits. Abortion was legalized in 1938.

While the prohibition of contraception indicated that effective techniques existed, the majority of women were still only marginally affected by the rise of new and safer birth-control methods. All classes practiced birth control in some form, but it was middle-class couples who were most able to exercise choice about when and how many children they might have. Those with limited resources – the poor, industrial workers – tended to have more children anyway. Prohibition of contraception, heavy penalties for abortions and pressure on women to have more children thus potentially affected most those who could least afford large families. It was among the poor that "backstreet" abortion was often the last desperate resort to restricting their brood of small children.

While the demands made by society thus came up against the limited resources of private families, the contradictions in the prevailing social and economic system became more obvious. The "Welfare State" was only in scaffolding in the 1930s; public assistance only helped the poorest. Thus during the interwar years the opposition to married women working or to planned parenthood came close to being punitive to many families. Meanwhile, however, many couples resisted public policy and quietly restricted the size of their families. Their attitudes began to create new values and expectations of family life which in due time would make an impact on public policy.

Women and the family under Stalin

From the Bolshevik Revolution of 1917 onward the Soviet Union had professed equality for women. Employment and education statistics suggest that the Soviet commitment to equality of opportunity continued during the 1930s. The total number of women workers rose from 24 percent of all workers in 1928 to 39 percent in 1940 and 56 percent in 1945. The female share of the greatly increasing numbers of students in higher education similarly rose from 28 percent in 1927 to 43 percent in 1937 and 58 percent in 1940. These changes, however, were forced on the Soviet Union and mainly resulted from the acuteness of urban labor shortages (engendered by forced industrialization) and, after 1937, by the drafting of millions of men into the armed forces.

Most female labor reserves lived in cities and were members of workers' families. Their recruitment was therefore cheaper than that of men from the countryside, since they could be brought into production without major outlays on new housing or social amenities other than child-care facilities. Women were mainly channeled into the least-skilled and lowest-paid jobs with the poorest promotion prospects. Any profession which acquired a preponderance of women became relatively low-paid, even if it had not been so at the outset – the prime example being medicine. Women remained greatly underrepresented in managerial and skilled positions, and continued to encounter considerable male chauvinism, resistance and harrassment.

Increased employment of urban women was not compensated by reductions in their household burdens: Soviet men rarely lifted a

▲ Soviet poster encouraging sport: "To work, build and not complain! We have been shown the path to a new life. You may not be an athlete but a gymnast you must be." Stalin's regime glorified physical prowess.

◄ Russian peasant woman suckling a child. By the mid 1930s the Soviet regime was alarmed by sharply falling birth rates and in 1935 outlawed abortion. But abortion had only been widely accepted by townspeople. In rural areas preindustrial forms of family limitation must have prevailed instead, such as amenorrhea (suppression of ovulation by suckling).

▼ Russian women plasterers. In 1935 women were surprisingly prominent among manual workers. They accounted for 24 percent of workers in coal mining, 23 percent in iron-ore mining, 32 percent in chemicals and 24 percent in engineering.

finger in the home. Urban housing was extremely cramped (urban housing space per person actually declined from 5.8 square meters in 1928 to 4.9 in 1932, 4.5 in 1940 and 3.9 in 1944. The Soviet Union had been very slow to develop and provide labor-saving household appliances, public laundries, efficient retailing and wholesaling, private automobiles and convenience foods, so Soviet women spent inordinate amounts of time on housework, shopping, public transport and queuing – looking after the men.

Until 1935–36 the family as a social institution was under attack as a custodian and perpetuator (in conjunction with organized religion) of pre-revolutionary and counterrevolutionary values. After 1935–36, however, the regime abruptly reversed its policies. In 1936 it was proclaimed that "the family is an important social institution under the protection of the socialist state....Disrespect toward parents, neglect of one's obligations towards father and mother...are psychological features of the social and moral decay of the personality, gravely harmful to...socialist society. Conversely, the strengthening of family relations...is one of the essential elements of consolidating the new order". The regime had suddenly rediscovered the usefulness of the family as

an anchor of social and political stability in a period of turmoil, as a prop for authority, as a means of disciplining and socializing Soviet youth, and as an inexpensive agency of social control and of care for the aged, the sick, the disabled and the orphaned. This was associated with an increasingly urgent perceived need for strong measures to raise birth rates to offset the disastrous demographic consequences of Stalin's Purges and of the liberal abortion policy of 1920–35. In 1936 there was a major tightening of divorce procedures. The Soviet state also mounted fascist-style glorification of motherhood, preparing the ground for the distinctly conservative Family Laws of 1944, which were also a response to the damaging effects of World War II upon family life and sexual responsibility.

In 1936 a much-publicized "Conference of the Wives of Engineers in Heavy Industry" endeavored to exalt and rehabilitate the role of the Soviet manager's "kept wife" as a hostess, housekeeper and charitable patron of downtrodden working-class women, an almost comical expression of the incipient "embourgeoisement" of the new Soviet ruling class. All in all, however, Soviet women gained significantly more duties and burdens than power or status.

◀ In the 1930s the Italian fascist regime adopted, as in Germany, a whole number of measures to boost Italy's birth rate. Family allowances, marriage loans, job discrimination in favor of men and punitive taxes for bachelors were introduced. The care of children also received new attention, as these stamps suggest. The "Opera Nazionale Dopolavoro" (national institute for recreation), for example, provided virtually free summer holidays for children, or handed out welfare relief in poor areas.

Young people are causing the...Party agencies much anxiety. Both boys and girls are trying by every means possible to dodge the year of Land Service.... There is a section of youth that wants the romantic life. Whole bundles of trashy literature have been found in small caves.

REPORT ON GERMANY, 1938

◀ In Nazi Germany pronatal family policies and eugenics (race care) were inextricably linked. Aryan women, as here the wife of a Nazi official proudly showing off her seventh child, were celebrated as the guarantors of racial purity and honored with medals. Although the principle of selection for the production of the "master race" was racial and medical rather than social, the pressure to reproduce fell hard on Nazi functionaries and officials who were to act as examples to the rest of the nation.

Youth Movements

By the beginning of the 20th century the particular problems of the phase of "youth" were recognized, and in Britain a contemporary expert wrote: "The miscellaneous associations represented by clubs, lads' brigades, boy scouts and the like, have all been called into existence for the express purpose of exerting some measure of control over the transition period which separates the boy from the man". Of all these youth movements the most important, which spread rapidly across the world, was the boy scouts. Founded in 1907–08 by Robert Baden-Powell, the scout movement arose in

◀ Italian youth magazine, 1932.

specific circumstances, reflecting the preoccupation of Edwardian England with the maintenance of its Empire. The Boer War (1899–1902) had shaken British self-confidence, and seemed to expose Britain's moral, physical and military weaknesses. These ruling-class fears, existing concerns about social order, and even specific problems about the fitness of army recruits, were addressed by the scout movement. Baden-Powell grafted ideas drawn from Ernest Thompson-Seton, who celebrated American Indian culture and woodcraft, as well as from his own experience of army scouting, onto those of Christian social reformers. It was an appealing mixture, but the rapid growth of the boy scout movement owed nothing to chance. Rather it was the result of skillful publicity, and thoroughly political. As Baden-Powell wrote: "Our business is to pass as many boys through our character factory as we possibly can" – inculcating in them obedience to authority, values of service and uncritical patriotism. It was an ideology rooted in the self-interest of the upper classes.

The youth movements of communist regimes, of the Italian fascists, and of the Nazis in Germany served quite similar objectives. In Nazi Germany the *Jungvolk* (for those aged 10–14), the Hitler Youth and the parallel organization for girls, the *Jungmädel*, bore the main responsibility for carrying out Hitler's exhortation "Be hard, German youth, and make yourselves hard" – through the mixture of sport, war games and propaganda. The ideological extremes of Nazism are reflected in this prayer of the Hitler Youth: "Adolf Hitler, you are our great *Führer*. Thy name makes the enemy tremble. Thy Third Reich comes, thy will alone is law upon the earth. Let us hear daily thy voice and order us by thy leadership, for we will obey to the end and even with our lives. We praise thee. Heil Hitler!" Yet it seems that as many adolescents were bored by it all as were fired with enthusiasm!

Women and family in Hitler's Germany

In the 1930s policies toward the family and women in the advanced industrial nations shared certain basic trends but differed strikingly in their commitment to their objectives. Under the National Socialist (Nazi) regime in Germany (1933–45) the revival of motherhood was carried to extremes. The pressures to which women were subjected were antagonistic; social welfare measures were antiemancipatory; and compared with reactionary policies in other countries women's oppression in Nazi Germany was antifeminist to the extreme.

Yet it would be wrong to dismiss Nazi policies toward women as purely reactionary. They never resulted in a true "bondage of pure housewifery" as envisaged by the famous slogan *"Kinder, Küche, Kirche"* (children, kitchen, church), which was to remind women of their proper place in the home. When Gertrud Scholtz-Klink claimed leadership of all the Nazi women's organizations, she also saw to it that "her" women would retain or even enhance their own "female sphere of action in society". Extraordinary contradictions were apparent in the Nazis' policies, which both

exploited women and subjected them to repressive protection. This suggested that both reactionary and progressive views were at work as the regime attempted to deal with the tensions within an economic and social structure in which "modernity" (city life, the small family, women's new freedom) coexisted uneasily with essentially preindustrial conservative political and social ideologies.

Antifeminism played an important role in the regime's attempt to enforce the unity of a conflict-ridden society, and ultimately, to generate mass support for its expansionist and population policies. Fueling antisemitic feelings, Adolf Hitler declared the concept of women's emancipation to be a construct of Jewish intellectuals. The repudiation of women's (much exaggerated) independence and the repeated attacks on the feminist movement also reassured conservatives and reactionaries for whom women's emancipation symbolized all they hated and feared.

The expansion of women's employment between 1925 and 1929 (20 percent) and the growing proportion of women students at universities had been sufficiently sharp to activate antifeminist

▲ Flight before the advance of war, in Spain during the Civil War (1936–39). These Spaniards forced on the move anticipated the fate of perhaps as many as 50 million Europeans who were to be expelled from their homes to become refugees during World War II. When the war was over Germany – in defeat and within reduced frontiers – found itself faced with the task of settling 10 million displaced persons. For all the destruction which it had wrought, World War I had not torn apart whole societies in the way that happened during World War II.

resentment. This grew during the Depression after 1929. In 1933 the Nazi regime simply turned the clock back and reduced the number of women students (from 18.9 to 12.5 percent) and removed women (where expedient) from the overcrowded labor market, especially from positions of responsibility or from well-paid jobs. Predictably too, it was the "new", allegedly mannish woman who came under attack – women who defied traditional conventions of femininity. To correct such unnatural development the Nazis channeled the education of young girls "into a deeper conception of the nature and values of womanhood, and of women's duties and responsibilities to the family and the 'Volk' [nation]" – a program that the Women Teachers Association had already formulated in 1921.

Yet the Nazis never urged the total exclusion of women from the labor market, nor was their objective of a separate curriculum for girls fully realized. Despite its antiemancipatory policy, by 1939 the regime was forced to encourage the return of some professional women into employ-

ment and young girls to take up academic study, if only to fill posts men had left empty as the war took them to the front. Women's employment as cheap labor was also essential to both the rearmament program and the war effort, especially after 1939, when labor shortages threatened the regime's war aims. By then the Nazis had failed to enthuse women into further service for the nation and their increase in employment between 1939 and 1945 was minimal. For various reasons the role of the housewife really did seem preferable to many women. As real wages had risen by some 30 percent by 1939 the family was financially better off than ever before and women experienced a real easing of their load. The Nazis' attempts to mobilize women for the war effort was also fairly half-hearted, threatening as they did to destroy a large part of the regime's basis of popular support.

The threat "to emancipate women from emancipation" (in the words of the Nazi ideologue Alfred Rosenberg) was real, however, as all notions of personal freedom and rights were to be replaced by total subservience to the state. Thus women were expelled from political office and stripped of their civil rights. A strict hierarchy of male dominance in public life was established, and while this served to appease male fears of female transgression, it also brought the regime closer to its real concern, which was with women as bearers of the future master race. Increasingly eugenic policies (gene and race care) were to expose the hypocrisy of the Nazis' cult of motherhood. While Jewish and gypsy women were portrayed as sluts and whores, the ultimate offer for women to partake in the reconstruction of society as "mothers of the *Volk*" was only directed at certain "valuable Aryan" women. Those who lacked in social value or were "racially and hereditarily impure" were vilified or murdered and excluded from bearing and rearing children (and men from begetting them) with compulsory sterilization as the principal deterrent, or by abortion of "defective pregnancies" (1935).

For the desirables, massive programs to revive motherhood were implemented. Propaganda projected images of the sturdy peasant family of lost times, of radiant mothers and healthy children exalting the family as the "germ cell" of the nation. This emotional appeal was enhanced by material incentives such as marriage loans, child bonus and benefits for large families and punitive taxes for the unmarried. Yet throughout the Third Reich the propagation of the strong family as a "bulwark against the tides of alienation" was flagrantly contradicted. Housing needs were almost totally neglected. The demand for absolute loyalty to the *Führer* (Hitler) undercut the authority of the head of the household. Children were encouraged to inform on the political attitudes of their parents. The socialization of children itself was concentrated outside the family in youth organizations. For the average and ordinary people the home was drained of its emotional meaning by Nazi policy. As the demands of the armamens drive increased, more and more men had to live away from home and women had to cope on their own. As unmarried women began to get official encouragement to bear illegitimate children, so (in the words of British historian T. Mason) "the official shining ideal of the integrated stable and prolific family began to look more and more like a monstrous deception".

World War II and social change

World War II caused enormous loss of life – 18 percent of the Polish population, more than 11 percent of the Soviet Union's, more than 7 percent of Germany's – and the displacement of many millions as refugees. Yet the war was less significant as a cause of social change than might have been expected. Arthur Marwick, a British specialist in this field, concludes that the class structures of European societies were little affected. The idea that the war brought about "social levelling" is justified to the extent that there were some gains in working-class living standards; and in Britain, for example, far from it being a "people's war", figures for strikes and absenteeism show that unions and workers took advantage of wartime full employment. Increased

self-confidence among workers was based partly on sharing of experience of the Blitz in the UK, the Resistance in France and service under arms. The mood of the time is reflected in the diary of a London bus driver in the early stages of the Blitz who wrote "We are all in the 'Front Line' and we realize it", and in the observation of a French trade unionist that "Within the Resistance prejudices tended to disappear, since people were united by something essential". Generally the experience of the war consolidated acceptance of the established order – nowhere more so than in Soviet Russia where the "Great Patriotic War" brought new social cohesion after the internal strains of the 1930s.

One area of social life that was affected concerned the status of women. Marwick argues: "The conclusion is inescapable that World War II offered women opportunities normally unavailable in peacetime to improve their economic and social status, and to develop their confidence and self-consciousness".

The war also confirmed the popularity of planning. It seemed in Britain that planning and the participation of all classes in the war effort were vital to victory, though this contemporary perception probably underestimated the significance of American money. The war years also saw the foundation of the postwar welfare state, in the report of the Beveridge Committee which was published in 1942. The critical new idea in Beveridge was that social security should be "comprehensive", not just for the poor. It was thus hoped to create a genuinely more united society.

▶ Soldier and children. Families were split up during World War II, even in countries which did not experience displacements of people. Many women became workers and carried responsibility for their families – some of them discovering that they were more capable than their menfolk. Yet the war did not bring about great change in the class and power structures of European societies. The sharing of experience by people from different backgrounds was part of a broader "social levelling", but also strengthened social cohesion.

LOVE AND MARRIAGE

How men and women display affection, engage in relationships and build economic security differ considerably despite the universal importance of ceremony to celebrate sexual union. In the West monogamy – no more than one spouse at a time – is universally the law and the nuclear family unit (man, woman, children) predominates though to a lesser extent than in mid-century. In large parts of Africa and Asia polygamous marriage – in which a man may take several wives – persists, and larger family groups live communally. Almost everywhere women are subordinated to the men of the household but their status and mobility vary considerably. The seclusion imposed on veiled Muslim brides of the Middle East and Asia is far from the experience of the liberated middle-class American women or West African women farmers and traders.

The age at which people marry and have children varies between societies, as it has in the past. In the west it often used to be later than it is now.

Love and marriage are associated with the most intimate and private parts of life and interference in them is strongly resisted. This has not stopped the state from intervening very directly in personal relations during the 20th century. The *kibbutzim*, the communal farms prominent in the Israeli state since the 1940s, offered a communal alternative to conventional Jewish marriage and family life. In socialist countries the ideals of "revolutionary love" and the proletarian family were promoted. These fell short of sexual licence, considered to be a bourgeois aberration, but inequality between men and women in the home was denounced. Collectivization (the move away from private property) was aimed not only at increasing agricultural and industrial production but also at undermining the authority of the male household head. Altered family forms were not sustained although personal relations were transformed. Following the communist victory in China in 1949, marriages arranged by parents for their children were outlawed. Here the youth brigades took on the task of educating young men and women in the mysteries of modern courtship in which they initiated and made the decisions.

In the West, the late 20th century witnessed a revolution in sexual relations and family forms. Young people claimed greater autonomy and independence for themselves. Choice of partner increasingly lay with the couples involved rather than their parents. Many lived together without formalizing their unions through religious or civil ceremonies.

Such changes do not go unchallenged and family lobbies promoting traditional and conservative values remain strong and vocal. The seductive promise of romantic love, popularized in films, ballads, novels and magazines as well as the enchantment of ceremony, ensures the enduring allure of Valentine cards, engagement rings and white weddings.

▲ An advertisement for skin creams. From the early 20th century advertising told Western young women that their skins had to be softer and younger. Ignoring such injunctions could preclude romance and love.

▶ From the 1930s the screen kiss of Hollywood films reinforced the idea of romantic love and after World War II spread it worldwide.

▲ The explosion of popular sex education from the 1960s is represented above all by the immense worldwide sales (in numerous languages) of the British book *The Joy of Sex*. The creation of new expectations of sexual fulfilment has also given rise to anxieties for many men and women.

▲ The wedding, in South Korea, of 6,516 couples belonging to the Unification Church (Moonies). Here the symbols of purity associated with Western weddings are employed as part of a religious creed that repudiates local custom.

▲ In India child marriages (as here) are less common than they were, and the age of marriage has gone up. In many societies marriage is the outcome of a contract arranged between families. Sometimes the marriage is formalized when the parties are children and becomes effective later.

◀ A divorcing couple at a Soviet court. The Soviet Union has usually pursued liberal family policies. Ensuing social problems were contained within the authoritarian structures of the state, but threatened to become overwhelming as state authority retreated in the late 20th century.

Datafile

The social and economic impact of the Great Depression in Africa, Asia and Latin America was mixed, depending on what raw materials were exported and to where. In general, however, the major effects were negative, driving many out of export production and reducing cultivated acreage and mining activity. Many rural producers experienced a new kind of crisis: one due to failure of markets instead of the rains. The turmoil which was caused contributed to popular risings against colonial powers. But the Depression and World War II also gave opportunities for some countries to industrialize further. Japan accelerated its drive to industrialize with success.

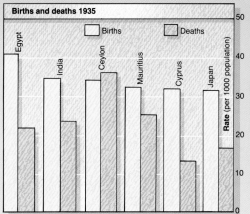

Births and deaths 1935

▲ Java's rubber output fluctuated with world output. Indochina, just starting real production, expanded slowly through the 1930s. Loss of export revenues led colonial governments to increase domestic taxation, sometimes provoking rebellion.

◄ The Japanese death rate was still characteristic of a poor country and worse than many. Ceylon's death rate exceeded its births. But for most, the tempo of growth in the birth rate was quickening.

▶ The Bengal famine was one of the worst famines ever. The rice price soared while wages stagnated. The capacity to buy, 100 in December 1941, fell as low as 24 in May 1943. Nationalists blamed the British for reserving the crop for its armies, and for preventing grain movement. Between 3 and 6 million perished.

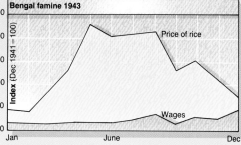

Bengal famine 1943

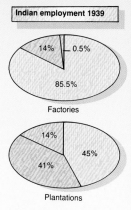

Indian employment 1939

Factories

Plantations

☐ Men
☐ Women
☐ Children

◄ Women and children were vital workers in India. The war boom increased the need for them in factories and mines, although on the plantations numbers declined. Women were paid much less than men for the same work and there was no provision for special needs (such as childcare), in spite of factory legislation.

▶ Bombay gangers traditionally recruited mill labor from their home villages, distant from the city. Many came from an arid district far south of the city, Ratnagiri. Rural poverty did not drive workers out, but social networks drew them in, fitting them to special tasks in the mills and special urban localities.

Cotton mill workers 1931

Origin (km from Bombay)
☐ 1–160
☐ 161–320
☐ 321–1,200
☐ over 1,200
☐ Unidentified migrants
☐ Born in Bombay

The Great Depression of the 1930s had contradictory effects on societies in Africa, Asia and Latin America. It was devastating for commercial farmers and for mining operations oriented to exports, but where governments had autonomy in setting tariffs it also stimulated industrial growth – notably in Latin America. These economic changes intensified social contradictions and helped to change the character of nationalist struggles. Meanwhile the whole relationship of the West to the rest of the world was profoundly affected by the remarkable rise of Japan.

The modernization of Japan

From the 1868 Meiji Restoration – a coup against the old Tokugawa dictatorship by a group of disaffected *samurai* (members of an aristocratic caste of warriors) – the new Japanese government strove to create a powerful modern state. It copied from Europe and America whatever social changes seemed best suited. The development of

DUSK OF EMPIRE

the armed forces was crucial, initially to defend the country against foreign intervention when all around the Great Powers of Europe were expropriating countries, but quite rapidly to prosecute the purposes of new Japanese imperialism. It was the drive to war, not for markets, which provided the basic stimulus to the economic transformation of the country.

Extraordinary sacrifices were required from the Japanese people, which was possible only through a combination of an ethic of heroic devotion with tight and fearful social control. Initially after the Meiji Restoration industrialization was entrusted to unemployed samurai rather than the old merchant class, so that the modern management cadre was instilled from the beginning with the ethic of service. Thus, a distinctive economic system was created, governed in part by quasi-feudal loyalties of warlords and retainers rather than market competition. In the first instance the fervor of patriotic sacrifice governed only the

▼ ▶ A Yokohama fish stall (below). By the 1930s Japan combined traditional dress and culture with elements of great modernity – such as this commuter train (right). Some found the combination hard to reconcile.

managers and owners of business; the mass of workers, recruited from poor village families and organized labor gangers (subcontracted by firms to perform particular tasks), were excluded. However, by the 1920s an increasing proportion of the work force in the largest corporations was being inculcated in the warrior ethic.

A dual structure was gradually emerging. On the one hand there was a class of extraordinarily large firms or groups of firms (the *zaibatsu*) with privileged subcontractual relationships to the state; on the other there was a mass of unstable small and medium enterprises that supplied goods to the large companies as subcontractors (or dealt with the local retail trades). In the first, companies moved to offering their work force a lifetime of employment. In the second, the turnover of workers was high, pay and levels of productivity were much lower, and conditions far inferior.

Education was a precondition for the rapid pace of growth. Only two years after the British introduced universal compulsory primary education, Japan followed suit. By 1904 98 percent of the relevant age group were in school. By the 1920s most farmers, for example, were literate. In higher education growth was equally impressive. In 1918 there were five universities and 104 high schools and colleges; by 1945 there were 48 and 342 respectively. Especial encouragement was

Life in Interwar Tokyo

City life in Japan had deep roots. In the early 19th century Tokyo (then called Edo) already had a million inhabitants and was probably the largest city in the world. With the great economic expansion of the 20th century cities grew quickly. By 1930 Tokyo contained almost 6 million people.

On the surface at least, city life for the majority was traditional. In new districts of Tokyo old class divisions were perpetuated on the ground – between samurai, merchants and artisans. Samurai areas, for example, were situated in the best locations, on high ground. Most people were packed in a dense mass of tiny crowded streets and higgledy-piggledy two-storey dwellings. Their traditional thin walls gave no privacy – even less during the day when they were removed. Families lived in one room. Washing was hung on bamboo poles pushed out from the first storey.

Most streets and lanes were unpaved and were muddy in winter and dusty in summer. Opening on to the narrow lanes were masses of shops, tiny restaurants and workshops for tailors, clogmakers and carpenters. In the lanes themselves stood tea, noodle and soup stalls. Street life was in continual movement, with itinerant craftsmen, story-tellers and hawkers of beancurd; with salesmen and junk-collectors; with children running free or at play, with girls carrying their infant siblings on their backs.

By the 1930s the urban birth rate was falling, but the majority in Tokyo were young and drawn from the lower classes. They were garrulous, warm-hearted and open and still embedded in traditional culture with its kabuki theater, suomo wrestling, geisha houses and traditional sentimental music.

By the 1930s there were increasing numbers of white-collar workers – managers, shop assistants, clerks. They wore western suits and aspired to escape from the old crowded cities. The great earthquake of 1923 encouraged dispersion of the population to new suburbs, with consequent commuting to work. The better-off were more westernized and formal in behavior. They favored orchestral music, modern drama, foreign films and ballroom dancing. For some of the intelligentsia the spread of new values was difficult to reconcile with Japanese traditions. Yet secular values had not eroded traditional beliefs in Japan as they had in Europe during early industrialization.

▲ **A Tokyo alley. Notice how narrow the lane is with dwellings virtually looking into each other. Most houses were made of bamboo or wattle – airy in summer but bitterly cold in winter. There was no heating. Most families depended on communal bathrooms and latrines. Most people, and virtually all women, wore traditional dress – like the woman in the picture with a baby tied to her back.**

given to military engineering, leading to the development of important Japanese prototypes.

In the 1930s Japan shared in the universal slump in agriculture which produced a rapid spread of rural indebtedness, but simultaneously, the value of industrial output soared and the dual structure of industry was even further exaggerated. Small enterprises took the full strain of the slump, while the large continued to make rapid growth. By 1932 the smallest companies paid wages which were only 26 percent of those paid by the largest firms and offered nothing like the large firms' stability of employment, health services, sports, educational and cultural activities. A male worker in a large company expected all his lifetime needs to be met by the firm; in return, he would expect to make whatever sacrifices were required to ensure the prosperity of the company. Sacrifices there were, and not merely in freedom of thought and action. Up to 1936 real wages fell almost continually. In textiles, an extreme case with a high proportion of women workers, the nominal average wage rate declined by 60 percent. Furthermore, as war production expanded and the armed forces vastly increased their recruitment, there were severe labor shortages. They were never allowed to be expressed in wage pressure; at most, during World War II, smaller firms moved to offering lifetime employment. Military discipline, expressed through wage and price controls as well as forced labor, now governed the civilian labor force.

From the late 1920s rightwing political views became increasingly important in shaping Japanese opinion, particularly in the armed forces. These views emphasized equality and anticapitalism: all should be equal under the emperor; the wealth of the zaibatsus was responsible for the impoverishment of the peasantry. They affirmed that military discipline ought to be the norm in society, not working for profit or pay. And finally, that Japan's cause was anti-imperialist – there could be no peace until the Anglo-American domination of the world had been overthrown and space made for the newcomers, Germany, Italy and Japan.

Japan was thus fully prepared when World War finally arrived, but to no avail, for in the end, despite the prodigious results of an extraordinary social discipline, the sheer economic weight of the giant American economy overwhelmed the country. The final spectacular triumph of feudal Japan was thus the prelude to catastrophe and the demise of feudalism.

The Depression and rural social change

As in Europe and America, rapidly and drastically falling agricultural prices had profound effects in Asia, where commercial cash cropping had grown in importance in the 19th century and had been booming in the 1920s. The slump brought a new kind of crisis to peasant cultivators who had been drawn into a greater dependence upon money and who, with the fall in prices for the commodities they produced, were left unable to pay for the essentials they needed. At the same time supplies of credit dried up, and the richer peasants, landlords and money lenders were also

hard hit. A South Indian proverb runs, "After ruin go to the city" – this was the fate of many members of the village elites in the 1930s. In Southeast Asia the Depression delivered the coup de grace to an agrarian social order already weakened by the effects of commercialization and colonial rule. As the fall in prices drove many households into deficit, the fall in exports led to a severe loss of government revenues from customs dues. To compensate for this the French in French Indochina and the British in Burma sought to increase head taxes, provoking peasant resistance in the Saya San rebellion in Lower Burma in 1930–31 and the brief establishment of peasant soviets under the influence of the fledgling communist party in northern Annam. The legitimacy of the colonial state and of the power of the rural notables of the old order were shattered as such guarantees of livelihoods as had existed in village economies were no longer honored.

It was also instability in relative prices rather than a fall in production which lay behind the terrible Bengal famine in 1943. In the circumstances of wartime inflation and the policy of restricting the movement of foodgrains imposed by the colonial government, fears about a shortfall in the rice harvest in Bengal provoked hoarding and a price spiral so that rice prices far outstripped the wages of agricultural laborers and rural artisans. They made up the majority of the three million or more victims of the famine. Famine resulted not so much from absolute decline in the availability of food as from price changes which eroded the spending power of those depending on wages.

▲ Women did much of the hard work in Japan's fields, particularly planting the rice seedlings in standing water. Conditions for peasant families were very harsh, and for women, even worse.

▼ Physical education at a Tokyo school. Strict regimentation in school and at work created a powerful collective discipline and spirit of sacrifice that stood Japan well in war. The country had a high level of education, practical rather than religious; it was intensely patriotic.

The rising tide of nationalism

In the colonial and noncolonial developing countries the Great Depression demolished the economic promise of empire and the two World Wars demolished the twin assumptions of the moral superiority and military invulnerability of the imperial powers. In the colonized countries, national movements were either created or grew into an increasingly significant force. In India the Congress mainstream, however, remained a loose coalition of interests that could not, until quite late in the day, confront social questions lest it undermine the coalition. Mass radicalization finally forced Congress to greater militancy to retain its position of leadership. It also forced the adoption of a social program to relate the national question to mass interests. Tenant farmers, sharecroppers and the landless were now offered agrarian reform, rent reductions, security of tenure and the abolition of zamindaris (a peculiar Indian form of landlordism, originating in tax farming). For the prosperous Muslim landlords, faced with the appalling prospect that the British could no longer be relied upon to protect them either at home or abroad, Congress's attack on landlordism, modest though it was, was frightening, and now the Muslim League at long last had an opportunity to recreate itself as an effective organization.

Latin American history in the independent period had always been dominated by caudillos (military dictators), based upon landed oligarchies, foreign investors and the use of military power. But by the 1930s the social structures of the more advanced countries had changed, providing the social basis for dictatorships based upon the new urban working classes, sometimes on the peasantry and or the army. The caudillos were now committed against both the landed oligarchies and foreign interests.

In Brazil a military coup brought to power a former governor of a southern state, Getulio Vargas, who established a popular dictatorship that lasted some 15 years. He strongly promoted industrialization (transport, paper, chemicals, steel), public works and some measure of popular welfare (an advanced labor code, educational and medical programs). In Mexico, Lázaro Cárdenas became president in 1936 and created a new political order, based upon organized workers, peasants and other groups. He nationalized the mainly foreign-owned railways in 1937, expelled foreigners and seized their assets and redistributed twice as much land as all the preceding administrations to some three-quarters of a million families. Finally, in Argentina the effects of slump had been a relatively rapid rate of industrialization; by 1943 more Argentinians worked in urban industry than in agriculture and herding. An army colonel, Juan Perón, with the strong support of the powerful trade union federation, built himself an immense base of popular support among the urban working class which not only frustrated an attempt by the army to arrest him in 1945, but also swept him to overwhelming power in 1946.

Jiang Jieshi would have liked to emulate the Latin Americans in China. But his rule depended

Life in Bombay Working-class Districts

There were more than 150,000 people employed in Bombay's cotton mills by the early 1920s. Most of them (more than 80 percent) had been born in distant villages, and would have been recruited as millhands by intermediaries known as "jobbers", men whose leadership and control of labor within the mills depended on the patronage they extended outside them.

Most workers lived within 15 minutes walking distance of their mills in three wards to the north of the old "native town" of Bombay. This working-class district, known to its inhabitants as *Girangaon* – "the mill village" – was dominated by ramshackle, jerry-built *chawls*, or blocks of small tenements with shared lavatories and washing places. Here perhaps as many as one-third of the residents lived in single rooms occupied also by six or more others. There were also boarding houses for single men (called *khanavalis*), which were sometimes organized by jobbers.

▼ Colonial rule and commercial development brought about the rapid growth of some Indian cities. Urbanization was a force for social change, though it could also reinforce caste identity, because these ties gave newcomers some security in the new environment of the town. Immigrants often retained links with their villages, sending back remittances from their earnings.

► Social patterns and beliefs were transplanted to the city. Astrologers (like these) remained important in the lives of Bombay's millhands, for it was still important to find the auspicious times for major events in the family and the life cycle of individuals.

►▼ The textile industry employed large numbers in the production and processing of cotton as well as in its manufacture, though usually in less well paid and secure jobs. Between the wars big cotton growers in other parts of India set up new mills.

earnings back to their villages. At the same time a mill manager said that "The millowners generally depend to break a strike upon workers who had lost connections with the land, as these people have no home to return to and hence are the worst sufferers at such times". Far from showing themselves less "committed" to factory work and quick to desert it, as observers supposed, workers who could fall back upon their villages were often the most resilient in maintaining industrial action – as they still were during the very long mill strike in Bombay in the 1980s.

The streets of Girangaon were the center of the leisure and the politics of the working class. The great majority of workers, asked in a contemporary survey to give "an account of their leisure activities... would not be specific and said they pass time roaming, which they consider a mode of relaxation". The street corners offered a meeting place, and liquor shops drew their customers, and gymnasiums their members, from particular neighborhoods, each of them with its own *dada* or local boss. Gymnasiums were an important focus of working-class culture. Leadership of a gymnasium was sometimes the basis of a *dada*'s eminence. Young men who became skilled at fighting through training at gymnasiums frequently provided a basis for community action. Neighborhood connections indeed greatly influenced the possibilities of industrial collective action, partly because workers' ability to stay out on strike depended upon the material resources of the neighborhood, and especially on their ability to command credit with shopkeepers and others. Public morality in particular urban neighborhoods could easily be mobilized against strike-breakers; and the balance of power on the streets – between different *dadas* – closely determined the possibilities for and outcomes of strikes. As unions organized they frequently dealt with *dadas* in order either to contain their hostility or

to negotiate their support. Workers were, generally, more effective politically outside the gates of the mills.

The growth of Bombay's industries has continued to draw in labor from villages outside the city and from farther afield. The social differentiation of the villages has tended to be reproduced in the city. Workers in more secure and better paid jobs are more likely to come from landowning families than those who are daily paid, casual wage laborers. The latter are recruited especially from "lower caste", landless groups. The employment in Bombay of large numbers from other parts of India, and increasing competition for jobs have given rise to a political party, the *Shiv Sena*, which aggressively promotes the interests of local "sons of the soil".

FERIENFAHRTEN RUND UM AFRIKA
DEUTSCHE AFRIKA-LINIEN

upon his army and his warlord allies, not a popular mass base. He nearly succeeded in liquidating the tiny forces of the communist party, but the fragment which survived the rigors of the Long March of 1934–35 to reach the remote base of Yunan was able to exploit the opportunity of the Japanese invasion to fuse the social issue with the national question, backed by independent military power. The communists came to inherit the mantle of Chinese nationalism.

Africa, by comparison with these turbulent events, remained relatively at peace, although strikes were now part of the force of opposition. For the white farmers who survived the slump, there was a short "Indian summer" of being idle rich, circulating between club, pools, dance rooms, races, polo and bridge.

Outside the charmed circle, tax systems continued to drive Africans off the land in search of work and into segregated colonies, rife with overcrowding, insanitary conditions and venereal disease, and where half the babies died below the age of one. There were protests, strikes, and even riots, but in nationalist terms they were more promises for the future than challenges in the present. In South Africa industrialization was already creating the need for a settled and more skilled black labor force, and for a time apartheid looked as though it might be reversed. But the postwar victory of the National Party (1948) ended that prospect.

Women in Africa, Asia and Latin America
The incorporation of Latin America, Asia and Africa into world markets, the continuing transformation of peasant economies by commercial agriculture and industrial production and the shifts in population to urban centers necessarily affected the organization and nature of the

household and relations between individuals within households. One common result was a deterioration in women's status in society.

The changes in sub-Saharan Africa were particularly significant as the acceleration toward a cash-oriented production system proceeded. In earlier periods gender relations had been based on a series of rights and obligations afforded to men and women in the context of production primarily for their own subsistence. Although there existed a wide range of property and other social relations in different African societies, it was common to find a system whereby women had customary rights to the use of specified fields, and control over the destination and distribution of their produce. These rights were complemented by obligations to work on the husband's fields, and to provide (some) staple foods for household consumption. Marriage contracts under such circumstances did not imply the subordination of women; marriage frequently implied specified individual rights and obligations, and required both husband and wife to engage in negotiated exchange of labor and produce for production, consumption and ritual purposes. In other words, far from having a "common" purse, men and women retained separate purses, and women were expected to establish and maintain granaries after marriage.

The privatization of land and the commercialization of agriculture destroyed the context of the existing sexual division of labor. Women's status declined as their access to productive resources became legally and formally mediated through the household head; their work on household land was no longer part of a reciprocal arrangement, but an obligation reflecting dependent status. Women lost control of the products they grew and processed. Cash payments for sales of crops were appropriated by men, who

◄ A German poster advertising cruises round Africa. For foreigners, Africa remained the home of the noble savage, living in innocence. Few saw ordinary African life for foreigners lived in segregated enclaves where Africans were only servants. When traces appeared of ancient civilizations – the Ghana empire, the Benin bronzes or the original Zimbabwe – whites denied that it was possible Africans could have created them and attributed them to foreign invaders.

▶ Malian women mashing millet. Africans depended overwhelmingly on cultivation for their livelihood, with staples including sago, millet, cassava and, later on, maize. The majority lived in villages, loosely associated in tribal groups and far from any cities or modern facilities. In parts of the continent, people migrated quite often between cultivating areas. Only in colonial enclaves was modern commerce and export-oriented farming developed.

▼ A village in West Africa in the late 1930s. African village life was composed of extended kinship groups, sons and their families sharing a compound with their parents, cultivating as a group. In West Africa women were important in both agriculture and trading. Elsewhere women were dependent upon men and upon their monopoly of the chief source of wealth: the ownership of cattle.

were legally responsible for the payment of taxes to the colonial authorities. While few would argue that women had equal status with men in the precolonial period, the evidence suggests that women's status deteriorated when the traditional basis of the sexual division of labor was transformed.

In Latin America, as in many parts of Asia, religion played a major role in circumscribing the role of women, and influenced the ways in which changes in the relations of production affected women's status. In Latin America it was the religion of the conquistadors (the Spanish conquerors of Latin America and their descendants) which emphasized the reproductive and domestic role of women and created an ideology which insisted that the women's production should be invisible.

During the interwar period, when large-scale urbanization began to accelerate throughout the continent, the sexual division of the urban labor force replicated that within the domestic sphere. New industries, especially chemicals and metal-based industries, solely recruited male workers who formed the basis of the organized working class. Women were confined to the traditional less skilled, lower-paid industries producing cheap consumption goods and to a variety of service

jobs – laundry, domestic servants, food preparation – which mirrored their role within the household. As the demand for clerical and administrative jobs grew within the state bureaucracy and nascent industry, it was men who were recruited as secretaries and clerks, reflecting in part the unequal access of women even to basic education.

In Asia religious tradition interacted with the changing social structure to reinforce gender codes which legitimized the subordinate social status woman.

The commercialization of agriculture and the beginnings of industrialization in many parts of Africa, Asia and Latin America thus had a profound effect on the position of women. It remains true, however, that women, particularly from the educated classes, were organizing to redress some of the more tangible inequalities, particularly in campaigning for women's suffrage, education and property rights. That these movements in Asia and Africa became interlaced with the nationalist and anti-colonial struggles does not detract from the reality that women did begin to organize against their increasing subordination, often in ways that prefigured some of the later feminist agendas in the West.

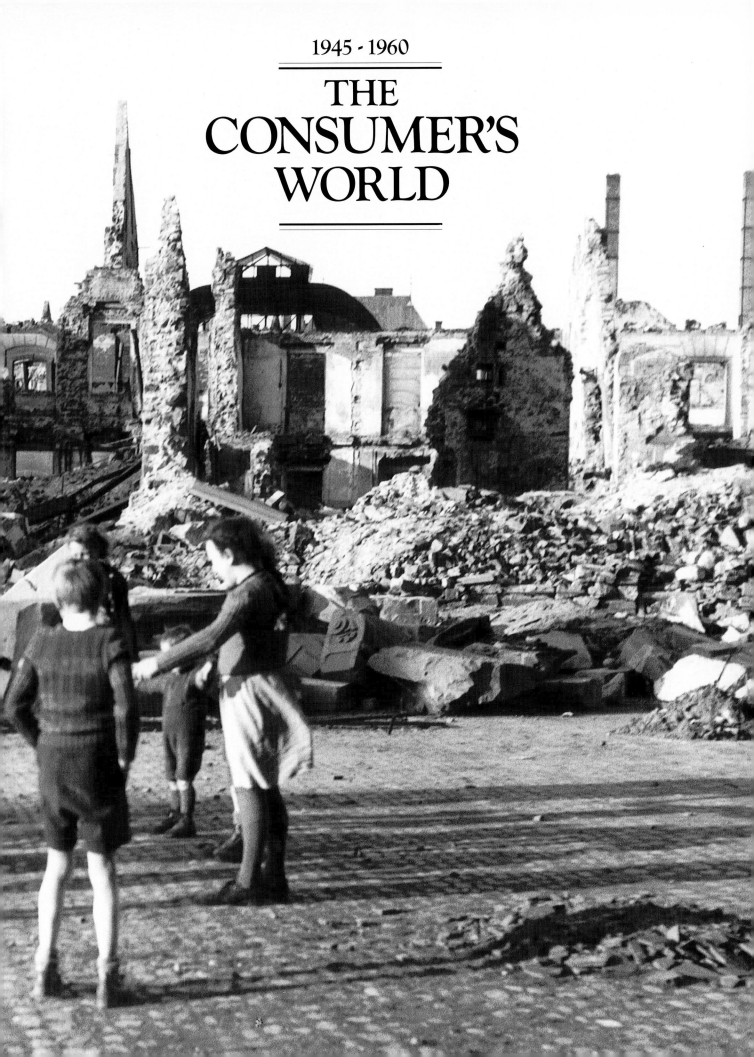

1945 - 1960

THE CONSUMER'S WORLD

Time Chart

	1946	1947	1948	1949	1950	1951	1952
Rural life	• TEEP (tetraethyl prophosphate), originally developed by the Nazis, is introduced as a pesticide by the American Cyanamid Company • Blizzards and storms destroy wheat crops throughout Europe	• May: Finland announces plans to experiment with Soviet-style collective farming • Warfarin (rat poison) is discovered by a University of Wisconsin chemist	• Jan: Agrarian reforms affecting various regions of Germany • Zoologist Fairfield Osborne expresses concern about increasing use of DDT in *Our Plundered Planet* (USA)	• US Secretary of Agriculture advances new plan to pay farmers the difference between the market and fair profit price • Latin America becomes a net importer of grain	• Beginning of agrarian reform in China • Average US farm worker produces enough food and fiber for 15.5 people	• 15 Jun: US Congress votes to loan $190 million to India to buy US grain • Two-year drought begins in Australia which kills off millions of head of livestock. Australian sheep farmers introduce the myxomatosis virus to kill off mushrooming rabbit population	• Feb: UK government offers farmers £5 per acre to plow up grasslands • Chinese grain production rises to 163 million tons, up from 110 million in 1949. Asia's rice crop falls below prewar harvests
Industry and labor	• Jan: Strikes during the month in the USA by 260,000 electrical workers, 263,000 meat packers and 750,000 steel workers • British Parliament nationalizes Bank of England (1 Mar) and coal industry (May) • Gulf and Anglo-Iranian Oil cofound Kuwait Oil Co, making Kuwait the largest oil producer in the Middle East • Air India is created in reorganization of Tata Airlines	• Jun: Shell (UK) and Gulf (USA) agree on exploiting oil fields • 23 Jun: Congress passes the anti-Union Taft Hartley Act over Truman's veto (USA) • Sep: Strike of 45,000 Yorkshire miners causes fuel shortage which closes Sheffield's steel works (UK) • UK government assumes control of the coal mines (1 Jan) and nationalizes electricity industry	• 1 Jan: British railroads nationalized • Jun: More than 10,000 doctors have joined the NHS after government assurances (UK) • Oct: Industrial production of plutonium begins in the USA	• 27 Jun–Aug: Australian coal-miners strike, but return to work after emergency legislation allows for the use of troops • 1–22 Jul: British dockworkers' strike closes ports • Volkswagen (Ger) begins commercial production • Saab-Scania AB is founded in Sweden	• 8 Feb: French National Assembly approves bill legalizing strikes and reestablishing collective bargaining • May: Schuman Plan, proposing the union of Franco-German coal, iron and steel, leading to the European Coal and Steel Community (1951) • 6 Oct: World's largest pipeline completed in Lebanon (1,068 miles) • Habloid Co produces the first Xerox copying machine (USA)	• 26 Jan: US Wage Stabilization Board freezes wages and salaries • 29 Apr: Zhou Enlai orders seizure of British Asiatic Petroleum Co assets (China) • May: Iran's new National Front government violates 1933 concession treaty with Britain by nationalizing the oil industry • First Five Year Plan begins in East Germany	• Jan: Farbwerke Bayer Leverkusen AG, BASF and Hoechst AG founded to continue the work of I.G. Farben (FRG) • Apr: US government takes control of numerous steel firms following strikes • General Dynamics Corp founded, and quickly expands in the defense industry (USA) • British Motor Corp created by a merger of Austin and Morris Motors
Government and people	• National Health Service Bill enacted by parliament making medical care free to all Britons (UK) • Indian Claims Commission created to settle lingering land disputes with the white man (USA) • Legislation closes brothels in Paris • Italian and Japanese women enfranchised	• Aug: Austerity measures imposed in Britain during financial crisis, including food rationing and a ban on foreign holidays • India outlaws "untouchability" but discrimination based upon the traditional caste system continues against harijans • Women given equal suffrage in China and Bulgaria	• Jun: Dr Daniel Malan comes to power on an apartheid platform (SA) • 25 Jun: Displaced Persons Act allows 400,000 homeless to settle in USA but according to a quota system • 30 Jul: British Citizenship Act gives Commonwealth citizens the status of British subjects	• Jun: Apartheid takes effect in South Africa; marriages banned between Europeans and Blacks/Coloreds • 15 Jul: Housing Act provides federal aid for slum clearance and low rent public housing (USA) • Equal voting rights granted to women in Costa Rica, Chile, India and Syria	• 8 Apr: India and Pakistan sign Delhi Pact creating a bill of rights for minorities • 20 Sep: McCarran Act passed by Congress, restricting suspected communists • Turkish Republic's first free elections (May) • Equal suffrage granted to women in El Salvador, Ghana, Haiti and Japan	• 23 Jan: US president Truman creates a Commission on Internal Security and Individual Rights • Apr: First health service charges imposed, leading to the resignation of Aneurin Bevan (22 Apr) (UK) • South African Dept of Interior issues cards to the population designating them by race	• 22 Apr: South African prime minister Malan makes parliament the highest court after the Supreme Court invalidates apartheid legislation • 16 May: House of Commons votes equal pay for women (UK) • 27 Jun: McCarran-Walter Immigration Act removes ban on African and Asian immigration (USA)
Religion	• Aug: Thousands die in Calcutta during Hindu-Muslim riots over British plans for partition of India • Palestine now has 650,000 Jews (including many illegal immigrants) and 1.05 million Arabs	• 29 Nov: UN votes for the partition of Palestine and the creation of a Jewish state • 400,000 Muslims and Hindus slaughtered in the aftermath of Indian partition. 8,500,000 refugees cross the Indo-Pakistani border	• 14 May: New State of Israel declared, which occupies 80% of Palestine and has an Arab population of 200,000 after 500,000 Arabs flee • 20 Sep: Israel outlaws Stern Gang terror group	• 17 Feb: Bulgarian government bill to cut church ties with foreign governments • 13 Jul: Pope threatens excommunication for any Catholic who aids communism • Preacher Billy Graham begins to gain prominence (USA)	• Dec: Dalai Lama flees from Tibet • Hungarian government begins closing university theology departments	• May: China proposes religious freedom for Tibet if it severs all ties with "pro-imperialist" nations	• 10 Sep: West Germany agrees to pay Israel compensation of £293 million for Nazi atrocities • 9 Nov: Israeli president Chaim Weizmann dies • Young Malcolm X joins US black Muslim leader Elijah Mohammed
Events and trends	• 4 Mar: France recognizes Vietnamese independence, but conflict continues with native Communists until 1954 • Nov: Foundation of UNICEF (Swi) • Worst inflation in world history in Hungary; one 1931 gold pengo now worth 130 trillion paper pengos	• Oct: General Agreement on Trade and Tariffs (GATT) is signed • US Congress authorizes the Central Intelligence Agency (CIA) (USA) • Widespread food shortages continue in the wake of World War II • Monosodium glutamate (MSG) marketed for the first time	• Foundation of the World Health Organization (WHO) in Geneva (Swi) • Original McDonald's hamburger stand becomes a self-service (USA) • US Congress decides to fund Voice of America broadcasts to foreign countries	• Establishment of the (West) German Federal Republic (23 May) and the (East) German Democratic Republic (7 Oct) • Simone de Beauvoir publishes *The Second Sex*, a seminal feminist tract (Fr) • Seven-inch "micro-groove" records become available (USA)	• Jan: Riots in Johannesburg as Blacks begin to protest against apartheid • 1 Mar: West German government ends all food rationing except sugar • US senator Joseph McCarthy begins his anti-communist witchhunt lasting four years	• 1 May: Radio Free Europe begins broadcasting from Munich to countries behind the Iron Curtain • Jul: Socialist International reconstituted at a conference in West Germany • Hydrogen bomb is developed by Edward Teller and other US scientists (USA)	• Jun: Blacks, Coloreds and Indians launch a massive campaign against the apartheid laws in South Africa • Oct: Mau Mau insurrection begins in Kenya; London declares a state of emergency • G.D. Searle Laboratories develop an oral contraceptive for women (USA)
Politics	• Aug: Civil war begins in China	• 15 Aug: India gains independence from Britain; the partition leaves India under Nehru and Pakistan under Jinnah • Jun: General Marshall proposes a European Recovery Program (Marshall Plan) (USA)	• 30 Jan: Mahatma Gandhi assassinated by Hindu extremist (Ind) • 14 May: State of Israel is proclaimed, with Dr Chaim Weizmann as president and David Ben-Gurion as prime minister	• 4 Apr: Formation of North Atlantic Treaty Organization (NATO) • 1 Oct: People's Republic of China declared	• 25 Jun: Korean War begins, as North Korean forces invade the South with Soviet backing. UN Security Council votes to intervene	• 4 Jan: South Korean capital Seoul falls to North Korean and communist Chinese forces	• 4 Nov: Dwight D. Eisenhower elected US president

1953	1954	1955	1956	1957	1958	1959	1960
● Khrushchev orders the plowing and planting of land in Kazakhstan despite poor rainfall (USSR) ● 13 states declared disaster areas as drought intensifies in US Midwest	● Large programs of hybrid grain planting ordered by Khrushchev (USSR) ● British report finds no link between pesticide use and human illness but recommends close investigation	● Mao Zedong proposes collective agriculture and the liquidation of peasant opposition (China) ● Grenada, which had supplied 40% of the world's nutmeg, loses three-quarters of its crop in a hurricane	● Agricultural Producers Cooperatives communize 100 million Chinese peasant families ● Attempts to collectivize agriculture in Poland are abandoned after 10 unsuccessful years	● Cereal grain output in China rises to 200 million tonnes; irrigation projects add a further 40 million hectares of cropland	● China's Great Leap Forward program begins with the creation of agricultural communes ● In response to an anti-trust suit, United Fruit Co creates a competitor in the banana industry (USA)	● Cuba begin agrarian reforms which include the confiscation of foreign property and the breakup of large land possessions ● China suffers disastrous crop failures	● Grain production in China falls below 1952 levels; rationing lessens the impact of the famine ● $6 billion of American grain is held in government storage facilities
● 1 Jan: China's first Five Year Plan comes into force ● Jun: East German workers stage anti-Soviet uprising; the uprising is crushed by Soviet troops ● Aug: Two million Parisians march in opposition to proposed civil service cuts (8 Aug); general strike five days later brings France to a halt	● 12 Jan: Foundation of Burma Oil after agreement between the Burmese government and three oil companies ● Jun: Rhodesia declares state of emergency as rail strike creates coal shortage ● Jul: USSR's first nuclear plant begins producing electricity at Obninsk	● 9 Feb: Compulsory military service takes effect in China ● Apr: France undertakes a ten-year plan for economic development ● 29 Sep: General strike called in Cyprus to protest against British control ● 2 Dec: Merger of the AF of L and CIO incorporates millions of workers (USA)	● 28 Jun: 100 workers killed in Poznan during riots against conditions under the Communist government (Pol) ● Production begins at the first oil well in Libya ● Getty Oil emerges from a reorganization of Getty's Pacific Company (USA) ● Britain's first commercial nuclear reactor is built at Calder Hall	● Mar: Strike movement begins in Britain and includes railroads, shipbuilding and machine industries ● 25 Jun: African National Congress calls a one-day general strike (SA) ● 22 Jul: Shell Oil and British Petroleum withdraw from Israel after Arab requests ● 4 Oct: USSR launches the Sputnik I satellite	● Jan: Nationalization of banks in the Netherlands ● 29 Jul: Creation of the National Aeronautics and Space Administration (NASA) (USA) ● Dec: UK government announces plans to close 36 pits and implement reductions in open-cast mining ● Unemployment in the USA reaches a high of 5.1 million	● Apr: Iraqi government begins nationalization of foreign oil companies ● 26 Jun: Opening of the St Lawrence Seaway (Can/USA) ● 15 Jul: Nationwide steel strike begins involving 500,000 workers (USA) ● 20 Nov: European Free Trade Association (EFTA) established by the "outer seven" (Aut, UK, Den, Por, Nor, Swi, Swe)	● Jul: Privatization of Volkswagen automobile company (FRG) ● 14 Sep: Organization of Petroleum Exporting Countries (OPEC) meets for the first time in Baghdad (Saud, Iran, Iraq, Kuw, Qat) ● 14 Oct: Nationalization of banks and industry in Cuba ● 29 US oil companies placed on trial, charged with conspiracy to fix prices
● 18 Jan: Administering the Mau Mau oath becomes an offence punishable by death in Kenya ● 24 Feb: South African prime minister Malan given emergency powers by parliament to oppose the anti-apartheid movement ● Women enfranchised in Lebanon and Mexico	● Apr–May: Thousands of Kikuyus detained as Kenyan police move against the Mau Mau ● 17 May: Brown vs Board of Education decision makes school segregation unconstitutional, ending the "separate but equal" principle (USA) ● 14 Dec: Legalization of divorce in Argentina	● 31 Jan: 60,000 blacks protest against forced eviction from an area designated white outside Johannesburg (SA) ● 7 Nov: Supreme Court makes segregation of public golf courses, parks, etc unconstitutional (USA) ● Abortion again becomes legal in the USSR but is conditional	● Jan: South African government announces its intention to remove 60,000 "coloreds" from the electoral register ● 16 Feb: British MPs vote to abolish the death penalty ● 13 Nov: Supreme Court strikes down segregation laws governing bus travel in Alabama (USA)	● Sep: Wolfenden Report suggests ending laws punishing private homosexuality (UK) ● 9 Sep: Congress passes legislation creating a Civil Rights Commission and federal safeguards covering voter rights, the first civil rights legislation since the Civil War (USA)	● Termination of China's birth control program by the Great Leap Forward ● Moroccan women gain the right to select their husbands ● Amended Food, Drug and Cosmetics Act of 1938 sets guidelines for food additives (USA)	● 1 Feb: Constitutional amendment to allow women to vote in national elections and run for office rejected by Swiss voters ● 20 May: Japanese Americans detained in concentration camps in 1942 regain citizenship (USA) ● Racial discrimination condemned by the UN General Assembly	● 21 Mar: 56 blacks killed in Sharpeville Massacre; four days later all black political organizations are outlawed (SA) ● 21 Jul: Mrs Sirimaro Bandaranaike sworn in as the first female prime minister of Ceylon
● Oct: Arrest of Cardinal Stefan Wyszynski brings protests from Polish Catholics ● 2 Nov: Pakistan decides to remain in the Commonwealth as an Islamic republic ● L Ron Hubbard begins the Church of Scientology (USA)	● 2 Jan: Television described as a threat to family life by the Pope ● Korean evangelist Sun Myung Moon creates the Unification Church	● 20 May: Argentinean government disestablishes the Roman Catholic Church	● 1 Oct: Report by Catholic Church in Britain proposes legalization of private homosexual activity involving consenting adults	● Apr: Johannesburg's Anglican bishop urges blacks to disregard a law forbidding their attendance of churches in white districts (SA) ● 11 Jul: Death of Aga Khan III, who had been the spiritual leader of the Ismailis for 73 years, succeeded by his son Aga Khan IV	● 7 Apr: Family planning receives the support of the Church of England (UK) ● Pope Pius XII dies and is replaced by John XIII	● 31 Mar: Dalai Lama flees from the puppet Chinese government in Tibet, finding refuge in India ● Dec: New republic of Cyprus elects Archbishop Makarios its new president	● Jan: Synod in Rome asks Catholics not to view TV programs not approved of by the Vatican ● 3 Mar: First Filipino, Japanese and black African Cardinals appointed by the Pope
● Britain announces intention to end all rationing next year ● L'Express begins publishing in France; Playboy magazine is first published in the USA	● US president Eisenhower outlines his "domino theory" of Communist aggression (USA) ● Cancer and cigarette smoking linked by the National Cancer Institute (USA)	● Feb: South-East Asian Treaty Organization (SEATO) has its first gathering in Bangkok ● Britain begins to fluoridate community drinking water ● "Coke" is adopted officially as a name by the Coca Cola Co (USA)	● Equal voting status for women in Vietnam, Laos, Cambodia and Pakistan ● Transatlantic cable telephone service begins ● Albert Sabin pioneers an oral vaccine for polio (USA)	● Study by University of Wisconsin shows 20% of Americans living below poverty line ● Eisenhower doctrine aids countries battling communism ● Jack Kerouac's On the Road brings the "Beat Generation" or "beatniks" to prominence (USA)	● 3 Jan: Formation of the West Indies Federation (until 1962) (Barb, Jam, Trin, Leeward Is, Windward Is) ● War against Britain begins in South Yemen (until 1967) ● Thalidomide is discovered as a cause of birth defects	● 2 Feb: Indira Gandhi (daughter of Pandit Nehru), elected leader of the ruling Congress Party (Ind) ● Jul: Communist anti-government rebellion begins in Laos ● In a decision which lasts 16 years, South Africa rejects the introduction of television	● World population surpasses three billion ● G P Searle Co introduces Envoid 10, a commercially-developed oral contraceptive (USA) ● Aluminum tins are first commercially used for food and beverages
● 5 Mar: Independence of Cambodia declared by Prince Sihanouk ● 27 Jul: Signing of an armistice at Panmunjom ends the Korean War	● 21 Jul: Geneva conference marks ceasefire in Vietnam with the division of the country at the 17th parallel ● Oct: Revolt breaks out in Algeria against French control	● 14 May: Signing of the Warsaw Pact creates a Communist military bloc in Eastern Europe	● 26 Jul: Colonel Nasser nationalizes the Suez Canal (Egy) ● Oct: National uprising in Hungary led by Imre Nagy is crushed by Soviet tanks and troops (4 Nov)	● 25 Mar: Treaty of Rome create the European Economic Community (EEC) (Bel, Fr, FRG, It, Lux, Neth)	● May–Sep: Rebellion of Algerian nationalists	● Jan: Fidel Castro declares a new Cuban republic after two years of rebellion	● Decolonization of French and Belgian colonies in Africa leads to the creation of numerous independent republics

131

Datafile

In the West economic recovery from the devastation of World War II was more rapid than contemporaries expected. Economies then began to expand at an unprecedented rate. The system of control of production and of management of consumption pioneered by Henry Ford at last reached its apogee. High productivity permitted high levels of welfare expenditure as well as giving rise to "the consumer society", first in the United States and then throughout Western Europe. Social and political stability rested on compromise between interventionist states, corporate capitalists and organized labor. The numbers of white-collar workers grew and, sharing in the general prosperity, some workers were influenced by middle-class values.

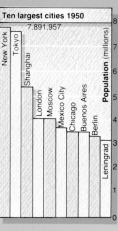

Ten largest cities 1950

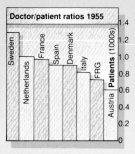

French agriculture

◀ European agriculture was transformed after 1945 as a result of government subsidies for farming and of the application of technology. The numbers of tractors in the Common Market countries (France, West Germany, Italy, Netherlands, Belgium and Luxembourg) increased seven times between 1950 and 1962; the use of fertilizers grew by more than 50 percent. By 1957 output was 35 percent higher than in 1939, and yet it was produced by a shrinking labor force. There was an exodus from the countryside.

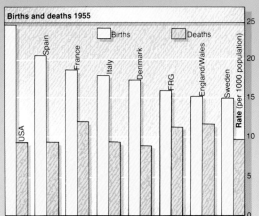

Births and deaths 1955

◀▲ Although Europe's "baby boom" was smaller than America's, the European population increased rapidly after 1945. This followed a period of stagnation before the war, and no one had anticipated the increase of 12 percent that took place between 1940 and 1955. Especially striking was the increase in France where the population had hardly grown for almost a century. The great European cities, however, were now generally surpassed in size by those of America, Japan and the "Third World" (above).

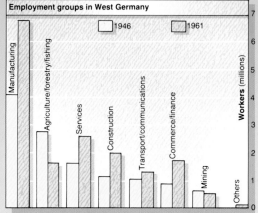

Employment groups in West Germany

▶ Affluence nurtured the notion that a college education was the birthright of all Americans. By the end of the 1960s more than 50 percent of 18–19 year olds were entering higher education, more than the economy really required. The education system had become an important means of controlling unemployment and absorbing manpower.

US degrees conferred

663,622

Doctor/patient ratios 1955

◀ Postwar improvement in public health was striking. The numbers of physicians doubled between the late 1920s and 1960, and more attention was paid than ever before to preventive medicine. Life expectancy improved; there was a dramatic decline in epidemic diseases though at the same time cancer and heart disease increased.

▲ As well as drawing in foreign workers, the rapid growth of the West German economy brought about expansion in the numbers employed in manufacturing. Even so there were still more people working in agriculture and the services combined than in industry, and manufacturing workers were never absolutely predominant.

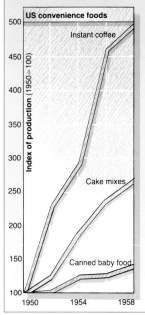

US convenience foods

◀ The accelerating development of a whole range of convenience foods marked the end of much food processing and preparation that had always taken place within the household. It also made possible greater manipulation of demand by advertising and thus opened up new opportunities for large-scale corporate enterprise.

▶ These poll data about how American adolescents spent their leisure time c. 1960 show how important television had become, molding ever changing tastes. Yet church-going remained important as the drift away from religion was reversed after 1945. Church membership was reaffirmed as part of the American way of life.

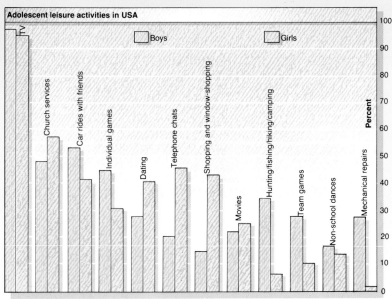

Adolescent leisure activities in USA

INDUSTRIALIZATION TRIUMPHANT

The affluent society and life-styles in the United States

Racial tensions and conflicts

The state of Europe after World War II

The changing life of the European village

Welfare states

Family policies in the 1950s

The baby boom

In World War II France and Britain both lost fewer lives than in World War I. Germany, however, lost many more (over 5 million) and throughout Europe the material destruction was incomparably greater. There was immense loss of housing and of transport infrastructure; industrial production in 1945 was perhaps a third of what it had been before the war; and the cereals harvest in continental Europe was little more than half the prewar average. There were deaths from starvation and in 1946 it was calculated that about 100 million people were being fed at 1,500 calories a day, or less (compared with estimated normal daily requirements of about 2,500). During and after the war, in Europe as a whole, some 40–50 million people were expelled from their homes and became refugees. According to the historian Walter Laqueur it was "the greatest migration Europe had known since the *Völkerwanderung* fifteen hundred years earlier".

Meanwhile, across the Atlantic, the war had brought to an end the stagnation of the 1930s. Very high levels of productivity were attained through government planning and direction. Living standards rose; life expectancy increased by three years between 1941 and 1945; and the American population entered a phase of both rapid expansion (by as much as one-third between 1940 and 1960) and relocation, as the West Coast became the center of demographic and economic growth.

To the surprise of many who were anxious for the future of Europe – even amidst their relief at the ending of the war – the western European economies demonstrated a remarkable capacity for recovery in the years after 1945. Soon they began to follow the United States toward a prosperity that had been undreamt of before 1939. In Europe, as in America, people's roles as consumers began to seem as important in determining their attitudes as their productive activities.

American society in the time of plenty

In 1950 the United States contained only 6 percent of the world's population but produced and consumed more than one-third of the world's goods and services. Despite drastic cuts in public spending after 1945 the massive wartime expansion in production was sustained, mainly because of pent-up consumer demand. Americans were encouraged to consume by manufacturers and advertising agencies, and assisted by an expansion of credit. In 1950 the Diners' Club introduced credit cards which became an essential attribute of the transnational culture of the late 20th century. The "consumer culture game" was born, of which the historian William Leuchtenberg writes "a minority of players held the bulk of the vouchers but most of the players had at least

▶ Some of the skilfully advertised convenience foods which became increasingly popular at this time established markets worldwide.

▼ The first self-service supermarket in Britain opened in 1948. It marked a revolution in retailing, which had been pioneered in the United States.

some vouchers to spend". Shopping became an avocation, spurred by the explosion of television. Regular television broadcasts had started in the USA in 1936. In 1946 there were under 17,000 sets; by 1949 a quarter of a million were being installed every month; by 1953 two-thirds of American families owned a set and American TV shows began their conquest of the world.

The pace of work seemed more easy-going as the "coffee break" became standard practice rather than an offence against industrial discipline. Production of instant coffee – archetype of the convenience foods which became characteristic of the West – increased ten-fold between 1947 and 1958. American teenagers became the pacesetters in a popular culture dependent on free spending and rapid turnover of fashions. By 1960 their expenditure was greater than the national product of smaller European states.

Consumer culture meshed with the other great influence in these years: the Cold War. Armaments expenditure fueled the 1950s boom (American gross national product increased by 51 percent in the decade) and some economists argued that the success of capitalism in averting a tendency to crisis (like that of the Depression) depended upon continuous high levels of such expenditure. Defense contracts became a major part of political patronage, and whole communities and regions came to depend upon them for their prosperity. The close connections between the industrial and military establishments, and their position as a "power elite" in American society, were recognized when President Dwight Eisenhower spoke of "the military-industrial complex".

The pattern of income distribution became increasingly diamond-shaped because of the expansion of the middle-income groups in American society, though extreme disparities continued to exist. In 1953 1.6 percent of adult Americans owned 90 percent of corporate bonds; but as late as 1968 some 30 million still subsisted below the poverty line in what one writer described as "The Other America". President Harry Truman's efforts to extend the New Deal with "Fair Deal" social reforms were constrained by Congress, and Cold War pressures limited the scope for liberal social interventionism. Eisenhower's "middle-of-the-road" conservatism did allow for extension of social security and unemployment benefits, however, for increases in the minimum wage and the creation, in 1953, of a Department of Health, Education and Welfare. These benefits and farm subsidies built a base of purchasing power, providing some of the "vouchers" of which Leuchtenberg wrote. They were not the fruit of labor activism, for though trade union membership had grown rapidly during the war, as unemployment gave way to labor shortages, and though two-thirds of manufacturing workers were union members by the late 1950s, less time was lost to strikes than to coffee breaks. Labor's stake in the weapons industry encouraged loyalty to government aims in the Cold War and protests in support of social reform were discouraged by union leaders. Labor was well organized but had been coopted.

These trends were assisted by the advent of the service economy. In 1956 the government announced that there were more white-collar (services) workers than blue-collar (manufacturing) workers. Though the ideal of individual entrepreneurship remained vital, fewer Americans were self-employed. Most had become "organization men", seeking security and finding identities in the service of large organizations. "Organization man" lived in the suburbs – as many people move to the suburbs each year as had arrived in the United States in the peak years of transatlantic immigration. The suburbanite became the representative American, valuing conformity, though he was probably still more active in the community than his counterpart in Europe. Though women, who had entered the labor force in large numbers during the war (and made up one-third of the labor force in 1943) by and large remained in employment, their purpose, research showed, was to increase family income rather than to find greater self-fulfillment. The notion of "home-making as a vocation" matched the values of "organization man".

The move to suburbia left a space in the big cities that was increasingly filled by blacks. Government action to encourage fair employment practices did nothing to ease racial tensions, which sometimes erupted in violence. Blacks had also joined the forces in large numbers, and their poor treatment and continuing segregation bred a new black militancy. After the war the consumer culture, projected into the ghetto by television, fueled black anger. By 1960 motels, lunch bars and laundromats had become battlefields of civil rights struggles. Meanwhile middle-class blacks pursued a strategy of seeking to end racial discrimination by action in the courts. One target was segregation in education. A challenge was launched against the legal support for "separate but equal" facilities (which were not equal in practice). The result was victory in the Supreme Court, when in 1954 Chief Justice Earl Warren

◀▲ During World War II more than one million blacks found jobs in the industrial cities of the north and west of the United States. Thereafter black family incomes rose sharply compared with white family incomes. Blacks' educational attainments began to catch up, too, and the proportion of blacks in professional and technical jobs rose faster than in the population as a whole. A black middle class emerged with a life-style like that of their white counterparts (as here, left, at a debs ball in New York), and its members led the struggle for civil rights. The movement developed a mass base toward 1960 as Dr Martin Luther King Jnr adopted Gandhian methods of nonviolent resistance. In February 1960 black students at Greensboro, North Carolina, began a sit-in at a lunch counter reserved hitherto for whites. This sparked a sit-in movement across the whole of the South (as above), which was ultimately successful in desegregating restaurants, hotels and public places like theaters and parks.

▼ The war brought about massive displacements of people. By 1945 there were 6 million displaced persons in Germany alone. Movements in many directions continued for several years, redrawing the ethnic map of central Europe. The social problems of absorbing refugees endured long after the war. Problems surrounding ethnic minorities also persisted.

announced that "in the field of public education the doctrine of 'separate but equal' has no place". Implementing the decision, however, proved to be more difficult, especially in the south. As attempts were made to enforce desegregation it even became necessary to use National Guard troops, as in the famous case of Little Rock, Arkansas, where troops were required to enable a handful of black pupils to attend a previously all-white school.

Reconstruction and conflict in Western Europe

By 1948 the industrial output of France and Italy had overtaken prewar levels; output in Germany did so in 1951. Yet the appearance of smooth recovery belies the bitterness of social and political conflict in the immediate postwar years. If, in general, the challenge to the established order was not as pronounced as after World War I, the reasons for this should be sought as much in the interventions of the United States as in the domestic circumstances of the European countries themselves.

The right was everywhere in disarray, tarnished by connections with fascism. The most radical challenges, however, whether for the socialization of industries, for more egalitarian distribution of incomes or, in the case of Germany, for the eradication of the remnants of Nazism, came not from the left political parties but from below. Groups of workers sought to bypass both legal channels and their own traditional organizations in hastening the process and expanding the scope of change. The parties of the left and the trade unions made a crucial contribution to the containment of this militancy, as when the postwar British Labour government used troops to break strike action. Where such moves did not suffice in continental Europe militancy was countered by direct American interventions and the regrouping of the right, around Christian Democratic parties, served the same ends.

Across Western Europe, first communists and then social democrats were soon removed from office and levels of unionization declined markedly. By 1950 the upshot was that levels of profits were comparable with those obtained before the war. The balance between the returns to capital and those to labor was extremely favorable to the employers.

The beginning of the Great Boom

During the 1950s the real gross domestic product of the UK grew at a relatively disappointing average rate of 2.4 percent, that of France at 4.5 percent, of Italy at 5.9 percent and of West Germany at a remarkable 7.4 percent. The performances of the French and Italian economies testifies to the fact that there is no necessary correlation between weak or unstable governments and weak economies. But the sluggish development of the British economy on the one hand, and the outstanding performance of the West German economy on the other demand examination for contributory social factors.

The UK's poor performance reflects not so much the economic muscle of a labor movement cutting into profits and thus reducing the potential for investment as the conservative, risk-averting culture of British entrepreneurship. British businesses preferred sharing out domestic and imperial markets among themselves to engaging in the uncertainties of competition. This in turn meant that employers failed to engage in the rationalization of their work forces which, for their European counterparts, was the prerequisite for the investment booms of the mid-1950s. Above all, the cozy overlaps of the political and the social with the industrial elite imposed

Population Movements in Europe 1939–45

Population movements
→ Refugees
→ Displaced workers

- - - International boundary, 1939
Greater Germany, 1942
Allied to or occupied by Germany, 1942

Scale 1 : 35 000 000

0   600km
0   400mi

Population Movements in Europe 1945–48

Population movements
→ Baltic peoples
→ Czechs
→ Germans
→ Poles

annexed by USSR 1945

- - - International boundary, 1948
Controlled by wartime Allies
Governed by Communist regime

Scale 1 : 35 000 000

0   600km
0   400mi

constraints on long-term prospects of growth. A powerful case has been made by the political scientist A. Gamble for linking political with economic stagnation and for protesting at the failure "to tackle the uncompetitive, status-ridden institutions of British society which assisted so much in ensuring the cohesion of the ruling class and encouraged conservative attitudes which impeded industrial rationalization".

Legend has it that for Germany 1945 was "zero year", when it began its industrial advance from scratch. An even greater legend claims that Germany experienced an economic miracle in the 1950s. In fact West Germany, whose fixed assets were actually higher in 1946 than they had been ten years earlier, in spite of the war, had clear potential for growth; growth was only held back because of US opposition. For Germany Marshall Aid was important not in itself as for the fact that it signaled an American change of direction: the United States had decided to see West Germany built up as a bulwark against Communism.

Within all the acquisitive societies in Europe created by the boom, as in America, essentially middle-class values set the tone. In seeking to share in prosperity, the working class endeavored to emulate bourgeois life-styles.

Elites, power and the state

In the UK the election of a Labour government in July 1945, with a large majority in the House of Commons, seemed to inaugurate a radical attitude to social change. Attacks were made on hereditary privilege. Thus, according to the British historian M. Beard, "it was with undisguised glee that Emanuel Shinwell, the Glaswegian Minister for Fuel and Power, ordered the continued excavation of the parkland in front of the largest country house in England...for opencast coalmining." Yet the aristocracy underwent an unmistakable revival during the 1950s. The landed interest reasserted itself forcefully in

Life in Postwar West European Villages

The European countryside underwent greater change in the 20 years after 1945 than in the whole of the preceding century. The farm population declined more sharply than before, even in the more developed countries. Parts of rural France became depopulated as people moved to towns, leaving behind farms and houses that later would sometimes be purchased by outsiders as second homes.

The history of one French village captures the movement of change throughout Europe as everywhere peasant production and ways of life declined. In Douelle-en-Quercy in central France in 1946 there were 534 people, three-quarters of them born either in the village or within 20 kilometers (12 miles) of it. Amongst them 208 were peasant farmers, operating on average no more than 5 hectares (12 acres) each. There were only two tractors, little fertilizer was used and yields of wheat averaged only 1200 kilograms per hectare (about 1100 lb per acre). There were also in the village 27 artisans, 12 shopkeepers, 19 white-collar workers and 12 people who were employed in manufacturing. On average people spent three-quarters of their incomes on food alone. Only 10 houses of the 163 in Douelle had inside toilets; only 3 had gas or electric cookers. None had washing machines; 5 had refrigerators. There were 5 cars and 2 television sets.

Thirty years later the same village had a population of 670 including many more newcomers than local people. Now only

one-third had been born in Douelle or nearby. There were still 53 farmers, now operating an average of 13 hectares (32 acres) each and owning between them 40 tractors. Thanks largely to intensive applications of fertilizers they now produced 3500 kg of wheat per hectare (about 3200 lb per acre) – almost three times as much as before.

There were still 25 artisans and 35 others employed in manufacturing, but these occupations, as well as agriculture, in Douelle and in Europe generally, had been surpassed in importance by the growth of the services sector. Now as many as 102 of those living in the village were employed in these sorts of jobs, in offices, banks and government posts. Of the 212 houses now found in Douelle-en-Quercy 150 had inside toilets; 197 had gas or electric cookers; 210 had refrigerators; 180 had washing machines. There were as many as 280 cars and 200 television sets. The village had been absorbed into the nation.

The writer John Berger describes the changing way of life in rural France in this way: "Ever since I could remember, everyone had always known who I was. They called me Odile or Blanc's daughter or Achille's last. A single answer to a single question was enough to place me. In Cluses [the town] I was a stranger to everyone. My name was Blanc, which began with a B and so I was near the top of the alphabetical list..." The whole person seemed to have been changed into a name on a list.

▲ The very neatness of this German village of the 1950s (as well as the automobiles in the street) suggests the passing of the old peasant way of life, and the steady replacement of agricultural workers by those employed in towns but who choose to live "in the country". Yet, in spite of the hard work it involves, small-scale agricultural production has survived in Europe, partly because of the political pressures exerted by farmers' organizations on the government of Europe under the Economic Community, which has subsidized small farmers.

the leadership of the Conservative party, while, simultaneously, the party retained the closest of links with commerce and industry.

Nowhere else in Europe was there so cohesive an establishment. In Italy *disunity* expressed itself politically – as it had done ever since the unification of the nation in the 19th century, which had divided the ruling classes. Christian Democrats were the main party, but could only govern in coalition with three small middle-class parties. They exacted a heavy price for their support. Their intransigence lay at the root of most of the political crises of the 1950s. In the Federal Republic of Germany (FRG) the sociologist and political analyst Ralph Dahrendorf distinguished a "multiple elite" within which there was surprisingly little overlap of personnel between business circles and parliamentarians. Despite the prosecution of some prominent Nazis, and as a direct consequence of the western Allies' decision to rebuild the FRG as a bulwark against communism, this multiple elite showed a marked continuity with that of the Third Reich in the judiciary, administration and the professions.

While the ruling classes of western Europe clearly succeeded in reasserting themselves after the challenges of 1945-48, they did so by making two kinds of adjustment. First, the establishment and growing supremacy of Christian Democracy marked the sacrifice of extreme and especially nationalist positions on the right. Both the Italian constitution and the Basic Law of the FRG explicitly banned fascist organizations. Secondly, significant sections of the moderate working class were given a role in business organization and a commensurate share in the fruits of capitalism – in West Germany through "codetermination", often seen as a model of successful corporatism.

The Welfare state

The years of growth in the 1950s coincided with a massive expansion of welfare provision, which helped ensure that prosperity was widely if unevenly shared. Although the right enjoyed an era of ascendancy throughout western Europe in the course of the decade, the principles of social justice and the development of the welfare state survived the change in the political climate. Welfarism, indeed, had not been an invention of the 1940s, nor had its terrain been exclusive to the left. Welfare policies thus developed along lines which had already been indicated before the war. In the UK the new scale of welfare provision (at first matched for comprehensiveness only in Sweden) had its roots in prewar and wartime arrangements. The exceptional circumstances of war had required state intervention in industry and social provision. It proved possible to perpetuate these into peacetime. The Beveridge Report of 1942 had formulated a scheme for comprehensive social security, "from cradle to grave" and family allowances were introduced during the war (1944). After the war the prewar unemployment scheme was consolidated in the National Insurance Act (1946) and a National Health Service was created (1948), which established the right to free treatment irrespective of means. In France, where social provision was also increased,

the social wage contributed one-fourth of the income of working-class households by 1958.

In West Germany the claims made on behalf of the "social market economy" by its Christian Democrat (CDU) protagonists belied a rather mundane reality. According to the *Düsseldorf Principles* published by the CDU in 1949, the motor of the German economy *and* social responsibility rested with the small business man. But the ideology of the "social market economy", for all its appeal, was never given legislative substance. Nor could small-scale business be the motor of the postwar economy. The need to compete in world markets combined with economies of scale and the importance of big enterprises (as employers or as exporters) made "the nurturing of large companies by the state a necessity rather than a crime" (J. Leaman). Increasingly, the

Only **Sunbeam**
TOASTS WITH
RADIANT CONTROL
. . . that gives you the same *UNIFORM* TOAST
whether bread is frozen or fresh, rye or white, thick or thin

Automatic Beyond Belief!

◄▲ **Expenditure on household appliances like this toaster (above), as well as washing machines and refrigerators, rose faster than any other items in domestic budgets. The socialization of care advanced, too, and here in Britain (left) a home-help looks after the children of an invalid mother.**

▼ **In Britain the aristocracy continued to thrive. This young woman, about to be presented at the royal court, belonged to a very exclusive elite.**

► The new domestic scene reflected in the cover of an American magazine, 1955. Arguably the most important change in women's circumstances in the postwar middle classes was the collapse of domestic service and connected with this, the rapid mechanization of housework. The major novelty of the 1950s was that it became acceptable for middle-class women to do the housework themselves. The mystery of the new machines did not for long, however, stave off the discontent many women felt with their assumed domestic destiny.

▲ A fairly general prejudice against the secretary of the 1950s was her disinterest in her work and her frivolous preoccupation with cosmetics. This pink typewriter from an American advertisement appealed to this stereotype – designed to bring a little color into an otherwise mundane reality of routine, tedium and unpaid overtime.

◄ After 1945 women were not expected to play an active role in public life. Real wages for women, as the £2 per week paid to this woman miner in Wigan, England, reflected employers' and trade unionists' reluctance to consider women's earning potential on an equal basis with that of men. It was not until women again became politically more active, especially in the trade unions, that greater attention was paid to equal pay issues. in 1957 the treaty of Rome provided a framework for equal pay rights and obligations which became binding for EEC member states.

proponents of the "social market" laid stress instead on the "social guarantees" provided by the State as the definitive element within their scheme. In spite of its purported uniqueness, the social component of CDU practice did not diverge significantly from the welfarism of other European countries.

For the bulk of the working class throughout western Europe, but also for substantial sections of the middle classes, welfarism brought real material gains. A rising standard of living was, from the point of view of capital, affordable under the prevailing conditions of growth. Social security and unemployment benefits certainly did not encourage work evasion. But they did give workers enhanced power in relation to individual employers and thus encouraged the mobility of labor. Poverty was by no means eradicated, nor was an era of perfect social harmony ushered in. In every wage settlement, the costs of the welfare state could provide a bone of contention: should the social wages, as employers argued, provide grounds for pay awards?

The net impact of welfarism in Europe was not so much the redistribution of resources between classes as redistribution within the working class which, taken as a whole, largely paid for the services and benefits it enjoyed through taxation. As the political scientist Ralph Miliband has suggested, this "does not make social and collective services any less valuable: but it does put in a different perspective the constant conservative laments that the welfare state is one vast gift which the 'middle class' makes to the working class."

A woman's "right to choose"

In France women finally achieved constitutional equality in 1946. Such "social promotion" of a fairer and more equal society was largely carried by the revolutionary spirit of the wartime Resistance. But practical considerations were mixed up with "revolutionary dreams" to establish true democracy. The need for the whole war experience of destruction to yield benefits for future society was put across by the *Défense de France* as "[the obligation] of every man and every woman...to transmit life". Thus it was possible for "the law [to] guarantee to women equal rights to those of men in every domain" while also protecting all mothers and all children "...guarantee[ing] the woman the exercise of her functions as citizen and worker in conditions which permit her to fulfil her role as mother and her social function".

This official reconciliation of equality of the sexes with specifically feminine characteristics was not peculiar to France alone. In West Germany women's legal equality, and equality "without ifs and buts" (in the words of the socialist leader Elisabeth Selbert) was included into the Basic Law of 1949 as "a fundamental principle of modern Democracy" (and as an antithesis to Nazi practice), yet with the understanding that women's social function as mothers needed recognition all the same. While Selbert claimed that motherhood should not stand in the way of women's equality and should not affect women's claim for equal pay, she also conceded

that women's equality built on a concept of equal worth, and not on men and women being the same. Thus after the war women in France and West Germany again began their long trek toward full equality via the road of sex differentiation.

In other countries the quite general lack of political importance attributed to the equality of the sexes during the war and after similarly precluded any radical change in the position of women. This was partly because of the erroneous assumption in the 1940s that where women's rights had been achieved it was up to individual women to break through the gender barriers and to grab what was on offer. Thus the noble aspirations for the sacrifices of World War II to result in a better world excluded equality issues. In the UK a comprehensive social policy which would make "want...unnecessary" (as envisaged by the Beveridge Report) did not propose positive measures that might include women in a "new world where everyone could develop to the full without constraint", except of course as mothers and wives. Within a framework of consensus politics and a collectivist approach to social policy, the "woman question" came under the category of "family policy". Women's pay was discussed in terms of secondary income, their work as short-term employment, and their status as that of a dependent on the "main wageearner". Women scored one success however: family allowances (introduced in 1944) were paid directly to mothers for fear that husbands might waste the money. In the UK commitment to the family and to protective measures for women was reinforced in the expansion of social welfare, which included assistance with expenditures arising from birth, marriage, illness or death.

The discussions about sexual equality together with the gender dimension in the development of social policy for the family after 1945 brought to the forefront the basic contradictions and potential tensions between the guarantees of individual equality for women on the one hand and, on the other, a very different set of assumptions which reconfirmed the family as society's fundamental social unit and women's reproductive role as an essential social function. These tensions had been ever present since the later 19th century. They had become more acute after World War I when one set of policies promoted the principle of women's equality while others, seeking to preserve "traditional" family life and restrict women from competition with men, tended to undermine it. From the Depression in the 1930s onward, but especially with the consolidation of the Welfare state after 1945, women in all modern capitalist nations experienced the "cumulative effect of a vast battery of laws and policies [which] directly and indirectly...reinforced women's dependence upon men and their responsibility for home-making and child-rearing" (V. Randall).

The baby boom

Greatly helped along by the psychological impact of World War II and the desire to reconstruct what was destroyed and feared lost, capitalist society entered, in the 1950s, its most family-oriented period of the century. It was the period of the famous "baby boom"; marriage rates shot up and people tended to have more children, almost as if to make up for lost time. This process of "re-privatization" (to use the term applied by the French historian Henri Lefèbvre) or retreat into the private or family life began in Germany somewhat earlier. Both men and women grabbed the opportunity to opt out of social and political life and to reclaim their private sphere which in the 1930s progressively got lost under Hitler's terror regime. As elsewhere, and perhaps to a greater degree in Germany, women were claimed as the supportive wives to war-beaten and disillusioned husbands and as caring mothers to children damaged by fascism or the terror of war. As one politician put it, women were needed to heal wounds, to stand in queues to claim rations, or to search out food to keep families alive. And above all they were needed to make good the loss of life through war.

France's population increased by 3 million between 1945 and 1954. In America the increase was even greater (and it was greater still in Japan). Ninety-six percent of people in childbearing years got married, and they married younger than ever before. The US pediatrician Dr Spock produced a new edition of his book on *Baby and Child Care*. Attitudes toward feeding, toilet training, and general child management, the author felt, had changed to such an extent that it had become necessary to warn parents against "permissiveness" in their attitudes toward their children. Everywhere perfect family life was extolled by the media and politicians.

Women themselves built on their role in the family, "dignified" it and secured the support of the state for it according to ideas which later came

to be dubbed by its critics as the "feminine mystique". Women's social role as the "hostess" to the successful husband (the organization man in America) was reborn. In fashion neo-Victorian ideas about a more delicate womanhood made an impact. During the war many women had dressed as if to suggest they were competent "comrades in arms". In 1947 the "dashing" wartime uniforms were replaced by new curvaceous lines (with a conspicuous consumption of materials) from Paris. From America came the "New Look" – corsettes, panty-girdles, gloves and accessories, longer skirts and new cosmetics to fight body odors. The new fashions all suggested disciplinary corrections for body and soul – as an antidote to the spirit of sexual liberation which women had begun to experience before and again during the war.

But women had increasingly higher expectations of married life, of achieving a partnership that came somewhat closer the that ideal of romantic love which American society in particular liked to project. By the end of the 1950s and early 1960s the marriage rate began to fall

▲ The new affluence and leisure of the 1950s also ushered in a new era of contests and competitions for a spot in the limelight of fame. Young girls would dream of becoming filmstars and new child protégés appeared in show business. Here proud mothers parade their babies during a baby contest in the United States. The famous baby boom of the 1950s also opened up a whole new world of design and mass-produced fashion for children – accommodating the most doting of parents. The longing for a certain glamor after the war thus found its way also into the nursery.

again and the divorce rate, which had shot up briefly right after the war and then leveled out, now accelerated its historical upward trend. Now it was claimed that women's work diverted girls from marriage, and that financially independent and "liberated" women were more likely to seek divorce. Against such a setting the expansion of women's employment did not lead automatically to an increase in social and political status, even if it managed to change women's own self-perception of their abilities, raising their expectations especially with regard to their relationships with men. Although more women had been drawn into the labor force during the war, often doing men's jobs, the patriotic label attached to their activities had tended to obscure the fact that they frequently did inferior work and were underpaid. After the war trade unions in the United States and elsewhere successfully conspired with management to oppose the principle of equal pay.

Thus the major stumbling blocks for women were old values and attitudes which remained largely unchanged, and the structural determinants of women's role and status (equal pay, equal promotional opportunities, career structures) lagged far behind formal equality.

Above all the housewife – the wife and mother – should be acknowledged as a full and responsible member of the community.... Her home is her factory, her husband and children a worthwhile job.... Let women make the most of their hard won freedom, not to build an independent women's world, not to escape from their family responsibilities, but to aim at building a family in which men and women act together for the sake of the children... a world built... on partnership.

CURRENT AFFAIRS
PAMPHLET, 1946

◄ Different ways of life, hopes and fears or parental values did not yet produce a more uniform model of parent–child relationships after World War II. In general, middle-class parents seemed to regard child-rearing as more problematic and were therefore more supportive of their children as this illustration suggests. Greater concern for security and respectability among working-class parents put greater emphasis on order and obedience and less on achievement or the personal advancement of their children.

► By the early 1960s the general conservatism and sexual repression of the previous decades began to show signs of relaxation. The advent of rock'n'roll music in the United States was one factor that helped trigger this shift. Black rhythm and the blues added depth and a more general appeal to the new music and dance for young people in Europe. Performing and listening to music were part and parcel of the "youth revolt". It was music that provided the stimulus for the development of an international youth culture, which gave rise to political protest.

Right now the basic insecurity the workers feel is this: they are haunted by the specter of the van driving up to the door to take away the TV set.

BESSIE BRADDOCK
BRITISH LABOUR
POLITICIAN

FESTIVALS AND CELEBRATIONS

Festivals show communities in celebration – they are times when the normal patterns of work and living are suspended so that peoples can come together usually in joy, sometimes in sadness, to commemorate past events or celebrate new ones.

Many festivals have their origins in the changing seasons – they welcome the coming of the rains, the safe gathering in of the harvest or the arrival of a New Year. The Chinese New Year, for instance, is celebrated by colorful processions in which evil spirits are driven off with light and the noise of firecrackers.

Religion plays a central part in many festivals, with the period of a festival seen as sacred and apart from ordinary time. The major world religions not only bring sacred meaning to the changing seasons – harvest festivals often take place in churches, for instance – they have their own commemorations. Christians mark the birth of Christ at Christmas and his resurrection at Easter. Jews commemorate the Exodus from Egypt in the Passover Feast each spring.

These may all be annual events but special rituals ("rites of passage" from one state to another) and celebrations also mark important moments in the life of an individual. Marriage celebrations not only commemorate a milestone in life they also anticipate the possibility of new life. At death funeral rites allow private grief to be merged into a public ritual.

In the 20th century new festivals have emerged to dignify important or traumatic events. Independence day celebrations affirm the birth and survival of new states. In Israel Holocaust Day commemorates those Jews exterminated in central Europe by the Nazis, and other Western nations have their own remembrance days for war dead. Old festivals have acquired new meaning or rituals as times have changed leading to complaints that increasing materialism in the Western world has overshadowed the traditional meaning of festivals such as Christmas.

The special time of a festival is usually marked with unchanging rituals which bring a shared sense of belonging to the community. Sometimes these rituals are extremely formal and solemn as in Remembrance Days with marching troops and moments of silence. At the other extreme festivals seem designed to allow a community to lose its inhibitions.

Festivals allow communities whether religious or ethnic to reaffirm their identity. For this reason festivals become particularly important for those in minority communities who wish to preserve their cultures.

▲▶ **Festivals can be spontaneous celebrations such as joy at the end of World War II (top) or dignified by careful rituals unchanging from year to year. The Passover Feast symbolizes the story of the Exodus of the Jews from Egypt, each food having its own significance.**

▶ **In the Western world Christmas has become the biggest religious and commercial festival of the year. A bewildering range of rituals have evolved in each national culture to celebrate the event. Here German crowds shop for gifts next to a traditional Christmas tree.**

▲ The Chinese New Year, at the end of January, is one of the world's most colorful New Year ceremonies. This celebration is in Rangoon, the capital of Burma, where the Chinese community has lost its commercial supremacy but has strongly retained its cultural beliefs, partly through such events.

◄ Halloween, celebrated by tradition on 31 October, originated in Celtic Britain and Ireland. It was a day when evil spirits were supposed to roam the world and bonfires were lit to frighten them away.

▼ Carnival in Bolivia. The carnivals of Latin America are among the most flamboyant and uninhibited of any in the world. They were developed by the Catholic Church as a period of celebration before the austerities of Lent.

Datafile

During World War II political arrangements made between the Great Powers assigned countries in Eastern Europe to Soviet influence. After the war the Soviet Union, by various means, brought most of these countries under the rule of a local Communist party. (Only Finland and Austria escaped.) The rulers of the new socialist states, many of whom had spent time in the Soviet Union and had close links with the Soviet Communist party, proceeded to reorganize their societies along the lines of the Soviet model. Where possible agriculture was collectivized, business and industry were nationalized, and the party was established as the controlling institution throughout society, overcoming strong opposition in some cases.

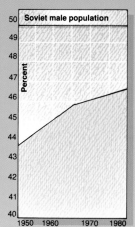

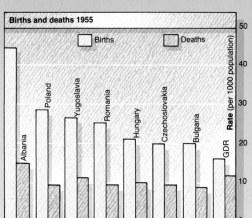

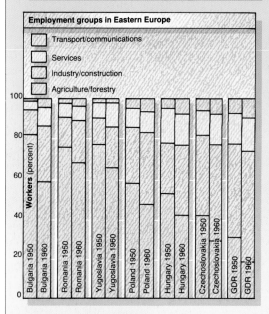

◀▲ Stalin's purges, collectivization and World War II killed 15 million more Soviet males than females. It took many years for the population to adjust (above). (One consequence was an increase in interethnic marriage.) Eastern block birth and death rates (left) reflect varying levels of development and the war. In the Soviet Union the birth rate was high, at 25.7, but the death rate freakishly low at 8.2: so many people who would have died in the 1950s had already perished.

◀ The share of the East European working population engaged in industry and construction rose by half between 1950 and 1960, under Soviet-style Five Year Plans. Big increases occurred in the least industrialized countries, Bulgaria and Yugoslavia; the smallest in East Germany and Czechoslovakia.

▼ In the 1950s the new Communist states attempted to impose collectivization of agriculture. Independent farmers were usually required to join large collective farms. In Poland and Yugoslavia, however, peasant resistance was so strong that collectivization was largely abandoned after 1953.

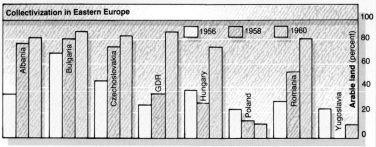

Victory in World War II gave the draconian and stultifying Soviet regime of the 1930s a new legitimacy, a broader base of popular support, new cadres and a fresh crop of heroines and heroes. It also established conditions that lasted for 40 years – until the "Gorbachev generation" arrived in 1985–87. From 1945 to 1985 the Soviet Union was administered by Communist party and state personnel (almost entirely male) who had risen in the wake of Stalin's prewar purges, but who had "won their spurs" and whose most formative experiences occurred during the War and postwar reconstruction. The memory of the war was assiduously cultivated by the regime – through hundreds of military bookshops and over 15,000 books – to maintain its legitimacy.

The triumphalism of Stalin's final years (1945–53) can easily obscure the fact that, in contrast to the burgeoning United States, the war-torn Soviet Union became a "superpower" largely by default, and that this status was vastly more burdensome for the Soviet people than for the Americans. While the US economy had expanded by 50 percent during World War II, Soviet national income in 1945 was about 20 percent below the 1940 level. The war destroyed 1,710 towns, 70,000 villages and 30 percent of capital stock. It left 25 million Soviet citizens homeless. As late as 1950, when Soviet reconstruction was pronounced complete, the United States was producing three to four times as much as the Soviet Union, on official Soviet calculations. Hence to pursue parity with US military forces, the Soviet Union had to devote a much higher proportion of its far lower per capita national income to military purposes. In other words, the burden of maintaining a huge military sector was a much heavier load for the ordinary Soviet citizen than for his or her American counterpart. The war-weary victorious Soviet people were in no mood to take on this burden. But successive postwar Soviet governments decided to impose it all the same, in their debilitating pursuit of military parity.

The human cost of World War II

The war took a terrible toll on the Soviet people. The number of "war deaths" is usually estimated at 20 million, but unofficial estimates have gradually crept up to 25–30 million – not all of whom perished at the hands of the Germans. The total includes several million who died at the hands of Stalin's mistrustful and vengeful Soviet regime. Since most of the casualties were men, enormous burdens were placed on Soviet women, both at home and at work. By 1946 there were 20 million or 52 percent more women than men in the 16–59-year-old age-group. Many of the surviving men were physical or emotional wrecks. So Soviet postwar reconstruction was

THE VICTORY OF SOCIALISM?

the heroic and stoic achievement of Soviet women, who constituted 56 percent of all workers and two-thirds of all *kolkhozniki* (members of collective farms) of working age in 1946.

Most families had suffered at least one bereavement. Many families had been forcibly parted. Many marriages were broken. Millions of children had been orphaned. Under an almost Victorian stipulation in the 1944 Family Edict, designed to protect married men and their families from the consequences of the husbands' sexual infidelities, millions of illegitimate children (mainly "war babies") were denied any right to their fathers' surnames, property or income and even to disclosure of paternal identity. In the immediate postwar years, the Soviet Union had around 11 million "fatherless" children, 4 million of whom were illegitimate offspring of fathers upon whom they could make no legal claims. There were also millions of war widows and unmarried mothers who had to bring up their children as best they could, aided only by a few generous relatives (if any) or by rather less generous state stipends. There were also numerous working wives who had to care for invalid husbands. The acute shortage of men in the postwar years also led to increased interethnic marriage and linguistic russification, which in turn made possible the ethnic russification of the next generation.

Social policies in Stalin's last years

In 1946 there began a repressive recollectivization of those areas in which collective farms had virtually disintegrated during war. In 1947–50 campaigns of "de-kulakization" (eliminating wealthier peasants) and rural collectivization (as brutal as those of 1929–35) were carried out in the newly annexed Baltic Republics (Estonia, Latvia, Lithuania), Moldavia, Western Belorussia and the Western Ukraine, which together contained over 20 million inhabitants. These annexations and the ensuing collectivization provoked violent resistance, including the emergence of armed guerrilla movements. They hid in forests and remote farms and carried out reprisals and assassinations against Soviet officials well into the 1950s.

Stalin's last years were the nadir of the collective farm system. Soviet grain output amounted to only 47.3 million tonnes in 1945 and 39.6 million tonnes in 1946 (compared with 95.5 million tonnes in 1940), causing widespread starvation. Most peasants only survived on produce from their miniscule private plots, but these too were subjected to increasing restrictions, charges, forced levies of produce and taxes. The performance of collective farms was also depressed by the destructive legacies of World War II, including heavy loss of buildings, equipment and livestock

The human cost of World War II for the Soviet Union

Renewed repression under Stalin

The "Virgin Lands" scheme

Living conditions in the late 1950s

Socialist reorganization in Eastern Europe

Life in East European cities

Workers and the workers' regimes

▼ Woman farmworker in the Ukraine. After World War II women made up nearly two-thirds of the Soviet agricultural work force.

and the sexual imbalance in their work force. Only those farms able to specialize in the more remunerative crops such as cotton, sugar and tea fared significantly better. Increasing numbers of peasants voted with their feet against the collective system by moving to the towns – 9 million in 1950–54. The urban population of the Soviet Union increased from 63 million (33 percent of the total) in 1940 to 108 million (50 percent) in 1961.

In 1946 the "People's Commissariats" became "Ministries", aptly coinciding with a transition from the roving, dynamic, trouble-shooting, mobilizing methods of management and administration of the 1930s and World War II to a more remote and sedate style of management and administration by faceless desk-bound bureaucrats who preferred the telephone to the microphone. This was the visible aging process of the Soviet regime, in which hard-line party ideologues and

internal security chiefs became more closely allied to the huge defense and heavy industry lobbies. A "military-industrial complex" emerged, comparable with that in the United States. Those involved – colloquially known as "steel-eaters" – put the interests of heavy industry and the military before those of farmers and consumers.

As the siege atmosphere of the Cold War developed from 1946 onward, prewar policies were revived. There were new purges, millions of arrests and deportations to forced-labor camps, Great Russian chauvinism and xenophobia, attacks on modernism and "cosmopolitanism" ("infection" with Western ideas), and overt anti-semitism and anti-Zionism. The latter greatly intensified when the state of Israel, established with crucial Soviet as well as US backing in 1948, provocatively allied itself to the United States and encouraged thousands of Soviet Jews to seek permission to emigrate.

World War II had, however, brought one major enduring concession. The Russian Orthodox church, which had been reduced by "militant atheist" antireligious campaigns in 1928–32 and 1936–39, achieved a remarkable resurrection. When Hitler's forces attacked in June 1941, the Russian Orthodox church (in contrast to Stalin's two-week stunned silence) immediately rallied the Russian people to the defence of the motherland. In 1943, in return, Stalin permitted a restoration of the patriarchate (kept vacant since 1925), a reopening of three theological academies, several seminaries and thousands of churches, and the dissolution of the thuggish "League of Militant Godless". A similar wartime "deal" had also been reached with the Baptists.

The "thaw" of the late 1950s

Stalin's death in 1953 was followed by a gradual "thaw". Over 5 million people were released from prisons and forced-labor camps and the armed forces were cut by 2–3 million men, incidentally boosting industrial growth rates. The harsh labor laws of 1938–41, which had criminalized unauthorized "quitting" and absence from work, were repealed in 1955–56, increasing occupational mobility. Minimum wages and pensions were raised. Top salaries were reduced. Social welfare spending was expanded. Abortion was legalized once more in 1955. Eight years' schooling became the compulsory minimum in 1958. Censorship and police surveillance were relaxed.

In 1954 Khrushchev launched the "Virgin Lands" program. It fired the imagination of the public and of the 300,000 volunteers mobilized by the Communist Youth (Komsomol) organization to bring into cultivation nearly 30 million hectares (75 million acres) of semiarid grasslands (steppes) in North Kazakhstan, West Siberia and the Volga basin. The increase almost equaled the total cultivated area of Canada and, together with Khrushchev's "new deal" for Soviet farmers (involving a more than five-fold increase in state procurement prices for grain and livestock products, reduced taxes and restrictions on private plots, and increased agricultural investment), induced a 50 percent increase in farm output and food supplies in 1953–58.

The problem of urban overcrowding was also tackled. In 1955 urban dwelling space amounted to 5.1 square meters (55 square feet) per person, still below the 5.8 square meters (62 square feet) per person available in 1928, and most urban dwellings consisted of communal flats whose shared kitchens, baths and toilets offered little or no privacy. Two-thirds of all urban families still obtained water from a communal tap or pump in 1953, and only 3 percent had access to hot water from a private tap. Hence the family laundry could take up two working days per week. However, the urban housing stock doubled under Khrushchev (1954–64). Millions of families felt the joy of moving into new system-built flats. Though they provided only half as much dwelling space per person as West European urban dwellings (on average), nevertheless each had its own toilet, bath, kitchen and privacy.

Crucially, for a decade or so, these advances somewhat revived party and public morale and public confidence in the party's capacity to deliver further advances in social welfare. This gave the Soviet regime a new wind, which helped to carry it through the 1960s.

▲ The wartime reconciliation of the Soviet state and the Orthodox church contributed to a religious revival. It was strongest in the western regions of the Soviet Union, which had experienced German military occupation. In this Ukrainian home the family is watched over by prominently displayed icons and a photograph of a son killed in the Battle of Kiev. The western regions were aptly called the Soviet "Bible belt", as 45–60 percent of inhabitants were practicing believers compared with 25 percent in the Russian Federation.

Eastern Europe: the consequences of war

World War II profoundly altered Eastern Europe and created conditions that allowed a Communist takeover. East European industrial and agricultural capacity, mineral resources and labor (including up to 6 million East European forced laborers) had been systematically plundered or harnessed to the Axis war effort. In Poland and Yugoslavia the depredations and loss of life were massive (far exceeding anything experienced in the West and comparable only with the experience of the Soviet Union) and help to explain why those countries produced Europe's greatest resistance movements. The Nazis not only exterminated three-quarters of Eastern Europe's 5 million Jews, they also saw Slavs as an inferior species, fit only to be hewers of wood and drawers of water, and treated them accordingly. Many Slavs joined resistance movements at least partly to evade arrest or seizure for forced labor. But resistance evoked barbaric German and Italian reprisals (sometimes "exemplary" massacres of whole villages), which in turn radicalized or polarized social and political attitudes, encouraging more people to join resistance organizations that were often communist-led or communist-backed. The prominent roles of communists in the resistance led many to see communists no longer as alien "antinational" subversives, but as stalwart patriots untainted by collaboration with fascism. Thus Communist parties gained the nationalist legitimacy and patriotic credentials they had lacked in the interwar years.

In Czechoslovakia after the war the Communists even emerged as easily the largest party, winning 38 percent of the votes in the freely contested elections of 1946. This enhanced standing was reinforced by the decisive Soviet role in the defeat of fascism and in the liberation of Eastern Europe in 1944–45. By contrast, except in liberal Czechoslovakia, the old establishments and many right-wing nationalists had been discredited by the

▲ "You will become a master". After the war young people were hastily trained by the older generations to replace the Soviet Union's "missing generations" (the victims of purges and the war). Formal training was usually inadequate.

Once I reproached [a collective farmer] for squandering the collective farm harvest, and I reminded him that he was a part-owner of the common property. He grinned sarcastically and sneered: "Nice lot of owners! It is all empty talk. They just call us owners to keep us quiet, but they fix everything themselves..."

SOVIET OFFICIAL, 1957

◄ A collective farm in Russia. A typical Soviet collective farm in the 1950s comprised 100–200 farmers in several villages and 1000–3000 hectares (2400–7200 acres) of land. Each farm household was permitted to work a small private plot or kitchen garden (usually under half a hectare or about an acre) on which to grow vegetables and fruit and keep a cow and a few pigs or chickens. Such private plots occupied under 1 percent of all Soviet farmland but produced one-quarter of Soviet agricultural output.

extent of their prewar and wartime flirtations and collaboration with fascism. East Europeans were thus psychologically prepared for a thorough-going postwar reconstruction in which radical peasant and worker movements would deservedly call the tune.

Within the antifascist "Popular Front" coalitions of communists, socialists, peasantists, liberals and Christian Democrats that had been formed before or during the war there was a broad consensus about Eastern Europe's postwar needs: radical land reform, expropriation of German and Italian property, expulsion of Hitler's German collaborators in Eastern Europe, public ownership of banks, the construction of large-scale "heavy" industries and public utilities, planned reconstruction and comprehensive social welfare systems. Most of Eastern Europe's major banks, industries and public utilities had already been taken into Nazi and/or state ownership by the Nazis and their collaborators. This, together with the circumstance that Eastern Europe's fascist and pro-fascist regimes had ended in collapse and disgrace, effectively cleared the decks for socialism of some sort, although it was not yet a foregone conclusion that it would take the form of Stalinist communist dictatorships. The center-left "Popular Front" coalitions which governed most

of Eastern Europe in 1945–47 simply inherited already state-owned or Nazi-owned industries, banks and public utilities. These assets were vested in the new East European states.

The peasantry and land reform

After the war the biggest challenge to the increasingly communist-dominated governments of Eastern Europe was posed by the peasantry. Peasants were still a majority of the population everywhere except in Czechoslovakia (36 percent) and East Germany (26 percent). Whereas the middle classes were deprived of property and economic opportunities and according to the historian David Mitrany were "rapidly reduced to poverty and impotence", the peasants "could neither be crushed like the middle class nor cowed and absorbed like the Socialists". As the socialists were too closely identified with Marxism and the workers effectively to resist Communist policies and methods, the Communist parties clearly saw the peasant parties as their major rivals. Therefore the Communists initially conciliated the peasant parties and "neutralized" the peasantry by backing radical peasantist land reforms in 1945–47 while behind the scenes they strengthened their grip on key state institutions (especially the security apparatus).

▲ Hungary's land reform in 1945 eliminated one of the last bastions of oppressive East European landlordism. This poster shows one Hungarian worker holding back expropriated landlords while another shows grateful peasants where to sign the title deeds for their newly received land.

Life in Postwar East European Towns and Cities

Between 1945 and 1960 many inhabitants of Eastern Europe experienced profound changes in daily life. World War II had itself left enormous devastation. In Poland and Yugoslavia the war had destroyed over one-third of the prewar housing stock and nearly half the factories. There had also been large-scale destruction of towns and cities in Hungary and in east-central Germany during the war's closing stages (most famously in Dresden, Berlin and Leipzig). In 1945 Eastern Europe's towns and cities faced a huge amount of reconstruction work to repair the ravages of war.

Problems were then compounded by the Communist regimes that came to power in the next three years. The new governments embarked on ambitious schemes for the high-speed development of heavy industry which in turn required fast expansion of towns and cities to house new workers.

Vast numbers of young male peasants moved from the countryside to the towns and cities, producing urban expansion far beyond natural rates of increase. Poland's total urban population, for example, nearly doubled from 7.5 million in 1945 to 14.4 million in 1960 (rising from 32 percent to 48 percent of the total), while Bulgaria's urban population rose from 1.9 million in 1948 to 3.0 million in 1960, or from 26 percent to 38 percent of the total. Eastern Europe's main cities showed spectacular growth. Between 1950 and 1960, for example, Bucharest grew from 886,000 to 1,226,000; Belgrade from 368,000 to 585,000; Budapest from 1,571,000 to 1,805,000; and Sofia from 435,000 to 687,000.

Eastern Europe's towns and cities became giant building sites. Economic austerity, functional "proletarian" priorities and the sheer magnitude of the housing problem resulted in a prevalence of cheap, drab, system-built blocks of flats,

which quickly became dilapidated. But those who moved to established cities at least had access to parks and other facilities: many millions of former peasants were forced to live in either muddy or dusty hut-camps near new giant industrial complexes or on the outskirts of soulless new industrial towns with few amenities and even less character. At the same time the grandiose plans for industrial development required the investment of up to one-third of national income. As a result urban consumption levels and living standards fell. Food shortages also persisted as peasants reacted negatively to rural collectivization, vilification of "rich peasants" and the imposition of unremunerative compulsory delivery quotas.

▲ Workers' housing in Leipzig, German Democratic Republic. While some East European cities (notably Warsaw, Prague and Budapest) were lovingly restored to their former beauty, in others, and more commonly, economic austerity and the magnitude of housing problems resulted in huge system-built apartment blocks.

The 1945–47 land reforms essentially completed those of 1918–23. However, they redistributed not only the still surviving large landed estates of Hungary, Poland and Eastern Germany, but also land from medium-sized farms (without compensation in the case of Romania, Yugoslavia and Albania), and they more strongly discriminated in favor of poor peasants and landless laborers. Also, while land was received as inheritable private property, it could not be sold, let or mortgaged without official permission. The transitory, tactical nature of these reforms was indicated by the lack of preparation (land registers and land surveys) and the speed with which they were carried out (within ten days in the case of Hungary

and Romania). At the same time, by their strong discrimination in favor of "poor peasants" and the most radical peasntist groups the Communists managed to foment some dissension and class conflict within the peasantist movements and reduce their influence.

Several factors thus prevented a repetition occurring in Eastern Europe of the huge human and economic costs of prewar Soviet rural collectivization. There was broader and more careful preparatory discussion and briefing on the precise forms and functions to be assumed by collectivized agriculture in each region. there was widespread use of transitional forms and differential compensation payments in recognition

▲ Unemployed workers in Budapest, 1947. After the failure of interwar governments to solve social and economic ills, millions of unemployed or insecure workers turned naturally after the war to communist movements. Marxism seemed to reject previous fascist, nationalist and religious bigotry and promised massive expansions of industry, industrial employment and upward social mobility.

▼ Polish women repairing railroad tracks. East European Communist governments proclaimed sexual equality and mobilized millions of women into the urban work force. They were heavily concentrated in construction and heavy labor.

that some peasant households were contributing much more land or capital or livestock than others. Peasants were often encouraged to join in cooperative farms by the offer of favors and privileges. Former landless laborers who had acquired land in the 1945–47 land reforms but lacked the means to farm it proved to be particularly susceptible to official blandishments. And whereas Stalin's regime in the Soviet Union had automatically branded successful farmers as "exploiters" and "class enemies" to be "liquidated" and banned from even joining collective farms, the East European dictatorships made more attempt to utilize such farmers in the formation of successful farming cooperatives, sometimes even making them farm chairmen or managers, secure in the knowledge that they would be surrounded and closely watched by their poorer brethren. Finally, Czechoslovakia and East Germany were much more industrialized than the Soviet Union and were in a position to furnish rapidly much of the equipment and fertilizer needed to make collectivized agriculture tolerably productive at home and, to some extent, in less industrialized neighboring states as well. In addition the already "tractorized" Soviet Union

exported over 100,000 tractors to Eastern Europe in 1946–62. Thus in Eastern Europe collectivized agriculture was better placed to realize its potential social and technical advantages than it had been in the Soviet Union in the 1930s.

However, fierce resistance from peasants who had recently formed part of Europe's strongest wartime resistance movements caused the early abandonment of wholesale rural collectivization in both Poland and Yugoslavia. The fact that Poland nevertheless carried out large-scale centrally planned industrialization with no more difficulty or lack of success than its collectivized neighbors further calls into question the social, economic and political "necessity" and desirability of rural collectivization.

Soviet-style communism in Eastern Europe

From 1947 to 1960 the East European states mobilized labor, capital, energy and raw materials to generate rapid industrialization. Overall rates of economic growth averaged 5 to 10 percent per annum in all countries. But there were high social costs: rapid urbanization, neglect of consumer and service sectors and housing provision, acute urban overcrowding, chronic shortages, long hours of queuing, extensive use of coercion, repression, show-trials, purges and intimidation, massive recruitment of women into low-paid occupations, and frequent errors and waste in centralized allocation of resources.

Nineteen-fifties social development in Eastern Europe also involved "totalitarianism", in the sense of total control: all-pervasive central control of all aspects of society (with the partial exception of religion), guided by a monolithic, all-embracing and ultimately stifling ideology. It provided no effective incentive or mechanism to control profligacy, costs, waste and inefficiency, no effective means of ensuring that what was produced was what users wanted, and very little public accountability for what was done.

Initial proletarian and socialist intelligentsia enthusiasm for the Stalinist economic strategy quickly wore off and turned to bitter disillusionment. Sociological studies of workers' protests and riots in East Germany, Hungary and Czechoslovakia in the summer of 1953 and in Poland and Hungary in the summer and autumn of 1956 have emphasized that the strongest protests came from precisely those elements which had originally provided the most enthusiastic support: young workers, socialist writers and intellectuals (many of whom had been imprisoned in 1949–53), peasants who had "risen" into the working classes, youth organizers, journalists and young men who had volunteered to "enlighten" the peasantry on the benefits of socialism and to instigate collectivization.

Thus the upheaval in Hungary in October and November 1956, which was crushed by Soviet military forces, was not simply an attempted "counterrevolution" instigated by Catholic, peasant and bourgeois nationalist opponents of Communist dictatorship, as Soviet interventionist propaganda maintained and as most Western observers wished to believe. It was partly a radical attempt by embittered and disillusioned

workers and socialist intelligentsia to bring about
a more authentic socialist revolution in Hungary,
with more far-reaching gains for the Hungarian
working class. The conflicting objectives and
ideologies of the rival leftwing and rightwing participants in the aborted Hungarian revolution of
October–November 1956 facilitated its suppression by the Soviet armed forces and their Hungarian collaborators, headed by Janos Kadar
(party leader from October 1956 to May 1988).
Kadar had underestimated "the bitterness and
determination with which the Hungarian
workers would turn against his regime" which
physically liquidated the workers' councils and
replaced them with "a bureaucratic hierarchy of
management installed under the intimidation of
the AVH [security police] and the... Soviet army".
According to the historian Bill Lomax, "Every independent organization of the working class had
to be smashed" and the working class bore the
brunt of the repression.

A network of workers' councils similar to that
which had been established before the rising in
Hungary arose in Poland in the wake of workers'
protests in Poznan in June 1956 (in which 113
people were killed by the Polish army and security police). Poland's workers' councils were taken
over by the regime, however, and became mere
"grievance boards", serving as barometers and
safety valves rather than as harbingers of authentic

industrial democracy and workers' control.
Workers' discontent was more muzzled than assuaged, but this did not provide a durable resolution of the recurrent conflict between the so-called
Polish United Workers' party and the workers in
whose name the party ruled.

Eastern Europe's Communist dictatorships
were less affected by counterrevoluttionary
"kulak", bourgeois, nationalist and religious discontent. This was not because such discontents
were absent, but because they lacked a strong
organized class base and because they could be
glibly dismissed as the death agonies of the
"former exploiting classes". Social unrest amongst
workers and the socialist intelligentsia, supposedly the twin pillars of the Communist dictatorships, was potentially much more damaging
and dangerous. It was nipped in the bud in
1953–58 by repression sugared with concessions
to the incipient consumerism of wage- and
salary-earners and to to the widespread desire for
social and economic security and stability. But the
price was the death of revolutionary spirit and
socialist idealism, which were superseded by
cynical "deals" and compromises and by pragmatic appeals to naked material self-interest. Buying off wage- and salary-earners' discontent was
the ultimate "sell-out", drawing most of society
into a deeply corrupting (implicit) social contract,
which also took a heavy toll on efficiency.

ALTERNATIVE SOCIETIES

Modern industrial society is society on a large scale. From its beginnings in the 19th century, individuals and communities felt threatened as personal and local identities became submerged in the strong nation state and under the centralized and large-scale organization of production. Two words express the experience of the large industrial city and of production based on a strict hierarchy with machinery at its core: "alienation", the loss of control over individual destiny and production; and "anomie", the loss of clear moral guidelines. The opposite image is that of the small rural community based on human labor. Inevitably industrialization and the nation state have provoked critical responses. Some have remained at the level of philosophical criticism; others have attempted to escape from (and even subvert) modern society by the establishment of alternatives, usually based on the idea of a lost rural communal spirit.

A powerful and influential movement based on an idealized rural life emerged in Russia in the 1860s and 1870s. Called *narodnichestvo*, it aimed to bypass capitalism and reform Russian rural life along socialist lines. In 1873-74 numerous *narodniki* ("populists") went into the countryside to persuade the peasants of their case, but found the peasantry unresponsive. In the 20th century all communal movements have had a core of protest but have been influenced by specific historical and political circumstances. Nationalist aspirations lay behind two famous communal movements, the Zionist *kibbutz* movement in Palestine (later Israel) and the Ghandian idea of a return to the village community in India. *Kibbutzim* are communal farms of 60–2,000 voluntary members. The first was founded in Palestine in 1910. Gandhia in the 1930s sponsored small-scale village-based craft manufacturing. In parts of the Pacific, "cargo cults" (movements that respond to Western goods as messianic interventions) were partly attempts by colonized people to struggle against loss of their traditions and identity.

In 20th-century Western society there have also been many different forms of alternative societies, such as the Spanish anarchist communities of industrial Barcelona and rural Andalusia. They had roots in the 1860s but found their fullest expression in the Spanish National Confederation of Labor in the 1930s. The mid 20th century saw a great flowering of hippie and libertarian communes in the USA and Europe.

Given the extent of social change in the 20th century, it is not surprising that there have been numerous attempts at creating alternative societies. Many have become famous, but none has succeeded in diverting the main directions of social change.

▲ ▶ **Jewish national aspirations became identified with manual work and self-sufficiency, which were epitomized in the *kibbutz*. Israeli *kibbutzim* remain important for Zionism.**

▶ ▲ **A Danish commune. Such concern with nature, physical health and sexual freedom questioned middle-class values based on urban life and concern about work.**

▲ Morning prayer at Taizé.
Religion has been a constant
source of social criticism.
Early Christianity questioned
aspects of Judaism and Islam
offered a purifying alternative
to previous Arab religion. The
modern Islamic world has
provided many movements
opposed to developments in
secular western capitalist
society. Sometimes responses
are meditative, as in the
Christian community at Taizé,
founded in southern France in
the 1940s.

◀ Amish Mennonite
communities in the United
States (in Ohio, Pennsylvania
and Indiana) are introverted
societies that reject the
philosophy, scale and much
of the technology of modern
America. Strict discipline,
linguistic separation,
insistence on self-sufficiency,
intermarriage and social
sanctions have enabled this
sect to survive from the late
17th century and into the late
20th century. However, while
many enclosed religious
communities have survived
through complete separation,
the Amish have managed to
do so while maintaining some
contact with the wider society.

Datafile

After World War II more radical social change occurred for many more of the world's people than ever before. Major schemes were begun for the reorganization of agriculture and for industrialization. New states were constructed in the newly independent countries, and nearly everywhere there was a sustained drive to spread education, especially primary schools, and some measure of health and welfare facilities. These changes, along with the improved consumption created by unprecedented growth in the world economy, generated striking declines in child deaths. Of course, the picture was not uniform. Vast numbers of people remained trapped in poverty, particularly in Africa and South Asia.

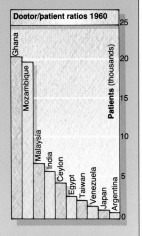

Doctor/patient ratios 1960

▲ Progress in extending health facilities – as measured by the ratio of doctors to population – was mixed, with Africa worse off, East Asia and Latin America better off. The availability of medical education was important – Ghana might be richer than India, but it had five times as many people per doctor. It was also possible to decline – as Argentina did – while Japan went in the opposite direction. But in 1960 Argentina was still significantly better off in health facilities than was Japan.

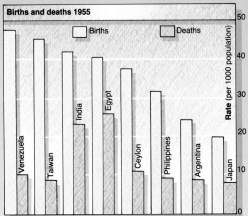

Births and deaths 1955

▲ By 1955 improved diets and health facilities led to decline in infant deaths and expanding populations. Birth control practices were slow to follow. They were more often accepted where women were educated (as in Argentina and Japan), but less so where the old survived only if they had adult children to support the aged.

▶ Newly independent governments tried hard to expand educational facilities to bind new nations together. The bottleneck was the supply of teachers. Where higher education had been long established – as in parts of Asia – it was less of a problem. In Africa, by contrast, there were few with qualifications.

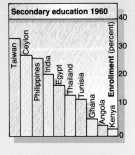

Secondary education 1960

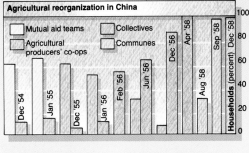

Agricultural reorganization in China

▲ Immediately after land reform in China, efforts were made to regroup the rural labor force in small mutual aid teams, and before this was complete, in larger cooperatives, which were themselves superseded by even larger collectives and finally giant communes.

▶ The Communists drove the Guomindang from China to the island province of Taiwan. In China the Guomindang had failed to reform land holding, but in Taiwan, they achieved it. Taiwan's agricultural exports expanded swiftly to support rapid industrialization.

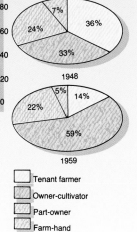

Land reform in Taiwan

At the end of 1945 much of the world lay exhausted and devastated after the terrible years of World War II. If there was hope, it was vested in the idea of creating a new world order. In the 1930s and before, it was said (and not only by socialists), unfettered capitalism had brought the world to ruin, to poverty and mass unemployment. State planning and organization during the war had shown that deliberate state intervention could reorganize any national economy in the interests of all its citizens, to produce full employment and prosperity. There were, of course, strong forces opposing the reduction of areas of private control, but even conservatives accepted the need for a measure of state direction and redistribution, publicly provided health and education services, and such public ownership as was required to balance private fluctuations and ensure cheap supplies to private industry. Planning was all the rage.

Planning in Africa, Asia and Latin America

Postwar attitudes and developments in Europe affected the colonies too and governments made efforts to increase the flow of investment to them. The British, for example, initiated what was at the time an enormous scheme to develop groundnuts (peanuts) in Tanganyika (now part of Tanzania) and a smaller one in the Gambia. Little attention was paid to the soil quality and pest dangers so that the project was a disaster. The "Groundnut Scheme" gave its name to derisive descriptions of the intelligence of government.

The independent and seen-to-be independent developing countries were no less affected by the enthusiasm for planning. Indeed, the argument became their own – at first in Latin America in the 1940s and 1950s, then in Asia in the 1950s, and finally in Africa in the 1960s. Everyone, it seemed, was now a socialist planner of one shade or another. It was argued that one solution for problems of national development was to block imports and stimulate industrialization at home – under state direction – an approach that came to be known as a strategy of import substitution industrialization.

Others had a more radical case. Backwardness only existed, they said, because the imperial powers had drained resources from their dependencies. Native capitalists had no interest in development, only in acting as the agents for foreign capital. Such dependency upon foreign power had to be broken and an autarkic (self-sufficient) economy devoted to domestic development established. Most of Latin America already had tariff protection in 1945, following reactions there to the Great Depression. After the war, however, protection became much more deliberate, complementary to industrialization. Both

NEW STATES, NEW SOCIETIES

before and after World War II the policy package seemed brilliantly vindicated in Latin America which enjoyed sustained economic growth and structural transformation over several decades. Few noted that this phase in the development of the world economy was also one of unprecedented growth, entailing a high demand for Latin America's raw material exports. Without the export revenue to make possible continued imports of both new technology and key components, growth could have been turned to slump.

For the newly independent countries, the validity of protected industrialization seemed self-evident. In India (independent from 1947) the second Five Year Plan in the second half of the 1950s radically curtailed imports and concentrated on building heavy industry in order to jump the stages of development through which western economies had passed. There were also measures to stimulate agriculture but these were of secondary significance. The state was to direct the process and to set up and run heavy industrial units. Indian planning amounted to an "Indian road to socialism", in which directive planning, unlike in the Soviet Union, would be combined with democratic parliamentary politics. These policies reflected the victory of Nehru's ideas, his belief in industrialization as the way to "develop", and his absolute dominance of Indian political life. Gandhi's ideas about sponsoring village-based, small-scale development – comparable with some of those of the peasantist movements of interwar Europe – were relegated to marginal significance.

Population and people in "developing nations"

At the same time as ambitious and optimistic planning schemes began to be implemented in the late 1940s and 1950s another development began that was to constrain if not undermine them. The problem is illustrated with particular sharpness by the case of Ceylon (now Sri Lanka). The demographic profile of Ceylon changed in a spectacular fashion in the later 1940s. Though the death rate among Ceylon's inhabitants had tended to decline in earlier periods, it declined quite dramatically from 21 per 1,000 people in the year 1943–45 to 14 per 1,000 in 1947 – a fall of one-third in only two years. This extraordinary change came about as a result of the use of the pesticide DDT to eradicate malaria, backed up with improved medical and health services. The birth rate did not decline in the same way. Between the beginning of the century and the 1950s the birth rate declined only from 38.1 to 37.6 per 1,000 while in the same period the death rate went down from 28.9 to 10.6 per 1,000. The population of Ceylon thus grew very rapidly as a result of the combination of a "modern" rate of death and a "traditional" birth rate.

▼ Clearing land for groundnuts (peanuts). The British groundnut project in colonial Tanganyika was a notorious disaster.

The same change took place throughout the new nations with increasing momentum after 1945, though it was not recognized until around 1960. India's first two Five Year Plans (covering the period from 1951 to 1961), for example, assumed a population growth rate of only 1.25 percent per year, whereas the 1961 census finally showed that the population had in fact been growing at around 2 percent each year. What came to be called "the population time bomb" had been set ticking. Population growth would, in time, increase the pressure on natural resources – though the extent to which "population pressure" has brought about the degradation of soils, in particular, has been exaggerated. It is poverty rather than sheer numbers which has led people sometimes to overexploit the soils they cultivate or to cut down forests; and high population densities in many cases are associated with labor-intensive

soil conservation practices. But population growth has compounded the problems of poor countries because of the social costs of maintaining large numbers of children. Increasing levels of investment have been required simply to maintain the level of services available to the population. From the point of view of the individual poorer person, however, having a large family might make very good sense, because it reduces the risk of being left without support in old age. As birth-control programs began to be introduced governments had to contend with the value – economic as well as emotional – that large numbers of children may have for many individuals. One family-planning slogan declared: "We are two; ours are two"; but its message about the economic advantages of small families was often unclear to those at whom it was aimed.

Population growth sometimes spurred development schemes. In Ceylon the government tried to tackle the problem of rural poverty in the island's densely populated southwest and to increase food supplies by moving families onto newly irrigated lands in the center and east. These "settlement schemes", here and elsewhere, proved to be very costly, though they helped to give substance to the idea of "building a nation".

Elsewhere there were extremely important land reforms. In Japan they were undertaken under American military occupation; in Taiwan they were made after the Chinese nationalists from the mainland reestablished themselves there. Land reforms were also carried out in South Korea. Land there was taken away from large estates and redistributed to smallholders to create a farm structure dominated by large numbers of

◀ Indian women at a birth-control clinic. The Indian government launched birth-control programs in the late 1950s despite much misgiving that these were irrelevant to the most urgent need – to increase output. But the programs spread very slowly for the status of parents depended on having many children, both to help in agricultural work and to support them in old age. Note that the posters seen here are in English, so they would not be understood by the overwhelming majority of Indian women.

holdings of small but economic size. Among the results was the creation of mass demand for the products of consumer industries, and land reforms played an important part in laying the foundations of the later economic success of these Asian countries. In India, meanwhile, in spite of the urgings of intellectuals and left politicians, reforms did not bring about a similar redistribution. In many villages it was common for a few families to own 50 percent or more of the land. It was argued that such concentration of landed wealth and the profitability of land renting and

▼ In 1960 a half or more of national output in developing countries came from agriculture. Often it took two-thirds of the work force, showing the low productivity, which was due to poor skills and lack of equipment, water, improved seeds and fertilizers. However, given such inputs, output could be expanded very rapidly as was shown in the following decade with the apparent success of the Green Revolution.

Importance of Agriculture c.1960

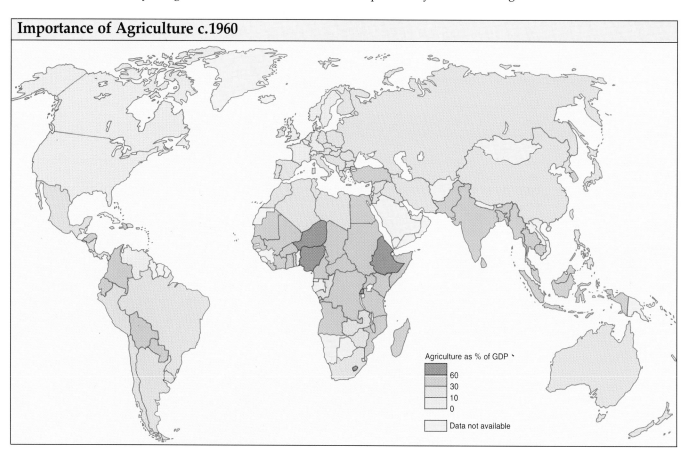

Agriculture as % of GDP

60
30
10
0

Data not available

moneylending accounted for the backwardness of Indian agriculture; redistributive land reform was economically as well as morally desirable. But in practice reform was opposed by the powerful political interests of the rural elite. It had been possible to ignore or overrule these in the circumstances of military rule in Japan and Taiwan. The only successful land reform in India in the 1950s was that which removed the topmost layer of land controllers from the colonial period. The richer peasants benefited, as they did also from government-sponsored attempts at "community development" and from participation in local government, which also enhanced their power.

In Africa colonial governments, convinced that local farming practices were unsound, sought to regulate agricultural production and rural society by legislating about cultivation and implementing soil-conservation schemes. These were sometimes fiercely resisted by people, sometimes simply ignored. With the advantage of hindsight

and a more critical awareness about colonial attitudes, it has come to be appreciated that African farmers were often right and the colonial "experts" wrong.

Almost everywhere development efforts extended both production for the market and people's dependence upon purchased items. The growth of market economies and the expansion of education did change attitudes, but often – as in Europe half a century or more earlier – encouraged consciousness of particular identities based on language, religion or region of origin rather than a commitment to the nation state and its ideals of modernity.

The Chinese road to modernization

In China the long period of internal war, which began with Japan's invasion in 1937 and continued with the civil war between the Guomindang and the Communists, ended in 1949 with Communist victory. At the outset the new regime

was committed only to a carefully administered land reform to establish its complete control of the countryside and eliminate landlords, but almost immediately it was faced with an international war in the northeast, in Korea (1950–53). This forced rapid economic centralization and the nationalization of a major part of industry.

By 1952 the government could initiate an ambitious Five Year Plan. It focused on industry, especially heavy industry. Only 8 percent of public investment was to be devoted to agriculture. The Plan imposed an intolerable strain on an already exhausted population. Food shortages remained severe and were exacerbated in the cities by the high level of immigration as a result of land reform. There were increasing controls to combat the strains – on wages, on movement, on food supplies.

These trends looked as if they were going to turn into slump, but this was postponed by an extraordinary and – as seen at the time – amazingly heroic attempt to break out of backwardness by sheer willpower, in the so-called "Great Leap Forward" after 1958. The party leadership sought to substitute for the lack of capital by mass mobilization under the slogan "Catch up with Britain in the output of major industrial goods within 15 years" (a target changed shortly afterward to "within 3 years"). Managers and technical staff were displaced by party cadres who

then forced – or induced, but without increased pay – the work force to abandon normal work practices and expand output by sheer effort at any cost.

In agriculture the existing cooperatives were merged into giant communes from which party cadres could mobilize labor for giant projects in irrigation, land reclamation, flood control and dam and highway construction. Men were taken away from cultivation to start rural industries;

▼ The 1950s were a time of enormous change in China. Modern marriage – celebrated with Western dancing in this photograph – became the norm, replacing concubinage and female subordination. But the puritanism of the new regime made marriage extremely rigid – divorce was virtually impossible. The clothes of these dancers show this puritanism.

600,000 tiny "backyard furnaces" became famous. Women were taken out of households to replace men in cultivation. Free canteen rations were supposed to supply the work force.

The cadres, in fear for their positions, reported unalloyed successes and ambitions soared. The leadership claimed that an entirely new social order was arising: China was on the very threshold of communism, and round the world many thousands of people applauded this heroic ambition. From the elements of the different phases of policy in China, but particularly from a version of the Great Leap Forward, foreign commentators derived an entirely new alternative strategy of economic development, which was said to be in marked contrast with what had happened in the Soviet Union. Now, it seemed, agriculture – the source of livelihood for the overwhelming majority of Chinese – was to provide the basis for development. The great masses of China's rural population would provide a labor force for giant projects of improvement without the need for capital, provided they were fully inspired by the task in hand. This required continual campaigns to mobilize people and others to prevent social differences reemerging, which would jeopardize the sense of common sacrifice. The government thus initiated purges to curb inequality, to beat back the growth of bureaucracy and privilege, to scourge the arrogance of power. It was thought that public authorities should supply a minimum level of welfare, health provision, food supply and housing to protect the population. (In fact these were provided only to the settled urban population, and then at increasingly poor standards.)

The conclusions about social development drawn from the Chinese case reflected the desires of observers rather than Chinese reality. In the Great Leap Forward reality swiftly caught up with

◄ In the "Great Leap Forward" of 1958 men were drafted into rural industry and women replaced them in agriculture. In expanding output no tasks were deemed impossible. People were motivated with a mixture of idealism and brute bullying – hence the young woman in the picture pulling a plow. These were age-old methods in China but in blunt contradiction to the claimed attitudes of the Communist party to people.

Restructuring Rural Societies

At the root of the social problems of most of Asia was inequality in the ownership of land, which condemned the large numbers of people who had either no land at all or only very tiny holdings to miserable living conditions. At the same time the small number of landlords could profit from money-lending. In the Chinese village of Ten Mile Inn, 440km (275mi) southwest of Beijing, for example, there were in 1937 eight households of landlords owning 48.5 hectares (120 acres) and 373 other families sharing between them only 88 hectares (218 acres). Peasants and landlords alike were poor, but there were still crucial differences between them. Seventy percent of the people lived for much of the year on husks, wild herbs and gruel "so thin you could see the reflection of the moon in it". The landlords meanwhile – supported by hired toughs – aimed to add to their estates through foreclosure on mortgages advanced to poor peasants.

Then in 1942–43, when northern China was occupied by the Japanese, Communist units organized the peasants to defend themselves. There was severe famine and the Communists set up a peasants' union linked to a campaign for "Digging Out the Landlords' Hidden Grain". The landlords' stores were distributed to those who most needed grain. The campaign did not save 59 people from death by starvation but it brought about the rallying of support to the Communists and initiated the process of reform. The levying of taxes disproportionately on the wealthy 30 percent of the village helped to release the poor peasants from the endless cycle of debt. So what was called *fanshen* began. Literally meaning "to turn the body" the word had the connotation of "standing up for one's rights". By 1947 the landlords held only one-sixth of the land they had owned in the past; their power was broken.

The land reform allowed some of the poor peasants to get a little better off, and a new class emerged. About one-third of the households in Ten Mile Inn became the so-called "new middle peasants". Later these people – now described as "feudal tails" – became for a time the object of a new land reform campaign. This of course alienated them from the Communists and, because they feared the loss of their land and ceased to fertilize it properly, also brought about

▲ A Chinese landlord, arms bound, kneeling before a People's Court. He was later sentenced to death for having exploited peasants. Land reform in China was thus carried out through local organization and struggle. It is not surprising that elsewhere, where landlords still held political power, land reforms, though legislated for, were only weakly implemented.

a fall in output. The party therefore sought rather to combine the labor power of the poor peasants with the few assets of these "middle peasants" under the slogan "Poor and Middle Peasants Are Two Blossoms on One Twig" – thus starting off the formation of "Mutual Aid Teams". These were based on the principle of voluntary cooperation especially to make use of labor to undertake such tasks as digging irrigation ditches and constructing terraces. They were the first step on the road to setting up production cooperatives in which people pooled their land and equipment whilst retaining ownership rights. Cooperatives were then succeeded by a more "advanced" form of collectivization in the commune system, under which individual ownership was suppressed. From this point onward acute problems in Chinese agricultural production began, mainly because of the loss of incentives for individuals.

heroic fantasy. The harvest of 1958 was apparently of record volume, yet there were grave food shortages later in the year. It was becoming apparent that the claims of the cadres were spurious, wild overestimates, and that the spectacular appearance concealed widespread discontent. The leadership began to attack a "negative leadership style" in the cadres, who stole the peasants' food and livestock to push up total procurements. Much of the industrial output turned out to be of too poor a quality to be used.

The economy and the country were in chaos. Mao Zedong, on behalf of the leadership, apologized to the party and retired as chairman of the Republic (he remained chairman of the party). Pay and conditions were restored, private ownership of livestock was guaranteed and incentives were restored. The giant communes were scrapped, reduced simply to county administrations, and much rural industry was abandoned.

Yet the damage was done. China plunged into three years of slump, made worse by the withdrawal of all Soviet aid and assistance (and the outbreak of the Sino-Soviet split). There was famine in the south (now estimated to have cost several million lives), rebellions and a major flight of minority people into the Soviet Union from the far western province; the rural militia mutinied in two provinces. The "Great Leap Forward" had in fact brought immense suffering to the people.

New states and social development
In India the end of World War II renewed demands for independence from Britain. By now the independence movement had split along the religious divide, with Muslims demanding a separate state and violence erupting between Hindus and Muslims. Britain's position became untenable: in March 1947 it was announced that the imperial authority would withdraw in August and two states would be inaugurated. The wonder was that, given the cataclysm of partition between India and Pakistan, it was possible to recover and to create in so short a time stable regimes dedicated to social progress (albeit in Pakistan, usually under military control).

Independent India and Pakistan, like most newly independent countries released social forces that had long been submerged by empire. It had perhaps been assumed by the Western-educated urban middle class that they were the natural heirs to their white equivalents. But almost immediately a vernacular educated middle class, often in alliance with rising castes of rich peasants, began to assert their ambitions. In the case of India, they forced the redrawing of the boundaries of Indian states to exclude from public employment those who spoke English or another Indian language. As the fruits of successive waves of development took place, the large cities grew, education and literacy spread, and new social strata emerged. Class conflict intermingled with caste rivalries and with the modern secularized fictions of political religion – Hindu, Muslim, Sikh – to produce a continuous cacophony of claims, conflicts and riots. The reality of independent India seemed remote from the dignity and moral integrity once envisaged by Gandhi.

◀ The overwhelming majority of Indians were illiterate, so elections in independent India required simplifications: symbols – shown here – were used for competing parties. Rivals fought to get the right symbol – Congress secured the sign of rural prosperity, the twin bullocks in the top-left corner.

▼ People in former French Togoland elect a new parliament in 1958. Voting made all equal and thus threatened traditional elder authority and subordination of women. Yet the independence struggle was dominated by the young and the urban, so traditional relationships were already weakened.

◄ Children of untouchables at school in Bangalore. Indian governments tried hard to outlaw elements of caste discrimination and to persuade Indians to treat each other with equality. But caste continued to be the bane of India. Efforts to raise or educate "untouchable" laborers provoked vicious assaults by upper-caste landlords. In the cities, caste remained a stubborn form of rigid snobbery and a principle by which jobs and occupations were allocated.

In the Dutch East Indies, which became independent as Indonesia in 1949, a similar transition took place. Compared with Indian nationalism, however, Indonesian nationalism was less well rooted. There was a severe shortage of educated people to lead the movement. Politics therefore tended to be those of Djakarta-based cliques who had little relationship with the rest of their enormous country of scattered islands. The price of this unstable structure was growing bureaucracy and armed forces. Between 1957 and 1960 an authoritarian order was constructed round the president (Achmed Sukarno) and the army, ruling through a system of populist corporatism known as "Guided Democracy", within which the army, the enormous Communist party and the Muslim nationalist parties competed.

In Africa the independence of the British colony of Gold Coast (Ghana) in 1957 was the signal

that what had happened in Asia would be reproduced there, though many Europeans were singularly unaware of these events, particularly in the settler colonies in Africa. Official encouragement of white emigration from Europe continued until the end of the 1950s.

Most of the newly independent countries faced grave problems of social stability after the ending of empire. Expectations could not fail to be very high but in conditions of poverty the new governments could deliver relatively little. Yet in some countries direct action had been shown to work. Thus in others attempting to establish order without improving material conditions for the majority incited opposition. In the worst cases this contributed to civil war or to successions of armed rebellions.

Sometimes old forms of social division – religion, "tribe" or language – became the unifying points for agitation; at other times new groups provided rallying points, such as sections of the armed forces, students, trade unions or even clubs. The new governments developed a variety of tactics to try to contain this. They exploited the prestige of the leaders of the independence movements, making them into godheads complete with ceremonies of worship. They made illegal all political activity except that in the government party; they censored the press; they gaoled, exiled or "eliminated" opponents. The means of physical control were expanded – armies, police forces. New symbols of national unity and new ideologies were created, based on careful selection from history. The young were drilled in their principles. For the former British dependencies the so-called "Westminster model" of multiparty democracy and a separate judiciary survived in a few cases, but when it disappeared British politicians lamented its departure without understanding the reasons why.

1960 - 1973

THE RESTLESS DECADE

Time Chart

	1961	1962	1963	1964	1965	1966	1967
Rural life	• Californian farmers plant a tougher-skinned tomato which can be picked mechanically, thereby cutting rising labor costs, and is used in processed tomato products • Crops fail again in China	• 14 Jan: EEC nations agree to formulating a Common Agricultural Policy (CAP) • Eight million Florida citrus trees are killed by 24 degrees F temperature (USA)	• In the aftermath of disastrous crop failures Khrushchev declares the Kazakhstan land experiment a failure, and seeks to buy two million tonnes of US wheat • 50% of Japan's crops destroyed by a typhoon	• New strain of high-yield rice introduced by the International Rice Research Institute for cultivation	• Starvation appears in India and Pakistan after the failure of the monsoon rains • USSR forced to purchase grain from Canada and Australia after another crop failure	• Food crisis becomes more acute as production falls by 2%; output in Latin America and Africa dips to prewar levels • US Department of the Interior publishes its first endangered species list	• China's Cultural Revolution reaches agriculture but peasants abandon collective farm in favor of private garden • Fruit and vegetable surpluses destroyed in Europe to maintain price levels
Industry and labor	• 3 Jan: One millionth Morris Minor is produced (UK) • US president John F Kennedy announces Alliance for Progress to spur economic and social change in countries which cooperate with the USA	• 13 Feb: General strike declared in Paris (Fr) • 29 Nov: Britain and France agree to construct the Concorde airplane • First industrial robots installed by General Motors (USA)	• 17 Jan: Industrial action by electric workers causes blackouts in London • 27 Mar: British Railway Board announces huge cutbacks including closing 2,128 stations and cutting 67,700 jobs (UK) • Phillips Petroleum Co and Pan American Oil Co sign a contract with the Egyptian government	• 24 Mar: Egyptian leader Nasser orders the nationalization of the Shell and Anglo-Egyptian oil companies • Jimmy Hoffa unifies all US truckers under the Teamsters Union banner	• Feb: Agreement between Krupp (FRG) and the Polish government over the construction of manufacturing plants in Poland • British MPs approve a corporation tax on profits gained by companies (UK) • Wages for US workers in building, trucking and transit have doubled since 1949	• Feb: New Five Year Plan begins in the USSR • Aug: Fiat agrees to build a $1 billion auto plant on the Volga (USSR) • 27 Sep–Nov: British Motor Co lays off 13,000 workers • Shell Oil announces oil finds in Muscat and Oman	• 22 Apr: United Autoworkers union, with 1.6 million members, disaffiliates itself from the AFL-CIO in protest again undemocratic leadership • 28 Jul: UK government nationalizes steel as British Steel Corp • Soviet engineers complete the world's largest hydroelectric power project in Siberia • Fiat (It) automobile production is now greate than that of Volkswagen
Government and people	• 13 Apr: South African apartheid policies condemned by the UN General Assembly • 1 May: Cuba proclaimed socialist by Fidel Castro and elections are suspended • 13–20 Aug: East Germany closes the Berlin border and constructs a wall along its length	• 7 Aug: Plans announced in the USSR to eliminate single family houses in urban areas • 7 Nov: Nelson Mandela imprisoned for five years (SA)	• 7 Apr: New Yugoslav constitution makes Tito president for life • 3 May: Haitian president Duvalier declares martial law after protests against him • Supreme Court rules in Gideon vs Wainright that states must provide attorneys for defendents who are unable to afford legal counsel (USA)	• 6 May: Amended Bantu laws further strengthen South African apartheid; eight black leaders including Nelson Mandela are sentenced to life in prison (14 Jun) • 20 Aug: US president Johnson signs the Economic Opportunity Act which commits $947.5 million to a war on poverty • Oct: East Germany grants amnesty to 10,000 political prisoners due to West German influence	• 4 Jun: US president Johnson presents his Great Society program to rid the USA of poverty • 1 Dec: USA begins the airlift of Cuban refugees • Busing of schoolchildren begins in North Carolina as a means of desegregation (USA)	• 1 Jul: Medicare health program, financed by social security payments, takes effect (USA) • Aug: Mao Zedong proclaims China's Cultural Revolution for the construction of an ideal communist state • 19 Sep: Bill introduced in South Africa to eliminate all interracial political parties	• 10 May: Road Safety B provides for compulsory breath tests (UK) • 25 Oct: Medical Termination of Pregnanc or "Abortion" Bill is pass by UK parliament • Birth control is legalize in France
Religion	• 20 Jan: Russian Orthodox Church is elected a member of the World Council of Churches • 31 Oct: Algerian riots marking the 1954 Muslim Rebellion claim 86 lives	• 3 Jan: Fidel Castro is excommunicated by the Catholic Church because of his anticlerical policies • 3 May: Hundreds of Muslims die in confrontation with Hindus in Bengal (Ind) • 25 Jun: US Supreme Court outlaws official prayers in school	• 3 Jun: Pope John XXIII dies and is succeeded by Paul VI (29 Jun) • 6 Jun: Martial law declared after riots protesting against the arrest of Muslim religious leader Ruhollah Khomeini (Iran)	• Mar: Malcolm X announces his intentions to split from the Black Muslim movement to form his own group (USA) • 20 Nov: Catholic Church exonerates Jewish guilt over the crucifixion of Jesus Christ	• 21 Feb: Organization of Afro-American Unity leader Malcolm X is assassinated in New York (USA) • International Society for Krishna Consciousness founded in New York	• 23 Mar: Pope and Archbishop of Canterbury meet officially for the first time, in Rome • 11 May: 100 priests protesting against police brutality in Barcelona are beaten by the police (Sp) • Vatican removes the rule forbidding US Catholics to eat meat on Fridays	• Death of Cardinal Francis Spellman, Archbishop of New York (USA)
Events and trends	• 1 Mar: US president Kennedy creates the Peace Corps of Young Americans for voluntary work overseas • 12 Apr: Major Yuri Gagarin is the first man to fly in space (USSR) • Angola begins a war of liberation against the Portuguese lasting until 1974	• Jul: Telstar satellite facilitates TV transmission between Europe and the USA • 15 Oct: Amnesty International created to investigate human rights abuses (UK) • Racial tension breaks out in the Deep South as a black student seeks to attend the University of Mississippi (USA)	• 28 Aug: 200,000 march through Washington in a civil rights demonstration (USA) • Britain is gripped by "Beatlemania" • Betty Friedan writes *The Feminine Mystique* (USA) • Valium is introduced by Roche laboratories (USA)	• 11 Jan: Surgeon General's Report links smoking with lung cancer and other diseases • 2 Jun: Palestine Liberation Organization (PLO) is created in Jerusalem • First Brook Advisory Clinic opens to give family planning advice to unmarried couples (UK)	• Feb–Mar: Extensive civil rights demonstrations in Alabama (USA) • UK government bans all cigarette advertising from television • First appearance of the Mary Quant-designed miniskirt, in London (UK)	• Betty Friedan founds the National Organization of Women (NOW) to fight for equal rights for women in the USA • US Food and Drug Administration report reveals no data to prove "The Pill" unsafe • London thrives as a center of world fashion trends	• 30 May: Eastern Niger secedes as the Republic of Biafra; the resulting ci war lasts two and a half years • 8 Oct: Revolutionary guerrilla leader Ché Guevara is murdered in Bolivia • 3 Dec: First human hea transplant successfully completed, in Cape Tow (SA)
Politics	• 20 Jan: John F Kennedy sworn in as US president • 17–20 Apr: Bay of Pigs invasion of Cuba ends in disaster and embarrassment for the USA	• 3 Jul: Algerian independence won after 132 years of French rule • Oct: Crisis over Soviet nuclear missiles found in Cuba; after a US embargo of Cuba, the missiles are removed	• 22 Nov: US president Kennedy assassinated in Dallas, Texas (USA)	• 7 Aug: US Congress passes the Gulf of Tonkin Resolution, allowing president Johnson to step up US action in Vietnam • Oct: Soviet leader Nikita Khrushchev is ousted and replaced with Leonid Brezhnev	• 29 Jun: US troops enter offensive for the first time in Vietnam • 11 Nov: Rhodesia announces Unilateral Declaration of Independence from Britain; Britain and the UN impose sanctions	• 19 Jan: Indira Gandhi is elected prime minister of India • 29 Jun: First US bombing of Hanoi (N Viet)	• 5-10 Jun: Israel wins a quick victory in the Six-Day War against Egypt, Jordan, Syria and Saudi Arabia

166

1968	1969	1970	1971	1972	1973
Crops in Saudi Arabia and other Red Sea countries destroyed by locust plague • United Farm Workers Organizing Committee leader, Cesar Chavez, organizes a national grape boycott (USA)	• Use of penicillin and tetracycline in livestock feed forbidden by the British Ministry of Agriculture • US FDA forbids the injection of most antibiotics into US livestock	• Much of the US corn crop is devastated by a fungus blight • World cotton production surpasses 50 million bales		• US prohibits the use of DDT pesticide because of damage to the environment • Soviet and Chinese crops ruined by severe drought; Moscow is forced to buy 4 million tonnes of milling wheat and 4.5 million tonnes of feed grain	• In response to high prices, US farmers plant 130 million hectares of wheat, an increase of 12 million on the previous year • US president Nixon orders a temporary embargo on the export of soya beans and cotton seeds (USA)
Jan: British Leyland Motor Corp created by a merger of BMC and Leyland Motor Corp (UK) • 14 May: French workers stage strikes in support of student protesters; worker grievances include poor state salaries and discrimination • 23 Aug: Czech workers stage a quick general strike to protest Soviet presence • Petroleum companies discover oil on Alaska's North Slope and organize the building of a pipeline (USA)	• 17 Jan: UK government publishes In Place of Strife, a White Paper on industrial relations (UK) • Jun: Phillips Petroleum discovers a massive oil field off the coast of Norway • With an unusual degree of unity Italy's trade unions use strikes and violence to gain pay increases	• 2 Nov: United Auto Workers initiate a 67-day strike against General Motors plants (USA) • Nov: UK figures reveal that days lost by strikes are equivalent to the number in 1926 • Dec: Shipyard and factory workers in Poland riot over high food prices • Libya nationalizes its oil companies	• 4 Feb: Rolls Royce declares bankruptcy (UK) • 7 Dec: Libya nationalizes the holdings of British Petroleum • Postal strike in favor of 19.5% pay increase halts deliveries for 47 days (UK) • Amtrak (National Railroad Passenger Corp) takes over almost all US railroad traffic	• May: Mexican prospectors strike oil; Chiapas-Tabasco oil field is the largest in the western hemisphere • 6 Nov: British government orders a 90-day compulsory freeze on prices and wages • Chile's nationalization of major industrial firms continues under president Salvador Allende	• 5 Feb: 20,000 black workers go on strike in South Africa • 3 Sep: TUC expels 20 unions which have obeyed the new Industrial Relations Act (UK) • Oct: US oil companies Exxon and Mobil are nationalized by Iraq • Energy crisis (triggered by the Yom Kippur War) contributes to the worst worldwide economic recession since the 1930s
Mar: Alexander Dubček's regime eases press censorship and arrests the former secret police chief (Czech) • 11 Apr: US president Johnson signs the Civil Rights Bill making it illegal to refuse housing on the ground of race (USA) • 13 Sep: Press censorship reimposed by occupying Soviet forces (Czech) • Nov: Shirley Chisholm is the first black woman elected to the House of Representatives (USA)	• Jun: Nigeria bans night flights supplying food and medicine to starving Biafrans. By November 300,000 refugees face starvation • 9 Jun: Enoch Powell proposes the repatriation of immigrants from Britain • 17 Oct: Passage of Divorce Reform Bill makes total breakdown of marriage ground for divorce (UK)	• 2 Aug: Mississippi has its first interracial marriage (USA) • 9 Oct: Italian Senate votes to legalize abortion • George Wallace, former governor of Alabama, asks other southern governors to defy federal integration orders (USA)	• 7 Feb: Referendum in Switzerland gives the vote to women • 20 Feb: Liechtenstein's male electorate denies women the vote • 20 Apr: US Supreme Court upholds the principle of busing schoolchildren to achieve a racial balance	• 22 Mar: Equal Rights Amendment passed by the US Senate • 6 Aug: Idi Amin reveals intentions to expel 50,000 Asians (Uga) • 26 Nov: Race Relations Act takes effect, making it illegal for employers to discriminate on the ground of color (UK)	• 22 Jan: US Supreme Court rules that states may not ban abortions during the first six months of pregnancy • 15 Oct: South African racial segregation is extended to cover all public gatherings • 24 Nov: Australian government enfranchises aboriginals
• 29 Jul: Papal encyclical declares any form of artificial birth control a violation of divine will (Vat) • 5–6 Oct: 100 Catholics in northern Ireland injured in demonstrations against discrimination regarding housing and employment (UK)	• 9 May: Vatican reveals plans to remove 30 "saints" from the Catholic liturgical calendar • Aug: Sectarian riots in Belfast and Londonderry lead to military intervention by British troops (UK)	• 16 Mar: New English Bible goes on sale; one million copies are sold in the first day (UK) • Jun: Methodist Church conference in Manchester announces that women will be permitted to become ministers (UK)	• Aug: 5000 Catholic and 2000 Protestant homes burned in four days of Belfast violence; 300 suspected IRA supporters arrested (UK) • State and federal aid to parochial schools ruled unconstitutional by the US Supreme Court	• 30 Jan: "Bloody Sunday": 13 Catholics shot dead by British troops during riots in Londonderry (UK) • 14 Sep: Tonsure, the circular head shave for monks, is abolished by Pope Paul VI	• 30 new cardinals named by Pope Paul VI • Attempt made by three Cypriot bishops to defrock Archbishop Makarios when he refuses to resign as president of Cyprus
4 Apr: Dr Martin Luther King assassinated in Memphis, Tennessee (USA) • May: Student rioting and protests spread to the civilian population; de Gaulle's regime is threatened (Fr) • Proctor and Gamble, Lever Bros and Colgate-Palmolive introduce enzyme detergent but the product creates environmental problems	• Feb: Human eggs are fertilized in test tubes for the first time (UK) • 17 Mar: Golda Meir becomes prime minister of Israel • 21 Jul: Neil Armstrong is the first man to walk on the Moon (USA) • 15 Oct: Millions across the USA protest against the Vietnam War	• Jan: Secessionist revolt in Biafra is crushed by Nigerian troops • Many US colleges are closed by student demonstrations over the Vietnam War • US Food and Drug Administration issues a warning that birth-control pills may produce blood clots	• 7 Jan: Announcement that long hair is now legal in the USSR • British College of Physicians compares cigarette smoking deaths to the great cholera and typhoid epidemics of the 19th century • US bans cigarette advertising from television	• 10 Jan: Surgeon-General's report reveals that nonsmokers exposed to cigarette smoke may suffer ill effects (USA) • 17 Jun: Watergate affair begins with a break-in at the Democratic Party national headquarters (USA) • Richard Leakey and Glynn Isaac find a skull which allegedly dates the first human at 2.5 million BC (Ken)	• 11 Sep: General Augusto Pinochet becomes president of Chile in a CIA-backed coup which claims 2700 lives • Steep rise in food prices throughout Europe, USA and Japan • Three-day working week ordered in Britain to conserve electricity
May: Occupation of the Sorbonne in Paris begins a month of student rebellions supported by a general strike, demanding the overthrow of de Gaulle's regime (Fr) • 20–21 Aug: Alexander Dubček's "Prague Spring" reform movement suppressed by Warsaw Pact troops (Czech)	• Sep: Colonel Muammar Qadhafi leads a military revolt in Libya	• 9 Oct: Cambodia becomes a Khmer Republic under Lon Nol after the overthrow of Prince Sihanouk (Mar); reign of terror begins against Vietnamese citizens	• 25 Jan: Idi Amin seizes power in a military coup in Uganda • 21 Apr: "Papa Doc" Duvalier dies and is succeeded as president of Haiti by his son "Baby Doc"	• 30 Mar: The British government assumes direct control over Northern Ireland • 11 Aug: Last US ground troops withdraw from Vietnam	• 27 Jan: Ceasefire in Vietnam ends direct US involvement • 6 Oct: Yom Kippur War begins in the Middle East with a simultaneous attack by Arab states on Israel

Datafile

In the 1960s unprecedented, rapid change began to affect many millions of people in Asia, Latin America and Africa amidst the emergence of new conflicts in their independent states. The creation of new governments and rapid industrialization swiftly increased the urban population. For masses of people ways of life changed as a result of migration to live and work in towns, often in the "informal" economy, or as agriculture was transformed by the impact of the Green Revolution. Education, newspapers, films and radio opened new horizons in both town and village, and offered moralities and family relationships that were destabilizing and, for the young, exciting.

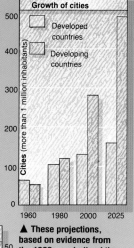

▲ These projections, based on evidence from the 1960s, underlined the speed of urbanization that had been initiated. Increasing numbers were now coming to live in the largest cities which were becoming characteristic of developing countries.

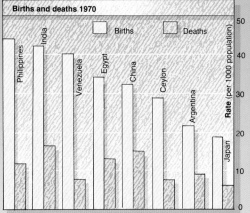

◄ Improved diets and a measure of public health provision cut down the infant death rate swiftly, leading to a rapid rise in populations and the growing youthfulness of developing countries, thus increasing employment problems.

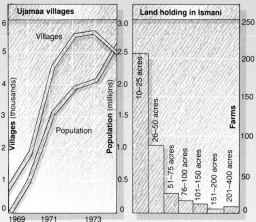

▲ Many countries introduced radical change in the countryside. Tanzania launched *ujamaa*, a key component in the pursuit of African socialism. The program sought to concentrate the farmers in selected villages where basic services and education could be provided for all. But force was required to persuade the farmers to move far from their fields and daily walk long distances. The services provided hardly justified the scale of sacrifice. In the end the scheme was discredited.

▲ Landholdings in Ismani in 1957 (in what was to become independent Tanzania) were quite unequal. But still roughly two-thirds of farmers cultivated more than 5 acres (2 hectares) and 30–40 percent over 10 acres (alongside the 26 farmers with over 100 acres or 40 hectares), which was much better than figures for Asia. Of course, land size does not indicate fertility or access to water or whether the land is afflicted with pests such as the tsetse fly, decisive factors for what the farmer could earn.

▼ Successful cultivation of new high-yielding varieties of rice (HYVs) required irrigation water, fertilizers and pesticides. This meant that they were first adopted mainly by richer Indian farmers who increased their wealth and power. But small farmers in the more favored areas soon caught up. The major problems lay in regions for which the new technology was inappropriate. Poor people, mainly laborers, gained so long as employment increased – as it often did – and as greater production reduced food prices.

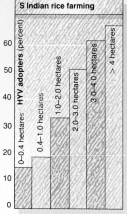

The 1960s were turbulent, giddy, exciting and fearful. The most powerful armed forces in the world, those of the United States, fought a brutal and bitter war in Vietnam and, while not defeated, did not win and were forced to withdraw with ignominy. China plunged into the extraordinary chaos of the "Cultural Revolution", when students mobilized as fanatical "Red Guards" attacked intellectuals and the communist establishment and were sent into the countryside to reinvigorate rural society with communist ideals. It excited worldwide interest as an experiment in mass emancipation, a vast refashioning of society by voluntary means and the self-scourging of a Communist party. It exercised enormous influence on young student activists in the West; Western intellectuals greeted Maoism as the model for social change, in the wake of the general discrediting of Bolshevism; and it inspired emulation elsewhere in Asia, notably in India. Its origins and operation were in reality less heroic than the posters and propaganda proclaimed, having to do with a power struggle in the Communist party leadership. It revealed the existence of an enormous and frustrated stratum of young people, grave discontents among workers and peasants, and a party that was apparently sclerotic.

Meanwhile much of colonial sub-Saharan Africa attained independence from colonial masters. Sometimes, as in the former Portuguese colonies, independence was only achieved through bitter wars that left countries wracked with continuing hostilities (especially Angola and Mozambique). But in others, Julius Nyerere's Tanzania (the old Tanganyika with Zanzibar) and Kenneth Kaunda's Zambia (Northern Rhodesia), there were experiments in development under the banners of "African Socialism", outlined most influentially in Nyerere's Arusha Declaration of 1967.

On the other hand emancipation seemed to be accompanied by savagery in some parts of the world: some regimes physically liquidated or exiled a significant proportion of the intelligentsia and trade union and peasant activists. The prototype was the military takeover in Brazil in 1964, followed a year later by an even more devastating one in Indonesia which led to the violent destruction of the Indonesian Communist party. So many of its supporters were killed, even among poor rural people, as to leave an imprint in the demography of Java and Bali. Eastern India experienced attempts at armed revolution on Maoist lines which deteriorated, however, in the state of West Bengal into individual acts of violence and murder and provoked a brutal response from the security forces. Educated young people, many of them facing the prospect of long-term unemployment, led this movement in India.

STRIVING FOR DEVELOPMENT

The same social group also led an insurrection in Sri Lanka in 1971 which was only put down by the government, which included communists and members of Sri Lanka's Trotskyist party, after the major powers from East and West had provided arms. There were also coups in Uruguay and in Argentina. In 1973 world social democracy and communism saw their most significant defeat in the overthrow of Salvador Allende's elected socialist government in Chile. The involvement of the United States in the fall of Allende was the most notable example of Western opposition to leftist regimes. This was the political context which gave rise to the theory that the "development" of the west had involved the systematic "underdevelopment" of the rest of the world through appropriation of resources and exploitation of labor; and that such underdevelopment continued even after the achievement of formal independence by erstwhile colonies, because of their dependence on Western capital backed by the use of power to support regimes sympathetic to capitalist interests.

▼ These people in an *ujamaa* village in Tanzania seem to show some enthusiasm for village life. "Villagization" did assist provision of such "basic needs" as clean water, health care and education, though collective agricultural production was unsuccessful and soon lapsed.

African socialism

Many of the newly independent states of Africa, led by intellectuals who had been educated in France or Britain and who had been influenced there by Fabian (gradualist) socialist or communist ideas, seemed set to escape the toils of dependence on the West by embracing doctrines of "African socialism". It was not universal – Félix Houphouet-Boigny of the Ivory Coast prided himself on his conservative pragmatism and close association with France; the new Nigerian governments and President Hastings Banda of Malawi also kept their distance. But others created an ideology from diverse sources to provide an inspiration for their peoples, a theory of what made Africa unique and potentially united and as a statement of aspirations. There were many variations, but at the heart was the proposition that traditional Africa was marked by cooperative communities, mutual self-help, not the exploitation of one class by another. This society, it was alleged, was in principle already a socialist order, and provided a basis for

Life in Latin American Shanty Towns

Rapid economic growth in Latin America in the 1960s stimulated the migration of masses of workers to the cities in search of better pay. The established classes were shocked and terrified; they needed the new workers to support economic expansion, but were most reluctant to meet the social costs, particularly in housing. Newcomers concentrated in the old dilapidated parts of the city in conditions of terrible overcrowding, turning them into slums. They replaced those born in the city and the better-off amongst them moved out to seize land, often publicly owned, to build their own houses with very much more space. They often filled up all the unoccupied areas, particularly where it was expensive to build legally.

Land occupations were often highly organized affairs, undertaken by "professionals", such as petty gangsters, who worked with corrupt policemen and local city politicians, anxious to secure reelection. The organizers found the land and, for a fee, organized the invasions and helped with building materials. Sometimes, they laid out a street plan with spaces for shops and other facilities because they wanted to attract the respectable working class to what would become a respectable residential neighborhood. The people who joined the invasions were usually young married couples with small children and reasonably secure jobs who desperately needed to escape from the slums to allow their children to grow up in better surroundings.

The original shanty towns were scarecrow dwellings of polythene, oil drums and cardboard, without water and sewerage services, subject to flooding and dust winds. Over the years many were transformed into areas with solid two-story brick and tile houses and schools and shops. The first inhabitants quickly tapped public electricity supplies (which led the electricity supply companies to recognize them so they could bill them), but had great difficulties in securing water supplies and sewage disposal, especially where dwellings were built across water courses or up steep mountain sides. Sometimes the gangsters continued to try to exercise authority and major battles were needed to oust them. There were also middle-class families who squatted – doctors, lawyers, architects – as the only way of getting an adequate amount of land when land prices had soared.

At first, governments reacted by attempting to clear areas, just to assert their capacity to reestablish order or to make way for major infrastructure projects, such as highways, bridges and parks. Much violence and great human misery were the results. In time some governments learned to tread with care. Then they provided new housing or sites with services for the displaced squatters. However, these shanty towns were usually developed where land was cheap because it was remote from where the jobs were located, so they were often quickly deserted by the original occupants and sold off to those who could afford to commute.

Eventually, many governments learned to tolerate the shanties, and some grew to considerable size, such as Netzahualcoyotl in Mexico City. The inhabitants did indeed upgrade them over time and turned them into decent neighborhoods. By 1990 a fifth of the inhabitants of the squatter settlements in the ring road round Mexico City owned cars and commuted to work in the great factory zones of the north.

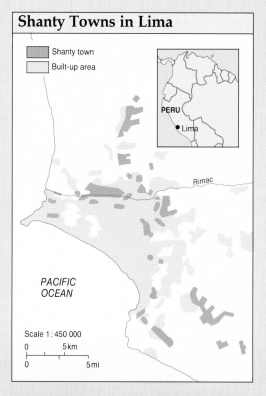

Shanty Towns in Lima

Shanty town
Built-up area

PERU
Lima

Rimac

PACIFIC OCEAN

Scale 1 : 450 000

0   5km

0   5mi

◄ Lima, capital of Peru, is not necessarily the most dramatic case of the growth of shanty towns. They spread very quickly in almost all the large cities of the Third World, ranging from thousands of families who lived most of their lives on the pavements of the central city area (as in Bombay) to solid respectable housing areas.

▼ Squatters occupied land that was usually empty because it was difficult to build on, such as the edge of rivers, beaches, or, as here, steep hillsides. Because shanty houses on such sites lacked adequate foundations, torrential tropical rains sometimes swept them away with considerable loss of life.

development different from either unregulated markets or naked state power. Several important African leaders – starting with Kwame Nkrumah in the Gold Coast – saw this doctrine as flowing from their Christianity and embodied in movements of community development, self-help and local participation, particularly when married, at the level of the state, to social democracy. Thus, the desperate shortage of capital could be compensated for by the use of cooperative labor. In Nyerere's Tanzania the *ujamaa* or "villagization" program regrouped the rural population in model new villages where voluntary labor was to create schools, shops, clinics, welfare and community centers, and churches.

The practice was very different. In Nyerere's original statements of *ujamaa*, for example, the formation of the new villages and the establishment of communal production were supposed to take place on a voluntary basis and be undertaken by people themselves. But very quickly the process became subject to coercion, marking the determination of the state to control agricultural production by subjecting the peasant population to its will. Tanzania was not alone in this effort in sub-Saharan Africa, though elsewhere the same result might be sought by different means – through agricultural settlement schemes or changes in land tenure. With single parties in such states, a censored press and controlled political life, few were available to speak the truth. While the rhetoric continued, efforts to industrialize led

to state trading corporations purchasing village output at low prices and selling it abroad at high ones, and diverting the surplus into industry, the salaries of the burgeoning bureaucracy, or private pockets. But exceedingly inefficient industry could not be sustained without imports, and impoverished cultivators could not forever produce exports to pay for them.

Urbanization and work in the "Third World"

After 1950 the speed of growth of the urban population of the world quickened. In 1950 there were 300 million town and city dwellers in the developing countries; by 1980 there would be 1.3 billion. These figures of course conceal enormous variety. Latin America became dominantly urban; most Africans were still rural dwellers in the 1970s. China and India had only about 20 percent of their people living in cities in 1965, but in absolute terms this was equivalent to the whole population of black Africa or South America.

The pattern of urban growth encouraged large cities rather than dispersed small ones. The world's largest cities, such as Mexico City and São Paulo, became characteristic of developing countries rather than, as in the past, of more developed countries. At the same time big cities spread their populations over much larger areas, and almost all experienced some decline in the numbers living in inner-city areas. Sometimes, with rapidly growing smaller cities up to 100 kilometers (60 miles) away from the large city,

▲ West African women are famous for traditionally dominating market selling and trading while the men farm. It sometimes gave women an important measure of independence and self-confidence. Trucks used as buses were called "mammy wagons" because they carried so many women traders round the country. Here, in Ghana, women operate a street market.

► From the 1960s high birth rates combined with a rapid decline in infant deaths produced a swift increase in the population of the Third World at a time when population sizes in Europe, North America and Japan were almost stagnant. This was especially true of the two great population giants, China and India, which between them had nearly two thousand million people.

▼ Officially, until the 1980s, China rejected birth control and its population increased rapidly. The urban minority was highly privileged, so the government tried to prevent an increase in their numbers for fear they could not be fed. However, apart from the early 1960s – when possibly 20 million died in famine – China's food supply has kept pace with population and diets have improved.

very large metropolitan areas began to emerge, dependent on the capacity to move increasing numbers of people and volumes of goods over long distances. One of the elements causing the spread of population was the tendency for larger modern manufacturing plants to be built well away from old built-up areas, leaving them with a mass of petty enterprises in what came to be called the "informal sector".

This term began to be used in the early 1970s following the recognition that many forms of employment, involving a high proportion of the work force of Third World cities, were missed out by official employment statistics. This "unrecorded" sector of the economy included a very heterogeneous set of activities, some actually illegal, though many not: from work in small engineering workshops using relatively sophisticated machinery to black-marketeering; from "moonlighting" work done by skilled electricians to collecting garbage in the streets for recycling; from informal money-lending to shoe-shining. The most obvious characteristic that such operations have in common is that they are too small to be captured in official statistics. But this is only an

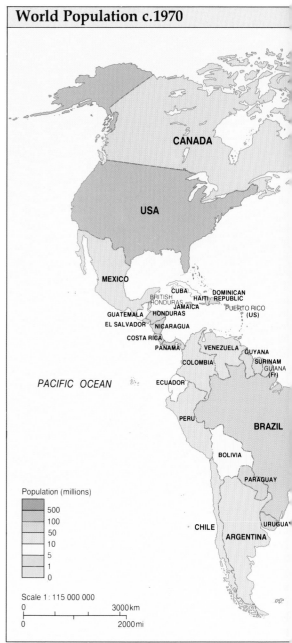

World Population c.1970

Population (millions)
500
100
50
10
5
1
0

Scale 1 : 115 000 000
0   3000 km
0   2000 mi

indicator of a more fundamental feature, which is that employment in these kinds of activities was "informal" in the sense of not being regulated by modern contracts. One of the main objectives of the organized labor movement, starting in the west in the 19th century and then spreading to the Third World, was to win legally enforceable rights to such benefits as sick pay, paid annual leave, protection against unfair dismissal, and to adequate standards of health and safety at work. The most important characteristic of work in the "informal sector" was that it is not subject to laws providing such rights.

However, it was often to the advantage of employers, in the West as well as in the Third World, to engage labor informally, because it was cheaper, unlikely to be organized and could thus be shed at will. Many activities, in manufacturing, distribution and in services, were carried on through various kinds of "putting out" arrangements: in engineering, say, by subcontracting

ALB	ALBANIA
AUST	AUSTRIA
BELG	BELGIUM
BULG	BULGARIA
CZECH	CZECHOSLOVAKIA
DEN	DENMARK
E GER	EAST GERMANY
EQ GUINEA	EQUATORIAL GUINEA
LUX	LUXEMBOURG
NETH	NETHERLANDS
SWITZ	SWITZERLAND
UAE	UNITED ARAB EMIRATES
UK	UNITED KINGDOM
W GER	WEST GERMANY
YUG	YUGOSLAVIA

to small workshops in which labor laws did not apply; in retailing through commission-selling; in the garments industry by employing women who worked at home. Even garbage picking was controlled by a small number of wealthy people who advanced money to collectors. It is not surprising, therefore, that the "informal sector" began to grow relatively as well as absolutely with the expansion of Third World cities in the 1960s.

Some development experts argued that the "informal sector" offered potential for employment-generating growth. They sought to implement programs of assistance for "small-scale entrepreneurs". There is no doubt that there have been small, informal enterprises with growth potential. But for those who were employed informally in Third World cities, though their wages were perhaps higher than they would have been in agriculture, their conditions of work and livelihood often compared very unfavorably with those of

the minority of workers who were employed in the public sector or by big companies. Such workers enjoyed considerable job security – to the extent that their jobs could sometimes become a form of property and be passed on to their descendants. They enjoyed a full range of benefits, including perhaps salaries pegged to a cost-of-living index. The number of such jobs in the manufacturing sector grew only slowly because of the capital-intensive nature of much of the industrialization in the Third World. This was the result of attempts to pursue "import-substitution" strategies of industrialization, which in fact required imports of capital goods and raw materials, and set up industries which survived only because of being protected by high tariff barriers. These allowed inefficient industries catering to very restricted elite markets to survive. Such features of "underdevelopment" followed from the policies of Third World regimes as much as from the dominance of Western-based, transnational capitalist corporations in the international economy.

Some social scientists argued that by the early 1970s the minority of workers in cities in the Third World who were in the "good jobs" constituted a "labor aristocracy" with strong interests in the perpetuation of the current situation and not in any struggle for social change to improve the lot of the mass of the people in their countries. Certainly the urban "working class" became, and has remained, divided by differences of job status which would often be reinforced by ethnic differences. The way in which urbanization and industrialization took place generally meant that jobs in particular industries, or in particular parts of a plant, became monopolized by people from a certain religious, regional or linguistic background. It thus became difficult for others, even with the same or better qualifications, to enter these jobs. A "principle of particularism" became established, extending even to very poor jobs. It was observed in Djakarta in the 1960s, for example, that those who survived by collecting cigarette butts came from a certain region and not from others. This kind of fragmentation of the "working class" lay behind the eruptions of violent confrontation between people of different tribal backgrounds, or as in South Asia, people of different religions.

Part of the informal sector was based in people's homes, and especially in the squatter settlements that came to surround the big cities of developing countries, or, in the case of Rio in Brazil, became interspersed with high-rise blocks of luxury apartments. Some of these so-called "informal settlements" grew to house a major part of the city's population. When such areas of illegal or irregular housing were first noticed, they were seen as a kind of physical "marginalization" of a section of the population from the established public society. However, measured against the life of the better-off minority, the poor majority had always been marginalized. There were continual interactions and exchanges, and the shanty dwellers often proved themselves capable of wielding power in the public domain. Furthermore,

► In the arid areas on the periphery of the Sahara Desert, finding and fetching water is a major activity. Social change is very remote, and most women and girls spend much time carrying water from distant sources. The arrival of cheap pumps powered by solar energy may one day change this.

▼ The Indian Punjab region was a main beneficiary of the new agricultural technology of the 1960s. As this scene in the town of Jandiali shows, much prosperity resulted. A minority of farmers became wealthy enough to own tractors as well as motorcycles and air conditioners. Punjab attracted rural laborers from the rest of the country.

quite dramatic increases in yields made possible by new cereal varieties which were especially responsive to fertilizers.

The impact of these higher yielding, modern varieties began to be felt from 1965 in the better irrigated parts of the developing world (and their successful cultivation has continued to be regionally concentrated). While some hailed "the end of hunger" as the output of foodgrains rose, other experts soon reached pessimistic conclusions. The extent of the "revolution" in agricultural production was contested and it was argued that the Biblical saying "To Him That Hath Shall Be Given" was borne out, because the water, fertilizer and pesticide requirements of the new varieties meant that they could be adopted successfully only by richer farmers. If poor farmers tried to grow them they failed to obtain much if any yield advantage because they could not afford to apply adequate amounts of the complementary inputs. Poor farmers suffered financial losses which led to increased indebtedness. There was then a tendency for these poor farmers to lose their land because of their debts to the rich people. Elsewhere, it was argued, landlords would find that it paid to evict their tenants and take over cultivation themselves. The rich peasants and landlords would also find it advantageous to invest in tractors and other machinery, leading to the displacement of labor, so that agricultural workers would lose out as well. Thus, it was felt, the Green Revolution would increase rural inequality and further impoverish large numbers of people.

By the end of the 1960s a wave of uprisings and violence swept across rural India, as in the infamous incident at the village in South India called Kilvenmani, in which 41 low-caste agricultural workers were burned alive by landlords' henchmen. An official report on *The Causes of the Present Agrarian Unrest* concluded that among the causes of such violence were the effects of changes taking place in agriculture.

There is no doubt that the introduction of new agricultural technology brought suffering to some rural people. In Malaysia's main rice-growing regions, for example, the use of tractors and combine harvesters meant the loss of their livelihoods for laborers and former tenant farmers, causing pockets of serious poverty in a relatively rich country. Elsewhere, in some cases, work burdens on rural women increased because of the continued high demand for their labor, while that for men declined. And there is no doubt that the political power of rich peasants increased. The widespread resistance from the rural poor such as seemed likely around 1970 did not occur probably because of the varying mix of welfare provision and of repression employed by Asian states. It has also become clear that there *have* been benefits from the Green Revolution, notably because of the effects of increased cereal production in lowering and stabilizing the prices of foodgrains (which account for 70 percent or more of the expenditure of the poor). Thus, because very poor people are especially dependent upon wage labor and the purchasing of food, they did benefit as consumers.

with the passage of time, the marginalized in the "informal settlements" might come to be the majority – between 60 and 85 percent in Addis Ababa, Luanda, Dar es Salaam and Bogotá. Quite often such areas lacked all services; households were obliged to buy water at high prices from private sellers, to dump garbage in the nearest available watercourse and steal electricity. Yet other millions were crammed in horrifying city slums, many families to a room. And yet others were homeless, eking out an existence by sleeping on the pavements, in railroad stations or under bridges.

The Green Revolution and rural societies

By the early 1960s it was clear that the social problems of Asia, stemming from inequalities in access to land, were far from solved. In some countries – notably India – programs intended to bring about redistribution of land had not been properly implemented, while in China, where redistribution had taken place, problems of organizing agricultural production in a densely populated, land-hungry country remained. Yet from the perspective of American foreign policy Chinese communism appeared a potent threat, capable of winning widespread support among Asia's poor people. There were political as well as humanitarian reasons for seeking to improve their lot.

This was the context in which the research foundations, endowed by two of America's greatest capitalists, J.D. Rockefeller and Henry Ford, increased their funding of agricultural research aimed at increasing the productivity of wheat and rice. Experts continued to press the importance of land redistribution, but it was clear that the existing regimes in most of Asia would not undertake it because of the importance to them of the large landowners' support. So finding ways of increasing food supplies without changing the structure of land ownership was essential. Agricultural research gave birth to what came to be called the Green Revolution – referring to the

OLD AGE

Growing old is a natural and inevitable process, however much people attempt to disguise or slow it down. What has been remarkable about the 20th century has been the increased number of people who survive into old age. A European born in 1850 might have expected to live for 40 years; now Westerners would expect on average to live for 70 years. This is not because people can live longer than they used to but largely because more survive into adulthood after the conquest of childhood diseases.

An important development in the Western world since the early years of the century has been the provision of old age pensions, starting at a formal retirement age of 60 or 65. One result is that the role of contributor to society can end abruptly. For many the chance to live freely without work responsibilities is a liberation. Often good health is maintained for 10 or 15 years after retirement and old age becomes a period of new interests and steady contentment.

For others, however, retirement brings a devastating loss of status. In a fast-changing society the skills and experiences of the old are rapidly redundant. Often income is reduced. Health problems are bound to increase gradually as the body ages. It becomes harder to accept change so that events such as moving house – perhaps into an old people's home – or the death of a spouse become all the more traumatic.

For society as a whole there is the responsibility of making the last years of life fulfilling ones. However, as the numbers of survivors increase and the birth rate falls, there are in many societies fewer young people to provide for the increasing costs of old age. This presents an enormous challenge.

In non-Western societies medical improvements have also led to longer life expectancy. In a poor agricultural society, however, old people may have a more defined role. Where change is slow, experience of the past is valuable in itself and thus confers status. Without state pensions the old may continue in productive employment simply by shifting to less arduous tasks. Even so, in a poor society old age is bound to be harsh. Some nomadic societies leave their old people to die when they can no longer contribute.

The end of human life, death, comes inevitably and every society has evolved rituals for coming to terms with it. In the West death often takes place impersonally in hospital, and many feel that traditional ways of coping have been lost. It is only recently that through the hospice movement and support groups that the West has learned again to face the reality of death.

▲ One hundred years young: Mrs Bowler of Reading, England, celebrates her birthday. Surviving to a hundred is still a rare experience – despite many medical improvements we still have not found the secret of extending human life far beyond this point.

▶▶ Exercises in the park. These Chinese old people go through a traditional exercise routine which should prolong active life. The benefits of such routines are increasingly recognized in an age when retirement can bring steady decline in body and mind.

▶ An 87-year-old woman sells lottery tickets in Tokyo. Old age does not necessarily mean ending on a scrapheap, even where old people are an increasing proportion of the population. Every society has a huge underused resource in its old people.

▲ The trauma of change: an old person faced with a housing crisis is comforted by a social worker. Sudden change can be particularly difficult for the elderly.

▲ Old people's lives can lack meaning, as the faces of these old men in a home suggest. Yet enormous resources are needed to provide fulfilling alternatives.

◀ Memorials to loved ones. Since the days of the pyramids and before the urge to commemorate the dead has been a strong one in human society – even when space is limited. Here mourners in Mexico decorate the resting places of their relatives. Some societies, especially perhaps those with Latin cultures, have retained a close association with the dead whereas others have tended to marginalize death, emotionally and physically, by removing cemeteries to discreet, hidden sites.

Datafile

The 1960s were a time of hope and experimentation in Eastern Europe and to a lesser extent in the Soviet Union. In places the "iron curtain" was lifted slightly, permitting increased East–West contact and dialogue. Communist regimes tried to legitimize their rule by promising, and to some extent delivering, increased social equality, real incomes, job security, social welfare and educational opportunities. For a while such experiments as Hungary's "market socialism" and Yugoslavia's workers' self-management aroused new enthusiasm for socialism. But hopes for reform were destroyed when the Soviet Union crushed Czechoslovakia's reform movement – the Prague Spring – in 1968–69.

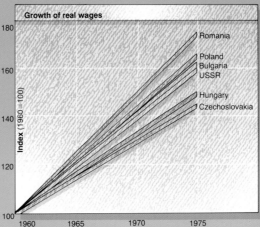

Growth of real wages

◀ For a while in the 1960s rising real wages assuaged or bought off workers' discontent, raised industrial morale and avoided repetitions of the serious workers' unrest that had shaken East European regimes in 1953–56 and the Soviet Union in 1962. In the longer term, however, the growth of real wages outstripped the supply of consumer goods, resulting in shortages, black-marketeering and hours wasted in queues for scarce goods. Ordinary people increasingly felt frustrated, disillusioned and alienated.

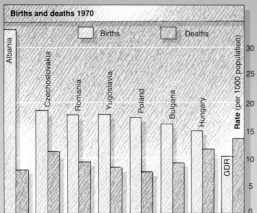

Births and deaths 1970

◀ In Eastern Europe industrialized East Germany had the lowest birth rate and the highest death rate. A large proportion of its population was elderly, partly because of the mass exodus of young people before the Berlin Wall was built in 1961. Opposite combinations were found in the least industrialized areas and where there had been great losses in World War II. Wartime losses partly account for the Soviet Union's birth rate of 17.7 and death rate of 8.7 in 1970. Some regimes did improve health and life expectancy.

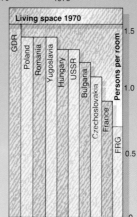

Living space 1970

◀ Increased investment in the 1960s reduced housing shortages and overcrowding. But in 1970 the average number of persons per room was still much higher than in the West.

▼ Access to Western television programs in east Germany and Czechoslovakia stimulated discontent with poor living conditions in Eastern Europe, whereas the backward communications infrastructure discouraged sought-after Western investment. The gap between east and west began to deepen.

Industrial employment in Yugoslavia 1972

◀ From the 1950s Yugoslavia's industry formally embraced the novel system of workers' self-management. But in practice the envisaged growth of workers' control of industry was impeded by the sheer magnitude of firms and their consequent complexity. In spite of intentions, managers remained remote from the shop floor. By 1972 over 60 percent of Yugoslav industrial workers worked in enterprises employing over 1000 workers and the average size of industrial enterprises was several times the Western average.

Mass communications equipment 1970

▶ A proclaimed goal of the Soviet regime in the 1950s and 1960s was to "catch up and overtake" the United States in consumption per head of meat, milk, eggs and other dairy produce. This goal was eventually achieved, but just at the point when Americans were becoming more aware of the health hazards caused by excessive consumption of fatty high-cholesterol foodstuffs and alcohol. The Soviet achievement resulted in increased susceptibility to heart disease, obesity, cancer and cirrhosis of the liver.

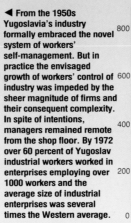

Soviet diet

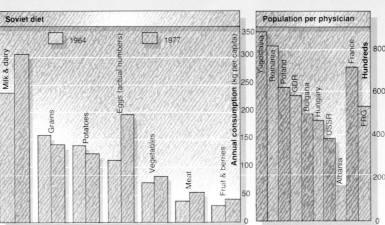

Population per physician

◀ By 1970 the Soviet Union and Albania boasted the world's most favorable ratios of physicians to population. But many physicians (most of whom were women) were over-specialized and had low social status, which led to poor morale and inflexibility. This contributed to a situation where a quarter of the Soviet population was hospitalized each year. The potential benefits were also offset by poor housing, insanitary water, low personal hygiene and inadequate medical supplies (even of basic items, such as dressings and syringes).

STAGNATION AND EXPERIMENTATION

The new Soviet optimism, vitality and experimentation fomented by the frenetic and unpredictable Khrushchev regime (1955–1964) was slowly suffocated from the mid-1960s under Leonid Brezhnev (1964–1982). The new "freeze" was brought about by a renewal of all-pervasive bureaucratic regulation, a reassertion of reactionary vested interests and ideological dogmatism, cat-and-mouse persecution and "show trials" of dissidents and Jews, widely-publicized violations of "human rights" and abuses of psychiatry. This climate strongly contributed to the widespread disillusionment, cynicism and corruption of the Brezhnev "years of stagnation".

The Soviet "gerontocracy" – the aging Soviet leadership of the Brezhnev era – was also a "kleptocracy", a regime that pocketed much of the people's hard-won wealth. Soviet Republics such as Georgia, Azerbaijan, Uzbekistan (where Brezhnev's notorious son-in-law was involved in billion-ruble agricultural frauds), Kazakhstan and

Tadjikistan, together with many local fiefdoms in the Russian Federation, were run by party mafias for their own benefit. The party "Godfathers" lived like millionaires on the proceeds of illegal trafficking, political jobbery, protection rackets and connections with the "second economy". Deprived of clear conceptions of the distinctions between private and public property and private and public goods, both rulers and ruled came to regard public property and public goods as gifts to be appropriated, or used profligately. This deeply corrupting situation gave rise to an increasingly amoral and feckless society, which would ultimately sap the strength of the superpower.

The Soviet Union's agrarian problem
Agricultural output, which had expanded by 50 percent in 1953–58, failed to expand any further in 1959–63, and the 1963 harvest was a disaster. The scope for easily achievable advances had been

▼ Soviet pioneers. Soviet education aimed to instill values in children, such as love of work and devotion to Lenin. All schoolchildren were expected to join the pioneers youth organization.

rapidly exhausted. When the official retail prices of meat and dairy produce were sharply increased in 1962 to help finance more sustained intensification of agriculture, there was major workers' unrest in several Soviet cities. Thereafter further improvements in Soviet food supplies were to be achieved, not by raising official retail prices but by vastly increasing state expenditure on food subsidies and on agricultural investment. In the 1970s food subsidies accounted for 10 to 15 percent of state expenditure and agriculture received 25 to 30 percent of Soviet investment. Massive resources went into this Soviet "black hole". Unfortunately, the forms in which urban food supply problems were tackled ultimately exacerbated rather than alleviated Soviet food shortages.

Reluctance to raise official retail prices of foodstuffs (for fear of provoking urban unrest), combined with the considerable growth of the disposable money incomes of the Soviet population fostered demand for foodstuffs which continually outstripped the moderate further growth of food supplies. Indeed, it was in the interest of the farm population to deliver only modest increases in production for the state distribution network and

the urban sector. For so long as agriculture remained a "problem" in the eyes of the state, farmers could expect to receive greatly increased farm subsidies, incomes and investment from the state. Conversely, if they had produced enough to satisfy growing urban demand and eliminate the need for large food imports from the West, agriculture would have ceased to be a "problem" and the state would have treated the farm sector less generously.

It therefore paid the Soviet farm population to provide only the most perfunctory fulfilment of their obligations to the state or collective sector and to concentrate on their private "home improvements" and increased private production of goods (not just food, but clothing, footwear, jewelry, drinks and the like) for themselves and for high-priced "free" markets. These private activities increasingly diverted material resources from the collective and state farms, often with the tacit approval of sympathetic farm officials who were "in on the game". Thus even after agricultural output stopped growing altogether in the late 1970s and through the 1980s, the real incomes and assets of the farm population nevertheless

▲ Peasant women visiting Moscow. Between 1930 and 1970 there was a massive exodus from the Soviet countryside. The urban population expanded by about 100 million, with the result that most town- and city-dwellers were of peasant stock, and continued to be linked with the countryside by family relationships. Moreover peasants were always to be seen in cities and towns, on the main streets, at railroad stations, and behind stalls at food markets.

continued to increase, as the state desperately pumped in more and more resources in a vain endeavor to reinvigorate Soviet collective farming and as persistent urban food shortages perpetuated rich opportunities for private profiteering. Quite simply, Soviet farmers gladly accepted more and more income and state support, in return for less and less effort.

The shrewd peasantry had at last won a sort of revenge for its sufferings in the 1930s and 1940s. In contrast to more recently collectivized peasantries in China and Eastern Europe, the Soviet peasantry gradually lost interest in "decollectivizing" or dismantling a system which they had learned to work and "milk" to their own advantage and which permitted levels of profiteering, alongside an absence of individual financial responsibility and risk, that privatized agriculture could not hope to match. This explains the very muted peasant response, other than in the more recently collectivized Baltic Republics and Western Ukraine, to 1980s proposals for decollectivization or privatization of Soviet agriculture. Thus, *through* the collective farm system, the Soviet state had in the end unwittingly erected an immense social barrier to any fundamental solution to the problem of chronic food shortages.

Economic stagnation

This institutionalized imbalance of supply and demand, reinforced by shortages induced by high military expenditure and by diversion of resources to inefficient heavy industry, was at the root of the luxuriant growth of blackmarketeering, corruption, pilfering and moonlighting under Brezhnev. Persistent shortages steadily diminished the value of rising money incomes, diminished work incentives and redirected energies from work to frustrating searching and queuing for scarce goods. People's increased dependence upon access to pilfered or black-market goods increased the value of the privileged access to special shops, services and accommodation reserved for key party and state personnel, and incensed and demoralized the unprivileged masses. The latter were being fobbed off with a superficially striking growth and equalization of money incomes, at a time when money income was being progressively deprived of real significance; position and "pull" ("*blat*") rather than money increasingly determined degrees of access to scarce material and cultural goods, services, housing and amenities. Most Soviet households accumulated large savings, frustrated at the dearth of attractive things to buy, although pent-up purchasing power was also channeled increasingly into alarmingly high consumption of alcohol and cheap cigarettes, to the growing detriment of health and family life.

During the 1960s and 1970s Soviet reformers devised elaborate bonus schemes, piece rates and pay scales in an endeavor to reward "each according to his work". But the intended incentives were largely nullified by shortages and erratic supplies. The Soviet workers' attitudes to work and remuneration were neatly encapsulated in an oft-quoted catch-phrase: "You pretend to pay us, and we pretend to work."

Women and the family

During the 1960s Soviet family legislation was brought more into line with that of the West, completing the reversal of Stalin's sexual counter-revolution. The December 1965 divorce law further liberalized divorce procedures; and the 1968 Family Code increased protection and financial safeguards for divorced women and their offspring. It also substantially increased the rights and status of children born out of wedlock. The number of divorces per thousand inhabitants (0.4 in 1950, 1.6 in 1965) reached a high plateau of 3.3–3.5 (or one divorce for every three marriages) in 1976–89. Other factors besides more liberal divorce procedures were at work. Nearly half of female divorcees cited male alcoholism and/or drunkenness as the chief reasons for divorce, reflecting the massive rise in Soviet alcohol consumption in the 1960s–70s. In addition, familial child-rearing functions were becoming less important as the importance of schools, peer groups and social organizations increased and as the average size of Soviet families declined to 3.7 persons in 1970 and 3.5 persons in 1989. Indeed, the average number of children per married woman decreased to two in the course of the 1970s, as Soviet couples adjusted to life in very cramped

▼ Apartment block in Moscow. The scale and monotony of most modern Soviet apartment blocks were no doubt intended to impress and to reinforce a sense of "proletarian uniformity". But the results were soulless and oppressive.

▼ A subway executive in Moscow, responsible for rolling stock. Since World War II women have been a majority of the Soviet work force, but most have been confined to low-status manual occupations. Some rose to supervisory positions, but even the most formidable Soviet matriarchs rarely attained positions of real power and authority.

▼ The recreational facilities in Soviet towns and cities were usually limited, but most of the older cities were well endowed with elegant and extensive parks (as here), many of which had belonged to the aristocracy or rich industrialists before 1917. In addition, most cities were well provided with cinemas and large "palaces of culture" (leisure centers). But there was a shortage of small, local, more informal venues (such as bars, cafes and restaurants).

urban accommodation or decided to forgo additional children so as to be able to spend more on clothing, footwear and consumer durables, which were expensive for Soviet citizens. The restraints of religion, social disapproval and pressure from the extended family were also being eroded, even in rural areas, where family farming of "private plots" was finally overtaken by income from "collective work" as the main source of household income, reducing the economic pressures to keep rural families intact. Increased urbanization and employment opportunities for women had also made it easier for formerly dependent wives to leave their husbands. Nevertheless, far from the family disappearing under Communist rule, families still embraced 94 percent of the Soviet population in 1970, and Soviet women were still far from achieving full emancipation and equality. In the 1960s–70s, average male earnings were 50 percent higher than those of Soviet women.

Absence of freedom of association and expression largely prevented the emergence of independent women's movements in the Soviet Union. Indeed the Soviet regime claimed that there was no need for independent women's organizations, because (officially) women's equality and emancipation had already been accomplished by early Soviet family legislation, universal education and the massive expansion of female employment. Soviet women who dissented from the official view stood accused of defaming the Soviet state. But while women did make up a majority of the Soviet work force, they were disproportionately concentrated in manual occupations and so-called "non-productive services", which conferred little power or status in the Soviet Union, and there continued to be a dearth of women in positions of authority. In secondary education girls were markedly higher achievers than boys, yet fewer girls were recruited to higher education and power-wielding posts. The meager provision of labor-saving household appliances and the two to three hours per day spent in shopping queues mainly affected women, as Soviet men still saw shopping and household chores as "women's work". Soviet power was still masculine!

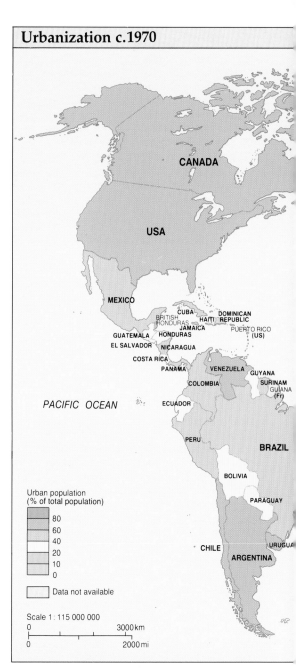

Urbanization c.1970

CANADA

USA

MEXICO

CUBA
BRITISH HONDURAS
HONDURAS
GUATEMALA
EL SALVADOR
COSTA RICA
PANAMA

DOMINICAN REPUBLIC
HAITI
JAMAICA
PUERTO RICO (US)
NICARAGUA

VENEZUELA
COLOMBIA
GUYANA
SURINAM
GUIANA (Fr)

PACIFIC OCEAN
ECUADOR

PERU

BRAZIL

BOLIVIA

PARAGUAY

CHILE
URUGUAY
ARGENTINA

Urban population
(% of total population)

80
60
40
20
10
0

Data not available

Scale 1 : 115 000 000
0   3000 km
0   2000 mi

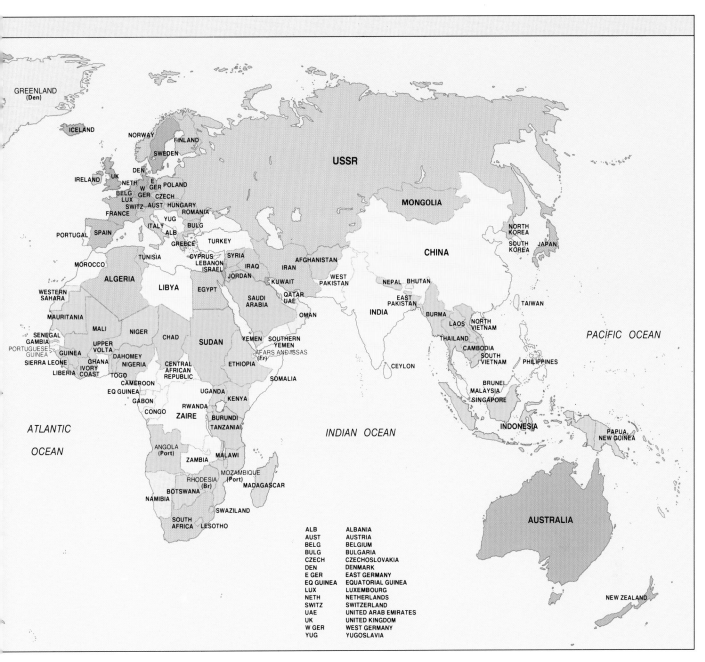

The map shows the nations of the world labelled, including GREENLAND (Den), ICELAND, NORWAY, SWEDEN, FINLAND, USSR, MONGOLIA, CHINA, and so on. A key in the lower portion reads:

ALB — ALBANIA
AUST — AUSTRIA
BELG — BELGIUM
BULG — BULGARIA
CZECH — CZECHOSLOVAKIA
DEN — DENMARK
E GER — EAST GERMANY
EQ GUINEA — EQUATORIAL GUINEA
LUX — LUXEMBOURG
NETH — NETHERLANDS
SWITZ — SWITZERLAND
UAE — UNITED ARAB EMIRATES
UK — UNITED KINGDOM
W GER — WEST GERMANY
YUG — YUGOSLAVIA

▲ By the 1970s the industrialized West had become substantially "suburbanized", leaving inner-city areas increasingly to the least privileged. Meanwhile the Third World was already experiencing the rapid growth of some very big cities, leading to the mushrooming of shanty towns. In the Soviet Union in 1950 only Moscow and Leningrad had contained more than 1 million inhabitants, but by 1970 the number of these big cities had increased to 20.

Eastern Europe: the search for change

Throughout Eastern Europe this was a time of unprecedented growth and, until the Soviet invasion of Czechoslovakia in 1968, of optimism and rising consumption. Between 1960 and 1970 private car ownership increased fourfold in East Germany and Poland and by as much as seven times in Hungary. Eastern European societies thus experienced consumerism, albeit on a modest scale by comparison with their Western neighbors; they too were marked by the rise of service employment and by expansion of welfare services and of educational opportunity. What was different was the formal commitment in Eastern Europe to the achievement of equality, not just equality of opportunity. The extent of social mobility was higher than in the west. Half the university students in East Germany were from working-class families in the early 1960s, when in Western Europe, outside Britain and Scandinavia, the proportion was less than 10 per-

cent. Yet important status differentiation remained between professional people, party apparatchiks and ordinary workers.

Different patterns of development and change characterized the states of Eastern Europe, resulting from their histories, cultures and the varying relationships between the Communist party and the people. East Germany, with an apparently successful economy, was influenced above all by its proximity to the West and anxieties over its relationships with the Federal Republic – symbolized by the building of the Berlin Wall in 1961. It became the most orthodox ally of the Soviet Union, the one most willing to toe the Soviet line. Poland, though it experienced comparatively high rates of growth of both industrial and agricultural output, remained an unhappy society. Even more than in the neighboring countries had the Communist party failed to become at all rooted amongst the people, and there was not much enthusiasm even amongst its members.

The party remained in power only because of the threat from the Soviet Union, offending the deep sense of Polish nationalism and giving rise to recurrent unrest and powerful antigovernment mobilization amongst workers. There was more popular support for communism in Czechoslovakia and Hungary, and it was perhaps for this reason that these two states saw the most serious attempts to remold socialism in the 1960s.

Czechoslovakia's "socialism with a human face"
The need for social reform in Czechoslovakia was widely accepted, even among members of the ruling party apparatus, as the remedy for the stagnation which had set in by the early 1960s, and brought disillusionment with communism in a country where it had known strong support.

Thus the Czechoslovak reform movement of 1963–68 did not aim to jettison "socialism" and the leading role of the party. It strove to achieve "socialism with a human face" by removing hardliners, democratizing the party and relaxing censorship. In keeping with the Czechs' reputation for being the most liberal, educated and sophisticated nation in Eastern Europe, the relatively large party and non-party intelligentsia dominated the Czechoslovak reform movement.

Intelligentsia hegemony in the Czech reform movement was both a strength and a weakness. The movement was exceptionally articulate and commanded great moral and intellectual respect and authority. On the other hand, because it lacked a mass base, the Soviet-led Warsaw Pact invasion of Czechoslovakia in August 1968 was

▲ A roadside trading depot in Yugoslavia. During the time of the postwar Communist regimes, rural Eastern Europe remained relatively untouched by modern amenities. There were few automobiles to be seen and most roads were dusty dirt tracks which became quagmires in wet weather. In the Soviet Union in the late 1960s the metaled road network was not much bigger than that of the UK, a country ninety times smaller.

not answered by widespread and tenacious resistance. This was another "Revolution of the Intellectuals", like that of 1848, and it was partly for this reason that it failed.

Hungary's "market socialism"

The happiest and most unexpected reversal of fortunes occurred in Hungary under Janos Kadar (party leader from 1956 to 1988). From late 1961 onward, after repression and recollectivization had brutally but effectively reimposed party control, Kadar's regime set out to conciliate Hungary's intelligentsia, workers, peasants and even Catholics, under the slogan "Those who are not against us are with us". Censorship and travel restrictions were progressively relaxed. Most political prisoners were gradually released and rehabilitated. Police excesses were curbed and there was increased observance of due legal process and the rule of law.

In the rural sector, which still accounted for about half Hungary's population in the 1960s, the new collective farms were granted unprecedented commercial and managerial autonomy, in equally unprecedented recognition of their (hitherto ignored) formal legal status as autonomous (self-managed) agricultural producers' cooperatives. Collective farmers responded by vigorously expanding Hungary's food output and exports, including food and wine exports to Western markets. The commercial and managerial autonomy which produced successful results in agriculture gradually spread to catering, food-processing, retailing, personal services, taxis, crafts and, lastly, factory industry.

In 1968, while Soviet and Western attention was nervously fixed upon the more highly publicized and provocative manner in which broadly similar socioeconomic changes were being introduced in neighboring Czechoslovakia, the low-key Kadar regime quietly inaugurated a comprehensive and carefully prepared "New Economic Mechanism" in Hungary – and got away with it. Henceforth, industrial productivity growth, innovation and responsiveness were to be promoted by encouraging industrial enterprises to establish direct contractual relations with one another and with their final customers at home and abroad, to become self-financing and to use repayable interest-bearing bank credits in place of outright grants from the state budget. By 1971 Hungary had effectively ceased to be a command economy, even though large-scale industry remained state-owned. Managers of large enterprises also remained party/state appointees who were not empowered to dismiss workers at will. The 1967 labor code gave the unions a "regularly used" right to veto management decisions, and industrial inefficiency and overmanning were to be dealt with more by redeployment than by painful plant closures and dismissals. Yet the sheer size of Hungarian industrial enterprises was more conducive to hierarchy, inequality and workers' alienation than to the growth of workers' participation, control and contentment. In 1973 Hungarian industry averaged 1070 employees per enterprise, 10 to 20 times the average for many Western states.

Workers' Self-management

The boldest social experiment in Eastern Europe was Yugoslavia's system of workers' self-management. It drew on earlier aspirations to give workers more involvement in industrial organization but emerged from particular circumstances. Tito's postwar Communist regime had initially tried to reconstruct Yugoslavia's economy along Soviet lines, with central direction and investment in heavy industry. The attempt ended in disaster and a new approach was needed. Instead the Communists devolved decision-making to the lowest possible level, partly in the hope of averting ethnic conflicts.

In 1950 workers' councils were established in most enterprises employing over 30 workers which elected teams to manage enterprises. The teams could make appointments and decisions about investment and salaries. At first their freedom was circumscribed by central regulation but in 1965–66 new life was given to the system. The economy expanded, but so too did bad investment decisions, wage inflation and imports. The system not only produced bad management, it also failed to prevent the alienation found in other socialist countries and in large-scale capitalist business: most enterprise directors were political appointees who remained aloof from the shop-floor.

▲ Heavy industries commemorated on Polish stamps. The postwar Polish Communist regime invested in such industries, which soon poisoned the atmosphere and alienated their workers. At the same time they neglected the development potential of Polish light industries.

▼ Catholic clergy in Zagreb, Croatia (part of Yugoslavia). The Croatian Catholic church remained a powerful force under Communist rule.

The early 1960s, while the long postwar boom continued, was a time of some moral fervor, epitomized by the presidency of John F. Kennedy in the United States. It was also a time when it seemed plausible to suppose that class conflict had come to an end and a new type of "post-industrial society" was emerging. Both the hopes of the establishment of a better society and these ideas about social change were shattered by the events of the late 1960s. Then, as economic growth faltered, America experienced a wave of social violence, of youth protest and of agitation for Black Power. In Europe the tumult of 1968 exposed deep discontents. A counterculture grew up which threatened established values.

Ten largest cities 1970

Tokyo, Mexico City, New York, London, Buenos Aires, Moscow, Los Angeles, Chicago, Shanghai, São Paulo — Population (millions)

▲ By now cities like Mexico City and Buenos Aires were growing very fast, drawing in migrants from rural areas to shanty towns and slums, and initiating tremendous problems of congestion and pollution.

◀ Western populations were still growing, though more slowly. In Germany the death rate exceeded that of births, foreshadowing the aging of the population which was to become a social problem in industrial societies at the end of the century.

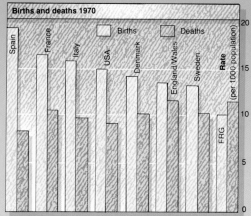

Births and deaths 1970

Births, Deaths — Rate (per 1000 population)

Spain, France, Italy, USA, Denmark, England/Wales, Sweden, FRG

▶ Labor migration into western Europe in the time when booming economies required more workers reached a peak around 1973. Then, with recession, limitations on labor migration began to be introduced and, partly as a result, ethnic tensions increased. But Switzerland exported some of its unemployment back to Italy!

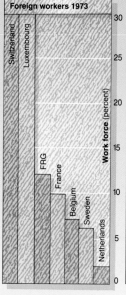

Foreign workers 1973

Switzerland, Luxembourg — Work force (percent)

FRG, France, Belgium, Sweden, Netherlands

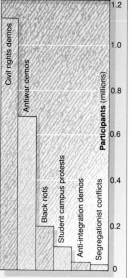

US civil strife 1963–68

Civil rights demos, Antiwar demos, Black riots, Student campus protests, Anti-integration demos, Segregationist conflicts — Participants (millions)

▲ These data show estimates of participation in different types of civil strife in the United States between 1963 and 1968, and reflect the violence of the time. There were most arrests associated with "negro riots" (nearly 50,000) but almost one-third as many in civil rights demonstrations which were mainly peaceful.

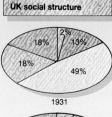

UK social structure

2%, 18%, 13%, 18%, 49%

1931

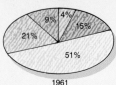

9%, 4%, 15%, 21%, 51%

1961

☐ Higher professional/managerial

☐ Intermediate nonmanual

☐ Skilled manual/routine nonmanual

☐ Semiskilled

☐ Unskilled

◀ Social structures in Europe had changed rather little. In Britain there had been decline in the relative importance of the lowest ranked, unskilled workers but little change at the top of the social hierarchy. Nowhere did economic growth bring a significant narrowing of the gap in incomes between richest and poorest.

For many in North America and Western Europe who were young at the time "the sixties" stand out as a distinctive period, one of greatly expanding opportunity and personal freedom. Others, looking back on this time, see it rather as one of decay, marked by personal and social irresponsibility. They link this to the "overdevelopment" of the state and especially of welfare provision. These, they argue, made for both a lack of responsibility and of enterprise and initiative which came to threaten the economic base of the freedom enjoyed by the young.

The contrasting moods of the early and the later 1960s partly reflected the tempo of the international economy. During the 1960s the long economic boom of the postwar period began to falter, substantially because the stimulus to growth in the reconstruction of Europe and Japan had by now been exhausted. Both productivity and the profitability of capitalist enterprise declined after 1965. The steep rise of oil prices in 1973 only delivered the final blow to an economic system that was already staggering. The inefficient rigidities inherent in Fordist methods of organizing production in very large-scale factories, with massive investments in specialized assembly lines, started to become apparent. The capacity to deliver collective goods – social welfare – had depended upon continuous growth in productivity and thus was threatened. For the moment states preferred to incur fiscal problems in maintaining welfare expenditure, but this did not restrain the mounting pressure from those who had been excluded from the political settlement of the 1950s – groups of marginal workers outside the big unions, blacks and members of the other ethnic minority groups, women and young people. The student movements of the time reflected anxiety about the future as well as the appeal of a radical counterculture which questioned the values of industrial society.

Post-industrial society?

In the 1960s sociologists began to argue that quite fundamental changes had taken place in Western society. These they sought to describe through such terms as "the service class society", "the knowledge society" or, most influentially, with Daniel Bell's term "post-industrial society". The main elements of these ideas were that whereas the business firm had been the key institution of advanced societies, and the principal social classes those of the capitalist entrepreneurs and the industrial proletariat, now theoretical knowledge was the crucial resource. Universities and research centers were the leading institutions (the "axial structures", according to Bell), society was increasingly run by technocrats rather than by capitalists, and the majority of people were

PROGRESS IN QUESTION

employed not in manufacturing but in personal, financial and social services. The values of hard work, encapsulated in Max Weber's concept of the "protestant ethic", were being challenged by a new ethic of fun and leisure. Some saw in these new conditions the possibility of greater social integration and harmony, resulting from the erosion of class differences; others saw potential for conflict between the old, liberal, humane values and those of the new technocracy (which the British writer C.P. Snow described as "the two cultures").

There was substantial evidence for all of these ideas. At some time in the 1950s the United States had become the first nation in which more than half of the employed population was not involved in producing food, clothing, houses, automobiles or other tangible goods. The United Kingdom followed suit in the 1960s. The increasing

▼ Boy meets girl in New York's Greenwich Village. Greater personal freedom challenged the protestant ethic in industrial countries.

importance of white-collar jobs apparently meant that people's experience of work was becoming more fulfilling, involving personal interaction rather than subservience to machines. More and more workers were described in official statistics as "managerial, professional or technical" (29 percent of male workers in the United States in 1970), and increasing proportions of the national product of the advanced countries were being spent on "research and development" (in the United States 9 percent in 1965, with another 7 percent going on education – compared with only 3.4 percent in 1949). Even in the most "class-ridden" of all Western societies – in Britain – the way in which the remaining industrial workers shared in the general prosperity seemed to show that they too were becoming "middle class" in their values and attitudes, in the process sociologists described as that of "embourgeoisement".

Change was more apparent than real. In fact only in Britain did manufacturing workers ever, at any point in the history of industrialization, constitute a majority of the work force. The long-run trend of change in occupational structures was rather a shift from agriculture to services employment with the share in industry remaining stable over long periods. In practice a great deal of employment in services involved office work which was as much subject to routine, to hierarchical authority and to "deskilling" through the breaking down of tasks into simple, mechanical operations, as manufacturing jobs. The "professionalization" of work was often a chimera: as Bell wrote, "the word engineer is now used to describe anyone from a salesman (a 'systems engineer' at IBM) to a garbage collector (a 'sanitary engineer' in the Chicago euphemism)". Similarly the expansion of education tended to increase the entry requirements for repetitive jobs. Above all the advanced industrial societies of the West were increasingly dependent, not less so, on largescale bureaucracies over which individuals had little control.

New estates and towns, and new suburbs where the working and middle classes lived side by side, seemed to lend credence to the notion of "embourgeoisement". But a famous study by David Lockwood and John Goldthorpe of British automobile workers found that not levels of income and consumption but work remained the definitive experience of class. The industrial worker was still dependent upon a wage, owed his relative affluence to overtime or his wife's ability to supplement the household income, and

generally held his labor to be not a vocation but drudgery. Even where working- and middle-class households lived in the same neighborhoods there was little sign of social integration. While the middle classes socialized primarily at home, working-class leisure activities continued to show strong communal characteristics, to hinge on kinship and community, on pubs and clubs, and to display a marked gender divide. Finally, the immediate impact of the secular decline of the share of the popular vote for the British Labour party after the mid-1960s was to make its supporters proportionately *more* "working class". The thesis of "embourgeoisement" was quite comprehensively rebutted.

The end of ideology?

The appearance of a more integrated society was enhanced, however, in Western Europe in the early 1960s by the ascendancy of a politics of consensus. This was described in Britain as "Butskellism", a term deriving from the elision of the name of the then leader of the Labour party (Hugh Gaitskell) with that of R.A. Butler, the principal Conservative theoretician. Both the major parties were committed in practice to much the same set of objectives, of welfarism, of increasing equality of opportunity and a "social market economy". In France the conservative government led by Charles de Gaulle was highly interventionist. In the Federal Republic of Germany the Bad Godesberg Conference of the Social Democratic party (SPD) in 1959 marked a historic change of direction. The party formally jettisoned its commitment to Marxism as an ideology and

▲ In the 1960s and 1970s employment in big office blocks such as this became more significant in people's working lives than factory jobs. There was talk of a "new service class society". But in spite of its apparently greater independence and "professionalism" a great deal of office work was as much subject to control and routine as that on an assembly line.

▶ Visitors at a motor show in Paris in the 1960s. Cars were more than ever a major status symbol. In the 1950s the purchase of a car and of major electrical consumer goods had become the aspiration of most citizens in the West. In the 1960s these aspirations were substantially satisfied. In Britain there were 2 million private cars in 1950; by 1964 over 8 million. Now smarter and faster cars became an increasingly possible dream.

Meritocracy

In 1958 the British sociologist Michael Young published *The Rise of the Meritocracy*, a partly satirical book which showed how some social scientists understood the changes taking place in western societies. Young wrote as if from the perspective of someone working in 2033 who was trying to explain the conflicts of that time by reviewing the history of the 20th century. He argued that "The fundamental change of the last century... fairly begun before 1963, is that intelligence has been redistributed between the classes, and the nature of the classes changed. The talented have been given the opportunity to rise to the level which accords with their capacities, and the lower classes consequently reserved for those who are also lower in ability". In societies dependent on high levels of skill large numbers of those of low intelligence were hardly employable. Fortunately there was a demand for their labor as personal servants of meritocrats. Young thus anticipated the renewal of domestic service by the end of the 20th century. Because of the widespread acceptance of the "merit" principle social harmony was established, for a time, with those of lesser merit finding fulfillment in handicrafts and games. Young pointed to a darker lining in some social democratic aspirations of his own time, which seemed likely to introduce new tensions in society.

◀ "Meritocrats" at work in a high-tech factory.

asserted that "Democratic Socialism" in Europe was rooted in Christian ethics, humanism and classical philosophy. Emphasis was placed on freedom and justice; the party favored "a free market wherever free competition really exists"; it stood for the elimination of privilege but made no mention of class struggle.

The takeover or participation in government by socialists almost all over Europe in the 1960s did not result in any dramatic changes in policy. Only in Britain did the old issue of the socialization of "the forces of production", through nationalization, remain a matter of controversy. Everywhere governments consulted different interest groups in society more extensively, following a pattern of corporatism marked out most strongly by the socialist parties in the Nordic countries. The stability of European societies was disturbed principally by strains induced by decolonization, especially in France. There de Gaulle's granting of independence to Algeria in 1962, bitterly resented by many though it was, finally caused the threat of disintegration to recede.

The events of 1968

In the calm consensus in Europe in the early 1960s few anticipated the convulsions of 1968, when for a moment France seemed at the point of revolution and there was strident social protest almost everywhere. These events lent force to the arguments of the American philosopher Herbert Marcuse that in the later 20th century the revolutionary class was no longer the industrial workers, who had been coopted into the management of capitalism, but students and the young more generally, who had the capacity to engage in social criticism and to organize on a large scale. The German students' union did not accept what was described as the "revisionism" of Bad Godesberg and remained active in social protest; Italian students in the early 1960s demonstrated against overcrowding in the universities and the rigidity of the curriculum; students in France mobilized around the same issues but were also powerfully politicized through their involvement in the struggles over decolonization and later by hostility to American imperialism in Vietnam. This was the immediate background to the events

of May 1968, when students and riot police confronted each other across barricades in Paris in an atmosphere which combined carnival and sense of fun (exemplified in the slogan "*Je suis marxist – tendance Groucho*"), with demands for university reform and for sweeping social change. When thousands and then millions of workers took part in a general strike in support of the students the Fifth Republic seemed near to collapse. But the sweeping Gaullist victory in the elections which followed in June showed that the political center had held in face of pressure from the extremes.

A survey of student participants in the revolt of May 1968 showed that for 56 percent of them the chief motive had actually been their concern over employment prospects; for 35 percent the focus was on poor educational facilities. A mere 12 percent thought of the events as a challenge to the structures of society. Student activism thus seems to have reflected some rather mundane concerns, and it was a more powerful force in France and Germany than in Britain partly, at least, because though recruitment to the elite in both countries was more dependent on academic merit than in

▲ Turkish *Gastarbeiter* ("guestworkers") in Germany. Germany was particularly dependent on immigrant workers because its own labor force was actually decreasing between 1960 and 1975. The aim was to recruit low-paid workers on a temporary basis; and it was assumed that the sending countries would benefit by the alleviation of their own unemployment problems, by remittances and by the eventual return to them of experienced workers.

Britain, the proportion of university students coming from peasant or working-class backgrounds was actually much *lower*.

The tumultuous year of 1968 thus crystallized social trends of the 1960s. There had been changes in European societies and a mood of criticism of capitalist industrialization. But old structures of power and authority persisted.

Migration and immigration

Settled and immobile, the traditional working classes of Western Europe failed to plug regional and sectoral gaps in the labor market. The problem was resolved by new waves of recruitment to the industrial work force. Young and healthy workers were recruited, with state support, mainly from southern Europe, Turkey and North Africa and at first left after short stays. They therefore claimed back little of what they paid in social insurance contributions. They also enabled the labor force to be adjusted to economic cycles. The recession of 1966–67 brought about a net loss of 800,000 jobs in West Germany, yet led to an increase in unemployment figures of only 300,000, because of the sharp fall-off in total numbers of foreign workers, euphemistically called "guest workers".

The indigenous work force was able to shift from old, declining or dying industries into new industries and the service sector. Above all, it was able to vacate the dullest, the poorest paid and the least secure jobs. Thus, the interests of migrant labor were generally underrepresented by trade union leaderships.

The presence of resident foreigners was not new to France or Germany, but in the course of

the 1960s the scale of employment of foreign workers increased dramatically. In the late 1940s there had been 1.5 million foreign workers in France; in the early 1970s their numbers had increased to 3.5 million so that they accounted for 7 percent of the total population. As early as the mid-1960s, foreign labor made up over 5 percent of West Germany's active labor force.

Problems of cultural assimilation, which were of a relatively minor order in the case of Italian migrant workers for instance, became acute especially with regard to Turkish workers in West Germany, to Algerians in France, and the relatively smaller numbers of migrant, from the West Indies and from South Asia who went to

▲ Families of Turkish *Gastarbeiter* in Berlin. Many immigrants settled down, wishing to stay a long time in the host country, though without necessarily changing their citizenship. This gave rise to problems in schools: should migrants' children conform to local cultural norms? Were local standards endangered, as some (host nation) parents feared? There were housing problems too. Segregation arose when Germans or Britons left inner-city areas and immigrants perforce settled in the places they had left.

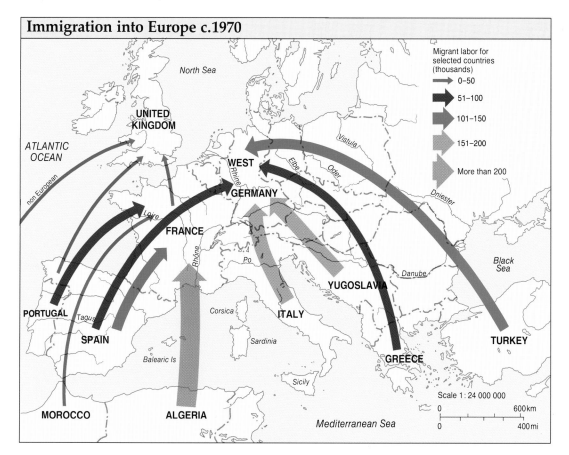

Immigration into Europe c.1970

North Sea

Migrant labor for selected countries (thousands)

0–50
51–100
101–150
151–200
More than 200

ATLANTIC OCEAN

non European

UNITED KINGDOM

Vistula

WEST GERMANY

Rhine

Elbe

Oder

Dniester

Loire

FRANCE

Rhône

Po

Danube

Black Sea

PORTUGAL

Tagus

Corsica

YUGOSLAVIA

ITALY

SPAIN

Sardinia

Balearic Is

TURKEY

Sicily

GREECE

Scale 1 : 24 000 000

0   600km
0   400mi

MOROCCO   ALGERIA   Mediterranean Sea

◄ By 1969 immigrants made up over 5 percent of the total population of Western Europe. Italians, Spaniards, Portuguese and (in Britain) the Irish were now rivaled in numbers by Algerians (in France), Yugoslavs, Greeks and Turks (in Germany) and Indians, Pakistanis and West Indians (in Britain). They shared the experience of being absorbed as a "reserve army of labor", in the least desirable jobs characterized by insecurity and poor working conditions, which had been deserted by indigenous labor. They also shared the experience of prejudice, though in varying degrees.

Britain. As West Germany's population of guest workers gradually became more settled, so the want of political as opposed to economic planning on the part of the government was exposed. Foreign workers and their families, enjoying no political rights in their "host" country and herded together in what were in effect to become ghettos, were vulnerable to prejudices activated by the experience of recession and unemployment which was to follow the oil crisis of 1973. Governments, instead of seriously confronting the issue of assimilation, resorted to restricting immigration – as Britain had already done as early as 1961. And so, intentionally or unintentionally, they seemed to legitimize the view that immigration was responsible for unemployment.

America: the triumph of liberalism

In the United States the early 1960s bear the stamp, above all others, of John F. Kennedy. His brief presidency (1961–63) encouraged the belief – not only in the United States – that a new and exciting age had arrived, and one above all of high moral purpose. "Ask not what your country can do for you", he said, "Ask what you can do for your country". This sense of purpose was extended into real accomplishment in the first years of Lyndon Baines Johnson's presidency (which began with Kennedy's assassination in 1963). In 1964 Johnson declared a "war on poverty" to carry out welfare initiatives which had been launched by his predecessor, and then announced his conception of the Great Society – "a place where men are more concerned with the quality of their goals than with the quality of their goods".

Johnson established the Medicare program of health insurance. Derided by the New England establishment as anti-intellectual, he saw through the Elementary and Secondary Education Act which provided grants for low-income pupils; and under his masterly leadership the 89th Congress, it was said, "brought to a harvest a generation's backlog of ideas and social legislation". At the same time the civil rights movement built up to a final push for racial equality. Already under Kennedy there had been a wave of desegregation of lunch counters, of "freedom rides" on interstate buses – testing a verdict of the Supreme Court that restaurants at bus stations could not discriminate against interstate travelers, and provoking violent opposition; and the southern universities were desegregated amidst bitter struggle. In August 1963 200,000 people gathered in Washington for a civil rights march, which was addressed passionately by Martin Luther King. "I still have a dream", he said, "It is a dream deeply rooted in the American Dream [that] one day in the red hills of Georgia, the sons of former slaves and the sons of former slave-owners will be able to sit together at the table of brotherhood".

King's vision came closer to being realized with the Civil Rights Act of 1964 which outlawed racial discrimination in public places, required equal access to public facilities, and prohibited discrimination in voter registration. A year later the Voting Rights Act effectively completed the enfranchisement of blacks. This was the apogee of American liberalism in the 1960s.

▲ Listeners to speeches at the great civil rights march in Washington, D.C., in August 1963. By this time the pressure from such demonstrations had pushed the administration into more resolute support for desegregation and the expansion of black voting rights; and troops had enforced court orders directing southern state universities to admit blacks. The achievement of civil rights was near.

◀ Even as the civil rights movement triumphed the black ghettoes erupted in the most destructive urban riots seen since the Civil War (1861–65). They showed the bitterness felt by blacks and signaled a new drive, not now for integration but for separatism and for self-help rather than reliance on white liberals. Some advocates of Black Power now sought to pursue a guerrilla war against white dominance.

◀ Tenements in Harlem. Once a genteel white neighborhood, Harlem became New York's largest black ghetto following the influx of blacks into the city early in the 20th century. In 1960 there was no part of Harlem in which more than 45 percent of housing was considered adequate. Only 7 percent of men were employed in professional or managerial occupations. It was said, "the negro has been left out of the swelling prosperity and social progress of the nation", echoing views that had already been expressed in the 1830s.

In 1965, only five days after Johnson had signed the Voting Rights Act, the Watts area of Los Angeles erupted in racial violence, leaving 34 dead, and signaling the first of four long hot summers which revealed the depths of antiwhite bitterness in American society. Watts shocked America, for it was so much *better off* than other black neighborhoods, and had been treated as a model of race relations. The even more intense violence in Newark and in Detroit in 1967 also happened in places where blacks had apparently been relatively favored. The common pattern running through Watts, Newark and Detroit was the cry for Black Power. The civil rights campaigners' idea of white and black togetherness was spurned. A new movement rapidly developed with features that were anathema to the civil rights activists – rejection of integration and also a willingness to employ violence. The looting that went on in the city riots was lauded as a political act. The Black Muslims, led by Elijah Muhammed and Malcolm X, jeered at Martin Luther King, and won a lot of support amongst young black unemployed and outcasts in the ghettos of the northern cities, offering a vision of a future society in which blacks would be on top. Part of their anger derived from the view that "The black man's burden [is] the white liberal!"

Thus it was that "In the smoking ruins of the gutted cities little remained of the sanguine expectations of liberalism" (Leuchtenburg), and the hope of the Great Society was smashed by violence, leading in the end to the election of the Republican Richard Nixon as president, by the "silent majority" of the American people, who were not black, who were not young students, and who looked to a man who answered the call to "Bring Us Together Again".

Youth protest and the "counterculture"

The affluence of the 1960s brought, amidst the wave of social and political protest, what has been called a revolution in morals – of a counterculture which in Theodore Roszak's words called for the "subversion of the scientific world view". While "modernity" sped ahead, new divisions opened up in Western society as hitherto silent social groups, ethnic or religious minorities, or immigrants demanded recognition and made their grievances felt. At universities the students' rebellion reflected the broader movement of change toward a more democratic and egalitarian society and a more humane personal and family life. Civil rights campaigns together with social critique advanced by the new left also gave feminism a new voice. In America gay rights activists began to campaign for the acceptance of an alternative sexuality.

Troubled by the prospects of a world that seemed increasingly bureaucratized and technologically driven, a new generation of young people rose to challenge entrenched institutions and the whole way of thinking on which the premises of Western consumer culture and meritocracy rested. Their protest against the establishment and its institutions and their revaluation of the value systems and symbols of authority which had prevailed in the West since the 18th century, had been foreshadowed by the so-called sexual revolution of the 1920s, and in America in particular also by a fervent critique of materialism in the same decade. After the war the "beats" of the 1950s, spreading also to Europe, picked up this theme. But it was to take that superabundance of worldly goods in the 1960s to produce a social and political protest movement which spread throughout the Western world.

The increasing presence of youth as a social and political force was crucial to this development. By the mid-1960s over half of America's population was under 30. According to a survey 80 percent of the under-35s were in some way involved in a search for "self-fulfillment", seeking an alternative life-style from that of their elders.

The icon-breaking counterculture of the young rejected the bourgeois catechism of the protestant

◀ The postwar boom in higher education created enormous problems. Since the establishment of new universities did not keep pace with the growing enrolment, most students had to be absorbed in the existing institutions. By the early 1960s the Sorbonne in Paris had almost 100,000 students. Student protest in France, as here in the Louvre, mixed issues of overcrowding and protest against an ossified university system with political grievances against the Gaullist regime.

ethic, fostering a rebellion against almost every aspect of traditional patterns of deference. The established churches which had until well into the 20th century preserved much of their importance as a mainstay of popular culture, and had continued to act as a bulwark of conservative social values, rapidly began to lose both their political and cultural influence. Official piety and church attendance were in decline. Yet religion was not. If anything, young people became more religious as they rejected the rationalism of the scientific age, replacing it with romantic, millennial or utopian dreams.

More harmful was the increasing consumption of alcohol and new experimentation with hallucinatory drugs to expand perception. Drugs

▼ Tupperware's range of plastic containers for the fridge and freezer and other uses was sold directly at home by organizing so-called "Tupperware parties", as seen here. Social gatherings of this kind, which mixed pleasure with the serious business of housekeeping, were a welcome relief for the relatively isolated housewife of the 1960s. Until the late 1960s public opinion averred that mothers should remain at home. Women generally obliged and actually tried to live up to the notion they could attain fulfillment only through rearing children and keeping house.

◀ The rediscovery of the pleasures of rituals and of festivity was an important part of the "counterculture" which erupted in America in the mid-1960s. At festivals such as this "live-in", usually held at urban parks, young people celebrated their new sense of personal freedom. When America's social reform movement came to a halt with the election of Richard Nixon toward the end of the 1960s, many of the once-utopian reformers of the counterculture turned away from their quest for fulfillment through a liberated community to fulfillment through the liberated self. This exploration and search for a true and autonomous identity later launched the "me first" protest movement.

were initially associated with performing or listening to rock music which was part and parcel of the youth revolt of the 1960s. "Acid Rock" made its appearance in San Francisco's light and sound shows. In Britain the Beatles' song, "Lucy in the Sky with Diamonds", clearly referred to the drug LSD. Drugs spread and marijuana became quite commonplace.

For many young people long hair and an unkempt appearance expressed the desire to escape the rigidity of a work-oriented existence. For the new "pot-heads" (in America) to be dirty was to be beautiful as they dropped out of school, drifting from "pad" to "pad". Alternative ways of living were found in so-called crash pads or communes, in the cities or away from them in the countryside, where the "flower children" and "hippies" of the 1960s and 1970s congregated.

Women and the family

In the new counterculture, with its focus on youth and hassle-free self-expression, there was little room for the very young or the mature or very old members of society. There was a certain cruelty in the way in which the old were declared to be obsolescent, part of that history that the young tried to shed. There was no tradition anymore, it seemed, and perhaps it is not surprising that initial bewilderment among the older generation eventually gave way to urgent calls for a return to "old fashioned decency and morality". How was one to deal with the changing position of women as they claimed the freedom to choose to have sexual experience and relationships both before, after and outside marriage; the free use of contraceptives and, if an unwanted pregnancy should occur, the right to abort? The really new and potentially liberating ingredient in women's lives had been the breakthrough in contraceptive technology. The contraceptive "Pill", developed by American scientists in the 1950s, became commercially available by the early 1960s.

Sexuality was possibly the most important preoccupation of radical feminism: it was sexuality which made men the "intimate" enemy. In the early 1970s abortion emerged as almost the definitive issue of the feminist movement. For radical feminists it symbolized women's sexual and reproductive self-determination; for other feminists it became an issue of women's individual freedom of choice. In the end even the Vatican proved incapable of stopping the distribution of contraceptives and the legalization of abortion in Italy in 1978. In Britain and a number of American states abortion had been legalized by 1970, though only Denmark (1973) and Sweden (1975) legalized abortion on demand.

The new degree of equality and independence that women sought to achieve was seen by many as an outright rejection of both marriage and the family. The rapid expansion in the numbers of married women in the labor force after 1960, and above all their changing attitudes to work or a career, seemed to confirm this fear. Women now no longer predominantly worked because they had to, in order to supplement family income, but because they wanted to; and they wanted to even if they had children.

So for the pro-family platform this was a difficult time as women seemed to move away from their central role as wives and mothers. Anxieties deepened when the family came under attack from "abolitionists", suggesting that the family stood in the way of progress – or from radical feminists who attacked it as the basis for women's oppression. New attitudes toward sex seemed to find expression in casual relationships and cohabitation rather than life-long commit-

ment. While divorce and separation rates started their long climb upward (more than doubling between 1960 and 1975 in many countries), indicating the growing fragility of the concept of "marriage for life", marriage rates also continued to drop. The birth rate within marriage also began to fall again, soon to reach zero growth rates in a number of countries; while the rate of births outside marriage began to rise more rapidly, especially among teenagers. In 1969 in Germany 37 percent of all first-born children were conceived before marriage. Social pressure to get married when pregnant was still high (to a lesser extent in Sweden). Until 1970 the number of single-parent families remained roughly the same

▲ A central issue of the "second wave feminism" of the 1960s was rebellion against the physical assertion of male power. This included the exploitation of women as sexual objects which is also the theme of these magazine covers. Sexuality was possibly the most important preoccupation of radical feminism. It was also gainfully exploited by the media, which sometimes ridiculed feminist arguments against sexual oppression and also expressed overt hostility to the whole notion of women's liberation.

Churches and Society

After World War II the long process of secularization – the decline of religious belief – accelerated. Although the great majority of people in western societies continued to express their belief in some kind of deity, active church membership dropped. By the early 1960s only about 10 percent of the British people – mostly the elderly, women and young children – went to church at all regularly. Religious observance was not much more active in Catholic France and Italy. Amongst the industrialized countries only the United States did not conform to the trend. A survey carried out in 60 countries showed that the United States had a higher level of religious commitment than any other, except for India. Outside America the cultural role of churches largely disappeared. Outside Ireland churchmen lost their political influence.

Throughout the earlier 20th century the Roman Catholic Church, in particular, remained a profoundly conservative influence. There were glimmerings of change after the war when a very small number of "worker priests" in France had a considerable impact. They took up manual jobs and, identifying with workers, opposed the

injustice of the existing social order. But their activities were stopped in the 1950s. Meanwhile Protestant theological reform exposed the Church, seeming to suggest that its message had become irrelevant. In this context the papacy of Pope John XXIII after 1958 brought dramatic change, The Ecumenical Council which he summoned (known as "Vatican II") and which met from 1962 to 1965 reformed much of the Church's social teaching as well as rewriting liturgy and lowering old regulations. The Mass, for example, was no longer said in Latin. After the Council the Church made strides toward ecumenism and became more open even on issues such as mixed marriage. Yet it still remained resistant to the practice of birth control, to abortion and to homosexuality, all condemned by John's successor Pope Paul VI, under whose leadership the pace of reform slowed down.

Later in the 20th century the Christian churches were to become more divided, between liberal theology and a return to "fundamentals", and between the pursuit of an active social role (as in "liberation theology", for example) or a conservative one.

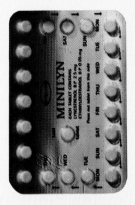

▲ Contraceptive tablets. Birth control changed dramatically in the 1960s with the arrival of the pill. In Britain it was initially issued by family-planning clinics and doctors. In America family planning as a public service was provided only to the poorest groups.

as in 1870 (10–12 percent – with national variations). After 1970, however, the single-parent family emerged as a more deliberate, intentional or less transitional life-style and the proportion of single-parent families was to double by 1980 (in America by that time to 21.4 percent of families with dependent children).

Attitudes to marriage
For a minority the significance of marriage as an institution began to diminish, demonstrating that different kinds of human sexual relationships were possible. The emergence of diverse family forms and life-styles, beginning with the "dual role perspective" (work and family) for women, single parenting, "common law" marriage or living in a commune also illustrated the fact that the very nature and range of possible ways of living together were products of social change. For many people, older (historical) family relationships became irrelevant. The so-called bourgeois family type (itself a product of social and economic change), which by 1900 had spread far beyond the middle classes to become the social norm, had centered on the mother and on the wife as a dependent. Love, the pivot of marriage,

had then had the character of a moral duty. All this was changing as the old dependents, wife and children, were now accorded new rights and women in particular achieved new independence. In Britain in 1974, for example, in over half a million couples the wife was the main earner; while in some seven million others wives contributed around a quarter of the family budget.

On the whole, however, the sexual revolution seemed not to have had all the consequences its earlier exponents claimed for it. There was no general consensus on sex roles, and traditional attitudes toward marriage remained pervasive – especially when it came to questions of fidelity in marriage. Despite the preoccupation with sex and its pleasures, sexual relationships outside marriage were not easily tolerated, by either partner. Sex may have been offered as a commodity by the amusement industry, the cinema or sex shop, but ideals of "true love" asserted themselves against "libertinism" in a number of ways. If libertinism did not materialize, then women's new independence and rights, and the reforms in divorce law toward the end of the 1960s and in the 1970s, certainly made it easier for women to make the break from marriages which had gone wrong.

▲ Feminist demonstrations such as this High School event in the United States were usually organized to raise women's consciousness of a shared struggle. Until the early 1970s consciousness-raising had a central place in feminist groups' activities, to help women to relate their personal experiences to wider issues of sexual oppression. By learning together women were to acquire a revolutionary solidarity of sisterhood. Among the more radical groups, this fueled anger and protest against male-dominated politics – eventually leading to separate organizations for women.

LAW AND ORDER

"Society" implies "order", but order is not synonymous with law. In many societies, both in the past and today, there has been no legal system, no laws, no courts, no prisons. Instead, order has been maintained by means of customary regulations and sanctions, though sometimes there have also been specialists in the settlement of disputes. With the development of large-scale societies and in particular of the nation state, standardization of law has been essential together with the development of the principle of citizenship, implying both rights and obligations. In the 20th century the extension of formal systems of law and of legal institutions has gone hand in hand with the spread of state organization. The great European colonial empires were of the greatest importance in this global change.

In many countries, however, different ways of maintaining social order continue to coexist. Thus in Papua New Guinea the institutions associated with Western law are part of the state, while in parts of the country order is still sometimes maintained between communities by means of traditional ceremonial warfare.

The principles of modern law are closely tied to the idea of the liberal democratic state. Equality of all before the law, separation of judiciary, executive and legislature, and public process are all part of what the law is supposed to be. There is also a darker side. While order may be desirable, it often implies conformity against the will of individuals or social minorities. Law also has an element of discipline which is enforced by means of punishment, and may thus be used to defend the positions of the powerful. Sometimes, as in Nazi Germany and communist states, the law has meant the defense of the position and beliefs of the party – political and ideological deviation were criminalized. In others it has been used to defend the privileges of the wealthy and powerful.

The law and the legal system are important aspects of the effective separation of the public and private realms. The criminalization of marital violence, corporal punishment of children by their parents, use of drugs, pornography – all arguably part of the "private" sphere – have been and continue to be important legal issues. While it has increasingly been recognized that different cultures may require different legal provisions, the experience of the 20th century has shown starkly that legal questions are also political questions and that the law can be used for illegitimate political ends – to discipline those who do not fit in with the mainstream of society.

▲▶ A stern but caring state: productive work and education are displayed in a Soviet "model" prison 1933. The aim is reform rather than punishment, preparation for return to society. This public face of Bolshevik penal theory was belied by the horrors of Soviet labor camps.

▶▶ A US prison, based on penal theory which confines the body and breaks the will. There is no pretense of reform here.

▶ Police in Boston in the United States. In face of protest, law and order may come down to force

◄ Legal majesty and impartiality are personified in these judges from Sierra Leone and symbolized by their special dress and remote bearing. Maintenance of these ideals in the face of powerful sectional interests is a constant struggle in all societies. The law is upheld not only by legal institutions; press freedom may be just as important. It is not yet clear whether Western legal systems work in non-Western cultures.

◄ The stark machinery of death in the United States: an electric chair. In many societies death continues to be the punishment for misdemeanors ranging through theft, murder, adultery, treason, political and sexual deviation. As with all law, the use of capital punishment may have more to do with politics than with justice or morality.

▼ Whose law, whose justice? The law in the hands of one section of society. Law has often been a means for control by a minority – by these whites in South Africa, by the party in the Soviet Union and in Nazi Germany. Censorship, the whip, the secret death, the panoply of control, a state without citizens, only degrees of prisoner – law can easily be used to build the prison state.

1973 · 1989

THE UNCERTAIN PATH

Time Chart

	1974	1975	1976	1977	1978	1979	1980	1981
Rural life	• Oct: India suffers its worst famine in 20 years	• Fighting in Ethiopia exacerbates continuing famine • Dutch elm disease begins to spread out from the Midlands and south of England; the disease has killed 6.5 million trees since the 1960s		• 19 Nov: In an effort to preserve wildlife, Jomo Kenyatta bans the hunting of big game (Ken)	• Apr: China purchases US wheat in bulk to supplement its supplies	• Jul: World agricultural conference to discuss the UN development program on the problems of developing countries	• Jun: Reports that ten million face starvation in East Africa; drought and wars create massive crop failures and refugee problems • Sep: Britain and France discuss a joint agricultural policy	
Industry and labor	• 6 Mar: UK miners' strike ends as miners gain a 35% pay increase • 18 Mar: Oil embargo on the US lifted by Arab states • May: Militant Protestants organize a strike which paralyzes Ulster (UK)	• Jan: UK wage inflation reaches 28.5%; in July the government passes a law to limit spiraling wage increases • May: nationalization of Gulf Oil de Peru • 5 Jun: Reopening of the Suez Canal • 11 Aug: British Leyland is nationalized	• 24 May: Concorde begins commercial transatlantic flights • Aug: 1.5 million reported unemployed in the UK • 15 Sep: 250,000 nonwhites go on strike in Capetown (SA) • 27 Nov: Four millionth Mini is produced (UK)	• 17 Jan: Workers in Cairo riot over increased prices (Egy) • Jul: "Social Contract" between the government and trade unions is destroyed by skyrocketing wage claims (UK) • French government takes control of subsidized steel	• 23 Jan: National strike is organized in opposition to the Somoza government (Nic) • Oct: Wave of strikes against the shah brings Iranian oil production to near standstill	• Jan: Britain's "winter of discontent" includes strikes by transport, hospital and local government employees • 28 Mar: Accident at the Three Mile Island nuclear power plant (USA) • 28 Jun: OPEC agreement to raise oil prices by 15%	• Aug: Polish workers strike and seize the Lenin Shipyard in Gdansk; two months of strikes and demonstrations bring concessions from the Polish government • 22 Sep: Polish workers launch Solidarność (Solidarity), a union led by electrician Lech Walesa	• 31 Jul: Strike of US professional baseball players ends after seven weeks • 3 Aug: Strike of US air traffic controllers • 7 Aug: One million Solidarity workers strike to protest at food prices and economic conditions in Poland
Government and people	• 15 Feb: Foreigners are banned from traveling within China • 1 Apr: Britain's NHS begins to provide free family planning service • Draft evaders and deserters during the Vietnam War are granted a limited amnesty by President Ford (USA)	• 1 Aug: US, Canada and 35 European countries sign the Helsinki Accord: a human rights agreement is signed; postwar boundaries recognized as fixed; USSR pledges to uphold human rights (Fin) • 29 Dec: Sex Discrimination Act and Equal Pay Act take effect (UK)	• Jun: Insistence that Afrikaans be an official language in Bantu schools leads to riots in Soweto (SA) • 4 Aug: 90% of political prisoners granted pardons by King Juan Carlos (Sp) • Sep: South Africa decides to allow multiracial sports teams to represent the country	• Jan: 240 Czech intellectuals, including playwright Václav Havel, sign Charter 77, a document proposing greater civil rights under the Communist government (Czech) • 17 Jan: USA restores capital punishment • 15 Jun: Spain holds its first democratic elections in 41 years	• Feb–Mar: Plans for moving Rhodesia toward black rule: all adult citizens enfranchised; Ian Smith and three black leaders sign an agreement to end white rule within a year • 6 Dec: Spanish referendum endorses the new democratic constitution	• Female prime ministers elected in Portugal (Maria Pintassilgo) and Britain (Margaret Thatcher) • 23 Jul: Ayatollah Khomeini bans the broadcasting of music, declaring it a corrupting force among the young (Iran)	• Feb: Margaret Thatcher recommends a 50% cut in strike benefits (UK) • 22 Feb: After anti-Soviet riots in Kabul, martial law is declared in Afghanistan • 30 Oct: Council tenants are now allowed to purchase their homes under the terms of the Housing Act (UK)	• 7 Jul: Judge Sandra O'Connor is the first woman ever appointed to the US Supreme Court • 18 Sep: France abolishes the use of the guillotine • 13 Dec: Martial law take effect in Poland
Religion	• 20 Apr: Sectarian violence in Belfast claims its 1,000th victim (UK) • Four Episcopal bishops disregard church law and ordain eleven women as priests	• Apr: Fighting begins in Beirut between right wing Christian Phalangists and Muslims (Leb) • 6 May: Cardinal Jozef Mindszenty dies in exile; the former Archbishop and Primate of Hungary was an outspoken opponent of Communism		• Feb: Idi Amin's troops murder the Archbishop of Uganda • Feb: Seven white Catholic missionaries massacred by guerrillas (Rhod)	• 6 Aug: Death of Pope Paul VI, succeeded by John Paul I, who dies 30 Sep, and is succeeded by John Paul II on 16 Oct • Nov: 913 followers of Jim Jones' religious cult, The People's Temple, commit suicide on the orders of their leader (Guy)	• 1 Apr: Khomeini declares Iran an Islamic republic • 20 Nov: Gunmen occupy the Grand Mosque in Mecca, Islam's holiest place; four days later, Saudi troops recapture the Mosque from the Shi'ite gunmen (Saud)	• May: South African police arrest 26 demonstrating churchmen • 19 Oct: Roman Catholic officials in Poland come out in open support of Solidarity	• 13 May: Turkish gunman attempts to assassinate Pope John Paul II in Vatican City • 12 Nov: Vote by Church of England General Synod allow women to become deacons
Events and trends	• Beginning of environmental fears about the condition and future of the earth's ozone layer • Mariner X satellite provides detailed views of Mercury and Venus • 11 May: Eleven million killed in an earthquake in China • 15 May: Dalkon shields contraceptive device is banned from the US market after fears about its safety	• 21 Mar: Monarchy is abolished in Ethiopia • Dec: US scientists claim to have established a link between oestrogen taken for period pains and uterine cancer	• 4 Jul: USA celebrates its bicentennial • 20 Jul: Viking spacecraft lands on Mars and sends back pictures to Earth • 24 Sep: Rhodesian prime minister Ian Smith announces a two-year plan to create black majority rule	• Sep: Study reveals that murder is the leading cause of death among young black Americans (USA) • 12 Sep: Black leader Steve Biko dies in police custody (SA) • Dec: Amnesty International human rights organization wins the Nobel Peace Prize • 800,000 people become refugees, "Boat People", from South Vietnam	• 29 Jan: Sweden is the first country to legislate against aerosol sprays which damage the ozone layer • 26 Jul: World's first test-tube baby born in the UK • 10 Dec: Millions of Iranians take to the streets in protests against the Shah	• 9 Feb: Fallopian tube successfully transplanted for the first time (UK) • 16 Jun: Exile of the shah of Iran • 11 Apr: Ugandan dictator Idi Amin deposed by a force of exiled Ugandans and Tanzanians • 4 Nov: US Embassy in Tehran captured by Iranians who take hostages (Iran)	• Jan: Surgeon General's report reveals lung cancer to be the leading cancer killer of women (USA) • 5 Jul: Iranian women protest in Tehran against the Islamic dress code for women • 4 Nov: Ronald Reagan elected president of the USA	• 16 Jan: National Cancer Research Institute in Tokyo reveals that the lung cancer rate is twice as high in women married to smokers (Jap) • Feb: Right wing of Guardia Civil attempt a coup in Spain • Dec: Alarm increases over a disease which affects the immune system and appears to be common among homosexuals in the USA
Politics	• Aug: US president Nixon resigns as a result of the Watergate scandal; vice-president Gerald Ford becomes the new president	• 16 Apr: Cambodia taken by the Khmer Rouge • 20 Nov: General Franco dies and is replaced by King Juan Carlos (Sp)	• 2 Jul: North and South Vietnam are united as a single socialist republic	• 5 Jul: Pakistani prime minister Zulfikar Ali Bhutto ousted by General Zia ul-Haq	• 18 Sep: Beginning of Camp David accords between president Sadat (Egy) and prime minister Begin (Isr)	• 7 Jan: Cambodia falls to the Vietnamese • 1 Feb: Ayatollah Khomeini returns to Iran after 14 years in exile • 26 Mar: Egypt and Israel sign peace treaty in the USA	• 4 Mar: Robert Mugabe is elected premier of Zimbabwe • Sep: Iraq attacks Iranian oil refinery at Abadan thus starting the Gulf War	• 6 Oct: Muslim extremists assassinate Egyptian president Sadat in Cairo • General Wojciech Jaruzelski declares martial law in Poland and bans Solidarity

1982	1983	1984	1985	1986	1987	1988	1989
	• Mar: Problems created by production surpluses lead to discussions on leaving farmland fallow (USA)	• 2 Jan: Environmental report stresses the threat posed by acid rain to English lakes and countryside • Global awareness of famine in Ethiopia; between 600,000 and one million die by the end of the year		• Apr–Oct: Food destroyed in Europe after contamination by fallout from the Chernobyl nuclear plant accident	• At current rates of environmental destruction, it is calculated that six animal and plant species are driven into extinction every hour	• Sep: Bovine spongiform encephalopathy (BSE) threatens British cattle in the West Country • Oct: Measures announced in Brazil to end the destruction of the rain forests	• 1 Jan: Trade sanctions imposed on EC after it bans import of US hormone-treated meat
• Jan: Unemployment in the UK surpasses three million • 31 Jan: Two- to five-fold increases in prices lead to riots at the shipyards in Gdansk (Pol) • Jun: Freeze on prices and wages in France begins and lasts four months	• Jan: Nigeria orders one million Ghanaian migrant workers to leave the country • 14 Mar: OPEC members agree to reduce oil prices by $5 per barrel • 20 Aug: Ban on sale of parts for the Siberian pipeline lifted by the USA	• 12 Mar: Beginning of a nationwide miners' strike (UK) • Jun: With the establishment of four designated economic areas, China seeks foreign investors • Dec: Leak of toxic gas from a Union Carbide plant in Bhopal, India, kills 2000	• 3 Mar: National Union of Mineworkers (NUM) votes to call off the miners' strike (UK) • 1 May: Police and 10,000 Solidarity supporters clash during a march (Pol) • US and Japan test process of energy production through laser-fired nuclear fusion	• Feb: Arab League agrees to establish a free trade area as the price of oil collapses • 1 May: 1.5 million black workers go on strike in Johannesburg • 30 Dec: Esso oil company announces that it will disinvest in South Africa	• 16 Jul: British Airways announces its intention to buy British Caledonian (UK) • 7 Sep: Ford obtains the luxury sports car company Aston Martin (USA/UK) • Boring of the Channel Tunnel begins at Calais (Fr)	• 8 Jun: Two million blacks go on strike to protest against apartheid (SA) • 17 Aug: Polish coal miners strike nationally • 7–12 Sep: Postal workers' strike causes tremendous disruption of the mail service (UK)	• Mar: Exxon Valdez tanker runs aground; 38 million liters of oil pollutes 160 km of Alaskan coastline • Jul: 300,000 Soviet miners strike for two weeks in protest over conditions and pay • 27 Nov: General strike brings Czechoslovakia to a halt
• 15 Mar: Constitution is suspended in Nicaragua; ten days later the Sandinista government declares a state of emergency • 8 Oct: Solidarity is outlawed by the Polish government although martial law is lifted in Dec	• 7 Nov: Chancellor of the Exchequer announces cuts in public spending of £500 million (UK) • 21 Jul: Martial law is lifted in Poland • 3 Nov: Referendum among white South Africans favors sharing some power with Indians and Coloreds, but not Blacks	• 12 Jul: Democratic Party selects the first woman, Geraldine Ferraro, to run for vice-president (USA) • 4 Sep: New constitution takes effect in South Africa, offering limited power to Coloreds and Asians but not Blacks, leads to violent rioting in Black townships	• 15 Apr: Racial sex laws are discontinued in South Africa • 16 Jul: 10,000 women from around the world meet at a conference in Nairobi to discuss progress on women's rights issues • 16 May: UK home secretary announces new police powers designed to control mob and picket-line violence	• 20 Jan: Martin Luther King holiday is observed for the first time (USA) • Apr: Bishop Desmond Tutu asks the world to impose sanctions against South Africa • 12 Jun: South Africa declares a state of emergency on tenth anniversary of Soweto uprising	• Jan: Soviet president Mikhail Gorbachev calls for greater democracy in the Communist party, his policies of perestroika and glasnost • May: South African liberals lose numerous seats to militant whites in the Conservative party (SA)	• 5 Jun: Burma introduces a two-month curfew after antigovernment protests • 29 Jul: Education Reform receives royal assent, introducing a national curriculum for schools in the state system as well as regular examinations (UK)	• 5 Apr: Communist officials agree to legalize Solidarity and hold democratic elections in Jun (Pol) • 26 May: Martial law declared in China; roundup of young "rebels" begins in Jun • 10 Oct: Hungary's Communist rulers vote to become social democrats
• 18 May: Sun Myung Moon, leader of the Unification Church, is found guilty on charges of income tax fraud (USA) • 17 Sep: Hundreds of Palestinian refugees massacred by Lebanese Christian militia	• Feb: Sectarian violence in Assam leads to the massacre of 600 Muslims refugees (Ind) • Jun: In a return visit to his homeland the Pope openly backs Solidarity (Pol)	• Mar: Week of religious riots in Yola kills up to 1000 (Nig) • May: Bombay is the scene of five days of bloody rioting between Hindus and Muslims (Ind) • 6 Jun: Indian troops storm the Sikh Golden Temple to release it from Muslim extremists	• Jan: Israel ends its secret airlift of Ethiopian Jews (Falashas) • 5 May: Jews angered by US president Reagan's visit to the Bitburg War Cemetery (FRG) which contains the graves of SS officers	• 12 Jul: Orange Day clashes between Catholics and Protestants leave 100 injured (UK) • 6 Sep: 21 killed in an Istanbul synagogue by Arab gunmen (Turk) • 7 Sep: Desmond Tutu becomes Archbishop of Cape Town	• General Synod of the Church of England votes in favor of ordaining women as priests • Terry Waite, Archbishop of Canterbury's special envoy seeking hostage releases, is himself kidnapped in Lebanon	• 21 Feb: Leading US televison evangelist Jimmy Swaggart is disgraced • 18 May: Siege of the Golden Temple at Amritsar ends when Sikh militants surrender (Ind) • 15 Jan: Beginning of the Arab uprising (intifada) in Israel	• Feb: Ayatollah Khomeini issues a fatwa condemning to death British author Salman Rushdie for offence caused to Muslims by the latter's novel The Satanic Verses (Iran) • Boston Episcopal church consecrates the first female bishop in history (USA)
• 1 Feb: US president Reagan announces the USA will provide emergency aid to the government of El Salvador • 2 Dec: Barney Clark receives the first artificial heart implant in an operation which lasts 7.5 hours (USA)	• 14 Jun: Nationwide protests over the rule of Pinochet in Chile • 18 Jun: Sally Ride, America's first female astronaut, goes into space as a crewmember on the space shuttle Challenger • 1 Sep: South Korean airliner shot down by Soviet fighter; 269 passengers killed • 22 Oct: Antinuclear protesters march in several European cities	• 18 Jul: Gunman shoots 20 people in a McDonalds restaurant for no apparent reason (USA) • 16 Oct: Archbishop Desmond Tutu (SA) wins the Nobel Peace Prize • UK scientists warn of the increasing threat posed by the "greenhouse effect" • French and American scientists discover the virus which causes AIDS	• 2 Jan: USA officially withdraws its membership from UNESCO • Live Aid concerts staged in London and New York to provide aid for the hungry in Ethiopia • 19 Sep: Mexico City devastated by an earthquake • Britain starts testing blood donors for the AIDS virus	• 28 Jun: US space shuttle Challenger explodes just after liftoff, killing its crew of seven • 27 Aug: US report says a hydrogen bomb was dropped on New Mexico by accident in 1957	• Aug: One person per day reportedly dying of AIDS • 10 Sep: 70 nations agree in Montreal to freeze current use of chlorofluorocarbons (CFCs) and to reduce their levels by 50% by 1999, in order to save the ozone layer • 16 Dec: Largest Mafia trial ever brings 338 convictions in Palermo (It)	• 19 Mar: According to US scientists the ozone protection treaty has come too late to save the ozone layer • 29 Apr: McDonalds announces that it will open 20 restaurants in the USSR • Sep: Flooding in Bangladesh leaves 20 million homeless • 10 Dec: Armenia rocked by an earthquake which kills up to 100,000 people	• 3 Dec: Presidents Mikhail Gorbachev and George Bush declare the end of the Cold War • 25 Dec: Execution of Romanian president Nicolae Ceausescu after the Communist regime is toppled in a bloody civil war • 28 Dec: Václav Havel is elected president of Czechoslovakia
• 2 Apr: Falklands conflict begins as Argentina seizes the UK territory; Argentina surrenders on 14 Jun	• 25 Oct: Operation Urgent Fury, as US troops land on Grenada after a Marxist coup there • Dec: Yasser Arafat withdraws PLO forces from Lebanon	• Feb: International peacekeeping force withdraws from Lebanon as the situation becomes chaotic • 31 Oct: Indian prime minister Indira Gandhi assassinated by Sikh bodyguards	• 10 Mar: Mikhail S Gorbachev becomes general secretary of the Soviet Communist party	• 25 Feb: Corazon Aquino drives Ferdinand Marcos from power in elections in the Philippines • 26 Apr: Fire at Chernobyl nuclear power plant contaminates most of Europe	• May: Beginning of hearings on the Iran-Contra affair, "Irangate" (USA) • 19 Oct: Black Monday: Wall Street share prices fall twice as far as in the 1929 crash; London and Tokyo are also affected	• 16 May: Soviet troops begin to withdraw from Afghanistan • Aug: UN ceasefire agreement between Iraq and Iran	• 4 Jun: Troops crush demonstrations against Communist rule in Beijing, with 2600 killed (China) • 10 Nov: Berlin Wall is opened, allowing free movement from East to West

Datafile

The sudden increase in oil prices in 1973 precipitated a crisis in the international economy which brought about a major restructuring. Features of this were the establishment of a "new international division of labor", involving the rise of newly industrialized countries led by Hong Kong, Taiwan, Singapore and South Korea. At the same time the old industrial countries saw "deindustrialization"; the further growth of services; and the introduction of new methods of work organization. "Flexibility" in labor markets meant greater insecurity for many workers and informal employment expanded. Decollectivization of agriculture in China heralded change in the socialist world.

Industrial countries 1988

22%
15%
11%
9%
6%
5%
32%

Pig iron output

- USSR
- Japan
- China
- USA
- FRG
- Brazil
- Rest of world

► At the beginning of the 20th century coalminers were the vanguard of the organized labor movement in Europe. In Western Europe they were no longer so. In Britain a strike lasting a year (1984–85) was unable to prevent large-scale job losses and pit closures. In France too the coalfields witnessed major job losses. In the Soviet Union and Eastern Europe, however, the miners of Silesia and the Donbas respectively were still able to force the hands of governments in the 1980s and 1990s.

Coal mining in France

174,000

Employees (thousands)

1963   1973   1983

▲ The industrial structure of the world in the late 20th century is reflected here in the output of pig iron in 1988. The raw material of the first industrial revolution was now produced widely. The leading industrial powers shared production with large but backward industrial economies. The Soviet Union's preeminence did not equate with economic leadership as US preeminence had done around 1914. Heavy industries, such as shipbuilding, had largely moved away from the old industrial centers.

Information technology

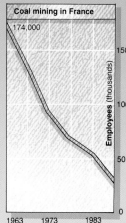

Massachusetts
California
New York
Illinois
Pennsylvania
Texas
New Jersey

Employment (thousands)

600
500
400
300
200
100
0

◄ Knowledge became a key commodity and the means of handling it by information technology (IT) a competitive industry. Concentrations of "high-tech" industry grew up in America, based on big universities. Leading centers were the Stanford Silicon Valley (California) and the MIT–Boston Route 128 (Massachusetts).

► The change in the economic structure of the West by comparison with the state socialist bloc is shown in the greater importance of financial services in Germany as compared with the Soviet Union. This reflected the expansion of services employment and the reorganization of the global financial system.

Employment groups

8%   1%
9%
10%
20%   28%
        24%

USSR 1984

7%
15%   33%
7%
6%
6%   26%

FRG 1985

- Manufacturing
- Services
- Agriculture
- Transport
- Construction
- Commerce
- Finance

► Alongside the growth of "high-tech" industry there was an expansion in second jobs, often involving "moonlighting" and household-based work. It ranged from casual work by the unemployed to highly paid consultancy, design and craft work, and was one of the ways in which labor markets became more "flexible".

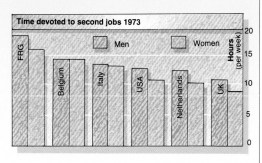

Time devoted to second jobs 1973

Men   Women

FRG   Belgium   Italy   USA   Netherlands   UK

Hours (per week)

20
15
10
5
0

The steep rise in oil prices in 1973 provoked an economic crisis that had been latent in the international economy for some time and brought to an end the long boom of the postwar period. The underlying causes of the crisis included the rigidity of Fordist large-scale methods of production and inadequate demand.

The responses that developed in the 1970s and 1980s saw a restructuring of the international economic system and of production methods. Labor was weakened by economic recession and employers made use of their greater power to make labor markets, production methods and patterns of consumption more flexible. The economies of scale that had been sought by Fordist mass production were countered by an increased capacity to manufacture a variety of goods in small batches, associated with more rapidly changing fashions. New production organization and the ability of firms to adjust rapidly to changing markets (to the point of adjusting markets) depended in turn on new information technology. This, for example, made possible the introduction of "just-in-time" production, whereby components were manufactured and delivered just as they were needed, which removed the need to lock up capital in the maintenance of large stocks of raw materials and finished goods. But the importance of information increased the advantages of large corporations even whilst often making production in smaller units desirable. At the same time more workers came to be employed on a variety of short-term contracts. This is what "flexibility" in the labor market meant – increased use of "informally" employed workers with few rights. The whole complex of changes was associated with aggressive neoliberalism in politics. It lauded the individual but its practitioners in government often proved to be centralist and interventionist. It was successful, however, in rooting a culture of entrepreneurialism deeply in Western societies and, in the early 1990s, extending it to formerly "socialist" countries.

The "new international division of labor"

The emergence of a new economic order involved the establishment of a new international division of labor following the rise of "newly industrializing countries". In the 1950s Hong Kong had begun to industrialize rapidly. For the first time, world demand for garments stimulated a poor city into frenetic growth. In the late 1950s Taiwan followed suit, and shortly afterward South Korea and then Singapore. In the last three cases – unlike Hong Kong – the process was initiated and supported by major state intervention. The process of rapid growth stimulated by the export of manufactured goods was not restricted to these

NEW DIVISIONS OF LABOR

four cases, although they attained higher rates of growth for a more extended period than many others. The phases of growth seen in South Korea – from garment exports in the 1960s to capital-intensive goods (ships, steel) in the 1970s to more skill-based goods in the 1980s (electronic, video and telecommunications equipment, vehicles) were replicated in some other developing countries in Asia and Latin America (though not successfully so in India).

The process did not so much indicate the peculiar merits of the four "little tigers" of Asia but rather a structural change in the world economy. In essence it reflected a decline in the comparative advantage of sectors of manufacturing in the more developed countries. By the 1980s the original Asian four had labor costs that were too high to compete in cheap garments, so other poorer countries took this over. China, for example, became a major exporter of garments. In Bangladesh employment in garment manufacturing for export grew to a quarter of a million. There was accelerated growth based on manufacturing for export in Thailand, Malaysia, Indonesia,

Mauritius, Botswana and elsewhere. Furthermore, while there was much fear that governments in more developed countries would block imports to protect their own manufacturing capacity (and, indeed, they did from time to time take such action), it seemed they had become increasingly dependent upon imports to produce their own output. To cut imports was thus to cut domestic employment, incomes and exports. Integration of a world economy had become a trend that could not be stopped at acceptable cost.

The process was seen most vividly in the burgeoning "offshore" production sites, particularly in the making of electronic components. In Southeast Asia and parts of Latin America, the same type of labor was involved: young women, literate, aged 15 to 22. Employers might say such workers were engaged because they had "nimble fingers" or were more conscientious and hardworking than adult men. A more obvious explanation was that, at a given level of education, this was the lowest-paid type of labor and it was subject in the factory to an extension of the patriarchal authority within the family.

▼ The employment of young women, supposedly because of their "nimble fingers", is not confined to modern industries, such as electronics. Here in a factory in Java vulnerable women workers make cigarettes under conditions of low pay and negligible job security.

Life in British Depressed Regions

In the 1970s and 1980s industrialized societies once again experienced high rates of unemployment. The burden was, however, shared unequally between regions. In Britain the gulf which had opened up in the 1930s between the North and South grew wider. This reflected the continued dependence of Scotland, Wales and the Northwest and Northeast of England on the old industries of the first industrial revolution. Now decline went so far as to represent "deindustrialization", and these regions knew persistent and long-term unemployment.

Those who had been vulnerable in the past were the least likely to escape unemployment now. Politicians urged people to move in search of jobs and, contrary to popular perceptions, many did. In 1980 600 workers a month were leaving the Northeast, mostly to look for jobs in Canada and Australia. But they were usually aged 25 – 35, and professional or skilled workers. For the least skilled who were most vulnerable movement was made difficult because of the availability of cheap public housing in the North, and the difference in house prices between declining and prosperous regions.

The hypothesis on "the psychology of unemployment", first developed in the 1930s, was borne out: "First there is shock, which is followed by an active hunt for a job during which the individual is still optimistic and

unresigned: he still maintains an unbroken attitude. Second, when all efforts fail, the individual becomes pessimistic, anxious and suffers active distress. And, third, the individual becomes fatalistic and adapts himself to his new state. He now has a broken attitude". One Tynesider, now back at work but in a less well-paid job, described his experience in similar terms: "When I was unemployed I was very worried: I thought that was it, I didn't expect to get another job. I slept in late until about 11 a.m. I got very bored. Hours in the early afternoon were the worst – hours when I thought that I used to be working. I wasn't ready for retiring yet: I can still work, I wanted to work. I got very jealous of those who were working. My wife is right when she said it affects me *as a man*: it isn't the money so much as the feeling men have".

Reduced budgets and enforced contact between husbands and wives led to increased tensions within some families. There was disturbing evidence of violent rows and family breakups linked to unemployment in the depressed regions. Young people also suffered acutely, the risk of unemployment for them being greater than for the remainder of the labor force. More stringent conditions for entitlement to social security benefits finally drove some of these youngsters to search for a living in cities where they slept rough or in "cardboard cities".

▲ An industrial landscape in the Northeast of England. With its old coal-mining, steel and shipbuilding industries in steep decline as a result of international recession, competition from newly industrialized countries, and public expenditure cuts, the Northeast was one of the declining regions of the older industrialized world. Changes in mining technology also contributed to the decay of coalmining communities. The British government said in 1986: "The North East is in the unenviable position of having the worst combination of unemployment blackspots in the country."

Why did this shift of manufacturing capacity to parts of the Third World take place? There are several reinforcing factors: expansion in infrastructure and improvements in health and education in developing countries; the creation of export processing zones, free of the bureaucratic restrictions so common in many developing countries and with taxfree access to imported machinery and raw materials; the rapid decline in the cost of freight movement by sea, road and air; and reduction in the restrictions on imports in developed countries. All these were "permissive" factors; they facilitated growth only if demand was expanding. What caused demand to expand? Here a key factor seems to have been the price of labor in developed countries which, from the mid 1950s rose relatively rapidly, making it impossible for many lines of production to take place when cheaper imports were available.

As barriers to trade declined, the old assumptions about how capital and labor were combined were transformed. It had been assumed that there would always be increasing scale of production and increasing use of capital relative to labor, culminating in automation. But that assumed a particular price for labor. When a *world* labor supply became available, the calculations changed – small and petty units of production, with very little capital, could defeat the giant automated factory. Women working at home with their children on a sewing machine to produce shoes could defeat the shoemaking plants of the United States. Thus the informal sector could now become highly competitive in a world economy when it was not in an isolated national one.

The change in the structure of production resulted in striking social changes. New urban working classes were created. At various times they became politically significant in strikes and agitations. Labor parties were no longer restricted to the developed countries. Indeed, in the 1970s, under the impact of the first slump (1974–75), there was a wave of major strikes, including general strikes, that affected equally both the more and the less developed.

The same seems to have been true of business classes. When, in the Philippines in 1986, Mrs Corazon Aquino challenged Ferdinand Marcos in the presidential election she did so with the strong support of the majority of Filipino businessmen. The symbol of her movement, the yellow shirt, became something of an inspiration to the similar movement that developed shortly afterward in South Korea. There were other cases – in Brazil and Mexico – suggesting that in a number of middle-income countries significant business classes had begun to exercise more independent political power. They seemed no longer willing simply to act as loyal retainers to an all-powerful state, but demanded the right to participate in the determination of policy.

Social structures had been transformed. There was no longer a massive peasantry with a powerful state and tiny business and working classes. In the newly industrializing countries, the urban classes – the mass of workers, the large educated middle class, and a self-confident business class – had come to dominate society.

◀ This Turkish woman in Paris carries on a tailoring business at home, working as a subcontractor for a large establishment. Such "informal" employment reduces the cost of labor, partly by undermining worker organization. This is one of the ways by which Western economies have been "restructured".

The onward march of deindustrialization?

In four of the six largest Western economies, real incomes fell between 1973 and 1975. Unemployment rates rose to what were, by postwar standards, unprecedented levels, such as had been thought incompatible with the postwar social order of a "corporatist" alliance of state, trade unions and employers. But it was not so. Indeed, unemployment rates resulting from the first slump, in 1974–75, were even exceeded by those of the second, in 1979–81. By then in many European countries there was little pretense of alliance any longer and governments were busy instituting market imperatives for all the supposed elements of the old social democratic pact – health, welfare and education.

The first slump, and even more the second, had particularly damaging effects in a major segment of manufacturing, much of it located in and around older industrial cities. The process, identified as "deindustrialization", was associated with another, "deurbanization" – the drift away from cities, especially large industrial ones. It was also associated with the further growth of service employment. The more advanced an economy, the higher the proportion of expenditure went on

▼ As the "young upwardly mobile professionals" (yuppies) of the Western world acquired more wealth in the 1980s, so sophisticated gadgetry such as this electronic diary came to meet their new market.

▼ These Swedish automobile workers form a workteam, with responsibility for several stages of construction. Their employer argues that with such arrangements "the small workshop atmosphere is built into the large plant", and seeks efficiency by creating "meaning and satisfaction in work".

▲ Blocks of flats and rows of East Germany's Trabant automobile reflect the social regimentation of centrally planned economies. The Trabant, produced by inefficient and dangerous methods, was much sought after. Hard currency exports, such as cameras, were also produced by uncompetitive methods. It was calculated in 1990 that only 8 percent of the work force was employed in internationally viable enterprises.

services, because people wanted to improve standards of relatively labor-intensive services – for example, health care, welfare and education. Even if they did not, the relative cost would rise because productivity in this sector does not increase as fast as it can in manufacturing.

The slump had the worst effects on old sections of industry, particularly heavy industry (steel, coal, shipbuilding, heavy engineering) which, with poor profit rates in the 1960s, had not received sufficient investment. Low-cost new producers with the latest technology, operating in the more advanced developing countries, scooped the markets.

Meanwhile, other sectors grew. In Britain the employment growth sectors between 1961/66 and 1976 were: insurance, banking and finance (52 percent growth); professional and scientific (56 percent); miscellaneous services (17 percent); and

public administration and defence (20 percent). These were the sectors in which, in the 1980s, so-called "yuppies" (young, upwardly mobile professionals) flourished in Britain and the United States. Implicit in the structural change in the economy was also a shift from full-time male employment in manufacturing to part-time female employment in services and a shift between regions.

There seemed to be another change of significance. For the black economy was said to have grown in a way similar to the expansion of the informal sector in developing countries. In the late 1970s Italy was famous for its major exports of garments, lace, shoes and some engineering products, much of which seemed to have been produced outside the statistical accounting of the Italian economy. The Los Angeles metropolitan region grew to be the largest manufacturing big city in the United States with one of the few competitive garment industries, based, it was said, on illegal Central American immigrants.

Stagnation and restructuring in the Soviet Union
In the Soviet Union the long-term deceleration of economic growth culminated in 1979–82 in absolute stagnation of key sectors – the nadir of the so-called Brezhnev "years of stagnation". President Leonid Brezhnev died in 1982, opening the way for diagnoses of the Soviet malaise. The most influential of these was the 1983 "Novosibirsk Report", written by the Soviet sociologist Tatyana Zaslavskaya and secretly discussed and circulated among senior Soviet officials. In Zaslavskaya's view, "the national economy long ago crossed the threshold of complexity when it was possible to regulate it effectively from a single center" and "the system of production relations which has been in operation over the course of many decades has formed a predominantly passive type

▶ In Eastern Europe the "second economy" of self-employment was deeply entrenched. In Hungary, according to one authority, 70 percent of households earned incomes from the second economy in the mid 1980s. With the collapse of official distribution systems in Poland, farmers sold their produce directly in the street. Though still fined by the police (as here), their activity came to be seen as one of the bases on which a market economy might be built in a post-socialist society.

of worker", characterized by "indifference toward work performed and its low quality... and a rather low level of moral discipline". The system (in her view) needed complete reconstruction, not piecemeal reform.

This trenchant and daring report became a manifesto for "*perestroika*", for the "restructuring" of Soviet society under Mikhail Gorbachev, who became party leader in 1985. The program put forward at that time by Zaslavskaya included an expansion of autonomy for state businesses and of small-scale cooperative and private enterprise (particularly in retailing, catering and other services), full legal and financial accountability and the rule of law, greater openness and freedom of expression, a shift from vertical (hierarchical) "command" relationships to horizontal contractual relationships. There was to be "socialist pluralism" and "democratization".

The year of the report, 1983, was also a high point in the "new right" counterrevolution in the West and in the resurgence of Western capitalism. In the United States President Ronald Reagan was denouncing the Soviet Union as the "evil empire" and unveiling his "Star Wars" Strategic Defense Initiative which envisaged massive extra expenditure on weaponry. The Soviet

chief of staff Marshal Ogarkov, among others, voiced the growing anxiety in military-industrial and KGB circles that the existing Soviet system could not catch up with the West economically, technologically or militarily. The advocates of *perestroika* won crucial support from the military and KGB by promising to liberate creative and innovative energies and increase investment and imports of Western technology and capital goods in order to accelerate Soviet development.

However, Gorbachev and his adviser Abel Agenbegyan raised too many expectations and gave too many hostages to fortune, by promising not only "acceleration" but also greatly improved supplies of consumer goods, a doubling of the housing stock and increased health-care provision by the year 2000, not to mention drastically increased salaries and educational provision. They remained dangerously susceptible to gigantomania, to the cult of the leader and to the "great leap" psychology of the first Five Year Plans and of the Khrushchev era. They were unwilling to face up to uncomfortable choices. Their commitments to over-ambitious goals were bound to overstretch and overheat the economy, exacerbate imbalances, undermine market and financial mechanisms and thus finally to reaffirm the role of the party-state bureaucracy and encourage the eventual reversion to central allocation, rationing and controls – as happened in 1990. Gorbachev's entire team retained the mind-set of enlightened planners, technocrats, reformers "from above". When they were challenged "from below", by Siberian oil workers, Siberian and Donbas miners, by ethnic separatists, by groups and movements who were outside the "charmed circle" and who aspired to move rapidly beyond reformist and centripetal restructuring of the Soviet system (*perestroika*) to more radical dismantling of the Soviet system, the Gorbachev regime apparently floundered. It was much more adept in dealing with foreign governments and unrepentant bureaucrats than with Russian workers and ethnic separatist movements. The weakness and disunity of the radical left, however, and the elitist nature of the dissident "human rights" movement left no politically effective alternative to the reformist technocrats as agents of social and economic change.

The economic squeeze in Eastern Europe
From 1973 to 1978, while the Western world went into economic recession, the East European economies grew even faster than they had done in the 1960s. This superficially impressive feat was made possible by the growing integration and interdependence of the Soviet and East European economies. In the long run this insulation from the recession further impaired their capacity to compete successfully in world markets. In addition, the East–West détente of the 1970s made available greatly augmented flows of Western capital and technology to the East European states. Intended to raise productivity and to expand the range of products available, it in fact increased reliance on Western capital and technology – Eastern Europe quickly ran up uncomfortably large hard-currency debts. It also had politically unwelcome social consequences. Increased contact with Western visitors, together with increased provision of amenities catering to their needs, helped to diffuse Western values.

▼ A Chinese peasant at a free market. Agricultural growth in China after 1978 reflected changes in the incentives offered to producers through the "responsibility system" and changes in prices and markets. The former effectively restored household farming, thereby tackling the problem of labor supervision in collective farming. The fact that periodic rural markets were again permitted led to resurgence of private marketing and facilitated increased specialization, but also provoked fears about increased inequality.

◄ **A motorcycle repair shop in rural China. In 1984 land sales were effectively permitted again in China. One reason for selling would be to go into more profitable enterprises such as small manufacturing or (as here) services. Some 13 percent of households had given up farming to become "specialized households". "The days are gone", it was said, "when peasants boasted about their digital watches. The new rich are building bigger houses and buying Japanese vans".**

The resulting "Westernization" of East European attitudes was, in the end, at least as dangerous and corrosive of party and state influence on the minds of the young as any formal change or "reform" in the socioeconomic system.

Increased reliance upon Western capital also proved to be economically hazardous. Debt service payments became very burdensome: in the late 1970s they began to exceed new inflows of Western capital. This time, moreover, the Soviet Union was unable to come to Eastern Europe's rescue. The 1979–82 world recession coincided with the nadir of the Brezhnev "years of stagnation" in the Soviet Union; Eastern Europe was thus caught in a two-way squeeze between a stagnating Soviet economy and a recession-bound West, from which it still had not fully recovered by 1989, when the "iron curtain" lifted and the communist dictatorships came to an end.

Between 1979 and 1989, with the possible exception of East Germany, the East European economies did not grow at all in real terms and, at least in the cases of Poland and Romania, experienced major reductions in living standards. Any prospect of economic development was made even harder by the fact that Eastern Europe, like the Soviet Union, had to a large extent "missed the bus" in the information technology, electronics and biotechnology revolutions.

Liberalization and decollectivization in China
After the death of Mao Zedong in 1976, the new Chinese leadership – increasingly under the direction of Deng Xiaoping – experimented with methods of overcoming the neglect of the years of Cultural Revolution in order to accelerate economic growth. In the late 1970s this increasingly entailed a liberalization of the economy, further decentralization and an orientation toward exports. The centerpiece of reform was the dismantling of the system of state-directed agriculture and the attempt to restore the close relationship between the cultivators and the soil.

The changes culminated in the abolition of the commune-brigade-team structure of agricultural organization and the effective restoration of a peasant-family-based system, with the right to acquire or dispose of land. The introduction of this "family responsibility" system went necessarily with the restoration of private markets.

The initial results were startling: agricultural output grew by 7.4 percent (and industry by 13.2 percent) in the 1980s. Village administrations were able to diversify into manufacturing, horticulture, services, transport and power. By the late 1980s there were said to be 80 million specialized rural manufacturing workers.

The pattern of decentralization made possible great diversification, but it also meant there were few flows between districts and provinces – poor areas stayed poor while rich ones grew richer. Furthermore, the stress on the need to make money allowed a rapid reappearance of unequal incomes and consumption. A new relatively rich social stratum emerged in the countryside, combining party cadres, rich peasants and rural industrial managers or businessmen. Corruption, never eliminated in China, grew at a prodigious rate. Loose controls on imports along with increasing demand for foreign goods, particularly from the newly rich, produced severe balance of payments problems.

In 1988–89 issues came to a head. After a run of good harvests that had sustained the success of the reform program, 1988 was a poor year. The total output of grain was well below requirements. Part of the decline was attributed to the government's relaxation of procurements and the introduction of more freely priced items while grain prices remained fixed and low. The peasants had therefore shifted cultivation out of grain to more profitable goods. The abolition of communes, it was said, had led to a neglect of rural infrastructure, particularly of irrigation and drainage networks and of rural roads, and this also had affected the harvest. It began to seem possible that decollectivization had brought only short-run benefits. "Noodle-strip", small-scale family farming might not lend itself, after all, to sustainable investment in land improvement.

Datafile

There were such major social changes after 1973 that some spoke of "the end of history". They referred to the triumph of neoliberalism and the collapse of socialist experiments. Throughout the West those who questioned the extent to which the state should intervene in social life were in the ascendant. Their ideas were found persuasive in Eastern Europe where communism was overthrown by risings in 1989–91 led mainly by the intelligentsia. Similar ideas motivated reformers in the Soviet Union. But amid the apparent failures of modernization in many countries, nowhere more so than in sub-Saharan Africa, Islam became an ideology of opposition to both socialism and capitalism.

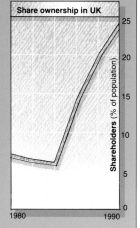

Share ownership in UK

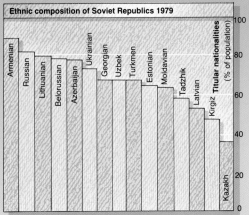

Ethnic composition of Soviet Republics 1979

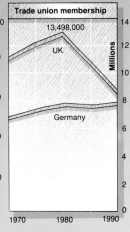

Trade union membership

13,498,000

UK

Germany

▲ The increasingly strident nationalism of the Soviet republics, to which Gorbachev's reforms gave space in the late 1980s, was complicated by the fact that in nine of them 30 percent or more of the population belonged to a group other than the dominant one.

▶ The extent of Communist party membership in the socialist bloc in 1989 bore little relation to the effective support the party received when free elections were held. It emerged strongly in Albania and Bulgaria.

Communist party 1989

▲ In the 1970s social democratic parties appeared to be the "natural" parties of government in Britain and Germany. Trades union membership grew (above). This trend was reversed in the 1980s and in Britain especially private share ownership was expanded enormously (top), assisted by the privatization of nationalized enterprises. It was argued that now the relatively prosperous "haves" constituted a majority over the excluded "have nots", changing the whole nature of politics.

▶ The apartheid system excluded non-whites from government in South Africa, in spite of their numbers. Elaborated after World War II, apartheid was challenged in the 1980s, mainly because of the development of the African working class.

Food supply 1977–79

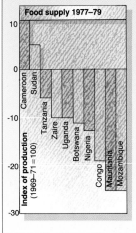

◀ Food production per head declined in a majority of sub-Saharan African states in the 1970s. This mark of economic decline was the result of attempts to subject agriculture to bureaucratic control, and its taxation through pricing.

S African population 1988

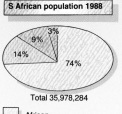

3%
9%
14%
74%

Total 35,978,284

- African
- White
- Colored
- Asian

By the 1970s the integration of the world economy was well advanced. The process redefined not only the role of the state and its capacity to administer a domestic economy in some isolation from the disturbing forces of world markets, but also the old intellectual arguments about appropriate policies. From the 1960s the "Keynesian" orthodoxy which, it was claimed, had guided government policies in Europe and North America since the 1940s went into decline. With it went the centerpiece of European social democracy, the tripartite alliance of state, trade unions and business. The alliance had assumed that there was some point in allying, that governments could determine full employment, the number of the poor and standards of education and health. But in an integrated world it seemed increasingly difficult to do these things at acceptable cost; external markets increasingly determined domestic activity. There was therefore little point in the politics of alliance. Corporatism became unfashionable.

Neoliberalism in the West

In the 1970s government policy began to reflect a revival of faith in unrestricted markets for goods, services and capital. Unlike the Great Depression of the 1930s, the two slumps of 1974–75 and 1979–81 did not lead governments to try to limit their relationship with the rest of the world. Rather they continued the process of integration. They did not try to sustain high employment so much as argue that this power no longer rested in their hands (and imply that, in reality, it never had). Implicitly, governments abandoned responsibility for the poor and homeless, arguing that "communities" should take over.

While virtually all governments in the more developed countries began to shift their policy stance toward the new orthodoxy in the mid-1970s, two political leaders in the 1980s became champions of neoliberalism: President Ronald Reagan of the United States (hence "Reaganomics") and Mrs Margaret Thatcher, prime minister of Britain (hence "Thatcherism"). Neither added anything new to its doctrines. Nonetheless, in the popular mind, the two supposedly fashioned an ideology which in the late 1980s became one of the inspirations for dismantling the Communist economic regimes of Eastern Europe and the Soviet Union and replacing them with market economies and a key issue in the debates in developing countries. Their social importance lay perhaps above all in the way in which they led a shift away from the collective norms and values which were pervasive in the 1950s and 1960s toward competitive individualism as a central value, which has penetrated into many walks of life.

REVERSES OF MODERNIZATION

The end of socialism?

Socialism began in the 19th century as a doctrine of revolt by the mass of the population in Europe to create a society based upon collective cooperation rather than the competitive individualism of a minority. In urban industrial society it became the code of an industrial working class, which sought power in order to establish the cooperative society. "Collective cooperation" became identified, however, with state intervention. Indeed, for many communists and socialists, state action itself constituted the whole community in action, even when no means existed by which the majority could influence the state (as with dictatorships). The Stalinist achievement in swiftly industrializing the Soviet Union in the 1930s added enormously to the authority of the idea that the state could be an effective agent of modernization and social reform. Thus, the original libertarian origins of the socialist idea,

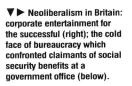

▼▶ **Neoliberalism in Britain:** corporate entertainment for the successful (right); the cold face of bureaucracy which confronted claimants of social security benefits at a government office (below).

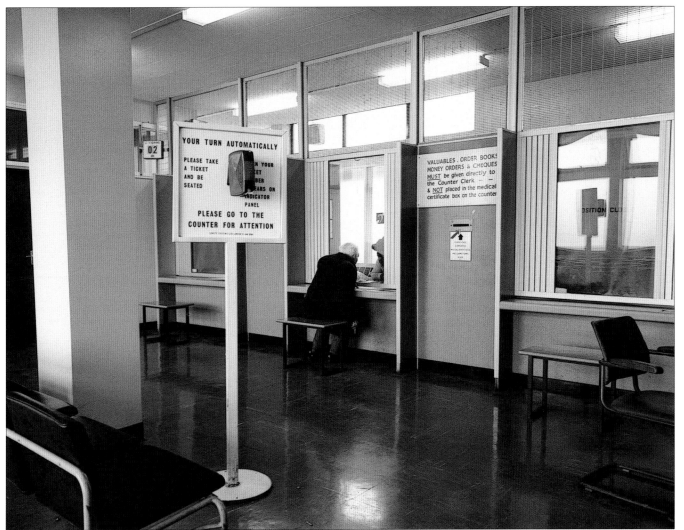

the common ancestry it had with the anarchists, disappeared. Indeed, socialism turned into its opposite: the doctrine of big government and bureaucracy.

In retrospect it can be seen that the emergence of Solidarity (*Solidarnosc*) in Poland in 1980 marked the beginning of the end of communist rule in Eastern Europe. Led by Lech Walesa, a shipyard electrician, Solidarity was born from the economic and social failure of Poland's so-called "United Workers Party" amid massive strikes in the shipyards on the Baltic and in the coal mines of Silesia. Elsewhere in Eastern Europe conditions may have been less grim than in Poland or (especially) in Romania. Nevertheless, there was widespread revulsion against all-pervasive corruption, concealment or perversion of truth, surveillance by internal security forces, police brutality and irksome restrictions. Citizens resented perennial shortages and hours spent queuing or searching for goods in short supply. Even in comparatively well-stocked East Germany, Czechoslovakia and Hungary, the spread of well-made Western goods produced a threatening escalation of expectations and discontent. Moreover, as growing numbers of nuclear weapons were stationed in Eastern Europe in the early 1980s and, more especially, after the nuclear power plant at Chernobyl in the Ukraine exploded in 1986, peace movements, green movements and Protestant churches intensified public concern about the military buildup, the growing reliance on Soviet nuclear technology and the

environmental costs of neo-Stalinist industrial development.

By 1989 the programs of the East European communist dictatorships had lost all credibility and even the ruling Communist parties had lost faith in their capacity to lead their countries out of the impasse. The cataclysmic changes of 1989, which ended Communist rule in most of Eastern Europe, were in large measure a "revolution from above", stage-managed by the intelligentsia, "reform Communists" and the Soviet KGB, concerned to retain Soviet influence in Eastern Europe by changing its regimes. But KGB interventions merely unleashed changes which it was unable to control. Even the apparently spontaneous demonstrations of popular hostility to the dying Communist dictatorships were preceded and prepared by the cultural and political dominance of the intelligentsia. Through their control of the media and information services, the intelligentsia and "reform Communists" committed to pluralistic democracy were able to manipulate the symbols and ideology of the incipient East European revolution and even to indicate what was taking place, how pressure could be most effectively applied, and where mass demonstrations should converge or assemble.

At the end of the 1980s a business class was just beginning to emerge in Eastern Europe but it was not yet politically effective. Thus the intelligentsia remained the leading force in East European society, though it was apparently entranced by the idea of creating market economies.

A poet was grieving because in work camps… young people dance to rock and roll in the evenings. But why shouldn't these youngsters dance after a hard day's work? After all, what is rock and roll? Chiefly it's rhythm. Why accuse rock of every sin? It's like decrying iambics. You can write marvellous verse in iambics or you can write trash. It's the same with rock… Young people want a new culture.

A. VOZNESSENSKY, 1987

◄ Soviet economists estimate that economic growth in their country virtually stopped in the mid-1970s. The daily lives of Soviet citizens became steadily more bleak; more and more time was spent in queuing for goods of poor quality. The failures of the system were inescapable and Soviet society inspired little enthusiasm. Here people searching for a flat scan notices on a city wall. In the 1960s most Soviet families in urban areas had been able to move into two- or three-roomed flats, but the standard of housing remained low. The situation was better in Eastern Europe, though there were still between two and three times as many rooms per inhabitant in Western Europe.

The mainsprings of *perestroika*

In 1985 Mikhail Gorbachev became secretary of the Soviet Communist party and immediately called for more *glasnost* or openness in Soviet life. With this and his subsequent policy of *perestroika* (reconstruction) he tried to please and to mobilize the Soviet intelligentsia, in order to broaden the social power-base of the Soviet regime beyond the increasingly discredited Communist party. The white-collar intelligentsia had monopolized higher education opportunities, becoming in effect a hereditary self-perpetuating elite in control of key sectors of society. Unfortunately most of the intelligentsia was unprepared for change and incapable of providing new ideas. The leading ideas were directed toward the past – to a return to "true Leninism" or "Christian values" or 19th-century liberalism, combined with an exposure of Stalin's crimes and a rehabilitation of the victims of his purges and show-trials.

The struggle for *perestroika* was the outcome not only of official recognition of the urgency of economic reform, but mounting public concern over widespread corruption, soaring crime rates and major ecological crises (such as the shrinkage of the Aral Sea). Other major concerns were the quadrupling of Soviet alcohol consumption in 1964–84, which led to the highest consumption per person of hard spirits in the world, increased crime, hooliganism, marital breakups and lowered life-expectancy. It was hoped that *perestroika* would reverse these and other adverse social trends. Except for temporary improvements in alcohol-related indicators, however, deterioration continued, contributing to various strands of the popular and official backlash against *perestroika* after 1988.

From 1985 to 1988 *glasnost*, *perestroika* and Gorbachev enjoyed considerable domestic as well as international acclaim. This helped Gorbachev to mobilize support and to surmount or outmaneuver conservative bureaucratic challenges, opposition and obstruction to a far greater degree than skeptics had thought possible. Legislation passed in 1987 and 1988 relaxed many economic restrictions. But economic changes were *smaller* in practice than they were on paper, due to the shortage of resources and the powerful inertia and passive resistance of central and local bureaucracies. Collective agriculture, command planning and

▲ Young people in Riga in Soviet Latvia. Such Western fashions were profoundly threatening to the old leadership of the Communist party. A counterculture of protest against bureaucratic regimentation had grown up. Some youngsters, however, followed Western fashions such as "heavy-metal" music while retaining a loyalty to the system which could bring them onto the streets to fight liberals.

central control of pricing, tax revenues and resource allocation were never really dismantled. The functioning of the command economy was gradually impaired, however, by the partial decentralization that did occur. In the political sphere, by contrast, the changes were much *larger* in practice than on paper. The whole climate was changed by the lifting of the veil of fear.

Contrary to the conventional wisdom that political liberalization was a *prerequisite* for successful economic reform, *glasnost* and political liberalization in practice became a *substitute* for successful economic reform. By unleashing social forces and national separatist movements which Moscow was ultimately unable to control, other than by reverting to the use of armed force and intimidation, *glasnost* and political liberalization were the undoing of Soviet economic reform.

Socialism in the Third World

There were also sweeping changes throughout the rest of the erstwhile socialist world. After the Cultural Revolution China was radically different. It had highly decentralized local administrations which constituted competitive conglomerates. When liberalization was set in motion it thus produced – in contrast to the Soviet Union – rapid economic expansion with a proliferation of small-scale private firms. The economic transformation produced, however, demands for political change to which the Communist party, retaining sufficient cohesiveness, again in contrast to the Soviet party, reacted with violence in Tienanmen Square in Beijing in June 1989, when students demanding democracy were massacred.

Elsewhere the ruins of what was called socialism were only too apparent. Zambia and Tanzania, twin pillars of African socialism, had long since become immured in permanent economic crisis, with corruption replacing all the old hopes.

In Latin America socialism had made a spectacular advance in 1959 with Fidel Castro's victory in Cuba. In 1979 Sandinista rebels took power in Nicaragua and implemented far-reaching social reforms, only to be voted out of government in 1990. By now the Castro regime was beginning to feel a need to move to a less authoritarian system.

The origins of socialism had been in the savage social divisions which were created by the unrestricted operation of market capitalism. These not only remained but were likely to be enhanced in a liberalized and integrated world economy. Thus the prospects for the survival of some form of socialism were not entirely dim.

Questions of nationalism

In the late 1980s much of Eastern Europe embarked upon an unexpectedly rapid triple transition: from communist dictatorship to pluralist democracy, from centrally administered economies to market economies and from supranational Soviet hegemony to fully independent nation-statehood. Previous attempts to build a new order in Eastern Europe on the basis of fully independent nation states (after each of the world wars) had provided abundant opportunities and a fertile breeding ground for extreme nationalism, and for fascist and communist authoritarianism.

▲ A desecrated Jewish cemetery in France. In the late 1980s the resurgence of antisemitism in Europe reflected fears about change at a time when national identities were in question. Ultra-right politics appealed to those bewildered by the changes taking place.

◀ In 1989 a demonstration in which thousands linked hands across the Baltic states revealed the strength of their demand for national autonomy. The Soviet Union had been held together more by coercion than by the creation of a "Soviet" citizen. Gorbachev's reforms allowed the expression of nationalism which was fed by the relative poverty of most non-Russians.

▶ Communist control submerged the ethnic patchwork of Central Europe. The stresses of the 1980s, associated with resurgent nationalism, meant that once again tensions built up around ethnic minorities such as the sizable Hungarian population in Romania.

Islam. In South Asia Muslim Kashmiris in India fought for their independence, as did some Sikhs in the prosperous state of Punjab following ill-advised meddling by the central government of Indira Gandhi. The events she unleashed, notably the storming of the Sikh holy places in Amritsar by Indian security forces, led to her assassination in 1984. Throughout much of India incidents of "communal" conflict between Hindus and Muslims became more frequent and more severe. Hindu nationalism (as opposed to *Indian* nationalism) became a force for the first time, threatening the secular principles on which Pandit Nehru had sought to build a modern India. In Sri Lanka Tamil-speaking people, as much "natives" of the island as the Sinhalese-speaking majority, fought a bloody guerrilla war for national sovereignty. In Africa there were comparable struggles as Eritreans and Tigrayans fought for independence in Ethiopia and black southerners fought Arabized northerners in Sudan. Almost everywhere in Africa the incidence of ethnically based conflict was high.

Such widespread events, occurring in very different contexts, have been associated with a variety of specific local circumstances. But there were common threads which help to explain the importance of nationalist and of other ethnic conflicts in the later 20th century. Nationalism, and other forms of ethnicity (such as "Hindu" versus "Muslim" or "Kikuyu" versus "Luo") which may indeed provide a base for nationalism, are to be understood above all as collective states of mind. They are, in Benedict Anderson's words, "*imagined* communities". The nation, Anderson says, "is distinguished as a community because, regardless of the actual inequality and

Unfortunately the changes set in motion in Eastern European countries rapidly and perilously created conditions and opportunities similar to those of 1918 and 1945. The national euphoria awakened by the ending of communist dictatorship heightened the importance of exclusive and potentially intolerant nationalism and national religions as the value systems and belief systems most capable of filling the void left by the demise of communism. Soon there was a resurgence of antisemitism, of discrimination against Gypsies and quite generally of tensions between majority and minority ethnic groups.

At the same time in the Soviet Union, as a result of *glasnost*, demands for national liberation began to be felt, especially in Latvia, Estonia and Lithuania, in Georgia, Armenia and Azerbaijan and even in the core republic of the Ukraine. Elsewhere in the world apparently similar forces were seen. In the West French-speaking Québecois in Canada again talked about parting company with Anglophone Canada; Basques and Catalans (in Spain), Flemings and Walloons (in Belgium) and Scots all sought greater degrees of autonomy or actual separation. Western Asia was a caldron of nationalist and ethnic conflicts, focused around the status of the state of Israel (founded in 1948) and the establishment of a homeland for displaced Palestinian Arabs, but exacerbated by old tensions between the Sunni and Shia traditions of

Ethnic Areas of Eastern Europe 1990

Ethnic majority over 50%
- Albanians
- Bosnians
- Bulgars
- Croats
- Czechs
- Germans
- Macedonians
- Magyars
- Poles
- Romanians
- Serbs and Montenegrins
- Slovaks
- Slovenes
- Turks
- Area of no majority

SWEDEN
DENMARK
Baltic Sea
USSR
Elbe
Vistula
Warsaw
GERMANY
Oder
POLAND
Prague
CZECHOSLOVAKIA
AUSTRIA
Budapest
HUNGARY
Drava
Sava
Po
ROMANIA
Belgrade
Bucharest
YUGOSLAVIA
ITALY
Danube
Sofia
BULGARIA
Black Sea
Scale 1 : 20 000 000
0   400 km
0   300 mi
ALBANIA
Tiranë
GREECE
TURKEY

exploitation that may prevail in each, the nation is always conceived as a deep, horizontal comradeship. Ultimately it is this fraternity that makes it possible, over the past two centuries, for so many millions of people not so much to kill, as willingly die for such limited imaginings". The idea of "nationalism" emerged in Europe in the 19th century in circumstances in which the old "face-to-face" communities, also imagined, but based on kinship and neighborhood, were eroded by the forces of modernization. The idea of the "nation", usually based on language, replaced older identities.

In the 20th century the small literate classes of colonial territories in Africa and Asia, mainly civil servants, professionals and some business people, for whom alone the idea of "the nation" could possibly have any meaning, sought to create independent nation-states in the pursuit of the political and economic goals of modernization. They had to build a sense of nationality among the mass of the people for whom "tribal" or religious identities had often been manufactured by the colonial powers. The failure of the elites in this effort, and the failures of modernization by industrialization, account for many of the conflicts considered here. There is almost invariably a crucial economic dimension: access to "good jobs" in the public sector (important in building up ethnic/national tensions in Sri Lanka, for example, or in Uganda); or control over other assets. But this is only one dimension of a broader cause: the inability of the political class to live up to its modernist ideals. Like the void left by the collapse of communism in Eastern Europe, the strains created by modernization, by "development", or its outright failure in much of the Third World, provides fertile ground for sectionalism which is easily made intolerant.

Islamic fundamentalism

Another significant social phenomenon of the later 20th century was the rise of Islamic fundamentalism, commonly associated with the revolution in Iran in 1979 which swept the Shah from power. In fact this is a misleading notion, both because fundamentalist movements represent a very old tradition within Islam, going back to its foundations, and because Saudi Arabia – ally of the United States – was a fundamentalist state long before the Iranian revolution.

All of the great religions of the world establish social charters or designs for the organization of society – setting out standards and norms for all aspects of life. Islam, partly because of the circumstances of its foundation by a militarily and politically successful tribal group in Arabia, offers the most powerful of such designs, embracing all

Once we thought that western society had all the answers for successful, fruitful living. If we followed the lead of the West we would have progress. Now we see that this isn't true; they [the West] are sick societies; even their material prosperity is breaking down. America is full of crime and promiscuity. Russia is worse. Who wants to be like that? We have to remember God. Look how God has blessed Saudi Arabia. That is because they have tried to follow the Law. And America, with all its loose society, is all problems.

MUSLIM WOMAN

Islam and Women

In Islam women are regarded with a mixture of fear – as a source of evil – and of paternalism – because they are vulnerable and in need of protection. They are seen as being dominated by "unruly passion", in contrast with the "calm and orderly nature of men". Men have thus been given a status above women and authority over them. Women are thought of as being threatening to the stability and good judgment of men. For this reason it is extremely important that their sexuality should be under the control of men. They must be modest, their "adornments" concealed by a veil except in the intimacy of their own bedrooms. They should be married as soon as possible and then "give themselves unquestioningly to their husbands".

There is justification in the Quran for these ideas. Yet it also contains what amounts to a charter for marriage as a flexible contract between two consenting adults. In spite of this, after the revolution in Iran, Quranic justification was used for the reversal of rights which Iranian women had won – rights to education; to leave off the veil; to vote; to contest the custody of children in case of divorce; to abortion on demand; and a ban on polygamy. Women were required again to wear the veil; their rights in marriage were annulled while men were allowed up to four permanent wives and were given exclusive rights to divorce at will. Some religious leaders equated unmarried women with terrorists; their approval of polygamy was in spite of a Quranic injunction "to marry only one wife" because a man cannot treat a number of wives with impartiality. One ayatollah, opposed to polygamy, nonetheless approved concubinage as a way of preventing women from being led astray.

◀ Some Muslim women supported Iranian fundamentalism.

who have accepted the faith. They constitute a single community of believers, the *ummah*, who must maintain the solidarity of the faith against unbelievers. Christianity, associated at its foundation with a subordinate, rebel group of people, makes a clear distinction between state and religion. Such a distinction is not made in Islam. *Sharia*, the sacred law of Islam, based on the Quran and *sunna* – the sayings and doings of the Prophet as recorded in the *hadiths* – is the framework for polity and society. But there have been many disputes within Islam, throughout its history, over whether the Quran and the *sunna* are the law, or the basis for the law. Broadly, how much interpretation is permissible? There has always been a tension between more pragmatic and more orthodox tendencies, with the Sunni tradition inclined to the former and the Shia to the latter.

Islamic fundamentalism always aimed to protect the purity of Islam from adulteration by speculative interpretations. It was thus directed against internal threats, from the superstitious beliefs of peoples absorbed into Islam, or from scholastic debate, as well as against those from outside. The external threats were derived from Western influences, and Islam was riven by disagreement between those who, perceiving the gap between Western and Muslim societies, argued for modernization and those who argued for return to the fundamentals of *Sharia*. It is not surprising that the ideas of the fundamentalists should have been found persuasive by those threatened by modern economic change, or who have been uprooted by it – migrants from villages to towns and members of the urban petty bourgeoisie. Such people, led by often low- or middle-ranking clerics, provided the main backing for movements like the Muslim Brotherhood, which had great influence in Egyptian politics in the 1980s and 1990s, or the movement which destroyed the Shah's regime.

Attempts in the 1930s by Reza Shah to modernize Iran created distance between the increasingly

◀ Islam extends from West Africa, across Asia into Southeast Asia. This mosque is in Malaysia, which has experienced progressive political Islamization since the mid 1970s. By then the Malay language had become the language of social communication for all Malaysians (for Chinese and Indians as well as Malays). Islam therefore became the last symbol of Malay ethnic identity. The government has emphasized economic development with spiritual regeneration and aimed at proving that Islam is a dynamic and adaptable creed.

▼ Arabs in the Gulf state of Dubai playing bar football reflect the tensions within the Islamic world between modernization and Western influences and the defense of the faith. Arabs are also tugged between different loyalties, a general one to "Arabism" and a narrow one to region, clan or religious sect. These tensions and conflicts are set in a context of inequality. In 1986 GDP per head in the Gulf states was $16,500 (Qatar), while some 50 million Egyptians had only $1100 per head.

westernized upper classes and the peasants and the people of the bazaars who continued to follow the *ulama* (religious-legal scholars). Reza Shah's son's reforms in the 1960s, his authoritarianism and repression of the *ulama*, deepened these tensions in Iranian society. In this context Ayatolla Khomeini's arguments for the subordination of political power to Islamic precepts, expressed in a simple and direct way and without any reference to western ideas, appealed to different social groups. He succeeded in welding together disparate forces – the urban working class and the traditional middle class of the bazaars, the modern middle class, which was by now resentful of royal authority and of foreign influence in the country, and the rural poor. Together they brought about the overthrow of the monarchy through massive demonstrations in 1978–79.

By the end of the 1980s Islam had become the central ideology of the Third World against the First. As the British political writer R. W. Johnson suggested: "In many parts of the world secular nationalism and socialism have failed in their project of modernization. The dream of surmounting poverty and drawing level with the West has, all too often, collapsed in despair and ruin. In that despair there is natural resort to a militant anti-Western ideology, to a creed that refuses the whole objective of 'modernization' – and Islamic fundamentalism has filled that need."

Crisis in Africa

In 1981 the World Bank published a major report which drew attention to the pervasive failure of economic and social development in sub-Saharan Africa. Four years later television viewers around the world began to become familiar with pictures of bands of emaciated refugees and of the victims of famine, especially (though not only) in northeast Africa. The hopes and expectations of independence had been utterly crushed. Of 34 countries described by the World Bank as "low income" in 1984, 21 were in tropical Africa. In the 1970s 15 African economies registered negative growth rates; population growth outstripped food production; life expectancy at 47 years was the lowest in the world; and in 1981 the region contained half of the world's refugees. Failure marked both those states which had espoused "socialism" and those which had explicitly sought a capitalist road. It was recognized that part of the reason for this situation was the way the continent had been torn apart by civil wars and other conflicts. In Uganda, for example, the atrocities of the regime of Idi Amin (1971–78) had ripped apart a society that had known relatively high standards of welfare and education. What had created this bloody turmoil and the "underdevelopment" of Africa?

When they became independent the states of sub-Saharan Africa were peasant societies. Their struggles for freedom had been won by small educated elites made up mainly of minor officials and teachers. There were few African businessmen; the most important traders were outsiders – Asians in East Africa, Lebanese in West Africa. The organized working class was generally small – less than 5 percent of the economically active

Life in South African Townships

Before dawn each day, streams of commuter trains disgorge black workers into South Africa's city centers. At dusk the workers are swallowed back into the trains and returned to townships such as Soweto, South Africa's largest township, situated outside Johannesburg.

South Africa's townships are the product of segregationist ideology. It defined cities as "white" and consistently sought to impede urbanization and to retain African workers in rural areas, where their employment options were confined to agriculture or factories and mines (as contract migrants). In 1923 the Natives (Urban Areas) Act provided for the establishment of segregated African townships by white municipal authorities on the principle that Africans "should only be permitted within the municipal areas in so far and for so long as their presence is demanded by the wants of the white population". African land purchase was curbed and, through the infamous "pass laws", a system of influx control was established.

Even so there remained only a grudging acknowledgment that a settled population of urban Africans was necessary. As late as the

▼ By the end of the 1980s overcrowding had reached crisis proportions in South Africa's townships, with densities of 15 people or more per four-room house. Those with jobs and housing accommodated unemployed relatives or took in lodgers to supplement inadequate incomes. Often they constructed makeshift extensions and corrugated shanties in their backyards. Even in the densely populated Witwatersrand area around Johannesburg, half the African population lived in informal rather than formal housing. Without electricity and adequate water supply, women's child-rearing and housekeeping tasks were burdensome.

1970s the state still attempted to restrict the proportion of urban African workers housed in family accommodation (as opposed to single-sex hostels) to 3 percent. It was even considered feasible to transport workers daily from new townships in the impoverished "homelands" up to 112km (70mi) away and weekly from points as far distant as 640km (400mi). In spite of the authorities' efforts a relentless inflow from impoverished rural areas continued.

By the mid 1980s 7 million urban people were housed in informal urban settlements. In Soweto alone, over 1 million people were subtenants. Moreover, juxtaposed with the makeshift extensions and tightly packed warrens of corrugated huts were middle-class suburbs, accommodating African bureaucrats, businessmen and professionals.

Township life has been characterized by resistance and struggle. In 1929 workers in Durban rioted against the municipal beerhalls whose monopoly over the sale of sorghum beer financed township administration. In the 1950s pass books were burnt countrywide. Education boycotts (as in Soweto in 1976) sparked off

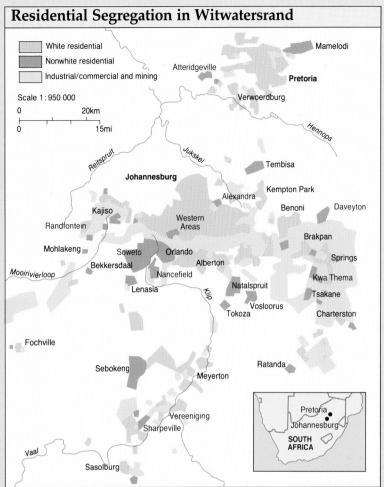

Residential Segregation in Witwatersrand

White residential
Nonwhite residential
Industrial/commercial and mining

Scale 1 : 950 000

0   20km
0   15mi

Mamelodi
Atteridgeville
Pretoria
Verwoerdburg
Hennops
Reitspruit
Jukskei
Tembisa
Johannesburg
Kempton Park
Alexandra
Benoni   Daveyton
Kajiso
Western Areas
Randfontein
Brakpan
Mohlakeng
Springs
Soweto   Orlando
Bekkersdaal   Alberton
Kwa Thema
Nancefield
Mooirivierloop
Natalspruit
Tsakane
Lenasia
Klip
Vosloorus   Charterston
Tokoza
Fochville
Ratanda
Sebokeng
Meyerton
Vereeniging
Sharpeville
SOUTH AFRICA
Vaal
Sasolburg
Pretoria
Johannesburg

organized campaigns, including bus, rent and consumer boycotts. In the 1980s township discontent was also directed against those who participated in black local authorities, many of whom used their positions to accumulate wealth and establish patronage networks.

During the 1980s the lives and property of the black accumulating classes came under attack by frustrated youths, intent on making the townships "ungovernable". Images of the charred bodies of "apartheid stooges" (victims of the "necklaces" of burning tires) flashed across the world's television screens. By the end of the decade township violence seemed endemic, with military and police occupation virtually the norm. Gangs of youth controled neighborhoods, entry to which was forbidden without the correct password or declaration of political allegiance. Workers reached their factories and offices exhausted and dazed, following sleepless nights peppered with sounds of gunfire and battles.

For all the horror of township life in the 1980s the townships continued to throb with assured energy. Popular civic associations had taken over as the effective instruments of local government; independent taxi services had replaced the state monopoly on transport; illicit "shebeen queens" had usurped the trade of the beerhalls; and a vibrant informal sector served consumption needs. South African townships have been isolated, but through this they have developed a language, music, culture and life of their own.

▲ By 1990 three-fifths of all South Africans lived in the country's urban areas. The mosaic of apartheid's segregated urban areas had been carefully designed and, moreover, designed to last. Spreading out from the central business districts were the affluent white suburbs, cocooned by buffer zones of vacant land or Indian and "colored" group areas. Flanking the peripheral industrial areas were the sprawling African townships, provided by the state to house its necessary but unwelcome urban work force.

▲ In the 1980s samples from the general population in eastern and central Africa showed levels of infection with Acquired Immune Deficiency Syndrome (AIDS) of up to 18 percent, representing a major social problem.

► There has been popular support for radical socialist policies in Africa as perhaps amongst these Angolan boys. Attempts to transplant Soviet methods to Africa have been disastrous however. Attempts to establish bureaucratic control over peasant agriculture have discouraged production in both socialist- and capitalist-style countries.

► Access to the luxury of an executive bed in Africa often depends upon being a bureaucrat, able to derive "rent" from control over regulatory activities and agencies of the state. These "haves" are among the favored clients of rulers, in systems of government which lack legitimacy and depend on force and a division of spoils through patronage. The members of the ruling classes, it is said, "respect the big belly squeezed under the steering wheel of a Mercedes far more than they respect talent, quality, and productivity."

population in most cases. In these circumstances the extent of organized, "civil society" beyond the state was limited. The political leadership was answerable to none but itself. The parliamentary institutions which had been transferred from the West were irrelevant in the absence of pressures from organized social classes, and in most cases they were effectively set aside quite soon. Power depended upon being able to command the personal loyalty of others, and this was secured through ties of kinship, "tribe" and region and by means of the distribution of patronage. "Jobs for the boys" meant the proliferation of bureaucratic roles which gave their incumbents the opportunity to appropriate bribes, or by using their powers to profit (for example, from the distribution of essential supplies like electricity). Because of these practices African bureaucracies no longer corresponded at all to Max Weber's model of the impartial, rational administration. In the absence of a secure legal framework and a working infrastructure, capitalism could not thrive.

It was also necessary for successful leaders to be able to use force and they needed either to have the army on their side, or to contain it by setting up rival forces. By the 1980s competitive party politics existed only in five countries and most of these were subject to personal rule by "strongmen" and were in practice dependent upon military power. The regular interventions, direct and indirect, of Western powers and their sales of arms only exacerbated the inherent instability of systems of personal rule. Public funds were looted; peasants were mulcted by taxation and by state marketing boards and tended to withdraw from the market; parallel or "black" economies thrived. These were the circumstances of decline in much of Africa. They proved generally resistant to the efforts of the World Bank and the International Monetary Fund in the 1980s to bring about economic adjustment, but the packages of measures enforced by these agencies often had the immediate effect of causing further deterioration in living standards as welfare services were cut.

One crucial factor in the future of Africa remained the fate of South Africa, the continent's only major industrial society. The expansion of industrial capitalism there was for a time encouraged by the policy of so-called "separate development" for people of different races under *apartheid*. But it also created the conditions for the challenge to white supremacy which began to be felt in the 1980s, and which depended substantially on the rise of the African working class. Pressures for reform emerged even in the Afrikaaner white establishment in the 1970s, leading to the fall from power of John Vorster in 1978. The modest efforts of P.W. Botha thereafter to reform the instruments of white supremacy eventually encouraged more opposition. By 1990 his successor, F.W. de Klerk, had begun to negotiate the demise of apartheid, though tragically amid increasing violence between the supporters of the African National Congress and those of Zulu Chief Buthulezi's *Inkatha* movement. In spite of appearances, the savage killing which took place did not stem from "tribalism". Johannesburg's *Business Day* newspaper wrote: "Fear, hatred, vengeance and depravity drive this bestial process" – which had its roots in the envy and resentments which accumulated in squatter camps on the fringes of the townships. It was a conflict between "haves" and "have-nots", not between tribes.

The future of South Africa was a vital issue for the future of Africa. A progressive regime in South Africa, based on the African bourgeoisie and the working class, would have the capacity to bring about change elsewhere.

THE ROLES OF RELIGION

In its varied forms, religion seeks divine guidance to make sense of the confusion and contradictions of everyday experience and provides identity, guidance about behavior and, in most cases, the prospect of a new beginning after death. The rise of a scientific world view in the late 19th century and the growth of the belief that beneficial social change can be brought about by human agency might be thought to have challenged the place of religion in the world.

The first half of the 20th century did indeed see a rise in popular secularism. Disbelief received a powerful boost through the Bolshevik seizure of power in Russia in 1917. The Bolsheviks' Marxist-Leninist doctrine saw religion as an illusory distraction and offered instead a new social order, rules for achieving a good life and the prospect of improved living standards. In some ways communism was a religion without a deity. But religion has survived, sometimes because it has been useful for rulers, sometimes because it has been able to identify with the underdog, and sometimes because the need for religious powers of consolation have continued.

The use of religion as tool of conservative and authoritarian regimes is well seen in the state promotion of Shintoism in Japan until that country's defeat in World War II. In Spain the Catholic church was used as a means of securing order after the overthrow of the republic an regime in 1939.

Religion as an element of resistance has been seen in numerous parts of the world in the 20th century. In Latin America the Roman Catholic church fought authoritarian states in the cause of the poor – often to the extent of coming into conflict with the papacy in Rome. In Poland the Catholic church helped to preserve Polish identity against communism and was at the core of the Solidarity movement in the 1980s. In the Middle East revivalist Islam has been at the heart of major social upheavals – from the Arab revolt against the Turks during World War I to the opposition to the Shah in Iran in the 1970s.

Among minority communities in Western Europe and North America – and for the majority black population of South Africa – pentecostal forms of Christianity have provided consolation and hope for the socially and politically marginalized.

Religion divides, religion unites. It may be revolutionary or conservative. Its strength lies in its unpredictability and flexibility, which suggests that it will long continue to resist the challenges of secularism.

▲▶ **Priests, generals and state power in Spain.** After his victory in the civil war in 1939, General Francisco Franco needed to unite a divided society. He looked to the church for assistance. Catholic organizations provided important support for his regime.

▶ **Church ceremony at the heart of the rural community:** a Lutheran church in Kansas, 1910.

▶▶ **Sikhs at the Golden Temple in Amritsar, India –** the focus for the sikhs' beliefs and their aspirations to be a separate nation.

◄ The old teach the young in the Jewish community in Morocco in the 1930s. Religious identity enabled this minority to survive in an Arab Muslim society.

▼ A newly baptized member of an evangelical Christian church in the United States emerges reborn in her new faith. Immersion demands commitment and symbolizes transformation.

▼ Desmond Tutu, leader of South Africa's Anglican church, inspires his followers (many of whom are not Christians) to fight for liberty from apartheid. Here religion moves from consoling the oppressed to becoming the vehicle for change.

Datafile

The late 20th century was a frightening time of increasing violence in cities, of rape and murder, drug abuse and drug-related crime, and of what seemed apocalyptic threats from AIDS and global environmental destruction. High divorce rates in the West, increased single parenting, and such phenomena as "dowry deaths" of women in India, resulting from the disappointment of bridegrooms at the size of the dowry brought by their wives, overturned cherished values. Yet there were also "new" social movements, depending more on mutual support than on hierarchy, reflecting deep moral concerns and which won wide support. They often depended especially on women who at last won greater individual freedom. All was not bleak.

▶ The largest cities in the world were now emphatically outside Europe and North America. World Bank projections showed that by early in the 21st century the populations of the developing countries would be more urban than rural, suggesting the scale of the potential problems of urban management. In the industrialized countries increased inequality of this time is reflected in the fact that, for example, in large US metropolitan areas more than half the children were living below the poverty line.

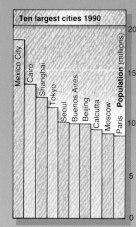
Ten largest cities 1990

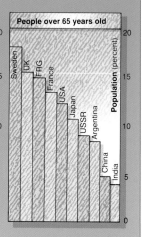
People over 65 years old

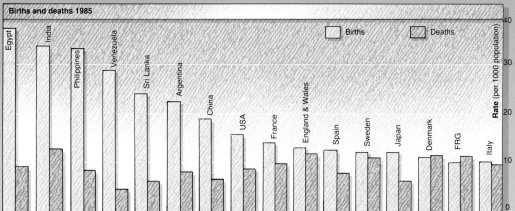
Births and deaths 1985

▲ In Western societies the problems of the "Third Age" – the increasingly significant period of people's lives spent in retirement – began to loom as large as those of youth. Between 1970 and 1990 the proportion of the population aged over 65 increased by more than 20 percent (36 percent in Japan). Already 15–16 percent of payrolls in America went in payments from the taxpayer to the elderly. How in the future, with costs rising to 25–30 per cent of payroll, would a smaller labor force pay for more care for the old?

▲ The disparity between birth and death rates meant that population growth was still high in developing countries, compounding the difficulties of welfare provision. One-fifth of their populations still went hungry every day. Yet a United Nations report on human development found that there had been improvement in levels of well-being in many countries, even in tropical Africa in the absence of economic growth. In most industrial countries population now grew only very slowly; in a few it even declined.

▶ In the industrialized countries the divorce rate was highest in the United States, followed by the Soviet Union, Canada and New Zealand. In the United States it declined a little in the 1980s, perhaps reflecting the renewed emphasis on family life in the ideology of the "new right". In times of economic insecurity it seems that the desire for stable values leads to greater emphasis on the authority of basic institutions such as family or religion, which it is possible to question or reject in "good times" such as those before 1973.

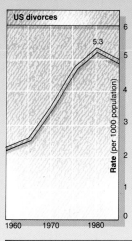
US divorces

▶ Single parenting was a positive choice for some in the West, mainly in the middle classes. Among the poor it was less deliberate. In 1987 three-quarters of black babies in the big inner cities of America were born to unmarried mothers. Meanwhile, because whites had fewer babies a shift in the ethnic structure of the labor force was underway. By 2007 perhaps 30 percent of recruits to the labor force will be blacks or hispanics. Will such underprivileged workers pay through taxes for the care of elderly whites?

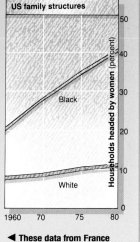
US family structures

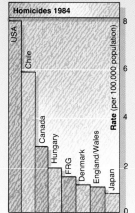
Homicides 1984

◀ High rates of crime in rich societies, especially of murder in the United States, of drug-related crimes (300 recorded cases for every 100,000 people in Canada, 276 in New Zealand), and rape (144 reported for every 100,000 women aged 15–59 in the United States, nearly 100 in Holland) perhaps reflected more accurate reporting. But there was no doubt of the distress in industrial societies, ascribed to "the weakening social fabric". Japan's low rates suggested a continuing sense of community and social cohesion.

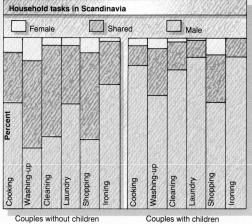
Household tasks in Scandinavia

◀ These data from France in the 1980s show that the sharing of household chores or the undertaking of them by men was higher in households where there were no children. The work loads of women in employment thus increased when they had children. It was still difficult, therefore, for women to combine pursuit of a career and raising a family. Even where men did help with housework their contribution was small and tended toward social activities (such as washing up) rather than hard work (such as cleaning).

SOCIAL TROUBLES AND HOPE

Attacks on the family
Alternative family forms
Legal reforms and social
relationships
Increasing violence and
AIDS
New ways of responding
to social problems

The 1970s and 1980s represented a major landmark in the public conception of the nature of marriage and the family, and of women's roles and their status. Extensive changes in marriage, divorce and family law were made in order to "modernize" what were thought of as traditional relationships. The legal status of women improved dramatically. Numerous laws were passed in support of equality.

Doubt about the role of the family

Amidst the eruption of so-called libertine values during the 1960s and 1970s, restrictions on the expression of sexuality were modified or ignored, conventional definitions of marriage were questioned and assumptions about sex roles were challenged. The long debate about the family and social change in the 20th century finally seemed to reach its culmination. The social unrest of the 1960s, which had brought forth the resurgence of feminism, had also thrown open many questions

▼ **Members of the "Third Age", the period after retirement, which became more significant in the late 20th century. Care of the elderly became a major charge on funds.**

about the family. Feminists attacked it as the bulwark of patriarchal society and the "new left" as a reactionary force that impeded progress. New research by historians and sociologists unfolded a whole host of misconceptions about the family and its history, which had been the premises of public policy for almost a century. There was now the new worry that the family might have become too self-contained – that in its intense privacy it had become "socially isolated", or as the British sociologist Ronald Fletcher wrote: "it seemed no longer to relate in a living way with the community". Others saw the community itself as but a "network of formal organization of people's wages, benefits, social services, rates and mortgages or taxation", while "being a person to others" had been lost. Why else would people have to turn to counselors or therapists?

There was new uncertainty, too, about the changed position of women and how that would affect family life – and new bewilderment when

▲ During the 1970s the single-parent family became a fairly common family pattern. Most of them were headed by women. But in the late 1980s there was an increase in single-father families (as here), due mainly to men's changing life-styles and desire to continue parenting. There is a general belief that single-mother families are "broken" and disorganized, the children deprived by their father's absence. This illustration seems to suggest that there can be warmth and deprivation irrespective of the sex of the parent.

▼ Homosexual wedding in Copenhagen. There have been a number of attempts by homosexual couples to obtain legal marriages which would give them the advantages of symbolic equality but also the usual social security or health insurance benefits due upon marriage. Denmark was the first country to institute homosexual marriage.

feminists attacked the myth of the happy home of patriarchal society and exposed wife-battering, sexual abuse and rape as the actual situation of thousands of married women. Others wondered whether the idealization of the family, the constant emphasis on love and sex throughout the 20th century had raised unrealistic expectations of marital relations – often leading to a breakup when not fulfilled. In the effort to raise women's awareness of their situation, feminist writing in the early 1970s indeed warned women against the pursuit of an ideal which was but a myth or a fantasy of fixed union and mutuality. The great anxiety over the rising separation and divorce rates certainly suggested a substantial gap between public expectations of marriage and the family and actual experiences. The emergence of more definite alternative family forms in the 1970s (usually associated with the emergence of the various countercultures of that period) similarly reflected this variance. The increase in single-parent families (which approximately doubled between 1970 and 1980) reflected to a high degree the steady rise in divorce rates but the number of people opting for "singlehood" also rose. The figures for one-person households also increased steadily, but mainly because of the higher proportion of elderly people living on their own – in Germany in 1982 they accounted for 31.2 percent of all households. "Cohabitation" (often seen as a temporary "trial marriage") became a preferred life-style for a significant minority of young or divorced people, though figures varied markedly from country to country (15 percent of couples in Sweden in 1979, 7 percent in Holland, 2.3 percent in the United States). Voluntary childlessness (in marriage), considered to be "atypical" until then, also made its impact in the 1970s. In the Netherlands in 1980 it was estimated that 20 percent of all marriages were deliberately childless. But although they were inconsistent with the patterns established in the "baby-boom" era, the lower marriage and high divorce rates and fewer children of the late 20th century were consistent with longer-term trends. They were not "abnormal" as was sometimes feared in the 1970s.

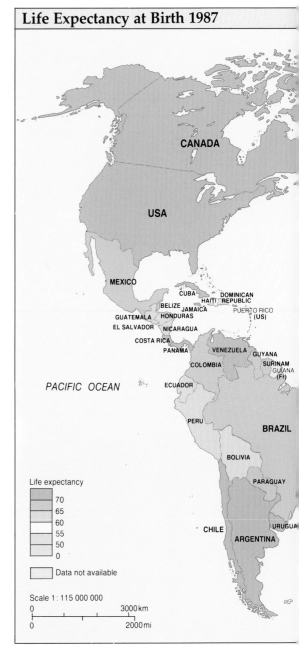

Life Expectancy at Birth 1987

CANADA

USA

MEXICO

CUBA

DOMINICAN REPUBLIC

BELIZE JAMAICA HAITI

GUATEMALA HONDURAS PUERTO RICO (US)

EL SALVADOR NICARAGUA

COSTA RICA

PANAMA VENEZUELA GUYANA

COLOMBIA SURINAM GUIANA (Fr)

PACIFIC OCEAN ECUADOR

PERU BRAZIL

BOLIVIA

PARAGUAY

CHILE URUGUAY

ARGENTINA

Life expectancy

70
65
60
55
50
0

Data not available

Scale 1 : 115 000 000

0 ———— 3000 km

0 ———— 2000 mi

In the end it was this "deviance" from conventional ways of life and the rejection of old "proven" values, together with associated symptoms of social disorder (rising illegitimacy, juvenile crime, baby-battering, incest and so on), that forced governments into taking a new and critical look at the traditional relationships of authority in the family and marriage and at discriminatory practices elsewhere. The reforms that ensued were a deliberate attempt at reconstruction, departing from earlier notions of family relationships, of male dominance or of women's dependency, and of their exclusive role as mothers.

Public policy and family relationships

Upon marriage young couples in some countries were now given the option of using the bride's maiden name as an official family name. In many countries child-rearing allowances were introduced for either parent, or fathers were given the option to take parental leave to look after a sick

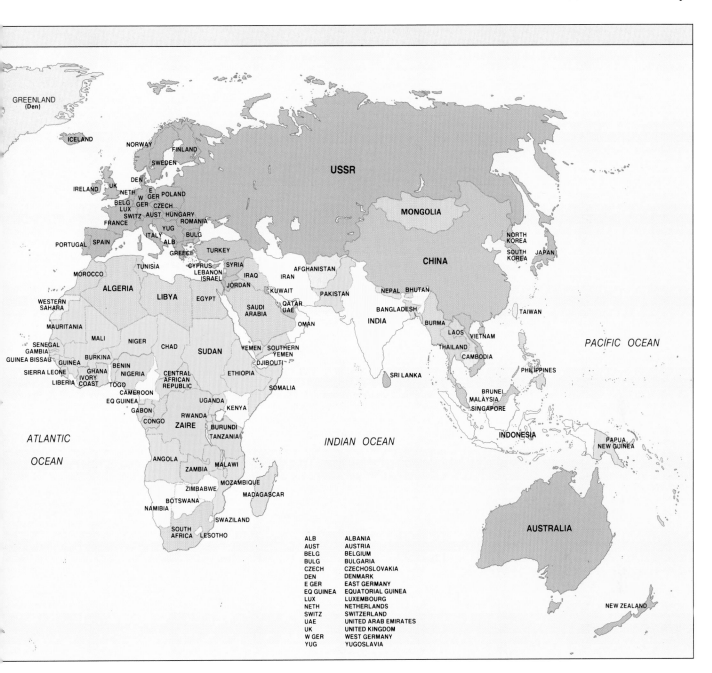

ALB	ALBANIA
AUST	AUSTRIA
BELG	BELGIUM
BULG	BULGARIA
CZECH	CZECHOSLOVAKIA
DEN	DENMARK
E GER	EAST GERMANY
EQ GUINEA	EQUATORIAL GUINEA
LUX	LUXEMBOURG
NETH	NETHERLANDS
SWITZ	SWITZERLAND
UAE	UNITED ARAB EMIRATES
UK	UNITED KINGDOM
W GER	WEST GERMANY
YUG	YUGOSLAVIA

▲ Economic development, social reforms, improvements in hygiene and social welfare together with advances in medicine have all contributed to the conspicuous increase in life expectancy in the 20th century. In developing countries average life expectancy increased by over one-third between 1960 and 1990, to 63 years (though only 52 in sub-Saharan Africa), even though 1.5 billion people still lacked basic health care.

child. Family law codes granted women equal rights in decision-making, in property and in work. Social policy was no longer to be punitive for working mothers but recognized women's right to work, attempting to ease rather than obstruct their dual role. Already by the 1970s women in Europe made up on average 37 percent of the labor force and 42 percent in North America – married women often outnumbered the unmarried. At the other end of the spectrum, women's "social invisibility" in the home (as "non-working" mothers who did housework) also received attention. Voluntary social security benefits were introduced for housewives, as for example in Germany. If things still went wrong, divorce was made easier too. Changes in existing laws generally replaced marital offenses as grounds for divorce with the principle of "irrevocable breakdown". Even in Catholic Italy the reforms of the Family Law Code (1975) granted spouses legal equality, permitted separation by

mutual consent and brought the long overdue equalization of the status of all children, legitimate or otherwise. In Ireland, however, divorce remained "unconstitutional".

After centuries of encouragement of childbearing, motherhood began to lose some of its centrality in public policy planning during the 1970s. Women were finally given leave substantially to control their own fertility, freeing them, as feminists saw it, from the tyranny of their reproductive functions. The wider availability of contraceptives and reform of abortion laws suggested that the separation of sex from procreation was now more generally accepted.

While reforms were intended to achieve greater justice in family relationships, allowing for greater "personal growth", rather than attempting to maintain family cohesion and fertility rates at all cost, the family's importance as the heart of society was never really questioned. The reforms were expected to strengthen the family once more, to make marriage more attractive and better adapted to modern times in order to shepherd straying lambs back to the fold, not to weaken it.

Nor did the old ambiguities and anxieties of public opinion about the changes in the family in the 20th century reach a conclusive resolution. Political debates on the family and divorce issues continued and if anything became more complex as new problems arose. After a decade of innovation, the family of the 1980s had to devise a new balance between new and old, adjust to the impact of women's employment on the pattern of childcare, care for the elderly, marital relationships – and the division of labor at home. Statistics for the 1980s suggested that the majority of people in fact continued to opt for a conventional family life, although many modern couples rejected a concept of marriage based on male dominance. The kind of sexual freedoms claimed within marriage in the 1960s and 1970s or other complex patterns of relationships proved for the majority simply too stressful to maintain.

A violent society: crime, drugs and destitution

One night in April 1989 there was a brutal assault and gang-rape of a white woman jogger in Central Park, New York, by a gang of 14- and 15-year-old poor and mostly black boys. The attack seemed to express for New Yorkers the fear and terror of city life. The state governor said: "This is the ultimate shriek of alarm. The ultimate signal that says none of us is safe". For a time the attack on this woman, a successful young investment banker, "was the symbol of what the mindless and brutish side of the city can do". Another 27 rapes that week went unremarked. "They weren't the stuff of myth; 80 percent of them involved, as

usual, people from the same race, from the same neighborhood, who knew each other".

This incident symbolizes a somber but extremely important aspect of life in the later 20th century – its increasing violence. There was an increase of drug abuse and of drug-related crime, both in the West and in countries involved in the supply of drugs. The numbers of murders increased, as did those of suicides and of family breakups. The figures for these sorts of events were reported in a United Nations report on human development, which led it to state that "the social fabric in the industrial nations is unravelling and shows starkly that higher national incomes are no protection against social tension and human distress". Some statistics probably reflect a greater determination to report and record incidents, but there is no doubt that they do reflect growing distress.

The causes are complex and poorly understood. The increased inequality of some industrial societies, associated with self-centered and self-seeking attitudes given licence by the aggressive ideology of neoliberalism, has played a part. This was perhaps the case in the tragedy of Central Park – though the connection was not direct. In the boys' own accounts of what happened, "It was fun. It was something to do". Inequality, even when tied up with racial differences, is an insufficient explanation. It was realized in Britain, for example, that the gangs of so-called "supporters" of famous football teams, whose interests were more in "doing over" opposing fans than in the game, were often not the unemployed (automatically suspect) but well-paid young men. Theirs was a culture of violence.

In this context the sudden appearance of a new epidemic disease in the 1980s seemed to some a

▲ Feminist badges were one way of creating among women a shared identity which reflected their case against sexual oppression and exploitation. When the United Nations proclaimed 1975 "International Women's Year", feminist movements began to shed their earlier culture-bound, single-country emphasis with a new awareness that the tension between the public image of women and their private lives had no national bounderies.

◄ The women's movement in India has been called the "most truly antipatriarchal and anticapitalist" of movements anywhere in the Third World and has often combined effectively with environmental movements. The impact of socialist ideology – with its impetus on egalitarianism – spread to feminism. Although these women trade unionists from the Punjab might not call themselves feminists, they are fighting for the same cause. The battle still to be fought for women's rights was shown by the increase of "dowry deaths" – caused by dissatisfied bridegrooms.

► This illustration may suggest that women have not come a long way: women worked in coal mines in the 19th century, usually for dismal wages. However, unlike some 30 years ago, this confident American female miner may have chosen to work in a pit, rather than having been forced to it by economic circumstances.

threat of an apocalypse. Epidemic diseases have profound social effects and AIDS (Acquired Immune Deficiency Syndrome), which appeared dramatically at the beginning of the 1980s, is such a disease. Its impact differed from one society to another, but in both poor and rich countries it strained health-care budgets. In some poor countries it reduced the number of adults who could provide food and care for young and old.

Fear of some social groups as especially prone to a disease results in stigma, never more so than when the disease is sexually transmitted and fatal, as AIDS often is. In the early 1980s doctors in the United States noticed an increasing frequency of an obscure form of pneumonia. The sudden appearance of many cases of this and also of a rare cancer, *Kaposi's sarcoma*, indicated that something unusual was afoot. Patients were dying because their immune systems were unable to combat these and other more common illnesses. The first victims were young homosexual men and early suggestions for a name for the disease indicated the prejudices so easily associated with it. GRIDS – Gay Related Immune Deficiency Syndrome – was a first attempt. Cases were soon found, however, in people other than homosexual men. In 1982 the name AIDS was coined, and identification of the disease agent and its mode of transmission presented a major challenge to medical science.

The 1960s and 1970s had offered prospects of sexual fulfilment. In Western societies, antibiotics, new forms of contraception and new ideas had facilitated freer sexual expression. In the West homosexual men claimed their own right to sexual and social liberation. As sexual expression became part of a political movement, the sexual climate of gay America in the late 1970s and early 1980s facilitated the spread of any sexually transmitted disease. HIV (the Human Immune deficiency Virus) is a slow-acting virus which can lie dormant for many years, enabling infectious people to appear healthy. This aspect of the disease meant that many people were infected before medical, social and political responses could be mobilized.

AIDS spread to every country and some of the highest rates were reported from the United States, France and Uganda. In Africa the disease spread heterosexually. The rapidity of spread can be partly explained by lack of health resources, poor general health, long periods of social unrest and economic disruption. Levels of infection were so high in some countries in the early 1990s – in Uganda perhaps about eight percent of the population were infected – that the number of deaths in subsequent decades might slow population increase or even reduce absolute population. This had serious social and economic implications. A disease mainly affecting people aged between 15 and 50 years of age will result in large numbers of orphans, shortages of labor, loss of expensively trained specialists, as well as increasing the burden of health and other forms of care.

Such effects were not restricted to the countries of Africa. In the rich world, hard decisions were going to have to be made about the allocation of resources between the care of people with AIDS and the care of people with other illnesses.

Movements of hope?

It would be panglossian not to acknowledge the severity of the social problems of the later 20th century. But it is also important to recognize the creative dynamism in peoples' responses to them. The foothills of the Himalayas, in India, are a long way from Central Park, New York. But they too have been the site of violence of a different kind – against nature and poor people's livelihoods, as commercial forestry operations exploited trees without regard to environmental sustainability. But from the early 1970s a popular movement, "Chipko" (which means "to hug"), was quite successful in checking this exploitation and served as a model for other movements elsewhere in India, such as those struggling against the social and environmental damage caused by some big dam projects. The name of the Chipko movement refers to its nonviolent strategy of resistance – that of embracing trees to prevent the lumbermen getting at them. Women were in the forefront, but the movement depended on the mobilization of community solidarity. It was also the vehicle for the expression of other grievances against the state, notably the lack of fulfillment of basic needs of health, education and employment.

Chipko exemplified the "new" social movements that grew up in developed and developing

◄▼ One of the homeless, mainly young people, living on the streets of London at the end of the 1980s. Such destitution had earlier almost disappeared. It returned because of changes in social security and the sheer cost of housing.

► In the 1980s "dropping out" was no longer fashionable as it had been in the 1960s. But the Hare Krishna movement retained a following and "holy men" from India still charmed Westerners eager to find meaning in their lives.

countries. They included especially women's movements, ecological movements and the peace movement. They shared the characteristics of being based on an individual sense of morality and justice which were mobilized socially and then directed at survival and the creation of identity and meaning. People sought greater empowerment through social movements which stood apart, however, from organized political parties. Their struggles were for greater autonomy rather than to take over state power. They were defensive rather than offensive, and they sought to distance themselves from both contemporary capitalism and so-called socialism. There were sometimes conflicts, but also complementarities, in the objectives of different movements. There were especially overlaps between women's, community, green and peace movements. Thanks to the preponderance of women in them they were more participative and mutually supportive than hierarchical in the way they organized. They offered one of the positive signs of a way ahead at the end of the 20th century.

▼ North Philadelphia, 1990. In a neighborhood which police call "The Land of Oz – where the abnormal is normal" a 13-year-old dealer lets a crack (cocaine) user inspect his goods. The young dealer, whose father died of AIDS, can sell 100 dollars worth of crack in an hour. On every corner are children, some only 8, hustling drugs, waiting for a chance to sell or deliver. This scene reflected the extent of crime, of random violence and death in cities in rich countries. Behind it lay international networks of extremely powerful criminals.

LEISURE

In preindustrial society leisure activities were fitted closely around work. They had to be cheap and available locally and this led to rich traditions of folk culture in song, dance and story-telling. People spent their leisure time together and reinforced their sense of community by doing so.

The 20th century has seen a transformation in leisure activity. First, there has been extraordinary technological change. By the 1930s the cinema had revolutionized social life in the cities, with millions attending "the movies" weekly and becoming dazzled by the glamor of the Hollywood studios. The wireless, which had spread to most middle-class homes by the end of the 1930s, and in the 1950s and 1960s television, broke down local cultures replacing them with news and ideas from a wider world. Of equal importance was the revolution in air transport which brought most parts of the world within 24 hours of each other and thus opened unlimited possibilities for mass tourism.

While these changes were taking place, working hours in the west were becoming shorter and incomes higher. There were many more opportunities for choosing one's own form of leisure, whether in sport, travel or cultural improvement. Leisure activities became big business. The package holiday industry boomed, with hotel complexes mushrooming along the world's more sundrenched beaches. Theme parks, such as Disneyland in the United States, offered complete entertainment for families. Youth cultures developed round rock and pop music.

Improvements in education helped lead to an increased interest in cultural activities. It became possible to visit the sites of ancient civilizations such as Egypt, Greece and Rome cheaply and easily. A fascination with the past led to interest in historic buildings and museums. Television helped introduce viewers to a wide variety of cultural activities such as opera and literature which before had been restricted to the richer classes.

Leisure could be used for relaxation and enjoyment but it also allowed participants to develop new roles outside the home and the workplace. It was possible to leave sophisticated life-styles in the city to go "back to nature", or live close to traditional cultures even if one had to fly by jumbo jet to find them. The results were not always beneficial. Poorer countries became increasingly dependent on the income provided by tourism while tourists themselves often undermined the cultures and ways of life they had traveled to see.

▲ ▶ Dancing was a traditional leisure activity which flourished in new forms as the latest tunes were spread by the gramophone and cinema. Dance crazes spread across the western world. These ballroom teachers in 1920s USA are coming to terms with jazz.

▶ Leisure centers became more sophisticated as the century progressed. In this holiday village an artificial tropical beach has been created under a vast dome. It is typical of the involvement of big business in leisure which has been dominant since World War II.

◀ In many warmer countries there is a tradition of families meeting outside the home to eat and drink together. This is a family in Barcelona, Spain, out enjoying a drink at a local restaurant. Many leisure activities have reinforced traditional family links but increasingly such activities have become aimed at one particular age group or specialized interest and may have served to undermine the cohesion of the family.

◀ These Russians use their leisure time to play chess, a peaceful, unhurried but also challenging way of spending the time. Such activities run the risk of being undermined by television and other less challenging forms of entertainment.

▼ The desire "to get away from it all" and explore the remoter parts of the world is a powerful one, particularly among young westerners. This picture was taken in the Peruvian Andes where a visitor comes face to face with a curious local people. However spartan the life-style adopted by the visiting westerner, gaps between cultures have remained wide and perhaps unbridgeable.

BIOGRAPHIES

Adler, Alfred 1870–1937

Austrian psychiatrist who founded Individual
Psychology and was strongly influenced by his
social concern. He studied medicine in Vienna
and became a prominent member of Freud's
psychoanalytical group before differences led to a
split in 1911. Emphasizing social factors in
personality development rather than sexual factors,
unlike Freud, Adler established his school of
Individual Psychology. He asserted that people are
motivated more by goals and expectations, even
though they may be unobtainable (fictional
finalism), than by their past, thus creating their
own personality. The principal human goal is
perfection; as this is patently unachievable,
inferiority feelings arise. Adler believed the unique
way in which an individual strives for perfection,
the "style of life", forms in early childhood. He
insisted that the individual should be considered
within the social context and that perfection can be
approached only by people striving collectively.

Atatürk, Mustafa Kemal 1881–1938

Soldier, statesman and first president of the
Republic of Turkey whose modernizing reforms
had a profound and lasting effect on Turkish
society. He reached the rank of general in the army
during World War I but resigned (1919) to fight for
independence and became president of the
National Congress. The British occupied Turkey
(1920) and dissolved the chamber of deputies,
allowing Atatürk to unite the first great national
assembly, which elected him president. In 1923
Turkey became fully independent, a republic was
declared and Atatürk was elected president. The
caliphate was abolished and sweeping reforms
launched, secularizing the state and promoting
nationalism rather than religion. He secularized
and modernized Turkey's education and legal
systems and codes of dress. Western-style
surnames were introduced and the Arabic alphabet
was replaced with the Latin. Women were
enfranchised. Foreign industry was nationalized
and national banks created to fund industrial
development.

Beauvoir, Simone de 1908–86

French feminist and novelist, de Beauvoir's work
has had an enormous impact on feminist thought.
After a private education she attended the
Sorbonne (1929) where she began her lifelong
relationship with Jean-Paul Sartre. Her most
famous publication is *The Second Sex* (1949) in
which she argues for the rejection of the myth of
women's femininity. In patriarchal society the
male and masculinity are held up as the norm,
while the female and femininity are seen as
abnormal or as "the other". Women's sense of
"the other", of their alienation, is predominantly
based upon their bodies and in particular their
reproductive role. As a novelist, de Beauvoir's

work focused on existentialism and feminism (*All
Men are Mortal*, 1946; *She Came to Stay*, 1949).
Eschewing marriage and motherhood while
embracing independence, de Beauvoir was active
in the women's movement, especially in the
campaign to legalize abortion in France.

Bernstein, Eduard 1850–1932

German socialist, the "father of revisionism" – the
movement away from revolutionary socialism.
Bernstein worked as a bank clerk and joined the
German Social Democratic party (SPD) in 1872. He
believed in German unity and democracy but
chancellor Bismarck's antisocialist legislation
pushed him into a radical stance. Expelled from
Germany and Switzerland he lived in London
(from 1888) where he was influenced by the Fabian
Society's belief in achieving socialism by gradual
change rather than revolution. Back in Germany
from 1901 he expounded a theory of socialism as a
natural manifestation of inborn human liberalism
and rejected Marx's belief in the inevitability of the
collapse of capitalism. His espousal of gradualism
was eventually accepted by the SPD. He became an
SPD deputy in the Reichstag in 1902, but left the
party in 1914 in protest at its support for World
War I. He rejoined on the outbreak of the German
Revolution in 1918 and supported the Majority
Socialists against the Independent Socialists and
Spartacists of Rosa Luxemburg.

Bevan, Aneurin 1897–1960

British Labour politician who, as minister for
health (1948–51), was the architect of the influential
British National Health Service (NHS). To create
this Bevan unified local authority and voluntary
hospitals into a single national system which
provided an entirely free service. It was achieved
against resistance from the medical profession
which he overcame by permitting private practice
to continue in tandem with the NHS. The service
began operating in 1948 and resulted in great
improvements in standards of public and private
health. When Hugh Gaitskell, then chancellor of
the exchequer, introduced NHS charges Bevan
resigned from his post of minister of labour (1951).
He subsequently became leader of the radical
"Bevanites" within the Labour party. His greatest
achievement was creating the NHS but he is also
remembered as a great orator, parliamentarian and
a man of high socialist principles.

Beveridge, William Henry 1879–1963

British economist and author of the famous
"Beveridge Report" on comprehensive social
security. As director of the government department
of employment (1909–15) Beveridge created a
national system of labor exchanges and the
administration for compulsory unemployment
insurance. After serving as director of the London
School of Economics (1919–37), chairman of the

Unemployment Insurance Statutory Committee
(1934–44), and Master of University College,
Oxford, from 1937, he was called into the ministry
of labour by Aneurin Bevan in 1940. In 1941
Beveridge chaired the committee inquiring into
social insurance which resulted in the report of
1942. It changed the prevalent understanding of
unemployment and demanded benefits without
means tests, the eradication of unemployment and
a system of family allowances. Initial government
response was slow but implementation began
during World War II and continued under the
postwar Labour government.

Binet, Alfred 1857–1911

French pioneer of experimental psychology and
developer of IQ (intelligence quotient) tests. In
1878 Binet turned from the study of law to
psychology, initially concentrating on hypnotism.
In 1892 he began work in a research laboratory at
the Sorbonne, becoming its director in 1894. He
specialized in child study, working first with his
own daughters as subjects; his collaborator was the
educational psychologist Théodore Simon. In 1895
Binet cofounded the journal *L'Anneé psychologique*.
In 1905 the first Binet–Simon intelligence tests were
conducted, the second series in 1908. In 1911 their
introduction of the concept of "mental age"
permitted the measurement of "IQ". Their findings
were published in *A Method of Measuring the
Development of Young Children* (1913). Binet was
the first to attempt a precise measurement of
intelligence and the first to include in such tests
questions demanding cognition.

Blum, Léon 1872–1950

French Socialist leader and, as head of the Popular
Front coalition government (1936–37), France's first
socialist prime minister, an office he held again
briefly in 1938. Arrested by the Vichy government
(1940), he was imprisoned in Germany (1942–45).
He headed a caretaker government (1946–47) before
withdrawing from active political life. Blum
advocated a combination of Marxist socialism with
French democratic traditions. His government
successfully introduced labor reforms, achieving
a 40-hour week, paid vacations, collective
bargaining, and the nationalization of the Bank
of France and several arms' industries. However,
his economic policies were less successful and
ultimately he failed to create a united
working-class movement able to resist the threat of
fascism.

Bonhoeffer, Dietrich 1906–45

German theologian. A student and teacher of
theology, Bonhoeffer was also a strong opponent
of the Nazi regime. As an active member of the
resistance to Hitler he was arrested, imprisoned
and hanged in 1945. Bonhoeffer's work has
influenced both ecclesiastics and academics and he

has been admired for his willingness to confront controversial issues. In *The Cost of Discipleship* (1937) he attacked "cheap grace", that which costs nothing in sacrifice to its followers, in the belief that real grace and the suffering it involves give truth to life. His best-known book, *Letters and Papers from Prison* (1972) calls for a "religionless" Christianity which should be aimed at the mature modern man and reject traditional religious predispositions. It also advocated a Christianity directed not at man in weakness but rather when he is strong. Such views have caused much debate.

Bowlby, John 1907–90
British psychoanalyst. Bowlby's study of 45 juvenile thieves in 1946 found that a common feature of their histories was prolonged separation from their mothers. He pursued the study of maternal deprivation and the idea that successful bonding between young child and mother may be necessary for healthy psychological development. He also studied the reaction of children to bereavement. His work amounted to a major contribution to developmental psychology and had wide influence on those working in mental health and medicine. For instance, it led in some countries to the practice of admitting mothers to hospital to accompany their sick children. However, his earlier findings have been criticized and new methods of analysis have provided alternative theories. His major works include *Maternal Care and Mental Health* (1951) and the trilogy *Attachment and Loss*, published between 1969 and 1980.

Cárdenas, Lázaro 1895–1970
Mexican politician and social reformer. Cárdenas rose to the rank of general in the Mexican revolutionary army before becoming governor of his native Michoacán (1928–32). He was instrumental in forming the Partido Nacionál Revolucionário (1929), of which he became chairman. As president of Mexico (1934–40) he was known for his introduction of social reforms. He inaugurated a successful six-year plan of agrarian reforms to distribute land to the peasants, establish credit systems and form communal village holdings (*ejidos*). He also extended education, established confederations to represent both peasants and workers, and nationalized foreign-owned industries.

Carnegie, Dale 1888–1955
United States author and teacher of public speaking. An active member of debating clubs at school and college, Carnegie became a salesman and an actor before he began to teach public speaking at the YMCA. A successful response and large attendances led to the publication of pamphlets, eventually collected in book form in *Public Speaking: A Practical Course for Business Men*

(1926). His most successful book was *How to Win Friends and Influence People* (1936). In this Carnegie presented common-sense advice for overcoming handicaps in order to become successful, emphasizing the importance of a positive attitude.

Castro, Fidel 1926–
Cuban socialist revolutionary. After becoming prime minister in 1959, Castro proclaimed a Marxist–Leninist program adapted to Cuban requirements. He expanded and improved educational institutions and established a free welfare state system. Employment was guaranteed and work compulsory; agriculture was reformed; US-owned property was nationalized. The reforms improved living standards and resulted in a more equal society but did not solve the country's economic and social problems. The economy remained inefficient and failed to cope with population growth. Cuba became dependent on subsidies from the Soviet Union and many of Castro's supporters became alienated by his authoritarian rule.

Ceauşescu, Nicolae 1918–89
Romanian dictator, Ceauşescu became secretary-general of the Romanian Communist party in 1965 and head of state in 1967. Within Romania he created an increasingly repressive regime based on the Securitate (an elite force with sole allegiance to the president) and a network of spies and informants. His forced industrialization policies took Romania from a position of relative prosperity to near starvation. To pay off external debt he exported manufactured goods and agricultural produce, creating domestic shortages of food, fuel and basic necessities. Food shortages were exacerbated when he pursued "systematization" – a policy to destroy villages and rehouse people in urban concrete apartment blocks. Other repressive measures included a ban on birth control and compulsory examinations for all women of childbearing age in order to ensure a high birth rate. Ceauşescu was overthrown by an army-supported popular rising in December 1989.

Chayanov, Alexander 1888–1939
Russian economist and student of peasant societies. Appointed assistant professor of the Institute of Agricultural Economy (1913), Chayanov directed the Institute until purged by Stalin in 1930. His research, both before and after the Communist revolution, focused on Russian peasant agricultural production. He advocated cooperation, reasonable incentives for peasants to produce and market their crops, and peasant control of the land. Not a supporter of forced collectivization, he nevertheless worked on the planning of Soviet state farms. Chayanov developed a theory of peasant farming based on household units of production.

Chomsky, Noam 1928–
US linguist, writer and political activist. Chomsky's theories led to the creation of a new school of linguistics and also had a profound impact on philosophy and psychology. Going against the dominance of structuralist thought, Chomsky argued that language is the result of an innate facility in the mind. Once this was fully discovered one could construct a grammatical framework to account for the vast range of sentence structures found in all languages (*Syntactic Structures*, 1957). Chomsky is also known for his involvement with New Left politics and for his opposition to US foreign policy, especially to US involvement in Vietnam during the 1960s and 1970s and in Kuwait in 1990–91. Chomsky's views on social and political affairs can be found in *American Power* and *The New Mandarins* (1969) and *At War with Asia* (1970).

Cohn-Bendit, Daniel 1945–
German Marxist/anarchist and student leader. Born in Germany, Cohn-Bendit studied sociology at the University of France, where he developed Marxist/anarchist theories opposed to all forms of authority and called for spontaneous action by the masses. He became the leader of student activists whose protests in Paris in 1968 included the occupation of university buildings. This unrest culminated in riots and Cohn-Bendit was seen as the compelling force behind them, but he preferred to be considered as merely a spokesman rather than a leader. He was expelled from France and returned to Germany, where he rejected his earlier standpoint: his theories took no account of the threat to man's future posed by destruction of the planet. He subsequently became a Green party politician in Germany.

Deng Xiaoping 1904–
Chinese Communist leader. An early supporter of Mao Zedong, Deng had a checkered career in the Communist party until 1977 when he made a final return to power. Concerned to concentrate on the modernization of China, he replaced the radical policies of Mao, which had caused turmoil, with a more pragmatic approach. He pursued an "open-door" policy of allowing foreign technology and capital to enter the country. Agriculture was decollectivized and managed to feed China's expanding population. The economy became more prosperous but Deng failed to introduce corresponding political reforms. As living standards rose, demands for political change increased – culminating in the prodemocracy demonstrations in Beijing in 1989. Deng met the challenge by ordering the army to put down the unrest – at a cost of several hundred deaths. Deng's reputation was damaged; the inflow of foreign investment fell. China ceased to look like a modernizing, politically stable country.

▲ Hans Jürgen Eysenck

▲ George Horace Gallup

▲ Marcus Garvey

Djilas, Milovan 1911–

Yugoslavian revolutionary leader who became an influential critic of communism and of the Yugoslavian communist regime. A leader in the World War II resistance movement in Yugoslavia, Djilas became a member of Tito's cabinet after the war. He reached high office by 1953 but political and personal disputes with the party leadership resulted in expulsion from political posts and resignation from the party. Imprisoned for accusing the regime of corruption and stating his support for the Hungarian uprising (1956), Djilas wrote and smuggled out *The New Class* for publication in the West (1957). This work was a bitter criticism of communism and its creation of a new privileged and corrupt class. Released in 1961, he was imprisoned the following year for publishing *Conversations With Stalin*.

Dubček, Alexander 1921–

Czechoslovakian reformist communist leader. A member of the Slovak resistance to German occupation during World War II, Dubček rose steadily in the Communist party ranks after the war and became first secretary of the party in 1968. Opposed to Soviet-style communism, which had led Czechoslovakia into economic stagnation, political purges and cultural repression, he proposed the most far-reaching reforms yet undertaken by a ruling Communist party. He increased the freedom of the press and rehabilitated victims of the purges. He also announced "Czechoslovakia's Road to Socialism" which would introduce basic civil rights and economic reform, remove centralism and reinstate democratic practices. Alarmed by the implications of liberalization, the Soviet leadership invaded Czechoslovakia after attempts to persuade Dubček to abandon his reforms failed. He and his supporters were ousted from office (1969). Dubček then worked for the forestry administration but was restored to public life after the collapse of the communist regime in 1989.

Durkheim, Emile 1858–1917

French sociologist. Durkheim taught at the University of Bordeaux and later at the Sorbonne in Paris. Believing that sociologists should study social facts rather than individuals, he argued that society has its own reality which cannot be reduced to the actions and motives of its members. In this social environment, with its constraints and pressures, the individual is molded and shaped. Durkheim's classic works included *The Division of Labor* (1893), which analyzes the basis of social order in preindustrial and industrial societies, and *The Rules of Sociological Method* (1899), in which he demonstrated that social facts, such as the rule of law, are not dependent upon individuals or upon any specific act of enforcement. In *Suicide* (1897) the apparently individual act of taking one's life

was explained in terms of different social settings, while in *The Elementary Forms of Religious Life* (1912) Durkheim suggested that the idea of society was celebrated in primitive religions and that objects only became sacred when they were seen to symbolize the community.

Egas Moniz, Antonio 1874–1955

Portuguese neurologist, statesman and founder of modern psychosurgery. Appointed to the newly created chair of neurology at the University of Lisbon (1911–44), Egas Moniz introduced and developed cerebral angiography. This involved injecting dyes that were opaque to X-rays into the arteries in order to make the blood vessels of the brain visible, a technique used in the diagnosis of brain tumors. He devised prefrontal leukotomy (1935), the severing of the nerve fibers between the prefrontal lobes in order to relieve severe emotional tension in psychiatric patients.

Eysenck, Hans Jürgen 1916–

British psychologist (German born). Eysenck stressed the importance of laboratory, statistical and questionnaire techniques in the study of human behavior. For example, he developed the Eysenck personality inventory and questionnaire. Famous for his vigorous and controversial criticisms of psychoanalysis, he argued that its theoretical explanations were redundant, its therapy suspect and its results could be achieved by spontaneous remission or resulted from placebo effects. Instead, Eysenck advocated "behavioral therapy" which rejects traditional explanations of unconscious motives and childhood experiences and uses practical methods such as relaxation in a process of unlearning undesirable responses. He also believed that intelligence and personality are mainly influenced by genetic factors.

Fanon, Frantz (Omar) 1925–61

West Indian psychoanalyst, social philosopher and revolutionary writer whose ideas influenced black leaders during the 1960s and 1970s. Fanon's work emphasized the conflict that exists between races. In *Black Skin, White Masks* (1952) he analyzed the effects of white colonialism upon blacks. He also wrote extensively on the Algerian revolution and in *The Wretched of the Earth* (1961) he extended his analysis of struggle to cover the Third World. Fanon urged colonialized people to overthrow imperialism by using violence, this being justifiable because violence was the vehicle used to enforce colonial rule.

Ford, Henry 1863–1947

US industrialist and exponent of industrial mass production. Ford had a flair for mechanics and built his first petrol-driven automobile in 1896. In 1899 he founded his own company and aimed to produce automobiles that most people could

afford. In 1908 the Model T appeared; by 1927 15,000,000 had been sold. The success was achieved by manufacturing a robust car by assembly-line mass production. Ford's attitudes to his workers, however, were paternalistic. He believed that high productivity could be achieved by high standards of employment. He introduced an 8-hour working day, paid higher wages than offered elsewhere, and ran a profit-sharing plan for employees. He was generally keen on supporting the individual against mass organizations and pressed his beliefs through involvement in politics.

Freud, Sigmund 1856–1939

Austrian founder of psychoanalysis. Freud studied medicine in Vienna and Paris. His first psychoanalytical work, *Studies on Hysteria* (1895), examined hysteria by using the technique of "free association". Freud went on to develop basic concepts of psychoanalysis: repression, the unconscious, conversion and abreaction. His major work, *The Interpretation of Dreams*, was published in 1900 and concluded that dreams are disguised fulfillments of unconscious wishes. Between 1900 and 1920 he wrote 80 papers and nine books and established the Psychoanalytical Movement. During the 1920s, Freud proposed the idea that humans possess a death instinct in *Beyond the Pleasure Principle* (1920) and wrote on his conceptions of the dynamics of personality in *The Ego and the Id* (1923) and *Inhibitions, Symptoms and Anxiety* (1926). He moved to London in 1938 and died of cancer in 1939. His work has had a profound effect on Western society.

Friedan, Betty 1921–

US feminist. Friedan advocates an individualist and liberal form of feminism. Her book *The Feminine Mystique* (1963) was one of the earliest and most influential books on the women's movement of the late 20th century. It describes the discrepancy between the ideals to which women try to conform and the frustrated reality of their lives. Friedan called for women to reject the "mystique" which regarded the highest achievement of women to be fulfillment through domesticity and motherhood and to develop fully as persons through education and work. Friedan herself had given up a career in psychology for marriage and a family. In *The Second Stage* (1981) she warned of the dangers of competing with men rather than insisting on the right to be different from them. Friedan also founded the National Organization for Women (1966), one of the most influential groups in the USA.

Gallup, George Horace 1907–90

US pioneer in the development of techniques for measuring public opinion, in particular the use of sample surveys for which the name Gallup Poll became the generic title. While director of research

at a New York advertising agency, Gallup used market research methods to conduct opinion surveys. He interviewed a small but representative sample of respondents across the country (approximately 1,000 to 1,500) in order to achieve a reliable gauge of national opinions. Gallup established the American Institute of Public Opinion (1935) and the British Institute of Public Opinion (1936). His technique was adopted in election forecasting and fostered an increased awareness of public attitudes by governments.

Gandhi, Indira 1914–84
Indian prime minister. After education at Somerville College, Oxford, and a political apprenticeship under her father Nehru (the first prime minister of independent India), Gandhi was elected president of the Congress party (1955) and became prime minister in 1966. Her resounding electoral victory in 1971 reflected public support which was reinforced by India's military defeat of Pakistan resulting in the creation of Bangladesh. Her election slogan "abolish poverty" raised expectations but these were disappointed as drought and international inflation led to economic crisis. Allegations of electoral corruption resulted in conviction by the high court (1975). Responding in the autocratic manner of which she had been accused, Gandhi imposed a national state of emergency, jailed political opponents, and assumed powers under which a series of laws restricting civil liberties were passed. During emergency rule she pursued programs of social reform, and sought to encourage further industrialization. In 1977 restrictions were eased and an election called, in which she was defeated. She returned to power in 1979 but was assassinated five years later.

Gandhi, Mohandas K. 1869–1948
Indian nationalist leader. Gandhi studied law in London before working in South Africa (1893–1914) where he campaigned against racial discrimination. Returning to India in 1914, he entered politics, becoming head of the Indian National Congress and, as a pacifist, advocating a policy of nonviolent civil disobedience to achieve *swaraj*, meaning "self-control" rather than just political independence. He was repeatedly arrested by the British, action which he followed by hunger strikes. During World War II the British sought cooperation (1942) but Gandhi insisted that India could only give effective support if complete independence was granted, which eventually occurred in 1947. India and Pakistan were partitioned into separate independent states and Gandhi's support for Muslim–Hindu understanding led to his assassination in 1948. Gandhi dominated Indian politics for nearly three decades. He was esteemed as a moral teacher and for his use of nonviolent protest.

Garvey, Marcus 1887–1940
Black leader and organizer of the first major US black nationalist movement. Garvey founded the Universal Negro Improvement Association (UNIA) in Jamaica but, unable to attract support, moved to the USA (1916). Establishing UNIA headquarters in New York, Garvey also founded branches in the main black communities of the North. He held the first UNIA convention (1920) with delegates from 25 countries present and spoke on Negro rights, achievements and culture, setting a precedent in encouraging blacks to be proud of being black. Garvey also advocated Negro economic independence and began various enterprises to forward this aim. However, his belief in racial purity and separation (which led him to endorse the Ku Klux Klan) and his dubious business practices brought him enemies. Garvey's influence declined and he was convicted of fraud (1925). His sentence was commuted by President Coolidge (1927) and he was deported. Despite attempts, Garvey could not revive support abroad and he died in obscurity.

Gompers, Samuel 1850–1924
US labor leader. Gompers, an immigrant to the United States, joined a union in 1864. In 1881 he established the US and Canada Federation of Organized Trades and Labor Union. He founded the American Federation of Labor (AF of L) in 1886, leading it, barring one year, until his death. A pragmatist, Gompers supported collective bargaining and strikes for basic necessities. He considered socialist ideology and intellectualism to be diversions from fundamental issues and deemed it necessary to work with capitalism to gain specific ends. Under Gompers, wages increased by 250 percent, working hours decreased, and the AF of L, with a membership approaching 3 million, became the USA's biggest labor organization.

Gorbachev, Mikhail 1931–
Reformist communist political leader. After a career within the Soviet Communist party Gorbachev became secretary-general of the party in 1985 and president of the Soviet Union in 1989. His first policy of *glasnost* (openness) resulted in greater freedom of expression, liberalization in the arts and the release of political prisoners. With *perestroika* (restructuring) he sought to tackle the Soviet economy's backwardness. *Perestroika* aimed to end the state's monopoly of the economy, modernize industry, encourage private and foreign investment and raise living standards. Expectations were raised but could not be fulfilled. Both industrial and agricultural production fell and living standards declined. Gorbachev's own position was threatened as republics pressed for independence from the Union and popular unrest grew.

Graham, Billy 1921–
US Christian evangelist. Converted at the age of 16, in 1939 Graham was ordained as a southern Baptist minister. In 1949 he began his preaching tours in America and by the following year was regarded by many as the main spokesman for the fundamentalists. He went on to preach throughout the world, including Europe (1954–55), Africa and the Holy Land (1960) and Korea (1973). His support widened from its narrow fundamentalist base to include all the major denominations. Graham used modern communications, especially television, to reach vast audiences. He also adopted modern business methods to arrange his appearances. Despite his highly developed capitalist methods, his preaching style is simple and direct and has won many converts for Christianity. He has also produced religious films, has published books and has developed friendships with several presidents of the United States.

Gramsci, Antonio 1891–1937
Italian Marxist. Gramsci joined the Socialist party (1914) and turned to Marxism after the Russian Revolution (1917). He formed a leftwing group within the party and founded the Socialist newspaper *L'Ordine Nuova* (1919). He became disillusioned with the Socialist party and in 1921 left to found the Italian Communist party (PCI). Gramsci then worked in the Soviet Union before returning to Italy to become leader of the PCI (1924) and an elected member of the chamber of deputies. In 1926 he was arrested and imprisoned by the fascist government. Released in 1937 due to ill-health, he died in the same year. Gramsci developed the concept of hegemony in which the domination of one class over others is obtained by both political and ideological means. While in jail he recorded his thoughts which were published posthumously and helped him gain the reputation as being one of the most important Marxist thinkers of the 20th century.

Greer, Germaine 1939–
Australian feminist. Greer took a first degree in Australia and then obtained a doctorate at the British University of Cambridge. She remained in Britain and lectured at the University of Warwick (1968–73). She shot to prominence with the publication of her first book, *The Female Eunuch*, in 1970, which sold millions of copies. Analyzing the prevalence of misogyny in society and culture, Greer attacked the misrepresentation and denial of female sexuality under patriarchy and portrayed marriage as a legalized form of slavery for women. However, by calling for women to act individually rather than for them to unite, her work did not create a practical agenda for feminism. In *Sex and Destiny* (1984) Greer diverged from current feminist theories about the family by advocating the return to large extended families.

► Václav Havel

► F. Theodor Herzl

► Carl Gustav Jung

Havel, Václav 1936–

Czech dramatist and dissident. Havel became a dissident through his desire to resist repression and uphold human rights rather than by a particular political attachment. After the 1968 invasion of Czechoslovakia by Soviet troops, the production of his plays and publication of his work were banned. During the 1970s he was repeatedly arrested and jailed. In 1977 he and many other intellectuals and artists signed Charter 77, a manifesto protesting at the failure of the Czech government to abide by the Helsinki Agreement on Civil and Political Rights. As one of the Charter's three principal spokesmen Havel was again imprisoned. Released in 1983, he was again jailed in 1989 for taking part in demonstrations against the government. His internment added to the growing unrest in the country and by the end of the year the communist regime had been overthrown and Havel was elected president. He insisted on the establishment of a multiparty system and free parliamentary elections.

Herzl, F. Theodor 1860–1904

Austrian founder of Zionism. A law graduate, Herzl was so shocked by the level of antisemitism in France exposed by the Dreyfus affair that, in 1896, he issued a pamphlet (*Der Judenstaat*) advocating the creation of a Jewish state. He displayed diplomatic genius in bringing together Jews from dramatically different backgrounds, in Eastern and Western Europe, for the first Zionist Congress, in 1897. First president of the World Zionist Organization, Herzl was convinced that only global cooperation would solve the problem of antisemitism. However, when the British government offered Jews a homeland in Uganda, he was unable to reconcile the differences within the movement, as many Zionists were immovably attached to the idea of Palestine as their only possible home.

Hitler, Adolf 1889–1945

German dictator. Born and educated in Austria, Hitler served with the Bavarian infantry in World War I. In 1920 he joined the Munich-based German Workers' party and in 1923 attempted to seize power in Munich. His *putsch* failed and imprisonment followed which he used to write *Mein Kampf* ("My Struggle"). In this he proposed a view of the world based on struggle between peoples rather than classes, in which the Aryan peoples were supreme and the Jews among the lowest. His renewed quest for power succeeded in 1933 when he became chancellor. His Nazi state, based on fascist "national socialism", restored full employment and developed Germany's infrastructure, but it retained authority through terror and dealt violently with communists, catholics and Jews. With the expansion of German territory from 1940 onward, Hitler's racial policies

were applied to conquered territories, culminating in the "Final Solution", the attempt to liquidate European Jewry by shooting and gassing. About 6 million Jews were murdered. Hitler committed suicide in Berlin in 1945.

Jiang Jieshi 1887–1975

Chinese soldier and political leader. Jiang failed to stabilize China but exerted a major influence on the continent in a period of major transition. After the death of the Nationalist leader Sun Yixian (1925), Jiang led the Nationalist movement and established a central government in Nanjing (1928). Continued opposition form war lords and communists undermined his power and contributed to his inability to achieve a consistent program of social reform. Jiang did reintroduce the state cult of Kongzi (Confucius) in an attempt to promote national unity and he initiated the "New Live Movement" (1934) in order to instill Confucian morals into society. War with Japan (1937–45), renewed civil war (1946–49) and corruption in government resulted in Jiang's defeat and the establishment of the Communist People's Republic of China (1949). He continued to challenge the communists from exile in Taiwan, where he was head of state until his death.

John XXIII (Angelo Roncalli) 1881–1963

Italian Pope. Ordained priest in 1904, Roncalli served as an army chaplain in World War I and afterward as a Vatican diplomat (1925–52). Appointed patriarch of Venice in 1953, he was elected pope in 1958 and was viewed by many as a "caretaker". However, in 1959 he announced the summoning of an ecumenical council, the first for almost a century, in order to reinvigorate Catholic Christianity and promote Christian unity. Pope John took an informal approach to the papacy and emphasized his pastoral role. In his encyclicals *Mater et Magistra* (1961) and *Pacem in Terris* (1963) was a reminder not to confuse error with the erring person; for example the philosophy of Marxism with the governments that espoused it. The former was to be rejected, the latter understood.

John Paul II (Karol Wojtyla) 1920–

The first non-Italian Pope in 456 years. John Paul II was a conservative who sought to underline orthodox Catholic positions on such issues as abortion, divorce and contraception, while as a populist he aimed to address the public in a direct manner avoiding the complexities of theological dogma. Born in Poland, Wojtyla was ordained priest just after World War II. He rose quickly through the hierarchy (bishop, 1958; archbishop, 1964; cardinal 1967) and was elected the first ever Polish Pope in 1978. He immediately began a global tour involving massive rallies at which he expounded the tenets of Catholic Christianity in relation to the modern world.

Jung, Carl Gustav 1875–1961

Swiss psychiatrist. His early works *Studies in Word Association* and *Psychology of Dementia Praecox* led to his introduction of the word "complex" into psychiatry and to his association with Freud. He became increasingly critical of Freud's insistence on the sexual basis of neurosis; the publication of Jung's *Psychology of the Unconscious* (1912) led to a final split (1913). He continued to develop his own theories, termed Analytical Psychology. The most important of these include the description of psychological types (extroversion/introversion); the discovery and exploration of the collective unconscious, with its archetype images and symbols; and the concept of the psyche as a self-regulating system. Jung spent much of his later work on the latter process which resulted in the widening of his investigations to include religious symbolism, myths, and historical studies.

Kadar, Janos 1912–89

Hungarian political leader. Kadar was installed as prime minister after Soviet forces had crushed the popular anticommunist rising in 1956. He had been a member of the Hungarian Communist party since 1931 and had served in the postwar communist regime. He quickly restored Soviet-style communism to Hungary. The party's authority was reimposed and agriculture was recollectivized. Thereafter, however, Kadar pursued a more conciliatory and innovative set of policies. Collective farms and industrial firms were given autonomy and encouraged to make direct contracts with each other. The country's intellectual and artistic life was encouraged. Living standards rose and Hungary's society was probably the most open within the Eastern block. Kadar remained in power for over 30 years, until 1988.

Kautsky, Karl 1854-1938

German Social Democrat leader. Kautsky, a graduate of the University of Vienna, became a Marxist in Zurich, where he met Eduard Bernstein. He also became a good friend of Engels, whom he met in London. In 1883 he founded the influential Marxist paper *Neue Zeit*, and cocreated (with Bernstein) the Social Democrats' Erfurt Program (1891), espousing an "evolutionary" Marxism, which was criticized by Lenin. A critic of leftwing radicalism and rightwing revisionism, Kautsky, at one time the German authority on Marxism, was isolated because of his moderate views and his opposition to World War l. He participated in the foundation of the Social Democrats' Heidelberg program (1925).

Kenyatta, Jomo 1889–1978

First president of independent Kenya. Involved in local Kenyan politics in the 1920s, Kenyatta lived in England (1931–45) from where he helped form the Pan African Federation. He returned to Kenya

in 1946 to become leader of the recently formed Kenya Africa Union, of which he was elected president (1947). By 1950 the Mau Mau terrorist movement had begun their violence and Kenyatta, despite his denials of involvement, was sentenced to seven years' imprisonment. In 1960 the Kenya African National Union (KANU) was formed, Kenyatta was elected president in his absence and they refused to cooperate with the British until he was released, which finally occurred in 1961. KANU won the May 1963 elections and on Kenya's independence in December 1963 Kenyatta became prime minister. A year later Kenya was declared a republic and a one-party state with Kenyatta as president. He emphasized racial and tribal harmony and managed to create the most stable black African country.

Keynes, John Maynard 1883–1946

British economist. Keynes was a graduate of Cambridge University, to which he returned as a lecturer in economics in 1908. He also advised the British Treasury during both World Wars and represented the Treasury at the Paris Peace Conference of 1919, voicing strong opposition to the draft treaty in *Economic Consequences of the Peace* (1919). The Great Depression inspired his most famous and most influential work, *The General Theory of Unemployment, Interest and Money* (1936). Against established economic theory Keynes argued that full employment was not a natural economic condition but could be achieved if governments provided "cheap money" and undertook programs of public investment. Many governments followed his advice and assumed responsibility for employment levels and instigated national economic planning.

Khomeini, Rubollah 1900–89

Iranian Muslim leader. Khomeini was exiled from Iran in 1964 after denouncing the modernizing and westernizing policies of the Shah, but continued to agitate for the Shah's overthrow from abroad. When the Shah was swept from power by a popular uprising in 1979 Khomeini returned to Iran and launched an Islamic revolution. He appointed a new government and introduced a new constitution which recreated an Islamic state. His new regime suppressed Western and non-Islamic aspects of society, such as pop music and alcohol. Women were forced to wear the veil and Islamic law and punishments were reintroduced.

King, Martin Luther 1929–68

US black campaigner for civil rights. A Baptist minister, King emerged as a champion of black people when he led a boycott campaign against segregation on public buses in Alabama in 1956. The campaign was successful and he formed the South Christian Leadership Conference (1957)

which became his vehicle for civil rights reform. Strongly influenced by Gandhi, King used nonviolent disobedience as his main tactic. He was a powerful orator and won massive support, especially from middle-class black Americans. His main achievement was the Civil Rights Act of 1964, which prohibited racial discrimination in many areas of life.

Koestler, Arthur 1905–83

Hungarian/British writer and philosopher. Koestler studied science in Vienna before becoming a journalist in Berlin and a member of the German Communist party. While serving as a war correspondent for the British *News Chronicle* during the Spanish Civil War he was imprisoned by the fascists. His experience in prison led to his break from the Communist party in 1938. One of the first to realize the similarities between Stalinism and Nazism, Koestler attacked the communist incompetence he had seen in Russia and Spain and Stalin's totalitarian displays of mass arrests and show trials. He wrote several books dealing with morality and political responsibility and his disillusionment with communism, especially *Darkness at Noon* (1940). Escaping from the Continent to Britain, he became a British citizen in 1948.

Kollontai, Alexandra 1872–1952

Russian revolutionary, feminist and diplomat. Kollontai advocated radical changes in traditional Russian society, including "free love", simpler marriage and divorce procedures, general improvements in the status of women, and ending the stigma attached to illegitimacy – policies which influenced the early Soviet Communist regime. The daughter of a general, she rejected her privileged status and became an active propagandist among women workers and, after the Bolshevik seizure of power (1917), a member of the Bolshevik central committee. Her prominent role in the workers' opposition, a group promoting the role of workers within the Communist party, won her popular support but resulted in an attempt by the central committee to expel her from the party, stopped only by Lenin's intervention. She continued her political career as a diplomat.

Lenin, Vladimir Illych 1870–1924

Russian revolutionary and political leader. Living mostly in Western Europe after 1900, he became leader of the Bolshevik wing of the Russian Social Democratic party. Returning to Russia after the 1917 March Revolution, he organized the Bolsheviks' seizure of power in November and founded the new Soviet state. Lenin began by making peace with Germany. He then won the support of non-Russians by announcing the right of self-determination; of industrial workers by making them the new privileged class; and of the

peasantry by giving them land taken from the gentry and the Church. The whole nature of Russian society was altered by the change from capitalism to communism. By 1921 the Communists had won the Civil War but discontent with the regime from the peasantry and workers led to Lenin's repression of opponents.

Levi-Strauss, Claude 1908–

French social anthropologist. Levi-Strauss's approach, drawing on Saussurean linguistics and in particular structuralism, viewed a social structure as a "model" rather than a concrete set of social relationships. This approach was used with regards to kinship, myth and primitive classification in an attempt to uncover underlying patterns, regularities and types. In much of his work the driving force behind much human behavior is seen to be communication, since this structures how we understand the social world. Having graduated in philosophy and law at the University of Paris, Levi-Strauss taught in Brazil, New York and later at the Collège de France. His major works include *The Elementary Structures of Kinship* (1969) and *The Savage Mind* (1956).

Lloyd George, David 1863–1945

British politician. The son of a Welsh teacher, Lloyd George grew up in poverty after his father's death. He qualified as a solicitor and became a Liberal member of Parliament in 1890. When the Liberals returned to power in 1905, Lloyd George became president of the board of trade and then chancellor of the exchequer in 1908. In 1909 his "People's Budget" proposed new taxes on the wealthy but was rejected by the House of Lords. The Liberals won a general election on the budget, which was then passed by the Lords in 1910. (The rights of the Lords were curtailed in 1911.) The budget was followed by the National Insurance Act in 1911, which introduced health and unemployment insurance based on the German model. It marked the early stages of the "welfare state" in Britain. Lloyd George was prime minister from 1916, when he was an effective wartime leader, to 1922.

Lukács, György 1885–1971

Hungarian Marxist philosopher and literary theoretician. Lukács's major work on Marx, *History and Class Consciousness* (1923), argued that the proletariat had a unique insight into history and that bourgeois thought was a "false consciousness". Attacked by leaders of the Soviet Communist party, Lukács soon repudiated this work and thereafter adhered more closely to the accepted Soviet doctrine. Lukács joined the Hungarian Communist party in 1918. After the failure of the Hungarian communist rising in 1919 he lived in Germany and the Soviet Union until he returned to Hungary in 1945.

▲ Rosa Luxemburg

▲ Joseph McCarthy

▲ Malcolm X

Luxemburg, Rosa 1871–1919

Polish-born German socialist leader and theorist. After a brief period as a leader of the Polish Social Democratic party she settled in Germany in 1898 and became an active member of the German Social Democratic party. She believed strongly in radical action and resisted the adoption of the gradualism urged by Bernstein. In 1906 she published the pamphlet *The Mass Strike*, advocating strike action to spearhead a proletarian revolution. Her more scholarly publication *The Accumulation of Capital* (1913) argued for her belief in the moral and economic unsoundness of capitalism. After the outbreak of World War I she and Karl Liebknecht broke from the Social Democratic party and founded the revolutionary Spartacus League. However, she spent most of the war in prison. Released in 1918 the Spartacists joined the German Communist party and the German revolution. She and Liebknecht were murdered on January 1919.

McCarthy, Joseph 1908–57

US anticommunist Republican senator. A circuit judge (1940–42), McCarthy served in the Marines in World War II and was elected to the senate in 1946 and again in 1952. As chairman of the Government Operations Committee of the senate he initiated a national anticommunist "witch-hunt". He rose to prominence in 1950 after his public announcement that 205 communists had infiltrated the US state department. Under President Eisenhower's administration McCarthy became chairman of the powerful Permanent Subcommittee on Investigations (1953–55) and, by using devices such as innuendo, smears, "guilt by association" and the media, especially television, he drove some out of their jobs and created an atmosphere of fear. Overreaching himself by accusing the army of subversion in 1954, he was formally condemned by the senate and the era of McCarthyism ended.

Malcolm X 1925–65

US militant black leader. The son of a Baptist minister, Malcolm X experienced the violence of the Ku Klux Klan at a young age when his family's home in Michigan was burnt down. During imprisonment for burglary and other crimes he was converted to Islam (of the Nation of Islam) and after his release (1954) led a mosque in Harlem (New York). In contrast to Martin Luther King, Malcolm X advocated direct and violent action by blacks against whites. He attracted the support of many black Americans, who were dissatisfied by the slow pace of reform, but was suspended from the Nation of Islam after referring to the assassination of John Kennedy as "the chickens coming home to roost". He founded his own religious organization (1964) but was assassinated the following year.

Mandela, Nelson R. 1918–

South African political leader. Mandela became involved in politics in the Youth League of the African National Congress (ANC). During the 1950s he was an activist of the ANC and organized campaigns of passive resistance to apartheid policies. However, the Sharpeville killings in 1960 and the subsequent banning of the ANC forced Mandela reluctantly to turn to violent methods. He was sentenced to life imprisonment in 1964 and refused offers of release if he would renounce the use of violence. He was eventually released in 1990 and as vice-president of the ANC led its delegation in talks with the South African government. Mandela's aim was the dismantling of apartheid, the establishment of a nonracial democracy in South Africa and the creation of means for making a fairer distribution of South Africa's resources among its people.

Mannheim, Karl 1893–1947

Hungarian sociologist. Mannheim taught at Frankfurt (1926–33) and the London School of Economics (1933–46). His writing includes *Ideology and Utopia* (1936) and *Man and Society in an Age of Reconstruction* (1941). His main contribution to his discipline was the creation of a new arena of debate called the "sociology of knowledge". He argued that all social thought was related to the class position of the social group; that all social thought was ideological. The implication of such a position was that objective knowledge and science were not possible. Mannheim attempted to surmount this problem by postulating that an independent intellectual class could achieve a disinterested knowledge. However, he eventually rejected this original position. His later work looked at contemporary mass society and the need for social planning.

Mao Zedong 1893–1976

Chinese political leader. Son of a peasant farmer, Mao helped to found the Chinese Communist party (CCP) in 1921, which at first cooperated with the Nationalist party of Jiang Jieshi. In 1934, after breaking with Jiang, Mao led his supporters on the "Long March" from southeast to northwest China and established his dominance over the party. The Japanese invasion of 1937 led to a truce between the Nationalists and Communists, but civil war broke out in 1945, in which the Comunists were victorious (1949). Mao developed his own brand of communism based on support from the peasantry and ideas about economic development based on the interdependence of agriculture and industry. He attempted breakneck economic modernization of China in 1958 with the "Great Leap Forward". It was a disastrous failure. In 1966 he attempted another rapid transformation with the Cultural Revolution, in which he unleashed millions of fanatical students, known as Red Guards, against

party elites and the intelligentsia and increased the cult of his personality. The consequent violence and deprivation damaged China's economy and society which had still not recovered when Mao died in 1976.

Mead, Margaret 1901–78

American anthropologist famous for her field studies in Samoa and New Guinea which resulted in such widely selling works as *Coming of Age in Samoa* (1928), *Growing up in New Guinea* (1931), and *Sex and Temperament in Three Primitive Societies* (1935). Mead maintained that cultural conditioning and environment, which were malleable, had a far greater influence than biological factors in determining human behavior in different societies. Her studies used this hypothesis in comparing the relaxed attitudes toward sex and child-rearing in these Oceanic societies with the more structured views in modern Western societies. Her work and methods have been criticized but her valuable contribution was recognized when she was elected president of the American Association for the Advancement of Science (1937) and posthumously awarded the Presidential Medal of Freedom.

Montessori, Maria 1870–1952

Italian educationalist. Montessori was the first woman to qualify as a doctor of medicine in Italy. She developed the educational system that bears her name which gained international recognition and had an enormous influence on nursery and infant education. The Montessori method sought to organize the child's environment and provide it with a variety of materials for development, including the climbing frame. She emphasized the importance of work rather than play but this work was to be undertaken at the child's own pace and in its own direction. Self-education was a key factor in her stategy and teachers were to remain in the background. Montessori also advocated scientific observation and induction. Her publications include *The Montessori Method* (1912).

Mosca, Gaetano 1858–1941

Italian jurist and political theorist. Educated at the University of Palermo, Mosca taught constitutional law there (1885–88) and at Rome (1888–96) and Turin (1896–1908). He was then a member of the chamber of deputies (1908–18) and made a senator for life in 1919. With Pareto he is regarded as having established the theory of political elites, arguing in his works, especially *The Ruling Class* (1896), that all societies have only two classes, the minority who rule and the majority who are ruled, whatever the form of government. The ruling class justifies its domination by legal and arbitrary means, using not only violence but also ideology. Mosca's theory was sometimes used as a justification for fascism but he opposed both Mussolini and Hitler and favored a liberal stance.

Mussolini, Benito 1883–1945

Italian dictator. Initially a journalist and socialist, Mussolini returned from World War I a fervent anti-Bolshevik and formed his own fascist party. Taking power after the fascists marched on Rome (1922), he established himself as dictator. He eliminated opposition by violence and threats, silenced criticism from the Catholic church with the Lateran Treaty (1929) and, in taking personal authority, aimed to mold a new society. He launched an ambitious program of public works and attempted to improve workers' conditions while retaining industrialists' and landowners' support. Mussolini also ensured that fascists took control of all educational, cultural, social, economic and legal institutions. However, his repressive and corrupt domestic policies were largely unsuccessful and in pursuing glory through dynamic foreign policies he led Italy to defeat in World War II and ensured his eventual execution.

Nagy, Imre 1895–1958

Hungarian political leader. A Russian prisoner during World War I, Nagy subsequently joined the Bolshevik party and became a Soviet citizen. Apart from a brief spell in Hungary, he stayed in the Soviet Union until 1944. He served in postwar governments in Hungary and became prime minister in 1953, when he embarked on policies that diverged from communist orthodoxy. He abandoned collectivization of agriculture and released political prisoners, but was forced to resign and was dismissed from the party (1955). During the popular rising of October 1956 he was reinstated as prime minister but could not prevent the Soviet Union from putting down the revolt. Nagy was captured and later executed. He was "rehabilitated" after the collapse of the communist regime in Hungary in 1989.

Nasser, Gamal A. 1918–70

Egyptian nationalist and political leader. An army officer who helped to overthrow King Farouk in 1952, Nasser became prime minister (1954) and president (1956). In 1956 he declared Egypt a socialist Arab one-party state with Islam as the official religion. In the same year he also nationalized the Suez Canal, resulting in an international crisis. He emerged with heightened prestige in the Arab world. Nasser's social and economic policies included modernizing village societies; limiting the land that could be held by one person; the extension of women's rights; industrialization; and the construction of the Aswan High Dam (with economic aid from the Soviet Union). However, Nasser also created a police state which curbed civil liberties and suppressed opposition. Conflict with Israel and involvement in other disputes strained Egypt's economy and limited the extent of Nasser's achievement.

Nehru, Jawaharlal 1889–1964

Indian nationalist leader. Educated in England, Nehru returned to India and joined the Indian National Congress (1919), of which he became general secretary and was elected president (1929). He subsequently developed a close relationship with Gandhi and in 1942 was officially named as Gandhi's political successor. When India gained independence and was partitioned (1947) he became the country's first prime minister and foreign minister. He sought to ensure that India was a secular state. He followed a policy of democratic socialism, emphasizing the need for social concern for the poor and outcast and the importance of democracy. He also worked successfully for equality for women in inheritance and property and for the industrial, scientific and technological modernization of India. On account of his modern outlook he attracted a following among the country's intellectuals and youth.

Nkrumah, Kwame 1909–72

Ghanaian political leader. Educated in America and Britain (1935–47), Nkrumah returned to the Gold Coast (1947) and formed the Convention People's party. Demanding "self-government now", the party won the country's first general election, though Nkrumah himself was in prison at the time. When released he became the country's first prime minister, negotiated his country's independence from Britain (1957), and became Ghana's first president (1960). Until 1960 much of the economy was allowed to remain in the management of foreign companies, but from then onward Nkrumah attempted to move in a socialist direction. The state became involved in the major sectors of the economy, but with disastrous effect. Using force to suppress opposition, Nkrumah was eventually overthrown by a military coup (1966).

Nyerere, Julius K. 1922–

Tanzanian political leader. After graduating from Edinburgh University, Nyerere became an active member of the Tanganyikan African National Union (TANU). The TANU enjoyed mass support and won the 1958 and 1960 national elections. Nyerere became prime minister (1961) and was elected president in 1962 when Tanganyika was declared a Republic. After 1964 he developed the new Republic of Tanzania as a democratic one-party state. Realizing the need for self-reliance and the poor response to requests for aid, Nyerere made the Arusha Declaration (1967), outlining his own version of African socialism based on what he claimed were the cooperative principles of earlier African societies. He stated that the rise of an elitist urban class would be prevented and that economic growth to industrial revolution was inappropriate for Tanzania. He nationalized major enterprises and created *ujamaa* villages: farming collectives with voluntary membership and the

goal of an egalitarian society producing for use, not profit. Villagization was in fact enforced and economic development was unsuccessful but Nyerere provided a stable regime and political independence.

Pankhurst, Emmeline 1858–1928

British campaigner for women's suffrage. Pankhurst formed the Women's Franchise League in 1889 which went on to attain the right for married women to vote in elections to local offices (1894). In 1903 she formed the Women's Social and Political Union (WSPU), gaining much publicity through its campaigns of civil disobedience. Pankhurst was arrested and jailed several times. During imprisonment in 1913 she went on hunger strike, was released and subsequently rearrested 12 times in the next year. With the outbreak of World War I suffrage agitation ended and suffragette prisoners were released. During the war Pankhurst successfully campaigned for the entry of women into industry and in 1918 women over the age of 30 received the vote. She died in 1928, shortly after the passing of the Representation of the People Act which gave equal suffrage for men and women.

Pareto, Vilfredo 1848–1923

Italian economist and sociologist. Pareto graduated in physics and mathematics at the University of Turin in 1868. He pursued a successful engineering career until turning in 1893 to social science, and was a professor at Lausanne University until his withdrawal from society to write. He held that economics must be studied in a social context; and in *Cours de l'économie politique* (1897) introduced his law, stating that inequalities of income in a society vary according to the number of incomes above a certain level. Pareto also propounded the "circulation of elites": that society consists of elites, who tend to become complacent, and non-elites, the more gifted of whom push to achieve, unbalancing the previous elite and replacing them. Elites must justify their existence.

Parsons, Talcott 1902–79

US sociologist. During the quarter century following World War II Parsons dominated sociology. A prolific writer, he sought to construct "general theory" of social action which would explain all human behavior ranging from the individual to the macrosocial. Parsons advocated the "structural functional" approach, which conceptualized society as an integrated organism with parts serving to maintain one another. Hence to understand each organ or each part of society, one must view it in its relation to the whole. The emphasis in Parson's work on integration led to widespread attacks and unpopularity from the late 1960s onward, with his work increasingly seen as being unable to provide a satisfactory explanation of social disorder and social change.

Perón, Juan D. 1895–1974

Argentinian political leader. A colonel who participated in the profascist military coup of 1943, Perón became secretary of labor and welfare and used his position to build up support among workers. He was forced to resign in 1945 and was imprisoned afterward, but his supporters demanded and obtained his release. He was elected president in 1946. In power he subordinated trade unions to the regime, but standards of living rose and welfare facilities were enlarged. He sought to obtain economic independence from the United States and the UK. Beef prices were increased and extra revenue was used to finance nationalization and industrialization. His policies were at first successful, but inflation soared. He gave his name to a brand of policies, which were pursued in various forms in different Latin American states. Perón was reelected in 1951 but deposed in a military revolt (1955) and went in exile. Almost 20 years later – in 1973 – he returned to the presidency but died the following year.

Piaget, Jean 1896–1980

Swiss psychologist. After studying biology, Piaget turned to psychology and specialized in the development of children's perception of the world. He argued that children do not simply absorb information but actively select and interpret what they experience. His central idea was that children initially lack the ability to be logical and that they gradually acquire this skill through informal experiences. Development occurs in stages, Piaget suggested. When a child discovers that it has contradictory explanations of the same event it is thrown into a state of disequilibrium. In trying to regain equilibrium the child will undergo intellectual change which leads on to the next stage of development, and so on. Although Piaget's ideas have been challenged, they have profoundly influenced education, psychology and philosophy.

Pius XII (Eugenio Pacelli) 1876–1958

Italian pope. Ordained priest in 1899, Pacelli rose to become papal nuncio in Germany during the Weimar Republic. He was appointed secretary of state (1929), drafted the Concordat with Hitler (1933), and was elected pope in 1939. Ineffective in his efforts to prevent the outbreak of World War II, during the war Pius used the Vatican's neutrality to carry out much humanitarian work, especially for prisoners of war and refugees. However, his attitude toward the treatment of Jews in Germany has caused controversy. Critics argue that Pius could have used his influence to prevent persecution whereas others contend, and he believed, that his intervention would have made no difference, or possibly made things worse. After the war he was concerned with the future of Catholicism in communist countries.

Reagan, Ronald 1911–

US president. A Hollywood actor from 1937 onward, making over 50 films in the following 25 years, Reagan was a Democrat supporter after World War II but switched allegiance to the Republican party in 1962. He was elected governor of California in 1966 and again in 1970. He increased taxes and cut state government spending. He won the Republican presidential nomination at his third attempt in 1980 and defeated president Carter in the elections. In 1984 Reagan was reelected for a second term by a large majority. As president, Reagan proposed to strengthen the national economy by cutting taxes and reducing Federal spending in every area apart from the military. He also decreased the social responsibilities of the Federal government and increased those of states and cities. Unemployment rose during his term in office and he failed to deal effectively with the country's social problems.

Reich, Wilhelm 1897–1957

Austrian psychoanalyst. Reich joined the Viennese Psychoanalytic Society (1924) and trained under Freud. In *The Function of the Orgasm* (1927) he advocated the need to achieve orgasm to obtain personal fulfillment and asserted that failure to do so would lead to neurosis. He subsequently combined Marxist politics with sexual freedom, founding the German Association for Proletarian Sexual Politics to provide advice on sex and birth control to the working class. Fleeing from Germany (1933), Reich lived in Scandinavia (1933–39) and then settled in America (1939). In his work *Character Analysis* (1933) he focused on character defenses which individuals used to resist the discovery of their underlying neurosis. In America he investigated "orgone energy", units of cosmic energy he believed to be found in the nervous system. The development and sale of "orgone boxes" to treat illness led to his arrest and a two-year sentence for contempt of court. Reich's theories were very influential during the 1960s.

Reith, John 1889–1971

British broadcaster. After an engineering apprenticeship in Glasgow, Reith served in World War I. In 1922 he was appointed general manager of the newly formed and privately funded British Broadcasting Company. He advocated the creation of a public broadcasting service and in 1927 the company was established as the British Broadcasting Corporation (BBC) with Reith as director-general. Reith aimed to give purpose and status to broadcasting and included cultural, educational and religious programs alongside information and entertainment. He demanded high standards of behavior from his staff. He left the BBC in 1938 to become chairman of Imperial Airways and later held numerous public appointments.

Rhodes, Cecil 1853–1902

British imperialist. Suffering from tuberculosis, in 1869 Rhodes went from England to South Africa where he became involved in diamond mining. In the 1870s he studied at Oriel College, Oxford, and graduated in 1881. During these years he formed ambitious plans for the extension of the British Empire, to create an Anglo-Saxon federation that would make war impossible. Returning to Africa he expanded his interests in diamond mining and became a powerful force in new gold fields. At the same time he became deeply involved in politics and from a base in South Africa expanded British territory to the north (including the modern Zambia and Zimbabwe). He left his immense wealth to fund Rhodes Scholarships, which enabled gifted subjects of Commonwealth and other countries to study at Oxford.

Roosevelt, Franklin D. 1882–1945

US political leader. Encouraged by family and friends to enter politics, Roosevelt was elected to the New York senate as a Democrat when 28 (1910) and was elected president of the United States in 1932 on a pledge to confront the problems caused by the Great Depression. His program, known as the "New Deal", extended Federal authority and expenditure. There was intervention in agriculture and industry; programs of public works; and social and labor reforms. Arguably the program's effect was as much psychological as practical, restoring America's national self-confidence. Roosevelt led his country into World War II (1941–45) and influenced the postwar settlement, though he died on the eve of victory in Europe. Roosevelt skillfully maintained popular support for his administration during a period of great social upheaval and his attitude to domestic social policies in the 1930s influenced American government policy for the next four decades.

Rowntree, Benjamin Seebohm 1871–1954

British industrialist and social researcher. Rowntree was a director (1897–1923) and then chairman (1923–41) of his Quaker family's confectionery firm in the British city of York, but Beatrice Webb described him as "more a philanthropist than a capitalist". He saw industry as a service and felt deeply responsible for the poor. As a businessman he introduced a works doctor (1904), a pension scheme (1906), a 5-day week (1919) and a profit-sharing scheme (1923). In 1921 he published *The Human Factor in Business*, which advocated humane management. His wider social concern was expressed in three influential surveys of poverty in York (1901, 1941, 1951). Concerned to use rigorous definitions, Rowntree distinguished between primary poverty (an absolute lack of means to sustain health) and secondary poverty (resulting from lack of expenditure on basic items).

▲ Albert Schweitzer

▲ Benjamin Spock

▲ Alexander Stambolysky

Russell, Bertrand 1872–1970

British philosopher. Russell was born into a famous British political and aristocratic family. As both an empiricist and positivist, a unifying theme throughout his academic work was that the scientific perspective of the world is on the whole the true one. Russell sought to simplify the basic claims of human knowledge; to link logic to mathematics; and to assert that conclusions about the world can be drawn from language. He was also known publicly as a pacifist, a personal standpoint which led to the dismissal from his lectureship at Cambridge and his imprisonment during World War I. His libertarian stance on sexual morality, education and war also led to his dismissal from a teaching post in the United States. Russell's later years saw him marrying his fourth (and final) wife and becoming involved in the formation of the Campaign for Nuclear Disarmament.

Sadat, Muhammad Anwar el- 1918–81

Egyptian political leader. A long-time supporter of Nasser, Sadat became president of Egypt on Nasser's death (1970). Its economy was in crisis, struggling under debts incurred by conflict with Israel. When Egypt's main ally, the Soviet Union, failed to deliver promised arms and assistance, Sadat expelled Soviet military personnel, repudiated debts, and turned to the United States. Sadat liberalized the economy, encouraged foreign investment and private enterprise. The economy expanded, but it failed to contain urban poverty and Sadat's policies provoked opposition. He was assassinated by Muslim extremists.

Sakharov, Andrei 1921–89

Soviet nuclear physicist and dissident. Sakharov's early years were highly successful. For his work on the Soviet hydrogen bomb he became a full member of the Soviet Academy of Sciences when only 32. However, in 1961 he openly objected to Soviet atmospheric nuclear tests and in 1968 called for a reduction in the nuclear arms held by the superpowers and for the integration of capitalist and communist social systems. The Soviet authorities responded fiercely. Sakharov was imprisoned and then exiled to Gorky (1980). With the accession of Gorbachev and the introduction of greater democracy in the Soviet Union, Sakharov was released (1987) and played a prominent part in Soviet politics. His courage won him respect worldwide and the Nobel Peace Prize in 1975.

Sanger, Margaret 1883–1966

US pioneer of birth control. As a nurse on the Lower East Side of New York City Sanger encountered the poverty, illness and death associated with uncontrolled fertility which, with her belief in a woman's right to control her own body, initiated a lifelong campaign to supply women with birth-control information and methods. Publishing the magazine *The Woman Rebel* (1914) and writing and distributing the pamphlet *Family Limitation* led to an unsuccessful prosecution for obscenity. In 1916 Sanger opened the first US birth-control clinic in Brooklyn, for which she served 30 days in the workhouse. She also founded the American Birth Control League (1921), organized the first World Population Conference (1927), was the first president of the International Planned Parenthood Federation (1953), and worked for birth control in many other countries, especially India and Japan.

Sartre, Jean-Paul 1905–80

French philosopher, novelist, dramatist and critic. Born in Paris, Sartre taught philosophy at Le Havre, Paris and Berlin. As the best known and most influential French intellectual of the postwar years, he was the exponent of Existentialism. At the heart of his world view was the concept of choice and the individual. He believed that human beings bring nothing into the world at birth and life is merely the sum of our past commitments. To put our faith in something outside our own will is to delude ourselves. We are imprisoned only by our absolute freedom and sentenced to live by our own moral judgment.

Schweitzer, Albert 1875–1965

German theologian, physician, philosopher and musician. Schweitzer studied theology and philosophy at Strasbourg, Paris, and Berlin. The publication of *The Quest of the Historical Jesus* (1906) established him as a major theologian. Concurrently he was an organist in Strasbourg and published a study of J.S. Bach (1905). Abandoning these studies (1905), Schweitzer qualified as a doctor of medicine (1913) and set up a hospital in French Equatorial Africa. Initially funded from his own income, the venture was later supplemented by periodic fund-raising visits to Europe, where he was interned by the French as a German during World War I. Schweitzer subsequently concentrated on world problems and in *Philosophy of Civilization* (1923) he put forward his ethical principal of "reverence for life" which he believed to be intrinsic to the survival of civilization.

Sorel, Georges 1847–1922

French social philosopher. In 1893, after an engineering career, Sorel wrote a critique of Marxism. He applied to politics many of Nietzsche's ideas, such as those of the will to power as the basic drive, science as a creative process, and excessive thinking (suppressing other functions) as decadent. He found Marxism spurious but invigorating. He agreed with Pareto that democracy does not banish elites. He believed that the best way of life must be fought for, and that violence is sometimes a noble expression of individuality. For a time a syndicalist, in 1909 Sorel lost faith in the initiative ability of the workers; he became a nationalist. His advocacy of the "social myth" as a means of activating the masses was appreciated by Mussolini, who fitted to his own purposes many of Sorel's theories.

Spock, Benjamin 1903–

US pediatrician and author. Spock graduated in medicine in 1929 from Columbia University and then trained for six years at the New York Psychoanalytic Institute. He practiced pediatrics in New York City and taught psychiatry and pediatrics at various universities including Minnesota and Western Reserve, Cleveland. Resigning in 1967 to become more active in the antiwar movement, he was tried for counselling conscription evaders but was subsequently acquitted. Spock's many publications include *The Commonsense Book of Baby and Child Care* (1946) and *A Baby's First Year* (1955, with J. Reinhart and W. Miller). His best-selling books, written in a relaxed, accessible style, advocated a flexible and understanding approach to child care and had an enormous impact on millions of parents.

Stalin, Joseph V. 1879–1953

Soviet political leader. After Lenin's death in 1924, Stalin eliminated his political rivals and won complete control of Soviet government by 1928. His chief aims were to maximize his personal power and to achieve rapid economic growth. These he accomplished by enforced industrialization and collectivization and by the "Purges" of the 1930s. These policies involved the execution of millions of real and imagined opponents and millions more being sacrificed as collectivization resulted in famine. By the time Stalin died (1953), the Soviet Union was a modern industrial, highly bureaucratized power with an educated population served by increased standards of social and medical services. However, he had achieved this by a system of slaughter and fear.

Stambolysky, Alexander 1879–1923

Bulgarian prime minister and agrarian reformer. After studying agriculture in Germany Stambolysky returned to Bulgaria, became editor of the *Agrarian Banner* and was elected to the National Assembly as leader of the Agrarian National Union (1908). Stambolysky's opposition to King Ferdinand's decision to enter World War I on the side of Germany resulted in imprisonment (1915) but, released (1918), he led an insurrection which forced Ferdinand's abdication. He became prime minister (1919) and, despite signing the unpopular Treaty of Neuilly, gained a majority in the 1920 elections. With virtual dictatorial powers, Stambolysky implemented policies favoring the peasantry – 80 percent of the population. The most important was redistribution of land.

▲ Marie Stopes

▲ Hendrik Frensch Verwoerd

▲ Lech Walesa

Stopes, Marie 1880-1958

Pioneer of birth-control clinics. After graduating in three subjects in 1902, Stopes taught and wrote botanical papers, becoming in 1904 Britain's youngest Doctor of Science. The distressing annulment of her first marriage in 1916 caused her to turn her attention to the desirability of birth control as liberating for married women and a factor in a successful and pleasurable marriage. She began to write on the subjects of sex and contraception, producing in 1918 *Married Life*, which was unprecedentedly direct, and *Wise Parenthood*. In 1921 she and her second husband Humphrey Verdon-Roe founded a birth-control clinic in North London. She wrote many more books, including *Contraception* (1923), the most comprehensive work on the subject. Stopes' frankness, practicality and commitment, romantically tinged by her view of sexual pleasure as the right of all women, were pivotal in the dramatic change of attitude toward women and sexuality which occurred in the later 20th century.

Sukarno, Achmed 1901–70

Indonesian political leader. A founder of the Indonesian nationalist movement, Sukarno became its leader in 1932 and cooperated with the Japanese during their occupation of the Dutch East Indies in World War II. After the war he and his followers succeeded in resisting the permanent reestablishment of Dutch rule. Indonesia became independent in 1949 under Sukarno. He pursued a modernizing program of social reform with investment in education and health, but was unable to construct a stable form of administration and government. When economic problems developed Sukarno was deposed (1966).

Tagore, Rabindranath 1861–1941

Indian poet, philosopher and educationalist. Tagore believed in "constructive nationalism", fearing the irrationality of mass action and arguing that independence must be preceded by renewal from within. He disagreed with Gandhi on civil disobedience and favored international cooperation. The two, however, remained close friends and Tagore was a strong influence on Gandhi. Tagore also supported rural regeneration, economic reconstruction, social reform and education, establishing a university which attempted to combine the best of Indian and Western educational and philosophical systems.

Tata, Jamsetji Nasarwanji 1839–1904

Indian businessman and philanthropist. Tata worked from 1858 with his father's export company, establishing branches worldwide, and in 1872 began to found cotton mills. Noted for efficient production, high-quality fiber and good treatment of employees, Tata introduced the production of raw silk to India and planned

hydroelectric plants. In 1901 he founded the first large-scale Indian ironworks, later (under his son's direction) the Tata Iron & Steel Co., one of the largest steelworks in the world. Land given by him for a research establishment later housed the Indian Institute of Science.

Taylor, F.W. 1856–1915

US theorist of management. Taylor trained as a pattern maker and machinist (1875–78), joined the Midvale Steel Company (1878), where he became chief engineer (1884), and obtained a degree in mechanical engineering through night school (1883). He successfully introduced a "time and motion" study at the Midvale plant in 1881 which provided the basis for his future theories of management science. Taylor believed efficiency of production could be increased by observation of workers and disposing of wasted time and motion in their jobs. Such rationalization of production methods, or "Taylorization", had a tremendous impact upon modern industry throughout the world. Taylor worked at a number of other firms including the Bethlehem Steel Corporation (1889–1901) where he developed high-speed steel and other innovations concerning metal production. Despite his skill as an engineer, he resigned in 1901 to devote more time to the spread of his ideas on scientific management.

Thatcher, Margaret Hilda 1925–

British political leader. The first woman to be prime minister of Britain (1979–90) Thatcher stood on the right of the Conservative party. She advocated a decrease of state responsibility toward the individual. In order to facilitate this, she froze welfare benefits and encouraged private enterprise. These policies directly opposed those of the majority of EC members and led to an abrasive relationship with members of the European Community. Her monetarist economic policies initially resulted in high unemployment which caused great unpopularity. As the world recession came to an end and Britain won the Falklands War (1982), Thatcher's popularity was regained. However, the introduction of the Community Charge to pay for local services in England and Wales in 1990 provoked strong opposition. This and her controversial lone stand against European monetary union eventually led to the loss of party confidence. She resigned in 1990.

Thompson, E.P. 1924–

British historian. A leading figure in postwar intellectual debate and involved in the rise of the "New Left" during the late 1950s, Thompson was a major influence in both historical and political thinking. He gained widespread prominence with his work *The Making of the English Working Class* (1963) which located the emergence of class during the industrial revolution and viewed it not as a

social structure but as a historical phenomenon. By drawing upon Marx, Thompson argued that class occurred when a social group, through their shared experiences, see their interests as in opposition to others. Rejecting traditional Marxist approaches, which viewed social behaviour as determined by powerful structural forces, Thompson emphasized the importance of human agency within history. He became an influential leader of the peace movement in the 1980s.

Tilak, Bal Gangadhar 1856–1920

Indian nationalist leader. Tilak, originally a math teacher, published his opposition to British rule, in order to politicize his fellow countrymen, in two weekly papers he produced. In 1893 and 1895 he organized big Hindu religious festivals, to arouse and deepen nationalist sentiments. Jailed by the British in 1897 for sedition, he won the name Lokamanya (beloved leader of the people). In 1905, opposing Curzon's partition of Bengal, he started a boycott of British goods which spread nationwide. He then initiated a program of passive resistance to British rule. Imprisoned again in 1907, he wrote a massive exposition of the Bhagavad Gita, the Hindu holy book. On his release in 1914, he launched the Home Rule League, and in 1916, back in Congress, signed the Lucknow Pact agreeing Hindu–Muslim cooperation.

Tito (Josip Broz) 1892–1980

Yugoslavian political leader. Leader of the Yugoslavian resistance movement during World War II, Tito established a communist regime at the end of the war and became prime minister (1945) and then president (1953–80). His determination to retain Yugoslavia's independence resulted in a split with the Soviet Union (1948). Despite immense pressure from the Soviet Union, Tito became the first communist leader to defy Stalin and succeeded in creating a national communism called "Titoism", which was not based on the Soviet model. He attempted to solve the country's nationalities problem by enacting a federal constitution whereby the five major Yugoslav nationalities each constituted a sovereign republic.

Vargas, Getúlio Domeles 1883–1954

Brazilian political leader. Vargas became president in a revolution in 1930 and was then deposed by military coup in 1945. He made notable changes in the Brazilian economy and society. He sponsored rapid industrialization to reduce Brazil's dependence on agricultural exports. His social policies included the establishment of labor organizations and a minimum wage, redistribution of land, and educational reform. His rule was authoritarian but he was seen as a "man of the people". In 1950 he again won office as president but eventually lost the support of the armed forces. Rather than resign he committed suicide.

Sidney and Beatrice Webb

Emiliano Zapata

Veblen, Thorstein 1857–1929

American economist and social critic. Hailing from an impoverished family of Norwegian immigrants, he took his PhD at Yale University in 1884. After several years of penury, he was finally given a teaching post at the University of Chicago (1892), where he produced his critique of capitalism, *The Theory of the Leisure Class* (1899). This study came to have great significance for later theorists such as Galbraith, particularly in its identification and critique of "conspicuous consumption". It attacked the ruling business class in the United States who made money and displayed their wealth in what he termed "conspicuous consumption".

Verwoerd, Hendrik Frensch 1901–66

South African political leader. Born in Holland to parents who emigrated to South Africa when he was two, Verwoerd became a professor at Stellenbosch University (1927–37). He then entered the political arena as editor of the nationalist newspaper *Die Transvaler* (1938–48), in which he publicized his racist and profascist views. After the National party's victory in the 1948 general election he served as minister of native affairs (1950–58) and prime minister (1959–66). Through these posts he became the chief architect of apartheid and the repressor of its opponents. he sponsored the numerous acts of parliament that created the legal separation of races. After the Sharpeville shootings (1960) he banned the African National Congress and Pan African Congress and introduced imprisonment without trial.

Walesa, Lech 1943–

Polish union and political leader. An electrician at the Gdansk shipyards, Walesa became leader of the workers there in 1980 and represented them in negotiations with the government which resulted in permission for workers to establish independent unions. The national federation of Solidarity was formed with Walesa as chairman. Walesa led Solidarity through the 1980s, even when it was banned under martial law. In 1988, with Poland's economy collapsing, Walesa was invited by the government to join negotiations. They led to recognition of Solidarity, free elections, and a Solidarity victory. As the union's senior figure, Walesa backed a radical and determined attempt to change Poland's economy from being centrally directed to one based more on free enterprise. Walesa was elected president of Poland in 1990.

Webb, Beatrice 1858–1943 and Sidney 1859–1947

British social reformers. The daughter of an industrial magnate, Beatrice worked for her cousin Charles Booth in his research for *The Life and Labour of the People of London*. Sidney was the son of an accountant who became a civil servant and one of the leading members of the socialist Fabian

Society. They married in 1892 and together researched and wrote numerous historical and social works, including *The History of Trade Unionism* (1894). They played a leading role in the foundation of the London School of Economics (1895), founded the socialist weekly magazine *New Statesman* (1913) and campaigned for the reform of the poor law. Sidney also became a member of parliament, president of the board of trade (1924) and colonial secretary (1929). After they retired from public life they visited the Soviet Union and wrote an account of Soviet society.

Weber, Max 1864–1920

German sociologist and political economist. One of the founders of modern sociology, Weber held professional positions at the Universities of Freiburg, Heidelberg and Munich. His work addressed both sociology's methodology and many issues within the discipline. Weber rejected the view that sociological study should be carried out in a way comparable to the natural sciences. Instead he emphasized the need to understand the meaning behind people's actions from which sociology could work toward formal models of action. Weber saw the process of "rationalization" as the dominant trend in society, with every area of human behavior being increasingly subject to both calculation and administration. In *The Protestant Ethic and the Spirit of Capitalism* (1920) he traced the development of modern capitalism back to the influence of Calvinist Christianity in Western Europe. This text along with much of Weber's other work is sometimes seen as a critical response to Marx's supposed emphasis on economic determination.

Weizmann, Chaim 1874–1952

Zionist and statesman. One of 15 children born to Jewish parents in Russian Poland, Weizmann showed an early flair for science. He was a successful student and then obtained a teaching post at the University of Manchester in England (1904). During these early years he became a prominent figure in the Zionist movement, which sought to establish a homeland for Jews. When World War I broke out, his scientific expertise and contributions to the war effort gave him access to senior politicians and he was able to secure the issuing of the Balfour Declaration (1917) in which Britain offered support for the establishment of a Jewish homeland in Palestine. In the interwar period he was president of the World Zionist Organization and after the creation of Israel in 1948 became president of the provisional government and then president of the country.

Wells, H. G. 1861–1946

British novelist, journalist, historian and prophet. Wells was a major figure in the spread of the new ideas at the start of the 20th century. After

studying biology and working as a journalist, he published scientific fantasies, such as *The War of the Worlds* (1898). Initially believing that science could create a perfect world, Wells subsequently realized it could also work for evil and felt that human civilization was likely to destroy itself. He outlined his socialist, internationalist and Utopian solutions to the ills of modern society in books such as *The Shape of Things to Come* (1933). Predicting modern technological achievements, such as the atomic bomb, he advised the public on the dangers of such progress. Wells also dealt with social issues. A strong advocate of world unity, he criticized the League of Nations and was involved in the Shankey declaration of the Rights of Man. World War II, however, destroyed his confidence in mankind.

Zapata, Emiliano 1879–1919

Mexican revolutionary. Zapata opposed the practice of landowners expanding their holdings at the expense of village lands in his native Morelos and became leader of a growing peasant movement. Under President Francisco Madero (elected in 1911), Zapata became leader in the state of Morelos. However, Madero failed to restore land under the old Indian communal system of the *ejidos* and Zapata proclaimed the "Plan of Ayala", which called for radical land reforms and condemned Madero as inadequate to the task. Adopting the slogan "Land and Liberty", he continued his campaign against subsequent governments and dictatorships while maintaining control in Morelos, where he carried out his own reforms. He drove out the rich landowners, divided the lands of their estates among the peasants, and established schools, social services, and agricultural credit organizations. The reforms were reproduced in the 1917 constitution and implemented under subsequent governments.

Zetkin (Eissner), Clara 1857–1933

German feminist and communist leader. Zetkin became a prominent and influential socialist theoretician on women's issues. She maintained that women's oppression originated from economic dependence on men and lack of employment. Recognizing the different roles of men and women and their equal importance, she also believed that women should be able to carry out meaningful work as well as function as wives and mothers. However, she did not advocate women's rights for their own sake but for the good of the working class as a whole. Her achievements included helping to found the Second Socialist International (1889); editing the socialist women's paper *Equality* (1892–1917); cofounding the International Socialist Women's Congress (1907) and the radical Spartacus League (1916); and serving the Reichstag (1920–33) as a member of the German Communist party.

GLOSSARY

African Socialism
Political vision of the 1960s and 1970s of supposedly traditional African life, based on the **extended family**, and seen as a naturally socialist system.

Alienation
A term originally used by Marx to refer to the projection of human attributes on to gods, and later to describe the loss of control by workers under **capitalism** of the work process and its products. Also the individual's sense of powerlessness in modern society.

Antisemitism
Enculturated prejudice against Jews, commonly legitimated by the assertion that they threaten the fabric of non-Jewish society, and used to justify discrimination and persecution.

Apartheid
(Dutch "apartness"). A system, established in 1948 in South Africa, of oppressive legalized discrimination against the black majority.

Apparatchik
A member of a Communist party's power structure, holding consequent privileges.

ASSR
(Autonomous Soviet Socialist Republic). A self-governing ethnically distinct unit within the Union Republics of the Soviet Union.

Blue-Collar Workers
Production workers in manufacturing industry, often required to wear protective clothing.

Bourgeoisie
The owners of wealth and productive assets in capitalist societies, or more broadly the sector of society benefiting from the development of **capitalism**.

Bureaucracy
A type of organization characterized by a hierarchy of authority and responsibility and by written rules which govern the conduct of salaried officials.

Cadre
A member of a core group of activists in a political organization such as a group.

Capitalism
A political and economic system based on private ownership of wealth and its investment in production for profit, involving the employment of waged workers.

Caste
A rigid system of status division, part of Hindu society. Caste is acquired by birth, defined by rules about marriage, and associated with notions of religious purity.

Christian Democracy
Political movement peculiar to continental Europe. Its 20th century form arose from church-linked World War II resistance movements, and is essentially a liberal **conservatism**.

Civil Rights
The rights properly accorded by law to a citizen to be treated fairly by the state regardless of status, race or creed.

Civil Society
Organized social life, outside the state, but defined in relation to it.

Class
A large-scale grouping of people who share characteristics relating to their ownership (or not) of productive assets and to their roles in production, which influence their life-styles.

Codetermination
In German, *Mitbestimmung*: the process, defined after World War II, of workers' participation in management strategy.

Collectivism
A system of social organization, or a business, with elements of collective responsibility.

Collectivization
The action of bringing property into collective ownership, especially as in the Soviet agricultural system under Stalin in the 1920s and 1930s.

Colonialism
The practice, common among Western European countries in the late 19th century, of annexing and imposing an economic, political and to varying degrees, social system on nonindustrialized, less politically unified nations in order to exploit their resources, human and otherwise.

Commercialization
The development of production for the market.

Commune
A group of people living together linked not by family ties but by shared ideology, associated especially with the "alternative" culture of the 1960s and 1970s in the West. Also the largest unit in the system of collectivized production established in China under Mao Zedong.

Communism
A set of political ideas associated with Marx, developed by Lenin and institutionalized in the Soviet Union, characterized by a high degree of **collectivism**.

Conjugal Family
A family unit based on a conjugal couple, usually with their offspring.

Conservatism
Politically, the tendency to value and maintain tradition and to promote organic and gradual rather than revolutionary change.

Cooperatives
Commercial enterprises jointly owned by workers, who benefit directly from the results of their labor.

Corporation
Any profit-making large organization; generally, a joint-stock company, which can be private, or public, the latter signifying a minimum capital value, and permission to issue shares.

Corporatism
A form of social organization in which key decisions are made by corporate groups (such as trade unions) or by these and the state jointly.

Counterculture
Any subculture based on values other than and often counter to those of the majority. Denotes particularly the set of ideas about sociopolitical organization espoused by radicals in the 1960s, featuring sexual and other permissiveness, and the devaluation of the family unit.

Craft Unions
Trade unions with membership limited to workers in one craft; cf. **industrial unionism**.

Cultural Revolution
The process activated by Mao Zedong in China in 1967–68, characterized by the fostering of a personality cult around himself, with indoctrination and coercion enforced by the "Red Guards"; its purported goal was to transform mass consciousness so that a socialist society could be firmly rooted.

Deindustrialization
A reduction in the proportion of national income generated by manufacturing industry, common in late 20th-century Western society; or, an absolute decline in industrial activity.

Demographic Transition
Alteration in population size and structure in the process of industrialization, with high birth and death rates giving way in stages to low birth and death rates.

Deskilling
Management strategy of reducing the skill level required by workers in production, often with the assistance of new technology, thereby reducing dependence on skilled workers.

Development
A complex term demoting social change which improves the living standards of the majority of people in a society. Thus it involves not economic growth alone, measured in terms of gross national product or per capita income, but also improved standards of health and education.

Division of Labor
The specialization of work tasks within a production system, or more generally, within society.

Drive System
The system of industrial management developed in the USA in the later 19th century involving mechanization, decreased reliance on skilled labor and closer supervision by foremen.

Embourgeoisement
The assimilation, via improved economic status and adjustment of value systems, of sections of the working class into the bourgeoisie.

Establishment
The group of those who hold positions of power and influence, usually conferred by tradition, in a society; it tends to promote the conservation of tradition and of its own power.

Ethnic Neighborhood
A residential area settled by people of a particular ethnic group, with their own culture.

Extended Family
Family group including three or more generations, or more than one **conjugal family** laterally related.

Fabianism
Ideology of the British Fabian Society (est. 1884), aiming to achieve a socialist order through gradual, democratic and nonviolent change.

Fascism
A political ideology often arising in capitalist crisis and usually embracing extreme nationalism and the rejection of liberalism, seeking national regeneration through a mass movement via a single-party state with strong leadership.

Feminism
A movement seeking equal rights and status, economically and socially, for women with men.

Feudalism
A hierarchical social order exemplified in medieval Western Europe, with a fixed hereditary ruling class, a stratum of lords and knights (vassals) owing allegiance to the rulers, and peasants and artisans totally dependent the upper orders.

Fordism
The revolution in management methodology introduced by Henry Ford, embracing mechanization of the production process, including the moving assembly line, a high minimum wage, under a paternalistic managerial eye, and market control through advertising.

Fundamentalism
Especially in religious practice, a movement to return to tenets perceived as essential, often in reaction against modern values and with aggressive and punitive elements.

Glasnost
(Russian: "having a voice, openness"). The innovative policy of political openness, internally and internationally, introduced in the Soviet Union by Mikhail Gorbachev in 1985.

Green Movement
Late 20th-century movement founded on concern about ecological issues and real value (quality of life) in the light of environmental degradation resulting from increasingly mechanized and short-term profit-seeking human activity.

Green Revolution
Dramatic rise in Third World agricultural production such as that in parts of India in the 1960s and 1970s, based on adoption of modern agricultural technology.

Hegemony
The exercise of control over a social group or society.

Import Substitution
Replacement of imports, often enforced by import tariffs, with domestic products, to stimulate industrial development.

Industrial Unionism
Unionism based on the representation of all the various workers in an industry in a single union.

Industrialization
The change from manual to mechanized production in a society, and consequent economic and social change.

Informal Economy/Sector
Economic activity which is not regulated by employment legislation, including a very diverse range of mainly small-scale manufacturing, trading and services activities, and self-employment. The informal economy accounts for 50 percent or more of employment in most **Third World** cities.

Intelligentsia
An intellectual elite, usually educated professionals.

Kulak
(Russian: "fist"). In Russia and the Soviet Union before **collectivization**, a powerful peasant who employed workers and carried on other economic activities as well as agriculture; kulaks were the object of Stalinist purges.

Landlordism
An economic system in which farmers rent their land from large-scale landowners.

Liberalism
A political system and attitude supporting the freedom of the individual above all, marked by tolerance and a wish to make society fairer, without losing the right of self-determination.

Maoism
The version of **Marxism** developed by Mao Zedong in China and influential in the **Third World**, focused on the needs and social importance of the peasantry, diminishing the power of a bureaucratic or intellectual elite, and promoting swift and sustained revolution.

Market Economy
An economy governed by the movement of supply and demand, characteristic of a capitalist system.

Marxism
The body of philosophical, economic and political ideas worked out by Karl Marx, which are guided by a concern with the conditions for human self-realization.

Middle Class
Social stratum between manual workers and those with wealth or status, consisting mostly of high clerical, administrative or professional workers.

Modernization
The process of social change, linked with **industrialization**, involving **rationalization**, secularization, and the development of the social division of labor.

Monopoly Capitalism
Form of **capitalism** which incorporates the domination of the economy by monopolies.

Nationalism
The belief that the needs, rights, privileges and separate identity of one's nation take priority over individual or wider interests.

Nationalization
The bringing under government control of any industry that was formerly privately owned.

Nazism
The ideology of the National Socialist German Workers' party, led from 1921 by Adolf Hitler, fascist in basis and characterized by a fervent belief in German (and "Aryan") racial superiority, aggressive expansionism and a virulent antisemitism.

Neoliberalism
Political belief in removing State control of the economy by returning ownership of businesses and public facilities to the private sector.

New International Division of Labor
The division of manufacturing tasks on an international scale, with assembly tasks allocated to low-paid **Third World** workers.

Nuclear Family
A basic family unit, consisting of one or two parents, with offspring.

Oligarchy
System of government where power is in the hands of a self-serving few.

Patriarchy
Sociopolitical system in which men dominate women.

Peasant
One who owns or rents land and produces on it using his/her own and family labor.

Perestroika
(Russian: "restructuring"). Mikhail Gorbachev's policy of reorganizing Soviet society along less repressive lines.

Petty Bourgeoisie
Influential social class comprising owners of small businesses.

Plutocracy
Government by the wealthy.

Police State
A political system where a police force and other coercive means are used to subjugate the population.

Populationist
A supporter of politically implemented measures to encourage population growth.

Proletariat
A term central to **Marxism**, signifying the landless **working class** in a capitalist society.

Rationalization
Weber's concept of the subjugation of all aspects of life to calculation and bureaucratization, seen as inevitable in a capitalist society.

Real Wages
Wage rates adjusted according to the retail price index, to denote their purchasing power.

Rural Proletariat
Landless agricultural workers.

Scientific Management
Early 20th-century revolution in management practice initiated by F. W. Taylor, involving increased **division of labor** (and consequent **deskilling**), full managerial responsibility for the fragmented production process, and time-and-motion study-based cost accounting.

Secularization
The process in which social structure and regulation becomes divorced from religion.

Serfdom
The state of being a serf, that is, a laborer dependent on and subject to the landowning class in feudal society, and without property.

Services
Intangible results of economic activity rather than goods.

Shanty Town
A slum settlement, usually of ad hoc structures, around urban areas especially in postwar **Third World** countries.

Social Democracy
Socialist ideology espousing democracy and advocating change through reform rather than revolution.

Social Estate
Rigid social stratum as in czarist Russia and feudal Western Europe, acquired by heredity and with legally defined rights and duties.

Social Market
Postwar Western European idea of "**capitalism** with a social conscience".

Social Order
The tendency to cohesion in a society manifest generally in social hierarchies and broad agreement on core values.

Socialism
Political doctrine based on the equality of individuals, with the state as administrator and protector of equal rights, and the removal of systems through which individuals can dominate others. In Marxist theory it signifies the stage of transition between **capitalism** and **Communism**.

Socialization
The process whereby the individual learns to conform to social norms.

Soviet
Any of the administrative councils forming the basic unit of government in the Soviet Union, existing at all levels, from village to national (the Supreme Soviet).

SSR (Soviet Socialist Republic)
Nominally independent, **soviet**-ruled, political unit within the Soviet Union, often with a strong ethnic identity.

Stalinist
Of a Communist regime, characterized by totalitarian rule with the use of terror and the cultivation of a personality cult around the ruler.

Suffrage
The right of an individual to vote in elections.

Technocracy
Government by those with greatest expertise in modern technology.

Third World
A term coined after World War II to refer to the world outside the industrialized "first" world of the West and the "second" world of the **Communist** bloc. Also known as "under-developed", "less developed" or "developing" countries, thay are those whose development has been affected directly or indirectly by **colonialism**.

Township
Urban settlement of poor, mostly indigenous people in postcolonial Africa.

Ujamaa
(Swahili: "familyhood"). This refers to the policy of **African socialism** as practiced in Tanzania, and especially to the formation of village settlements intended to be run on a communal basis.

Upper Class
The social stratum distinguished by wealth and power, usually inherited, and exclusivity.

Urbanization
Progressive increase in the proportion of a country's population living in cities.

Village Commune
The social unit which in pre-Revolutionary Russia was responsible to landlords for peasant rent payments, administered by a council of elders (*mir*), and embodying collectivist principles.

White-Collar Workers
Nonmanual workers, especially at the lower levels of responsibility.

Working Class
The social stratum consisting of those who work, usually manually, for wages.

FURTHER READING

* indicates an important source for this book;
** a major source.

General Overview

Alavi, H and Harriss, J *Sociology of "Developing Societies": South Asia* (London, 1989)

Allen, C and Williams, G, *Sociology of "Developing Societies": Sub-Saharan Africa* (London, 1982)

Archetti, E P, Cammack, P and Roberts, B R *Sociology of "Developing Societies": Latin America* (London, 1987)

Asad, T and Owen, R *Sociology of "Developing Societies": The Middle East* (London, 1983)

Duus, P (ed) *The Cambridge History of Japan: Volume 6 – The Twentieth Century* (Cambridge, 1988)

Freund, B *The Making of Contemporary Africa* (London,1984)**

Hosking, G, *A History of the Soviet Union* (London, 1990)**

Jones, M A, *The Limits of Liberty: American History 1607–1980* (New York, 1983)**

Laqueur, W *Europe since Hitler: the Rebirth of Europe* (London 1982)*

Sarkar, S *Modern India 1885–1947* (Delhi, 1983)

Stearns, P N *European Society in Upheaval: Social History since 1750* (New York, 1975)*

Taylor, J and Turton A *Sociology of "Developing Societies": South East Asia* (London, 1988)

Tipton, F B and Aldrich, R *An Economic and Social History of Europe from 1939 to Present* (London, 1987)*

Background and Theory

Anderson, B *Imagined Communities: Reflections on the Origins and Spread of Nationalism* (London and New York, 1983)*

Barraclough, G *An Introduction to Contemporary History* (London, 1964)

Giddens, A *Sociology* (Cambridge, 1989)

Harvey, D *The Condition of Postmodernity* (Oxford, 1989)**

Kitching, G *Development and Underdevelopment in Historical Perspective* (London, 1982)

Kumar, K *Prophecy and Progress: the Sociology of Industrial and Post-Industrial Society* (London 1985)*

Sayer, D *Capitalism and Modernity: an Excursus on Marx and Weber* (London and New York, 1991)*

Work

Beynon, H *Working for Ford* (Harmondsworth, 1973)

Braverman, H *Labor and Monopoly Capital* (New York, 1974)*

Freund, B *The African Worker* (Cambridge, 1988)

Gordon, D et al. *Segmented Work, Divided Workers: The Historical Transformation of Labor in the United States* (New York, 1982)*

Sandbrook, R *The Politics of Basic Needs: the Assault on Urban Poverty in Africa* (London, 1982)

Roberts, B *Cities of Peasants* (London, 1978)

Family

Anderson, M *Approaches to the History of the Western Family* (London, 1980)

Ariès, P *Centuries of Childhood* (Harmondsworth, 1973)

Evans, R J and Lee, W R (ed) *The German Family* (London, 1981)*

Fletcher, R *The Shaking of the Foundations* (London, 1988)

Gillis, J R *Youth and History: Tradition and Change in European Age Relations 1770 to the Present* (New York, 1975)

Mitterauer, M and Sieder, R *The European Family: Patriarchy to Partnership from the Middle Ages to the Present* (Oxford,1982)*

Women and Feminism

Atkinson, D, Lapidus, G, and Dallin, A (eds) *Women in Russia* (Brighton, 1978)**

Buckley, M and Anderson, M (eds) *Women, Equality and Europe* (London, 1988)

Degler, C *At Odds: Women and the Family in America from the Revolution to the Present* (New York, 1980)

Evans, R J *The Feminists* (London, 1977)*

Flexner, E *Century of Struggle: the Women's Rights Movement in the United States* (Cambridge, Mass, 1969)

Lapidus, G, *Women in Soviet Society* (Berkeley, Calif, 1978)**

Massell, G, *The Surrogate Proletariat: Moslem Women and Revolutionary Strategies in Soviet Central Asia* (Princeton, NJ,1974)**

Randall, V *Women and Politics: an International Perspective* (London, 1988)*

Rendall, J *The Origins of Modern Feminism: Women in Britain, France and the United States* (London, 1985)*

Rowbotham, S *The Past is Before Us: Feminism in Action since the 1960s* (Harmondsworth, 1989)*

Stites, R *The Women's Liberation Movement in Russia* (Princeton, NJ, 1978)**

Literature

Berger, J *Once in Europa* (London, 1989)

Berger, J *Pig Earth* (London, 1979)

1900–1914

Clark, M *Modern Italy 1871–1982* (London, 1984)

Gutman, H *Work, Culture and Society in Industrializing America* (New York, 1977)

Hobsbawm, E *The Age of Empire* (London, 1987)**

Magraw, R *France 1814–1915: The Bourgeois Century* (London, 1983)

Marwick, A, Waites, B, Emsley, C and Donnachie, I *Europe on the Eve of War 1900–1914* (War, Peace and Social Change: Europe 1900–1955, Book I) (Buckingham and Bristol, PA, 1990)*

Nelli, HS *From Immigrants to Ethnics: the Italian Americans* (New York, 1983)*

Weber, E *Peasants Into Frenchmen: the Modernization of Rural France 1870–1914* (Stanford, PA, 1976)

1914–1929

Bequai, A *Organized Crime: the Fifth Estate* (Lexington, Mass, 1979)*

Braeman, J, et al. *Change and Continuity in America: the 1920s* (Columbus, Ohio, 1968)

Cowper, H, Emsley, C, Marwick, A, Purdue, B and Englander, D *World War I and Its Consequences* (War, Peace and Social Change: Europe 1900–1955, Book II) (Buckingham and Bristol, PA, 1990)**

Golby, J, Waites, B, Warner, G, Aldgate, T and Lentin, A *Between Two Wars* (War , Peace and Social Change: Europe 1900–1955, Book III) (Buckingham and Bristol, PA, 1990)**

Jászi, O *The Dissolution of the Habsburg Monarchy* (Chicago, Ill, 1929)**

Kaiser, D (ed) *The Workers' Revolution in Russia, 1917* (Cambridge, 1987)**

Koenker, D *Moscow Workers and the 1917 Revolution* (Princeton, NJ, 1981)**

Maier, C S *Recasting Bourgeois Europe: Stabilisation in France, Germany and Italy in the Decade after World War I* (Princeton, NJ, 1975)

Marwick, A *The Deluge: British Society and the First World War* (Basingstoke, 1991)

Mitrany, D *Marx against the Peasant* (Chapel Hill, NC, 1951)**

Rothschild, J *East-Central Europe between the Two World Wars* (Seattle, Wash and London, 1974)**

Trotsky, L *The Revolution Betrayed* (New York, 1937)**

1929–1945

Chandavarkar, R "Workers' Politics and the Mill Districts in Bombay between the Wars", *Modern Asian Studies*, Vol 15, No. 3 (July 1981)*

Filtzer, D *Soviet Workers and Stalinist Industrialization* (London, 1986)**

Fitzpatrick, J *Education and Social Mobility in the Soviet Union, 1921–34* (Cambridge, 1979)**

Golby, J et al. – see above

Muhlberger, D (ed) *The Social Basis of European Fascist Movements* (London, 1987)

Peukert, D *Inside Nazi Germany* (London, 1987)

Polonsky, A *The Little Dictators* (London, 1975)**

Scott, J *The Moral Economy of the Peasantry: Subsistence and Rebellion in Southeast Asia* (New Haven, Conn., 1976)

Stevenson, J *British Society 1914–1945* (Harmondsworth, 1984)

Tannenbaum, E R *The Fascist Experience: Italian Society and Culture 1922–1945* (New York, 1972)

1945–1973

Bell, D *The Coming of Post-Industrial Society: A Venture in Social Forecasting* (London, 1973)

Berghahn, V R *Modern Germany* (Cambridge, 1987)

Castles, S with Booth, H and Wallace, T *Here for Good: Western Europe's New Ethnic Minorities* (London, 1984)

Crook, I and D *Ten Mile Inn: Mass Movement in a Chinese Village* (New York, 1979)*

Franklin, S H *The European Peasantry: The Final Phase* (London, 1969)

Hinton, W *Fanshen: a Documentary of Revolution in a Chinese Village* (New York, 1966)

Kerblay, B *Modern Soviet Society* (London, 1983)**

Leuchtenberg, W E *A Troubled Feast: American Society since 1945* (Boston, Mass, 1973)**

Lomax, B *Hungary 1956* (London, 1976)**

Marwick, A *British Society Since 1945* (Harmondsworth, 1990)

Rothschild, J *Return to Diversity: East Central Europe since World War II* (London and New York, 1989)**

Worsley, P *The Third World* (London, 1967)

Young, M *The Rise of the Meritocracy* (Harmondsworth, 1958)

1973 to the present

Afshar, H (ed) *Women, State and Ideology in the Third World* (London, 1985)*

Connor, W D *Socialism, Politics and Equality: Hierarchy and Change in Eastern Europe and the USSR* (Columbia, NY, 1979)*

Gellner, E *Muslim Society* (Cambridge, 1981)

Gorz, A *Farewell to the Working Class* (London, 1982)

Guha, R *The Unquiet Woods: Ecological Change and Peasant Resistance in the Himalaya* (Delhi, 1989)

Harris, N *Of Guns and Butter: The World Economy in Crisis* (Harmondsworth, 1983)

Harris, N *The End of the Third World: Newly Industrializing Countries and the Decline of an Ideology* (Harmondsworth, 1987)*

Hiro, D *Islamic Fundamentalism* (London, 1988)*

Kagarlitsky, B *The Dialectics of Change* (London and New York, 1990)**

Sandbrook, R *The Politics of Africa's Economic Stagnation* (Cambridge , 1985)*

Sinfield, A *What Unemployment Means* (London, 1981)*

Sword, K *The Times Guide to Eastern Europe* (London, 1990)**

Zaslavskaya, T *The Second Socialist Revolution* (London, 1990)**

ACKNOWLEDGEMENTS

Picture Credits

1   An Indian Christian family before World War I: SOAS
2–3   An American migrant family of the 1930s: LC
4–5   Mexican women in 1911: Museum of Modern Art, Oxford/Casasola Archives
6   A Chinese family of the 1960s: M/H. Cartier Bresson
20–21   A street market in East London, c.1910: HDC
56–57   Soviet members of a collective farm: PF
92–93   A "Hooverville" on the outskirts of Seattle, USA: Special Collections Division, University of Washington Libraries, Photo: Lee
128–129 Children in postwar Germany: M/Werner Bischof
164–165 An illegal political meeting in South Africa: M/Ian Berry
220–201 Street scene in Baku, USSR, in the late 1980s: Camera Press/Dimitry Sokolov

9, 10–11 HDC **12–13, 15** SV **16** Format/Maggie Murray **18–19** M/Abbas **25** Ford Motor Co. **26** RV **27** Victoria and Albert Museum **28t** Cadbury Ltd **28b** AA **29t** RV **29b** Musée de l'Elysée, Lausanne **31** HDC **32–33, 33tr** LC **33tl** SV **34–35** Greater London Photograph Library **34** HDC **35** SV **36** MEPL **36–37** RV **38–39, 38t** HDC **38b** PF **39t** RV **39b** M/Pinkhassov **41** Mansell Collection **42t, 42b** International Museum of Photography at George Eastman House **43** Hapag-Lloyd AG **44** RV **45t** MEPL **45c** AA **45b** HDC **46t** MEPL **46b** PF **46–47** State Historical Society of Wisconsin **47, 48–49** SV **48, 49t** HDC **49c** FSP **49c** Sally and Richard Greenhill **50–51** RV **51** MEPL **52t** HDC **52b** RV **54t** SOAS **54b** SV **55** Museum of Modern Art, Oxford/Casasola Archives **61** Jürgens Photo **62, 63t,63b** RV **64t** Collection of Beryl Williams, University of Sussex **64b** Jürgens Photo **65** RV **66t** Jürgens Photo **66b, 67b** Collection of Beryl Williams, University of Sussex **67t** MEPL **68,69** AA **70–71, 70t,70c** HDC **70b** Otto Dix Private Collection **71t** PF **71b** FSP/Noel Quidu **73** RV **74t** AA **74b, 75t** HDC **75b** RV **76–77** Bocarnville Village Trust **77** HDC **78** LC **79t** Brown Brothers **79b** HDC/Bettmann Archive **80t** The Advertising Archives **80b, 81** SV **82t** The Robert Opie Collection **82b** UPI/ Bettmann Archive **83t** Barnabys Picture Library **83b** Angelo Hornak **84–85** The Robert Opie Collection **84t** Shirley Baker **84c** Museum of Childhood, Edinburgh **84–85b** Brown Brothers **85t** PF **85b** IKON **87** IWM **88** Barnabys Picture Library **89** HDC **90, 91** SV **97** LC **98** AA **98–99** LC **100** PF **101t** Weimar Archive **101c** Robert Hunt Library **101b** Edimedia **102t** Bodleian Library **102b** RV **103** M/H. Cartier Bresson **104l** RV **104r** Beryl Williams **105** MEPL **106,107** PF **108–109** Roman Vishniac **108** SV **109t** FSP **109c** Juhan Kuus **109b** Sally and Richard Greenhill **111** LC **112** AA **113t** Beryl Williams **113b** RV **114t** AA **114b** SV **115** MEPL **116–117** M/Robert Capa **117** HDC **118–119** Culver Pictures **118t** The Robert Opie Collection **118b** Courtesy of Mitchell Beazley **119t** FSP/Kim Chow **119c** M/Raghu Rai **119b** M/Eve Arnold **120–121** RV **121** AA **122** LC **123t** Camera Press **123b** AA **124–125** The British Library **125t** M/H Cartier Bresson **125b** HDC **126** Deutsche-Afrika Linien **126–127** HDC **127** PF **133tl,133tr** AA **133b**HDC **134** M/Eve Arnold **135** Washington Post © reprinted by permission of the D.C. Publishing Library **137t** HDC **137b, 138** SV **139t** Saturday Evening Post **139c** HDC **139b, 140** PF **141l, 141r** Saturday Evening Post **142–143** US National Archives **143t** HDC **143b** SV **144–145** Zefa/Damm **144t** Culver Pictures **144c, 145t** Zefa **145c** HDC/Bettmann Archives **145b** M/Salgado **147** M/Robert Capa **148–149** PF **149b** M/H. Cartier Bresson **149t** The Soviet Political Poster, V. Suryaninov, 1954 **150t** National Szechenyi Library, Budapest **150b** PF **151** M/Werner Bischof **152** M/Erich Lessing **153** 153 M/David Seymour **154–155** PF **154t** Middle East Centre, Oxford: Jerusalem and E. Mission

Collection **154b** Mark Edwards/Still Pictures **155t** Cephas Picture Library/Mick Rock **155b** M/Ernst Haas **157, 158** HDC **159** M/Werner Bischof **160t** M/H. Cartier Bresson **160b** M/M. Riboud **161** PF **162t** Press Information Bureau, Government of India **162–163** United Nations **163** PF **169** Hutchison Library/Sarah Errington **170** LC **171** Hutchison Library/Crispin Hughes **172** M/H. Cartier Bresson **174–175** Mark Edwards/Still Pictures **175** Hutchison Library **176–177** M/Martine Franck **176t, 176b** PF **177tl** Sally and Richard Greenhill **177tr** Euan Duff **177b** South American Pictures/Tony Morrison **179** Format/Brenda Prince **180** Camera Press/Armand Latourre **181** Camera Press/Klaus Lehnartz **182t** Camera Press/John Launois **182b** M/H. Cartier Bresson **184** Barnabys Picture Library **185t** AA **185b** Topham Picture Source **187** HDC **188, 189b** M/H. Cartier Bresson **188–189** Paul Trevor **190** SV **191** M/G. Peress **192** M/B. Davidson **193t** Bettmann Archive **193b** M/B. Glinn **194t** Rex Features **194b** Courtesy of Tupperware Home Parties **195** Bettmann Archive **196t** AA **196b** John Webb **197** M/Leonard Freed **198–199** FPG International **198t** PF **198b** M/Alex Webb **199t** M/Jean Gaumy **199c** Culver Pictures **199b** Juhan Kuus **205** Format **206** M/C. Steele Perkins **207t** M/Steve McCurry **207c** Psion UK PLC **207b** Volvo Concessionaires Ltd **208t** Wolfgang Mezger **208b** Camera Press **209** Format/Melanie Friend **210–211, 211** Sally and Richard Greenhill **213t** Format/Melanie Friend **213b** Paul Graham **214** Network/Ignatier **215** Camera Press/TASS **216–217** HDC **216** FSP/Vladimir Shone **218** Network/Karen Golestan **219t** Sally and Richard Greenhill **219b** Network/Lewis **220–221** Camera Press/Hilton Hamann **222t** FSP/Al Venter **222b** Mark Edwards/Still Pictures **223** Hutchison Library **224–225** M/Raghu Rai **224c** Jesus Lozanzo **224b** Kansas State Historical Society **225tl** Israel Museum **225 tr** FSP/Duclos Alexis **225b** M/McCurry **227** Sally and Richard Greenhill/Sally Neal **228t** Sally and Richard Greenhill **228b** FSP/Noel Quidu **230t** AA **230b, 231** Format/Raissa Page **232** Mark Edwards/Still Pictures **232–233** M/Eugene Richards **233t** Zefa **234–235** Center Parcs Ltd. **234t** Bettmann Archive **235t** Image Bank/Terry Williams **235c** M/C. Manos **235b** Image Bank/David Brownell **236l, 236r** PF **236c** M/Elliott Erwitt **237l, 237c, 237r, 238l, 238c, 238r** PF **239l** HDC **239c, 239r, 240l, 240c** PF **240r** HDC **241l** PF **241c** Jürgens Photo **241r** M/H. Cartier Bresson **242l** HDC **242c** PF **242r** M/Eve Arnold **243l** M/Cornell Capa **243c** Camera Press **243r** HDC **244l,244c,244r,245l,245r** PF **245c** HDC **246l,246c,246r,247r** PF **247l** HDC

Abbreviations
AA   Andromeda Archive
FSP   Frank Spooner Pictures
HDC   Hulton Deutsch Collection, London
IWM   Imperial War Museum
LC   Library of Congress, Washington DC
M   Magnum, London
MEPL   Mary Evans Picture Library, London
PF   Popperfoto, London
RV   Roger Viollet, Paris
SOAS   School of Oriental and African Studies, London
SV   Süddeutscher Verlag, Munich

t = top, tl = top left, tr = top right, c = center, b = bottom etc.

Editorial and research assistance
Steven Chapman, Robert Dewey Jnr, Andy Overs, Michelle Von Ahn, Philip Waller

Artists
Alan Hollingbery, Del Tolton

Photographs
Shirley Jamieson, Joanne Rapley

Typesetting
Brian Blackmore

Production
Stephen Elliott

Color Origination
Wing King Tong Co., Ltd, Hong Kong

Index
Ann Barrett

Acknowledgement
The general editor would like to thank the production editor for his outstanding forebearance and good humor.

INDEX

Page numbers in *italics* refer to illustrations or their captions. **Bold** page numbers refer to the subjects of special or ancillary text features.